DOMESTICATING ORGAN TRANSPLANT

Domesticating Organ Transplant

FAMILIAL SACRIFICE

AND

NATIONAL ASPIRATION

IN MEXICO

MEGAN CROWLEY-MATOKA

Duke University Press   Durham and London   2016

Printed in the United States of America on acid-free paper ∞
Typeset in Quadraat Pro by Westchester Book Group

Library of Congress Cataloging-in-Publication Data
Crowley-Matoka, Megan, [date] author.
Domesticating organ transplant : familial sacrifice and national
aspiration in Mexico / Megan Crowley-Matoka.
pages cm
Includes bibliographical references and index.
ISBN 978-0-8223-6052-0 (hardcover : alk. paper)
ISBN 978-0-8223-6067-4 (pbk. : alk. paper)
ISBN 978-0-8223-7463-3 (e-book)
1. Kidneys—Transplantation—Mexico. 2. Organ donors—Mexico.
3. Transplantation of organs, tissues, etc.—Social aspects—Mexico.
4. Transplantation of organs, tissues, etc.—Moral and
ethical aspects. I. Title.
RD575.C77 2016
617.4′610592—dc23
2015031550

Cover art: Collage by Martyn Schmoll; heart photo © Eduard
Lysenko, istock; locket photo © juicybits, istock.

For my father, James Swenney Crowley

And my mentor, Arthur J. Rubel

Their lively intellects and love of debate are dearly missed

Contents

Acknowledgments

First and foremost, there are not words sufficient to express my gratitude to the patients, family members, and transplant professionals in Mexico who so graciously let me into their lives and shared so generously of their time, energy, space, ideas, joys, frustrations, hopes, doubts, and everyday habits. The most astonishing and deeply moving thing about anthropology is that people allow us to do it, and I feel profoundly privileged to have been allowed to do it in this place with these particular people. Although their individual names do not appear here for reasons of confidentiality, their stories and words are the lifeblood of this book. I hope I have done them justice.

My entrée into the transplant community in Guadalajara, as well as my efforts to make sense of that world, were profoundly enabled by Dr. Javier García de Alba García at the Unidad de Investigación Social, Económica y en Servicios de Salud, along with his colleagues Ana Leticia Salceda-Rocha, Juan Antonio González Barrera, Evangélina Herrera Solís, and María Faustina Campos-Arciniega. With great generosity and good humor, they provided me with an institutional home and a lively intellectual community, as well as guidance both sensitive and candid in navigating the scholarly, political, and personal challenges of fieldwork in Mexico. Through their friendship and the many adventures (culinary, literary, musical, matrimonial, and otherwise) into which they invited me, I came to experience Guadalajara in a way that would not have otherwise been possible. In addition, the

Bontield family with whom I lived throughout the course of my fieldwork sustained and enriched this work immeasurably by so warmly enfolding me into their family. I cannot even imagine navigating the emotional terrain of this fieldwork without Doña Tere's incredible cooking, the soul-restoring pleasure of playing with the family's beautiful babies after long and often grim days spent in the hospitals, and the joyous chaos of long Sunday afternoons filled with family of all ages, barbacoa, music, tequilítos, and fútbol.

Long before I got to Mexico (and long after I left) this project was supported and shaped by more people than I can ever hope to do justice to here. First thanks must go to my advisor, the late Art Rubel, whose wisdom and guidance in matters theoretical, ethnographic, and practical nurtured the course of this work and my own development as an anthropologist. The abiding curiosity and deep generosity of his intellect made him one of those rare mentors who are able to both demand rigor and encourage freedom of thought in equal measure. It has also been an enormous privilege to have Margaret Lock bring the depth of her insight and the warmth of her friendship to bear on this project as it has grown from the tentative kernel of a graduate student's idea to a finished book. Her own brilliant work provided early and enduring inspiration for the fascinating and useful things one might be able to do with anthropology, and I feel outrageously fortunate to have shared ideas, laughter, and good meals with her over the years. I would also like to thank Bill Maurer, whose inspired teaching led me to my first exploration into the world of organ transplantation, and whose intellectual spirit and sense of serious play is utterly ingrained in the beginnings of this project. Jim Ferguson also had an important guiding hand in the early development of this work, and I remain indebted to and admiring of his precision of thought and language. In the beginning stages of this manuscript, Susan Greenhalgh was the kind of reader one scarcely dares hope for, with an uncanny ability to attend to issues of theory, politics, logic, organization, and aesthetics simultaneously and with a razor-sharp eye.

In making its circuitous way from dissertation to book, this project benefited immeasurably from support of all kinds from many different sources. The fieldwork itself was enabled by funding from the Fulbright Fellowship Program, the National Science Foundation, the Social Science Research Council, and the UC MEXUS program. Preliminary write-up was supported by a University of California Regents Dissertation Writing Fellowship. During the lonely work of dissertation writing, Patty Marshall and Elisa Gordon, both then at Loyola University Chicago, offered much-needed anthropological fellowship that kept me going as I toiled far from my home graduate program. A postdoctoral fellowship and a later visiting faculty appointment with the MacLean Center for Clinical Medical Ethics at the University of Chicago provided invaluable time for thinking and writing, as well as an abiding network of intellectual comradeship upon which I still depend. From that network, ongoing engagement with Mark Siegler, David Cronin, and Lainie Ross in particular have continued to hone my thinking and interest in transplantation, while Debjani Mukherjee and the late Melinda Gordon became cherished friends on the academic road. My time at the University of Chicago was also greatly enriched by the warm support offered by Jean Comaroff, whose sponsorship of a Visiting Research Scholar position with the Anthropology Department helped to ensure that I did not become too lost among the doctors while training in bioethics.

My first faculty position at the University of Pittsburgh and the VA Center for Health Equity Research and Promotion provided vital intellectual and institutional support during what became a drawn-out phase of manuscript revision, as I learned to find my way in the world of academic medicine while striving to keep at least one foot firmly in anthropology. I cannot imagine having been able to do so without the keen intellect and unstinting support of Bob Arnold, who throughout my time in Pittsburgh and ever since has been the kind of mentor with whom it is just a joy to work. Wickedly smart, irreverent, and deeply kind, thinking with him has been not just productive but awfully good fun as this project has wound its way toward an end of which he never let me lose sight. Pittsburgh was a marvelous and storied place in which to think about organ transplantation, given its place in the history of the field, and I benefited greatly from my engagements with the rich community of multidisciplinary scholars and clinicians engaged in transplant work there, particularly Galen Switzer, John Fung, Mary Amanda Dew, Andrea DiMartini, Larissa Myaskovsky, Henkie Tan, Ron Shapiro, and Mark Unruh. In anthropology, Nicole Constable and especially my dear friend Gabi Lukacs provided much-needed connection to my home discipline.

My time in Pittsburgh was also marked by becoming a mother, and I had the incredible good fortune to be surrounded by a group of whip-smart, accomplished, and unsparingly frank, funny women colleagues who were doing the same, particularly Judy Chang, Winnie Teuteberg, Amber Barnato, Molly Conroy, Cindy Bryce, and Kelly Hyman. Their companionship made figuring out the new balancing act of our lives and work both more possible and a great deal more fun.

My current colleagues in Medical Humanities and Bioethics at Northwestern University make up the most engaging, nurturing, and challenging academic home I could wish for—I don't know how I got so lucky. Katie Watson and Debjani Mukherjee accompanied every single step of the final round of rethinking and rewriting the manuscript in our wonderful writing group, doing so with just the right combination of unflinching, spot-on critique and unwavering enthusiasm. Kathryn Montgomery and Catherine Belling provided insightful, generous readings of the whole manuscript at the crucial final stages, and to have the eyes of such clear thinkers and fine writers on my work was truly a gift. Tod Chambers and Alice Dreger have been wise, savvy, and sometimes savagely funny sounding boards for title ideas and much else about the book writing process. Other members of our MH&B community, especially John Franklin, Sarah Rodriguez, Bryan Morrison, and Myria Knox, as well as our inspiringly committed graduate students have been crucial in creating what is the special alchemy of this place. The wonderfully collegial Department of Anthropology has provided me with a welcoming second home at Northwestern, for which I thank our chair, Bill Leonard, in particular. My attachment to the department and my work on the final version of this book have been immeasurably deepened by Rebecca Seligman, who went chapter-for-chapter with me in an intensive writing partnership as we finished our manuscripts together. Without her incisive comments, careful eye for argument, and motivating companionship, it is hard to imagine where this book would now be.

I have been so fortunate that my array of anthropological interlocutors and dear friends keeps expanding, from graduate school Christina Schwenkel, Jennifer Heung, Selim Shahine, Kimberley Coles, and Tom Douglas remain treasured fellow-travelers, and since then I have been particularly lucky to work and think with Elizabeth Roberts, Sherine Hamdy, Gala True, Harris Solomon, Sharon Kaufman, Lawrence Cohen, Ciara Kierans, and Betsey Brada along the way. More specifically, different versions of this work have benefited greatly from the insight of many generous reviewers, both formal and informal. In particular, three brilliant, engaged, and enormously patient reviewers for Duke University Press provided theoretically challenging and rigorously thoughtful reviews over an extended time period that profoundly shaped the final manuscript—I am able here to thank Lesley Sharp and Emily Wentzell directly. Without all three reviewers, this would have been a very different and surely a far weaker book, and I am grateful to Ken Wissoker at Duke not only for his wise guidance and unflagging support for this protracted project, but for finding me such constructive and meticulous readers. Elizabeth Ault at Duke has also been crucial in helping to navigate the review and revision and production process, and I remain in awe of her skills at navigating the bureaucratic world of cultural patrimony permissions in Mexico—this book has been profoundly *agilizado* by her efforts in particular, as well as by those of her skilled colleagues in production and marketing at Duke, in particular, Susan Albury. In addition, Donald Joralemon, Luis Alberto Vargas, and Alan Harwood all provided insightful and critically helpful reviews of an earlier version of the manuscript, and generous early readings by Valentina Napolitano and Lynn Morgan also provided trenchant comments and additional food for thought. Feedback from Carole Browner, Betty Wolder-Levin, and two anonymous reviewers for *Social Science and Medicine* on an earlier version of chapter 4 helped to focus and tighten that analysis in critical ways. In addition, presentations of portions of this material to audiences at the University of California, Irvine; the University of Chicago; the University of Illinois, Chicago; the University of Pittsburgh; Northwestern University; the University of Pennsylvania; Brown University; and various annual meetings of the American Anthropological Association, the Society for Medical Anthropology, and the American Society for Bioethics and Humanities all generated lively discussion and thought-provoking insight for grappling with this material.

Finally, and most fundamentally, I am so very thankful for my family, who has supported me throughout this long process with such enthusiasm, grace, and good humor. Having been raised by my parents, James and Margaret Crowley, to love books deeply, it is a particular pleasure to have produced one of my own. And while I wish my father were still alive to read it, I am grateful to have had my mother—an astute reader and a beautiful writer in her own right—as such an engaged companion along the way. From visiting me in the field to reading a seemingly endless stream of chapter drafts, she must surely feel as if this book is partly hers as well. My husband, Derek Matoka, has been on this ride with me from the very beginning, celebrating my admission to graduate school despite the three-thousand-mile separation it required, spending his med school vacations visiting the Mexican hospitals that were my field sites, creating time and space for my writing over many years, and accompanying me in this long, strange journey into the world of medicine in which we are both, in our own ways, engaged. He not only sustains and continues to challenge me, but has given me our two splendid daughters, Kathryn and Ellie, who over the course of this project have grown old enough to fall in love with books themselves and have helped to alternately harangue and hearten me on through the final stages of finishing this one. They are, as they know, my deepest joy.

Introduction

During my first fieldwork visit to Mexico I found myself encountering the same striking story again and again, a story centered on a young boy in kidney failure, the son of a Mexican father and a German mother. Initially diagnosed in the city of Guadalajara, the boy was then taken by his (relatively affluent) parents to Germany for additional consultations. In both places they were told that a kidney transplant was the best hope for their son. In Mexico, a *living* donor transplant was all that was offered, given the local scarcity of organs obtained from brain-dead (or *cadaveric*) donors.[1] In Germany, however, physicians strongly advised a cadaveric transplant—a recommendation based, in part, on an aversion to the instrumental use of living bodies in the long aftermath of the Nazi era (Hogle 1999). After much consideration, the German mother decided to give a kidney to her increasingly ill son, motivated by the somewhat higher success rates with living donor transplants over cadaveric ones.[2] Once so decided, went the story, German physicians advised the couple to return to Mexico, deferring to the greater experience and expertise of their Mexican transplant colleagues with living donation. The mother's German natal family, by all reports, was horrified and angered by her decision, and vehemently opposed the donation. It seemed inconceivable to them that she would risk herself when another option existed. The mother, however, determined to do everything possible for her son, rejected their pleas that she reconsider. The family returned to Mexico where the donation and transplant were carried out successfully in a private hospital in Guadalajara.

This was a story that seemed nearly ubiquitous during that first field visit to Guadalajara, offered up in turn by many of the various transplant surgeons, nephrologists, nurses, and transplant coordinators I was making the rounds to meet in the several institutions where transplantation took place across the city. In each telling, it was almost invariably emphasized that the mother's decision to donate reflected the fact that she had become "*más mexicana*" (more Mexican) through her willingness to potentially sacrifice herself in order to save her son. Her German family's horror at her decision, in contrast, was used in the storytelling to exemplify a colder, more individualistic ethos. The key reading being offered here indexed a particular valence of national identity and pride, one that highlighted—and celebrated—an iconic vision of the self-sacrificial Mexican mother. For my interlocutors this was clearly not just a story about motherhood, but one about nationhood as well. That is, it was a story that reversed typical modernist narratives in which the technology and skill of the putative first world are always superior. It was a story in which what we might call the *cultural technology* of the Mexican family (and of that self-sacrificial mother in particular) was imagined as a resource that has enabled Mexico to develop its own kinds of expertise, its own forms of superiority both technical and moral. For the anthropologist, it was a story that forced me to think from the very beginnings of this project about the bodies of mothers, about the pull of suffering and the calculation of risk within families, and about the fashioning of both individual and national identity as they emerge and converge in the context of transplantation.

Both the content and the insistent recurrence of the story remained with me, and I have found myself returning to contemplate it again and again since those exhilarating, often bewildering early days of fieldwork. Over time, the story has come for me to both situate and condense many of the central concerns of this book. The tale of the German mother highlights the degree to which transplantation is a deeply cultural and biopolitical enterprise. An enterprise, that is, that both reveals and enacts situated notions of who can and should risk their bodies through organ donation, as well as who can and should benefit from that risk. After all, it is striking that it was the mother's—never the father's—body over which those debates about donation took place. Equally striking is the way that ideas about the desirability of living versus dead organ donors, as well as what constitutes acceptable risk and worthwhile gain, shift as the family moves between the Mexican and German contexts. Clearly neither the clinical practices nor the biopolitics of transplant are everywhere the same (Crowley-Matoka and Lock 2006). And indeed, it was precisely those differences that were so deftly leveraged in the service of national identity in the proud, repetitive recounting of the story that I encountered during those early days in the field. Moreover, such issues of national identity surface not only in the content of the story, but in the context of its telling as well. Perhaps it should not be surprising that so many of those transplant professionals shared a common impulse to be sure that one of the first stories this gringa anthropologist heard was *not* one that conjured "developing world" tropes of inadequate resources and incomplete expertise.[3] Instead, this was a story that deliberately touted cultural, technological, and even ethical triumph through the medium of transplantation.

Attending to the striking repetition of this story during my first field encounters seems telling in another way as well. For this insistent recounting seems to suggest a certain symbolic, representational power at work here, a way in which this particular story usefully captured and succinctly communicated something my interlocutors wanted to be sure that I grasped. Indeed, the emblematic nature of the story of the German mother who became más mexicana—emblematic both for those telling the story, and for me in hearing and continuing to ponder it—embodies another central concern of this book. That is, it crystallizes a concern with the way in which organ transplantation is so often made to stand for something—or for many things—larger than itself. And so, taking a cue from that recurrent, resonant figure of the German mother, in this book I am interested also in exploring how organ transplantation serves—more broadly and across a range of different registers—as a kind of icon.

In one register, organ transplantation clearly stands as icon for the wonders of science, as well as for its dangers. Lesley Sharp, for example, has described transplantation as an "icon of medical achievement," in which the considerable powers of biomedicine to repair ailing bodies and defy death are dramatically manifest (Sharp 2006: 1).[4] Not always triumphal, however, transplant has also frequently played a more sinister role in the scientific imaginary, serving as iconic of the processes of bodily commodification and neoliberal exploitation made visible in what Nancy Scheper-Hughes has so vividly termed the "neo-cannibalism" of global organ trafficking (1998a: 14). In another register, the ability to wield transplantation often figures as an icon of national progress and pride; this is much the way it is made to work in that story of the German mother who becomes más mexicana. Yet transplantation—when it is perceived to go awry—has also often stood as emblematic of developmental failure and even national shame, as in the global media frenzy over India's black market "organs bazaar" (Cohen 1999; Das 2000). And within anthropology itself, organ transplantation has become iconic of a certain set of theoretically central and often politically charged divides between nature and culture, self and other, life and death, gift and commodity, science and spirituality (see Ikels 2013 for a recent overview of the burgeoning anthropology of transplant).[5]

In each of these registers it is intriguing to ask, why does transplant seem so readily to condense and capture a core set of meanings about biomedicine, about national identity, and even about anthropological theory? To draw on Claude Levi-Strauss's famous formulation, why are organ transplants not just so good to think (with), but so good to symbolize with (Lévi-Strauss 1962)? And further, what might be the localized, material effects of being pressed into such symbolic service for how organ transplantation is enacted and experienced—as well as for how it is analyzed? Such questions of iconicity resonate with Judith Butler's notion of *coming to matter* as a process of acquiring both materiality and importance through repetitive acts of meaning-making (Butler 1993). Indeed, we might think of those eager tellings and retellings of the story of the German mother in just this way, providing initial insight into how transplantation has come to matter in Mexico both through the materiality of living donor bodies and as a sign of national identity and pride. Taking transplant as a kind of icon helps to illuminate these processes of signification and materialization, focusing our attention on how organ transplantation operates as both an idea and a practice.

I take up the notion of the icon advisedly here, aware that the term has a rich and varied history of usage, from its most prosaic employment as simply a kind of symbolization, to its precise deployment in semiotic analyses as a form of representation specifically based on likeness and similarity, to its religious meaning as an artistic representation of a sacred Christian figure. Mindful of this range of meanings, I find that each of these incarnations of the notion of the icon lends a useful analytic—and sometimes affective—dimension to the way I use the term throughout this book. In exploring the representational resonance that organ transplantation seems to bear, it will be critical to ask a set of semiotics-inspired questions about what key features, what specific forms of likeness are foregrounded when transplant is made to stand in for biomedical achievement, for national aspirations, or for particular kinds of anthropological problems (Mertz 2007; Peirce 1974). Equally important will be the question of what gets lost in such foregroundings—that is, what complexities are elided in the simplifying processes of symbolization? Beyond this, the religious form of the icon usefully evokes a sense of both the sacred and the profane, as the fervent devotion that icons inspire is so often tempered by fears about their tendency to become a form of false god (Vrame 2003). Such moral duality, such a simultaneous sense of both the miraculous and the potentially corrupt, is aptly attuned to the complex ways in which transplantation is both enshrined as a pinnacle of biomedical (and sometimes national) achievement *and* persistently haunted by intimations of profiteering, criminality, and butchery.

As Lynn Morgan has pointed out in her recent work on the figure of the fetus as icon in American culture, the most powerful icons are often the most polysemic ones, those which can be read to divergent effect by different constituencies (Morgan 2009; see also Nelkin and Lindee 1996; Taylor 2008; Verdery 1999). In such readings and counterreadings icons are rendered not just representational but deeply political, a site of both assertion and contestation. An analysis of the iconic thus requires remaining alert to the particular stories of the way things stand being put forward in such condensed representations, as well as to the other sorts of possible stories they work to quell. Listening carefully for both the stories voiced and the stories silenced in iconic renderings of transplant is an approach that borrows also from Homi Bhabha's insight into stereotypes as a "complex, ambivalent, contradictory form of representation, as anxious as they are assertive" (Bhabha 1994: 70). And in retaining a feel for the exertion as well as the anxieties of power at work in symbolizing processes I draw too W. J. T. Mitchell's ruminations on representation. For Mitchell, the icon as a form of representation is never (just) an object but is always an act, a process, that is at once aesthetic and political (Mitchell 1986).

Exploring the polysemy of transplant as icon in the pages to come requires attending to *what* transplant is held to symbolize: what are the particular images, figures, objects, ideas that are made to emerge out of and stand in for the diverse network of practices, actors, and forms of relation that constitute transplantation? How do the particular aesthetics and histories of those images and figures matter? What are the interests, values, constituencies, and hierarchies that are served—or undermined—in the process? These are the questions that the notion of organ transplantation as icon serves to foreground. I take these questions to the ethnographic ground of Mexico—a place where transplant is dependent on living kidney donors and informed by a rich religious and political iconography of bodily sacrifice. In doing so, the chapters that follow explore how transplant gets caught up in particular ways of imagining and enacting both individual and national selves—and how such imaginings, in turn, materialize transplantation in locally specific ways.

More broadly, focusing on iconicity provides a useful angle of inquiry into a range of issues—conceptual, political, and ethical—that emerge at the intersections of embodied experience, subjectivity, medical practice, and state power. Moving organs from one body into another inescapably poses a set of thorny questions with reach beyond the boundaries of transplantation itself, questions of the relation between self and other, of the biotechnical possibilities for human connection and exploitation, and of the rights and responsibilities we have both in our own bodies and to the bodies of others. Locally specific arrangements governing from whom organs come and to whom they go—as well as who gets to decide and who gets to profit—are consequential at the level of individual, lived bodies as well as for how the wider social body operates as both symbol and site of governance (Scheper-Hughes and Lock 1987). The transplant endeavor is literally dependent on making some bodies give up organs in order to provide treatment for others, thus providing a starkly immediate and material example of how ailing physical bodies and the larger sociopolitical body pull upon and shape one another. In tracking how transplant, as an iconic form of medicine, has come through particular kinds of meaning into particular kinds of being, I am informed by the long trajectory of scholarship that has illuminated the body as a potent site and source of social meaning (see, among many examples, Douglas 1966, 1970; Foucault 1963, 1976; Haraway 1991; Lindenbaum and Lock 1993). Understanding the body as a fundamentally contested terrain, constituted by ever-shifting relations between power, knowledge, and practice, I take organ transplantation as an analytic site where those contestations are rendered unusually, usefully visible.

Technology Out of Place?

> Organ transplantation in Mexico—interesting . . . So you're studying black market stuff, organ selling, that kind of thing?
> —Anthropology colleague, United States

It has been a common initial response to my research, an assumption fielded time and again from academic colleagues and nonacademic friends and family in the United States. I found the response first amusing, then irritating, and then—as it became utterly predictable—intriguing in the regularity with which so many assumed that research on transplantation in Mexico must involve the illegal, must invoke a story of transplant gone awry in some dangerous and disordered way. Engaging what Stuart Youngner has called the "dark side" of transplant's iconic image (1990), such assumptions were surely fueled in part by influential work on the global organ trade by anthropologists Lawrence Cohen, Nancy Scheper-Hughes, and others (e.g., Cohen 1999, 2002, 2005; Moniruzzaman 2012; Scheper-Hughes 2000, 2002a, 2002b, 2004, 2005). Recurrent and unsettling stories in the popular media about organ sales and organ theft also surely colored such reactions (e.g., Finkel 2001; Rothman and Rothman 2003; Sack 2014; Schemo 1994). But Mexico, notably, has never featured centrally in either academic or more popularized versions of such accounts. Indeed, this explanation seems insufficient to explain the pervasiveness of this assumption that organ transplantation in Mexico must not work in the expected and respectable ways. The implicit subtext here, of course, is that transplantation in the developed, postindustrial world *does* work in ways (at least reasonably) proper and just. Mention of cross-cultural research on organ transplantation in Japan and Germany (Hogle 1999; Lock 2001), for instance, typically elicited expectations of cultural difference, but not this knee-jerk assumption of illegality and exploitation.

We might think of the underlying logic here in terms borrowed from Mary Douglas's famous formulation of dirt as "matter out of place" (Douglas 1966: 36): in an almost automatic sort of way transplantation in Mexico seemed to strike many of my U.S. interlocutors as *technology out of place*. This borrowing seems helpful for capturing how transplantation in Mexico was thought (by some) to transgress the boundaries of an implicit global hierarchy, violating the imagined geographies and chronologies of a developed versus developing world divide. "Out-of-place-ness," of course, is always a relative matter, and so the presumed dangerous disorder of transplantation in Mexico necessarily invokes a moral and social order that it has contravened. Captured also in this notion of technology-out-of-place is the powerful pull of not just fear but fascination contained in those (often almost eagerly made) black market assumptions. For as Mary Douglas explored long ago, both danger and desire are often compellingly commingled at the fertile site of such transgressive boundary crossings.

At work in those technology-out-of-place reactions seemed to be a set of assumptions about both Mexico as a place, and transplantation as a particular form of medicine. On the one hand, such responses resonated strongly with Nancy Stepan's analysis of the ways in which science and technology are so often presumed to move from a (Western) center outward to a "problematic periphery," such that Latin America historically has figured typically as a (faulty) receiver of scientific knowledge and practice, rather than a producer of such in its own right (Stepan 1991: 3; see also Soto Laveaga 2009). Such flows of technology from center to periphery are reversed in the way people in search of the stuff of life (both jobs and health care) are often understood to move instead from periphery to center. This is a dynamic and a set of expectations that operate with particular power in the context of the highly charged and hierarchical history of U.S.-Mexico relations (Chavez 2013; Wailoo et al. 2006).[6] Such entrenched expectations about flows of both technology and people are precisely the context against which that proudly told story of the German mother deliberately spoke back, asserting the expertise of Mexican over German transplant surgeons in the use of living donors and tracking the family's surprising, circular movement first away from and then back to Mexico.

Also surfacing in the conversations that stemmed from those initial technology-out-of-place reactions were questions not just of technological expertise, but of priorities as well. Underlying concerns about the wisdom of practicing transplantation in a country where other more basic life needs (such as clean water, adequate nutrition, and simple primary medical care) often go unmet was an assumption that such high-tech biomedicine is a luxury, one that ought to be permitted only after a certain level of general development and widespread well-being has been attained. This is a defensible critique, to be sure, but one easily leveled at the United States as well, a country that currently supports 245 transplant centers, yet until very recently has permitted some fifty million of its citizens to go without basic health-care coverage (UNOS 2014a).

Yet in the context of such technology-out-of-place reactions, understanding transplantation as a form of inappropriate health-care luxury rests not just on the costly, high-tech nature of transplantation, but on a particular global health imaginary as well (Livingston 2012).[7] This is an imaginary in which Mexico—despite its relatively privileged positioning within the global South—is a place more likely to be characterized by illnesses of infection, malnutrition, and poverty, rather than those of aging and chronic disease so often associated with both first world status and transplantation itself. Yet a vision of transplantation as something most needed in places where people are able to live long enough and, in some sense, healthily enough for their organs to wear out and need replacement is distinctly out of sync with the epidemiological shape of kidney disease in Mexico. For chronic disease is hardly a first world prerogative. Diabetes—which leads to kidney failure—is a public health problem of epidemic proportions in Mexico: it is the leading cause of death among women (Rull et al. 2005), and afflicts one quarter of all those between twenty-five and forty years old (Correa-Rotter and González-Michaca 2005). Indeed, chronic kidney disease specifically is among the top ten causes of death in Mexico (García García et al. 2010). A key contributor to this massive disease burden are toxic exposures to kidney-damaging chemicals from a range of poorly regulated agricultural, manufacturing, and pharmaceutical sources—exposures only on the rise under the privatizing pressures of deregulation in Mexico, as in many other places around the world (Hamdy 2012; Kierans 2015; Ramirez-Rubio et al. 2013).[8] And in many such places, as in Mexico, a medical treatment like transplant that relies so intimately on the readily available bodies of family members may come—as we shall see—to register more as pragmatic necessity rather than high-tech luxury.

Ultimately, encountering those recurrent technology-out-of-place reactions—and the set of assumptions that underlay them—reinforced the disquiet I felt over the way that the "problematic periphery" so frequently figured in accounts of transplantation primarily as the exploited source of organs for transplant. Troubled by the sometimes sensationalistic, even orientalizing, affects and effects of such accounts, this project was thus motivated in part by a commitment to asking not just what happens when people in "Other" places give (or sell or are robbed of) their organs, but to following closely what happens when they get them as well. In the process of asking such questions, the notion of technology-out-of-place serves as a sort of mnemonic device, a reminder to stay always alert, à la Mary Douglas, to how particular categories are being constituted and to the boundaries thus delineated, defended, and sometimes disrupted.

Iconic Mexico

It is within the context of such technology-out-of-place assumptions that the story of the German mother with which I began signified so strategically. Acutely aware of the particular, privileged gaze from the North given voice in those initial reactions to my research, both the moral power of the más mexicana mother and the prowess of Mexican transplant surgeons highlighted in that story speak back with pointed precision to such assumptions. Such speaking back asserts that transplantation in Mexico cannot be presumed to be merely a flawed reproduction of what occurs in higher income countries, but has its own forms of expertise and merit. Not merely reactive, however, such speaking back also works to highlight some of the key dimensions of the local context critical to the particular ways in which organ transplantation has come to matter in Mexico.

The story of the German mother who gave a kidney to her son has already alerted us to one of the most distinctive features of transplantation in Mexico—an overwhelming dependence on living related organ donors. In fact, upward of 80 percent of kidney transplants in the programs I studied were performed using organs from family members. This stands in sharp contrast to other settings where reliance upon cadaveric donors is far greater (such as the United States or, even more markedly, Spain), or where the use of living unrelated donors/sellers is more common (such as India, Egypt, or Israel). One effect of this dependence was to render kidney transplants the only routine form of solid organ transplantation then practiced in Mexico, because hearts, livers, and lungs from brain-dead donors generally were too rarely available to support active transplant programs.[9] As such, kidney transplantation (with its organ-specific set of physiological, institutional, and imaginative dimensions) often functioned in Mexico as an icon of the transplant endeavor as a whole in local imaginings and politics.

Thus it is that transplantation in Mexico was not only itself iconic in important ways but was deeply bound up with—indeed dependent on—one of the key iconic features of Mexican culture, la familia mexicana. Much has been written about the central place of the family, both in the political economy of the Mexican state and in the symbolic imaginings of Mexican national identity (Diaz-Loving 2006; Keller et al 2006; Lester 2007; LeVine

1993; Lewis 1959; Lomnitz and Pérez-Lizaur 1987). Often posed in explicit contrast to the cold individualism thought to characterize the United States, la familia mexicana is typically imagined as large, multigenerational, cohesive, and intensely loyal, a collective body that serves as the center of social, economic, and moral life. The notion of la familia mexicana indexes a social world where individual autonomy is not enshrined as both social good and personal goal, but rather where personhood is most meaningfully enacted and experienced through relatedness, materialized through dense ties of love, responsibility, and interdependency and the endless give-and-take of family obligation. This is, of course, an idealized (and ideological) imagery, but one that nonetheless retained considerable cultural force in the making of both Mexican identity and Mexican transplantation.

Powerful ideas not just about family but about mothers in particular emerge in the story of the German mother, of course, and indeed the image of la mujer sufrida or la mujer abnegada (the suffering or selfless mother) was also both an iconic one in Mexican culture writ large and crucial to the way transplantation was locally enacted and interpreted. Clearly bound up with highly gendered notions of kinship, la mujer sufrida is also a deeply religious figure, inevitably invoking the image of the Virgin Mary whose sorrowful pain is linked to human salvation. The frequent subject of religious iconographic paintings throughout the Christian world, the Virgin Mary offers a vision of Mexican motherhood with considerable cultural currency in a setting so thoroughly (though sometimes contentiously) suffused with both Catholicism and newer forms of evangelical Christianity.[10]

Yet feminine self-sacrifice is hardly all that the Virgin Mary may be made to embody. In the distinctively Mexican figure of La Virgen de Guadalupe, whose exuberantly ubiquitous image adorns not only church altars but community murals, cars, flags, belt buckles, and vivid tattoos throughout Mexico, she is also a powerful and empowering symbol of deep national pride (Baez-Jorge 1995; Brading 2001; Lafaye 1976; Wolf 1958). La Guadalupe's miraculous sixteenth-century encounter with an indigenous peasant outside of Mexico City marked an unprecedented appearance of the Virgin on New World soil, signaling the emergence of the Mexican people and nation into "full-human" status at a colonial moment when there was little room for either Indians or mestizos ("mixed blood" descendants of Indian and European parents) in the existing spiritual, social, or legal orders. This deep history renders La Guadalupe a richly polysemic figure in Mexico, signifying self-sacrifice and self-assertion, cherished tradition and

Figure I.1 *La Virgen de Guadalupe* hangs on a truck; image from pilgrimage to the Basílica of Guadalupe, December 2014. Photo by Miguel Tovar, Getty Images.

aspirational modernity all at once. As such, she retains a contemporary currency distinctive from the way other situated incarnations of the Virgin Mary may be waning in relevance, as Jane Collier has explored in rural Spain, for example (Collier 1986). Also signaled in her much-reproduced figure is the vibrancy of a popular Catholicism in Mexico that has since its very beginnings been engaged in the lively creation of new saints of all kinds—including a compelling contemporary figure known as El Niño *Doctor de los Enfermos* (Baby Jesus, Doctor of the Sick), whom we will meet in the pages to come. As we shall see, such saintly figures of La Guadalupe and El Niño Doctor form part of a local grid of intelligibility through which both women and men made sense of—and hence made possible—the bodily sacrifices required by transplantation.

Not merely a sanctified, celebrated figure, however, La Guadalupe in Mexico is always shadowed by a darker double as well, a double given flesh in another iconic representation of Mexican womanhood consequential for local interpretations and materializations of transplant: *La Malinche.* La Malinche, the indigenous woman who stands accused of having betrayed her people by enabling the Spanish conquest through her relationship with Hernán Cortés, represents the other side of the feminine coin in Mexico

(Alarcón 1981; Diaz del Castillo 1956; Glantz 1995). As such, she is also linked with other powerful, painful images of womanhood, such as La Llorona (the Weeping Woman), a famous ghost in Mexican folklore burdened with guilt over killing her own children for the sake of a lover, said to appear on lonely roads late at night to terrify unwary travelers (Candelaria 1993; Ingham 1986; Paz 1959). If the Virgin Mary represents woman's potential for nurturance and self-sacrifice, this shadow figure reveals the simultaneous potential for betrayal and destruction also inherent in the roles of wife and mother. In the chapters to come we will find the suffering, powerful figure of La Guadalupe (as well as her dangerous twins) echoed in the complexities of the role played by—and expected of—mothers in the processes and politics surrounding living organ donation.

La Malinche stands as a central figure in a national imaginary not just of gender in Mexico, however, but of race as well. For it is from the originary violence of her relationship with the Spanish conquistador Cortés that a new nation is imagined to have been born in the racially mixed figure of el mestizo. An image deliberately crafted as an act of political imagination in the aftermath of the Mexican Revolution in the early twentieth century, el mestizo figures the nation as a kind of hybrid body, incorporating both ancient indigenous and modern European selves into a vigorous new race (Alonso 2004; Knight 1990; Vasconcelos 1979 [1925]).[11] Meant to overcome the fragmentation of a vast cultural and geographic landscape torn apart after a decade of devastating civil war, the notion of Mexico as a mestizo nation has had enduring power, and the figure of el mestizo (which is, notably, typically rendered as a masculine figure) has been mythologized throughout Mexican art, literature, and political discourse. A site of both celebration and contestation, however, critiques of el mestizo abound. Contemporary indigenous Mexicans, for example, indict the way the discourse of mestizaje slyly celebrates heterogeneity as means of enforcing homogeneity, pointing out that they are not merely part of Mexico's past (Stephen 2002). Caught up in such disputes, the hybrid mestizo body nonetheless remains an iconic sign of Mexican national identity. And the specific politics and aesthetics of this figuring matter for the way the bodies wrought by transplant may—as in the story of the German mother—become similarly caught up in imaginings of a national self. For this is an imagery that brings particular inflections of race, of gender, and of underlying violence to the local shape of transplant practice. In the chapters to come we will see how the legacy of mestizaje may haunt the emergence of this new form of hybrid body in Mexico, a body wrought, this time, by the biomedical marvels and uncanny conjoinings of transplantation.

If imaginings of Mexico as a mestizo nation turn out to be somewhat ambivalent—born out of both colonial violence and hopes for postrevolutionary cohesion and peace—so too is the state itself an ambiguous figure in the story of how transplant has come to matter in Mexico. Following the decades-long single-party rule of the Partido Revolucionario Institucional (PRI), a period characterized by socialist ideals, authoritarian oppression, and the exertion of political power through a capillary-like system of patronage relations, the Mexican State has been facing a profoundly unsettled contemporary moment. Widespread neoliberal reforms enacted under the pressures of global capitalism in the late twentieth century—including the structural adjustment policies of the 1980s and the North American Free Trade Agreement (NAFTA) of the 1990s—have been followed by upheavals of various kinds: from the peasant uprising of the Zapatistas in southern Mexico, to the defeat of the PRI in the presidential election of 2000 for the first time in nearly seventy years, to the rising regime of a brutal drug economy in which Mexican police, military, and political officials have been deeply implicated (Campbell 2014; Gledhill 1999; Muehlmann 2013; Stephen 2002). It was amid such pervasive political uncertainties that transplantation in Mexico took root primarily in the public health-care system—a system that was at once one of the last remaining vestiges of the Revolution's commitment to the collective well-being of the people and a key site of recurrent public scandals about official abuses both physical and financial. The particular institutional shape and clinical practices of state-supported transplant in Mexico thus served as a site where the biopolitics of making live (or not) and risking life (or not) were sometimes starkly visible, condensed in the bodies of those chosen to receive organs and those called upon to provide them (Foucault 1976).

As such, I attend in the chapters to come to the notion of Mexico as a kind of *slippery State*, a deeply biopolitical body of governance that operated as a source of both life-giving, practical benefits and everyday experiences of insecurity and disillusionment. Such unsettled, unsettling political conditions rendered actors in the transplant endeavor often illegible to one another—as well as to a wider public—in both practical and moral terms.[12] This was a world in which the figure before you in the doctor's white coat might be dedicated healer, greedy profiteer, ambitious politician, groundbreaking scientist, or dangerous *traficante* (trafficker of drugs, of organs, of other coveted, illicit goods). Or he or she might, at different moments, in different relational contexts, inhabit some complex combination of those roles. These forms of illegibility and the pervasive political uncertainty that produced them also had, as we shall see, palpable consequences for how the transplant endeavor did—and did not—come to matter in the slippery State of Mexico.

Taken together, this series of figures—la familia mexicana, the suffering mother (who is both La Guadalupe and La Malinche), el mestizo, and the slippery State—animate a complex iconography of gender, ethnicity, religion, and nationalism in Mexico. They serve as evocative shorthand for some of the distinctive features of the Mexican setting that have shaped how transplantation there has taken clinical shape and produced meaning in both personal and political registers. Yet invoking such iconic figures is both useful and always an already compromised endeavor, for simply identifying their potency—the way they represent ideas that travel and carry force in the world—runs always the risk of reifying it. Contested, contradictory, and incomplete as they are, these figures nonetheless form part of a symbolic idiom upon which people—patients, families, medical professionals, politicians, and others—draw in diverse ways on imaginings of self and nation. And so, in the pages to come, we will watch for how these figures are evoked and instrumentalized in the stories, logics, expectations, and images with which people made meaning of transplantation—and hence *made* transplantation—in locally particular ways.

Tapatío Transplantation

While it is possible—and sometimes useful—to traffic in notions of culture and identity at a national level, Mexico is an immense, sprawling, and hugely diverse country, rife with sharply drawn and dearly held regional differences. The iconic figures of La Guadalupe, el mestizo, and others explored above operate as a set of widely shared symbols, a sort of national idiom on which people in different social and geographic locations draw in distinctive ways. Yet beyond these broad strokes of the larger context, the particularities of the local setting where this study was conducted are crucial as well. This research was based in the city of Guadalajara, Mexico, and the project has extended over a twelve-year period from 1998 to 2010, with the most intensive period of yearlong fieldwork occurring at the turn of the millennium. Guadalajara, whose inhabitants proudly refer to themselves as *tapatíos*, is Mexico's second-largest city. Located several hundred miles northwest of Mexico City, Guadalajara serves as a major resource and service hub to the six surrounding states (Jalisco, Michoacán, Nayarrít, Guanajuato, Colima, and Aguascalientes). Reflecting the extreme urban concentration of health-care resources in Mexico more generally, Guadalajara maintains two elite tertiary-level hospitals that draw people seeking specialized care—such as transplantation—from all over western Mexico and beyond.[13] At the time of this research, Guadalajara housed the most active kidney transplantation program in all of Mexico, an unusual coup over the typically dominant Distrito Federal of Mexico City. It was an achievement of which the local transplant community—composed of a diverse, unevenly articulated array of social actors including patients, donors, family members, clinicians, social workers, administrators, pharmaceutical salespeople, and government officials—was understandably proud.

Appealing as a research site for this reason alone, Guadalajara also occupies a very particular cultural and political economic space in Mexico. Although a major metropolitan area, Guadalajara at the turn of the millennium did not come close to either the sprawling growth or the high crime rates of the capital, something for which its inhabitants regularly pronounced themselves grateful. A common refrain in casual conversation was that Guadalajara was *más tranquilo* (more calm) than Mexico City, offering a more civil and gracious pace of life. Guadalajara is often represented both by its own inhabitants and by other Mexicans as a deeply traditional city, and the region has long served as the source of various emblematic symbols of "Mexican-ness" including mariachi music, tequila, and *charrería* (a form of rodeo known for its athleticism and dramatic showmanship). These are much loved—and also much caricatured—symbols of Mexican culture that signify and circulate powerfully both within and across national borders. In keeping with this image of traditionalism, Guadalajara is also widely known as a politically conservative and deeply Catholic city, one that has retained much of the gracious architecture and wide boulevards of the colonial era (Carrillo 2002). Simply riding a bus around the city could quickly reveal these characteristics—passing one of the many beautiful churches and cathedrals often elicited a startlingly immediate response as many on the bus would rapidly touch forehead, sternum, and each shoulder in the sign of the cross, sometimes murmuring a quiet prayer.

Yet the particular inflection of traditional Mexico conjured in commonplace representations of Guadalajara was a decidedly mestizo one—unlike the southern region of Mexico, there was a relatively small population in the Guadalajara region that was visibly marked or marked itself as indigenous. With the exception of a small contingent of Huichol people who were most visible in the city as street vendors of artisanal crafts, indigenous dress, customs, and language did not generally provide public lines of demarcation along an axis of race or ethnicity in Guadalajara. Such lines were marked out in more subtle ways, however, by reference to physical features such as the shorter stature, darker skin, and strong "Mayan" nose thought to place someone closer to the Indian than to the European end of the mestizo spectrum. Cowboy boots and hats on men, and long, full skirts and shawls used as both bodily wrap and modest head-covering for women comprised other such markers by which people in Guadalajara referred obliquely to notions of race or ethnicity via an idiom of urban/rural and class distinctions. During my fieldwork I only rarely heard anyone use the pejorative *indio*, however references to a particular patient as *muy típico* (very typical, very traditional) or *muy folklórico* (very folkloric) might be delivered in a somewhat sly aside, often meant to contextualize what might then be described as a "superstitious" mind-set or an "inadequate" living situation in the context of transplantation. Given this local context, race or ethnicity does not make the kind of overt appearance as a key axis of differentiation in this research that it surely would have made had this work been conducted in a more explicitly ethnicized setting like Oaxaca in southern Mexico. However, local assumptions about race or ethnicity are intimately bound up with the more commonly employed distinctions of class and urban/rural identity that recur throughout the book.

Despite being so powerfully imagined as a site and source of Mexican tradition, Guadalajara is also a profoundly global city with long-standing connections to complex flows of money, people, and technology from all over the world. Reflecting a trend of growing investment by multinational firms, for instance, Guadalajara at the turn of the millennium was the site of some 20 percent of IBM's world production (Napolitano 2002: 198). The city also boasts an excellent university and a well-known medical school, which attracts a large number of international (especially U.S.) students. In addition, the area is the site of a well-established U.S. retirement community centered on nearby Lake Chapala—a development that has enticed some Guadalajara physicians (including one of the transplant surgeons we will encounter in the pages that follow) to begin to contemplate entrepreneurial schemes for attracting the private health-care dollars of this aging population.[14] In fact, the retirement community's English-language newspaper ran an interview with this particular transplant surgeon in which he suggested that, in the not-too-distant future, North Americans might find the local health-care system a source of convenient and lower-cost organ transplantation (Miller 1999).[15] Global connections flow outward from Guadalajara as well, from the long-standing migration of manual laborers through the formal U.S. Bracero Program of the mid-twentieth century up to the present-day routinized but risky border crossings of undocumented workers. And elites from the region in business, politics, and science also circulate widely through international networks of training, employment, and leisure travel. Although the above-mentioned transplant surgeon's hoped-for future flow of transplant-seeking North Americans had not yet materialized at the time of this research, Mexican patients in fact proved to be quite adept at mobilizing global ties of various kinds in pursuing and managing their transplants. In the chapters to come we will encounter living donors who return from the United States in order to provide a kidney to a family member, as well as patients who rely on a constant flow of both money and information provided by family in the United States in order to negotiate the process of seeking a transplant.

Such global linkages carry transplant professionals away from Mexico in search of training, to elite centers of transplant medicine in the United States, Europe, and Japan, and also work to bring transplant experts in from elsewhere. During my research one of the local hospitals hosted two prestigious conferences organized around visits by transplant surgeons and organ procurement professionals from Spain—a country that served as an important model for the transplant endeavor in Mexico, not just because of the close linguistic, cultural, and historical ties between the two countries, but because Spain boasted the most successful cadaveric organ donation program in the world.[16] As a visiting American researcher, I sometimes found myself enrolled in the complicated politics of these global professional networks in unexpected ways. In one such instance, a rival department chairman arrived on the transplant ward to proudly (and pointedly) introduce a visiting American cardiac surgeon. Before I quite knew what had happened, I found myself being pushed forward by the transplant program director (in a parrying move) as "his American scientist" here to study and work with him. Hardly used to being summoned as a source of scientific prestige in quite this way, the moment felt to me like an edifying twist on the discredited anthropological habit of proprietary references to the places we have worked as "my community," foregrounding just one of the potential ways in which my gringa positioning might be instrumentalized by those I sought to study. Highlighted also in that slightly awkward, somewhat funny moment was the complexity of the multidirectional flows of people, ideas, and resources of all sorts that make up transplantation as a set of practices (and ideas) that are at once powerfully global in their circulations and inescapably local in their instantiation.

A Tale (Mostly) of Two Institutions

Transplantation in Guadalajara at the turn of the millennium was highly centered in the city's two elite tertiary-level public hospitals, both of which housed active kidney transplant programs (as well as nascent liver transplant programs). These hospitals represent the two major government-run health-care systems in Mexico, the Instituto Mexicano de Seguro Social (IMSS—Mexican Institute of Social Security) and the Secretaria de Salud (SSa—Ministry of Health).[17] Other key elements of the health-care landscape in Mexico, including private hospitals and the panoply of "alternative" health-care services provided by *naturistas, curanderos, homeopatas* (naturalists, folk healers, homeopaths), and others, are also part of the local story of transplantation and will make occasional appearances in the pages to come. And yet part of what was so striking about transplant in Mexico was precisely its emergence as a phenomenon primarily of the public health-care system, rather than of the profiteering private sector.[18] Private hospitals in Guadalajara at the time of this research engaged only passingly in transplantation as a matter of marketable prestige—trading on the iconic, high-tech mystique of transplant to bolster a hospital's cutting-edge reputation—rather than of direct profit (see also Cohen 1999 on the marketing allure of transplant in the Indian health-care landscape). As one private hospital director told me quite bluntly: "It's not worth it to us, from a financial perspective. We do a few for the prestige, but we're not really that interested in getting into the business of transplantation" (Dr. Alvarez). Transplantation in Mexico was thus fundamentally both a family matter, deeply dependent on the bodies of those living related donors, and a public affair, rooted in the institutions of an increasingly eroded but still essential national health-care system.

Broadly speaking, the IMSS system at the time of this research was the largest of the federal health-care systems, providing coverage for slightly over half of the Mexican population and serving primarily working- to middle-class people whose employment in the formal sector paid into the national Social Security system (INEGI 2000).[19] Nationally, the IMSS possessed the best-developed infrastructure of clinics, hospitals, and specialized equipment of any of the Mexican health-care institutions—including the private sector. Yet the IMSS clinics and hospitals were typically overburdened and undersupplied, and many patients who had rights to the system often opted for private care for minor ailments when they could afford it, in order to avoid long waits, out-of-stock pharmacies, and care that could be notoriously brusque. Deeply flawed but also deeply necessary as the primary source of health care for the majority of Mexicans, the IMSS was regarded by many as one of the last remnants of the largely abandoned hopes of the Revolution, representing a national commitment to at least the promise (if not the reality) of health care as a universal right of the people.[20]

At the time of this study, the IMSS Centro Médico de Especialidades (Specialty Medical Center) in Guadalajara housed the country's most active kidney transplant program. Although the hospital's first successful kidney transplant was carried out in 1976, until the mid-1990s transplant activity remained sporadic at best, and in some years not a single transplant was performed. While the demonstrated ability to do transplants was valued as a mark of scientific achievement, any sizable expansion was thought to be unrealistic. In 1995, however, a nephrologist fresh from training in the United States took over with an ambitious vision for dramatically building the transplant program and growing the yearly transplantation rate. His plans, which leaned heavily on the wooing of donations from multinational pharmaceutical companies, were deemed so outrageous by his IMSS colleagues that he was dubbed "MonteAlbán" in a derisive play on his own name that cheekily invoked both the massiveness of the famous pre-Columbian archaeological site in southern Mexico and the Mexican actor, Ricardo Montalbán, who played host on the old American television program *Fantasy Island*. Over the next five years however, those monumental, fantastical goals were achieved, and at the time of this research, the program was performing approximately two hundred kidney transplants per year and was beginning to build a liver transplant program as well. Worthy of a study all its own, this growth involved the complex interplay of dogged determination, politics both institutional and personal, the costly economics of kidney therapies, surgical charisma, and the glamorous media-grabbing cachet of transplantation, among a host of other factors.

The IMSS transplant program was housed in the tall hospital tower of the IMSS Centro Médico, a stark concrete landmark in the generally low-slung cityscape of Guadalajara. The scale and the scuffed marble floors of the building reflected a former grandeur that has been slowly worn down by day-to-day use and the unending passage of the sick and their families. Upstairs, the transplant program occupied the better part of an entire floor, sharing space with the dialysis and hemodialysis programs that served the hospital's kidney patients. Patients, family members, and staff bustled their way in and out of patient rooms and staff offices, frequently crowding the hallway as they lay in wait hoping to catch an elusive physician or the constantly-in-motion transplant coordinator. Patients and their families were a varied lot, ranging from urban factory workers and small-business people to rural campesinos (farmers) to the occasional well-heeled housewife. There was constant activity as patients came in and out of the coordinator's and doctors' offices, clutching charts and X-rays, setting up appointments, seeking information, bureaucratic forms, and reassurance. As patients interacted with transplant staff, there was also occasional emotional chaos—tears, anger, fear, recrimination, but also laughter, joy, and fervent gratitude.

More loosely organized than the IMSS, the largely state-run SSa system was essentially a public charity system designed to care for the most vulnerable members of society. Estimates suggest that approximately 10 to 15 percent of the population depended primarily upon the SSa for health care (INEGI 2000). Patients in the SSa system paid "quotas" for their care, based on a sliding scale assessment of income, and many paid nothing at all. Though patients required neither the ability to pay nor an outside referral to access the SSa system, interminably long waits for hospital beds and services greatly restricted access, sometimes catastrophically so. Regarded by many as a "poor people's hospital" where those without hope go to die, the SSa hospital's university affiliation meant that it was also a site for academic teaching and research, as well as for sometimes cutting-edge medical care such as transplantation.

The SSa hospital's transplant program was also under the direction of a U.S.-trained nephrologist. Although the program was officially launched in 1988, the first kidney transplant was not carried out until December 1990—a delay characteristic of this perpetually resource-strapped hospital. Subsequent growth was halting, never quite achieving the goal of one transplant per month. A major limitation of growth was the hospital's inability to provide patients with the immunosuppressive drugs required after transplant surgery, due to the SSa mandate to provide coverage for in-patient care only. All too aware of the lifelong and extremely expensive commitment these drugs represent, the program director was reluctant to transplant patients without a plan to guarantee ongoing medication access. Such plans ranged from cobbling together money from private benefactors to brokering discounts with the pharmaceutical companies to finding post-transplant employment for patients that would entitle them to access to the IMSS system and its drug benefits. Despite such limitations, however, the SSa hospital not only maintained an active kidney transplant program but was also the site of the country's only successful liver transplant program during the study period.

The SSa transplant program in Guadalajara was housed in the Antiguo Hospital Civil (Old Civil Hospital). Itself a hybrid structure, one half of the hospital consisted of the "old wing"—a structure built by the Spanish bishop of the city nearly two hundred years before. This older section of the hospital combined graceful open courtyards with long, echoing, grim hospital wards lined with narrow cots and makeshift curtains. In a dense layering of histories of suffering and stigma, the ward that had once served as the leprosy wing in the hospital had become, during my time there, the AIDS unit. This original structure was connected to a newer medical tower, a dingy concrete structure with overcrowded waiting areas and perennially out-of-service elevators. The SSa transplant program was somewhat splintered between these sections of the hospital, and transplant program staff, patients, and their families shuttled constantly between the nephrology floor, the transplant program office, hemodialysis, and the intensive care unit. Like the IMSS patient population, the SSa patients were also a mixed lot, although Mexicans with various markers of both rural life and Indian ethnicity were much more common than in the IMSS hospital—cowboy hats and boots on the men, women with shawls drawn carefully and demurely over their heads, and the stature, skin tone, and facial structure of indigenous Mexicans were ubiquitous. Urban, working-class mestizos also abounded, however, and occasionally there appeared patients or family members whose clothes, cell phones, and style of speech signaled a more prosperous economic stratum. Patients and their families waited propped up against walls, or, if they were lucky, in flimsy plastic chairs, to be called into staff offices and consultation rooms. Many people brought blankets, food, even pillows, knowing from experience that the wait could be a long one. A certain camaraderie often grew up among them as they waited or wandered the halls, sharing information and frustrations, hope, and the occasional piece of fruit.

Though sketched out here as separate entities, any neatly drawn distinctions between the social security setting of the IMSS, the public charity setting of the SSa, and even the presumably privileged setting of the private health-care system proved hard to maintain once on the ground. Both physicians and patients were mobile elements within the matrix of health-care options, constantly and strategically shifting back and forth between different institutional settings as they tried to maximize the relative advantages of each. Physicians often juggled jobs in the public and private sector— holding positions in the government hospitals for the prestige and access to more advanced technology and equipment but needing a private practice as well in order to make ends meet.[21] Patients too, across the socioeconomic range, moved—sometimes deftly, sometimes haltingly—across the complex health-care landscape, making use of a mix of private and various public health care services, and often combining biomedicine with homeopathy, naturalism, and/or *curandería* (folk healing) in ways that to them felt complementary rather than contradictory. Such constant interconnections between institutional settings, as well as the relatively small size of the still-in-formation local transplant endeavor, created a degree of social intensity and often face-to-face interaction best captured by the notion of transplant community I use throughout this book. Indeed, it was precisely these interconnections that surely made the story of the más mexicana German mother so widely shared among so many of those I first met as I began this work. Ultimately, this was the complex, shifting institutional ground upon which the complex nexus of relations entailed in what Lesley Sharp so usefully terms "organ transfer" has come to matter in Mexico (Sharp 2006: 3).

Tracking Transplantation

In approaching a topic as layered with fantasies, fears, embodied desperation, and institutional complexity as organ transplantation, I was committed to the familiar anthropological approach of staying put, convinced that long-standing strategies of showing up, hanging out, riding the daily rhythms, and sharing meals, frustrations, emergencies, tedium, and endless conversations with the same group of people for an extended period could produce a richness of data and insight hard to come by otherwise.

And so, employing the classic ethnographic methods of participant observation and in-depth interviewing, I devoted much of my time in Mexico to
the IMSS and the SSa hospitals, ensuring that I was an ongoing presence
in both throughout the course of my fieldwork. Observations took place
everywhere I could think to go in the complex social world of the hospital, in the perpetually overcrowded offices of transplant coordinators and
physicians, in patient rooms and operating rooms, at nurses' stations and
pharmacy lines, in clinic rooms and waiting rooms, and at patient support
groups and staff meetings. Time spent around the transplant wards allowed
me to develop a nodding acquaintanceship with patients that often grew
into conversations and, when they were willing, formal interviews. Often,
in fact, patients approached me first, full of curiosity about what such an
obvious gringa was doing hanging around in the hospital all the time—the
little notebook that served as my constant companion frequently prompted
initial assumptions that I was a reporter. The relationships that grew out
of those early interactions allowed me, in many cases, to follow patients,
families, and the clinicians who cared for them out of the hospital and into
their lives, spending time with them in their homes, workplaces, favorite
restaurants, nearby parks, and even a local bowling alley where a group of
us met on Sunday afternoons for a few games and lots of laughter.

The field notes I took by hand each day and recorded and expanded on
my laptop each evening eventually accrued observational and interview data
on 323 transplant patient cases, and on 74 potential cadaveric organ donation cases. These qualitative data were augmented by quantitative statistics
shared with me by each transplant program from its own patient databases.
I conducted in-depth, taped interviews with 50 transplant patients, divided
between the IMSS and the SSa programs, and including patients already
transplanted, patients awaiting transplantation with a live donor, and
patients on the waiting list for a cadaveric transplant. In all, I formally
interviewed 22 female patients and 28 male patients, with ages ranging
from seventeen to sixty-two. Patient socioeconomic status varied widely,
and interview participants ranged from college-educated upper/middle-
class (engineer, small business owner) to high school–educated working-
class (factory worker, food vendor) to grade school–educated marginalized
poor (farm laborer, unemployed single mother). In addition, I interviewed
key transplant professionals in both hospitals, including physicians, surgeons, transplant coordinators, and nurses, as well as administrators responsible for policy and budget decision-making. I pursued questions of

policy outside the hospital walls as well, through interviews with regional government officials involved in transplant-related policy, including members of the nascent statewide Consejo Estatal de Trasplante de Organos y Tejidos (State Council on Organ and Tissue Transplantation), a politically contentious body still in formation at the time.

Another tactic for tracing the movement of people, practices, and ideas outside of the hospitals themselves was attending a number of conferences and training courses (some for the general public, some for various types of medical personnel) on organ donation and transplantation. Other public-education events were also important sources of ethnographic experience and information, including several publicity stunts planned by patients to draw attention to their plight. Toward the end of my main fieldwork stint, I was invited to present two papers on my research at a national conference on transplantation held for medical professionals from around the country, an opportunity that allowed me to reflect some of my preliminary findings back to the local transplant community and opened up further avenues of discussion.

And finally, I sought to extend my research outside of the transplant community itself—beyond the countless conversations with friends, street vendors, taxi drivers, and random acquaintances in which all anthropologists engage. Such efforts included systematically monitoring the popular media for news stories about transplantation in particular and health care more generally, a task greatly aided by the IMSS hospital's news media clipping service.[22] I also conducted a small series of interviews with Catholic priests—including the bishop of the main cathedral in Guadalajara—about the Church's attitudes toward transplantation and donation and about priests' own experiences and beliefs in dealing with such issues in their own congregations. Another window into a wider point of view was provided by a new state initiative in Jalisco to record willingness to serve as an organ donor on drivers' licenses—a program that generated data on donation attitudes of upward of 120,000 new license recipients.

Doing anthropology entails not just collecting all of these variegated forms of data, of course, but deciding how to make sense of and represent them. At a practical level, I have followed anthropological convention in protecting the identities of research participants. The names of all patients, family members, transplant professionals, and government officials have been changed throughout, and in some cases individual details have been combined, elided, or altered in order to disguise distinguishing characteristics. Although individual identity is protected, the identity of the city and primary institutional sites where this research was conducted clearly has not been. This was a decision made in consultation with the directors and other staff members of the transplant programs I studied, who agreed that because of the programs' elite status in Mexico the location of this research would be difficult to disguise. Such pragmatic considerations aside, however, my interlocutors also made it quite clear that their interest in promoting awareness about the existence of successful transplantation in Mexico outweighed their understanding that the study goal was not to present the programs in a promotional or even necessarily flattering light (nor, I should note, was it a goal to present them in an unflattering light). This was a decision we came to together toward the end of my main fieldwork stint, after months of ongoing contact and conversation had increased their confidence that they understood both me and my project better, and after I had the opportunity to present some preliminary research findings to them. Throughout the book, direct quotations are cited (and translated by me) from either individual taped interviews or from my field notes, and quotes and individuals are identified by name, a brief occupation descriptor (e.g., engineer, street vendor, surgeon) and main institutional affiliation (e.g., IMSS, SSa, private hospital). These identifiers are intended to provide some approximate markers of socioeconomic status and class positioning, and to help the reader track individuals as they appear in different places throughout the text.

Such familiar anthropological writing conventions help both to protect those who participated in this research and to orient those who will read it. With similar goals in mind I also provide markers throughout the book of my own presence as an actor in the field I aim to describe. Doing so is meant to serve as a recurring reminder that what I can offer here is but one possible story of the way things stand. This account of organ transplantation in Mexico at the turn of the millennium is a story that—like all forms of knowledge—is situated, fundamentally conditioned by the storyteller herself (Haraway 1991; Harding 1991). My own ethnographic gaze is shaped in ways I can mark and challenge and try to expand but can never fully escape: I remain female, white, well educated, a person raised in the middle-class suburban world of late-twentieth-century North America (among many other identifications). So too did the gazing back of those I sought to study—those who spoke and interacted with me, as well as those who chose not to—inevitably apprehend and respond to me in their own situated ways that I can strive to comprehend, but for which I can never fully account. What I can do is try to frame the ethnographic stories I have to tell in terms of the conditions under which I learned them, attending throughout the book to questions of context as well as content, to how and when and by whom certain narratives, certain kinds of experiences were made available to me in the field.

Also worth marking are the conditions under which I produced this account from those field experiences, for this book has had a long gestation. Since I first began this research transplant medicine, Mexico, and anthropology itself have continued to move through time and change of various kinds. Though some sense of those changes is surely, necessarily incorporated into the book, the central story I have to tell is unabashedly focused on a particular moment, just at the turn of the twenty-first century, when organ transplantation was truly coming to matter in Mexico in clinical, ethical, and political terms. This is, of course, an ongoing story, some dimensions of which are now being picked up by Ciara Kierans, who has been studying the course of kidney patients specifically without IMSS access in Guadalajara more recently (see, for example, Kierans 2015). My own account—like all ethnography—is thus particular to a time and place, but it also speaks to a larger set of processes of biotechnical emergence, proliferation, and incorporation (into both individual and national bodies) that we are bound to see recur in the ongoing march of medicine as scientific endeavor, clinical practice, and capitalist enterprise. Organ transplantation is neither the first nor the last example of medicine's interventions into bodies, selves, politics, and ideas urgently calling for anthropological attention.

How I have come to think about that millennial moment in Mexican transplantation has been shaped by the fact that I too have hardly remained static since those first, heady days of fieldwork. In the process of conducting this project so unavoidably engaged with the politics of families and the bodies of mothers, I have extended my own forms of embodied experience and familial attachment, becoming both a wife and a mother myself. I have also become a professional, not just in anthropology, but in medicine as well by virtue of the hybrid academic appointments where I have made my institutional homes. In the process, I have experienced the sometimes unexpected, uneasy ways that being an observer of transplantation can pull one into being a participant—even a form of professional—in the transplant endeavor. I have had to pick and choose my way carefully among invitations not just to share my research, but to collaborate with or even (in a move I chose not to make) to become wholly institutionally assimilated with the transplant clinicians that I study. In thinking through such charged choices, as well as through the material that my time in Mexico yielded, I have been immeasurably aided by the growing community of scholars in the anthropology of transplant that has emerged over the past decade, providing evocative, provocative comparative examples against which to sharpen my own ethnographic observations, as well as cherished intellectual companionship along the way. All of these expanding forms of attachment, familial, professional, and intellectual, have deepened the resources available to me for thinking through the complex pull of emotion, obligation, desperation, and aspiration on those who need organs, those who are called to give them up, and those who work to make such organ transfers possible. Though the years elapsed since I began this work have rendered this book less timely in a journalistic sense, they have also, I hope, produced an account much richer than I would otherwise have been able to tell.

Mapping the Chapters

This book explores how organ transplantation gets caught up in particular ways of imagining both individual and national selves and how such imaginings materialize transplant in locally specific ways that have crucial consequences in clinical, social, and political terms. More broadly, the book takes up the way that organ transplantation is so often made to stand for something—or for many things—larger than itself, not only in millennial Mexico, but in anthropology itself. Seen in turn as a triumphal example of modern medicine's death-defying powers, as miraculous proof of God's work in the world, and as the horrifying extension of capitalism's voracious commodification of the human body, I argue that transplantation serves as a kind of icon, as a site where many different—and sometimes conflicting—commitments, claims, and anxieties are condensed and instrumentalized.

The book is divided into three sections, each containing a set of paired chapters. The first section explores the question of what kinds of bodies were—and were not—made available in Mexico to transplantation's demand for organs. Chapter 1 examines the dependence on living related organ donation in Mexico, delving more deeply into the questions of gender, risk, and responsibility first raised in the story of the German mother, and arguing that the feminization and familialization of transplantation in Mexico produced a powerful effect of familiarization. Framing this as a kind of *ethical domestication* of the transplant endeavor as a whole, this chapter traces out some of the resulting material, political, and ethical effects on the way transplantation has come to matter as both practice and idea in Mexico. Chapter 2 turns from the abundant bioavailability of living donors in Mexico to explore the relative biounavailability of brain-dead donors, interrogating both the conditions and consequences of this scarcity of cadaveric organs in terms of an all-too-familiar politics of blame that we might see as its own form of ethical domestication. I argue that beneath easy indictments of "superstitious ignorance" and "family refusals" as the barriers holding back further flourishing of the transplant endeavor lies a much more unruly story about the situated difficulties of materializing brain death both *as* a slippery state, rife with conceptual ambiguities and practical difficulties, and *in* a slippery State, where institutional and interpersonal trust may be hard to come by.

The next section moves from the donors who provide organs to the patients who need them, exploring the lived experiences, institutional politics, and symbolic dimensions of seeking and (for some) of living over the long term with a transplant. Chapter 3 focuses on the complex ways in which certain patients came to be deemed worthy of transplantation and others did not, attending in the process to the representational powers and pressures exerted by transplant's iconic status. Such decisions about who should (and should not) be transplanted are also, critically, decisions about what kind of clinical and moral enterprise transplant itself should be. Chapter 4 picks up the story of posttransplant life, resisting the romance of transplantation's standard salvationary narrative to examine the lived challenges of posttransplant health, productivity, and reproductivity over the longer term. These challenges produce for many transplant recipients what we might call a form of persistent patienthood, a state-of-being much more contingent than the familiar happily-ever-after story of transplantation. Eliding this more complex and uneasy lived reality in the iconic story line of transplantation is, I argue, another form of strategic simplification—indeed a domestication—of the transplant enterprise itself.

The last section moves away from the iconic dyad of organ donor and organ recipient to consider two other key nodes in the set of relations through which transplantation comes into being. Taking up in turn the figure of the kidney itself and of the transplant professional who works to make it move between bodies, these last two chapters engage—and also question—some of the iconic analytic frames that anthropology has brought to the study of transplantation. Chapter 5 delves into the social life of the kidney, examining and complicating the moral and affective politics (as well as the analytic effects) of the gift/commodity frame and arguing for a more expansive temporal and relational approach to tracking the complex, unstable meanings of organ transfer. Chapter 6 explores the dense intermingling of notions of the sacred and the profane and of insiders and outsiders in how the iconic figures of scientist, saint, and monster persistently haunt not only the professionals who enact transplantation, but also those of us who study them. Drawing on but also stepping back from the ethnographic specificity of Mexico, these final chapters together explore a set of broader conceptual questions regarding how transplant has come to matter in anthropology itself and how, conversely, anthropology comes to matter in particular ways through its engagement with the transplant endeavor. A brief Coda looks back to the figure of the German mother become más mexicana with whom we began in order to look forward to an emerging biopolitics of global health that we might frame as also, in a sense, más mexicana in its growing dependence on the intimate resources of body, family, and culture to fuel the survival of some at the risk of others.

PART I

GIVING KIDNEYS (OR NOT)

1. Living Organ Donation, Bioavailability, and Ethical Domesticity

Opening Bodies

Transplantation in Mexico was overwhelmingly a family matter. During the time of my research, well over 80 percent of all kidney transplants were performed using organs from living, *related* donors. Less than 10 percent of kidney transplants relied on organs from living, *unrelated* donors—a number that included friends, neighbors, coworkers, and coreligionists, as well as sometimes murkier forms of relationship. And a scant number of brain-dead donors provided the remaining 10 percent or so. This material fact of familial donation in Mexico stands in sharp contrast to other settings around the world, where different configurations of what Lawrence Cohen has so usefully termed "bioavailability" predominate (Cohen 2005). In the United States, for example, kidneys come in roughly equal measure from the brain-dead and from living donors (UNOS 2014b), while in Spain brain-dead donors enable an astonishing 90 percent of all transplants, and *any* use of living donors is both limited and lamented (Matesanz et al. 2009; Matesanz and Miranda 1996a). In yet other settings—India and Israel, perhaps most infamously—there has emerged a strong reported preference for living unrelated organ sellers as a source of "fresh" organs, unencumbered by familial entanglements and made immunologically acceptable by

Figure 1.1 *Las Dos Fridas* (The Two Fridas), Frida Kahlo (1939) © 2015 Banco de México Diego Rivera Frida Kahlo Museums Trust, Mexico, D.F. / Artists Rights Society (ARS), New York. Photo by Schalkwijk/Art Resource, NY. Reproduction authorized by the Instituto Nacional de Bellas Artes y Literatura (INBA), 2015.

increasingly powerful immunosuppressive medications (Cohen 1999, 2005, 2011; Moniruzzaman 2012; Scheper-Hughes 2005). Such situated forms of bioavailability are central to how "global" biotechnologies like transplantation come to matter—materially, discursively, and ethically—in locally distinctive ways.

While the global traffic in human organs has rightly drawn much critical anthropological attention, the view from Guadalajara pushes us to explore a somewhat different set of logics mobilizing local forms of bioavailability. In Mexico, the erosive effects of neoliberal reform on the public health infrastructure have been widely felt (Laurell 2001, 2011). Yet neither the profiteering private hospital nor the money-hungry organ broker—so notoriously familiar from accounts of transplantation in other settings—dominated the local transplant scene. Rather, transplantation in Mexico took root primarily in the public institutions of the IMSS and SSa hospitals. And it was materialized largely through the intimate, domestic relations of kinship. Rather than rendering human organs into a kind of "bare life" commodity form (Agamben 1998), in millennial Mexico it seems that transplantation both produced—and was produced through—kidneys that were thoroughly "encultured" and individuated, saturated with and drawn forth by the weight of specific social relationship and cultural expectation.[1] Taking up the thread of our previous encounter with the German mother who became más mexicana through donating a kidney to her son, this chapter thus delves into how particular kinds of bodies were rendered most appropriate and available to the corporeal demands of transplantation in Mexico. In the next chapter I invert this question of the bioavailability of living related kidney donors to interrogate the biounavailability of cadaveric donors in Mexico that necessarily underlay and conditioned it.

The painting of The Two Fridas (figure 1.1)serves as a thematic guide of sorts, for it condenses some of the key symbolic connections and tensions we will need to navigate.[2] Frida Kahlo, one of Mexico's most prominent twentieth-century artists, is known for her intensely personal depictions of physical and emotional suffering, suffering wrought by both the severe injuries sustained in a catastrophic bus accident early in her life and by the tumultuous course of her marriage to the Mexican artist Diego Rivera. By its very rawness and power, however, much of her work conveys not just suffering and vulnerability, but a ferocious strength as well. There is an aggressive potency produced by pain rendered so viscerally visible. The Two Fridas conjures up this complex mixture of suffering and strength, of sacrifice and the fearsome power it can engender. It depicts an open, wounded feminine body—a twinned body in which the intimate connections made possible by medical technologies seem to be both life-giving and violating. The exposed doubled hearts both evoke the theme of agonizing love that dominated much of Kahlo's work and echo the imagery of Christ's similarly exposed "sacred heart" so ubiquitous throughout Mexico. Moving between these hearts, blood appears to circulate on ambiguous pathways, suggesting the promise of life sustained through the body of another (which is also self), but also the threat of death with the spill of blood onto the lap of one of the figures. It is difficult to tell if the relationship between the two figures is symbiotic or vampiric. Differences in dress between the two Fridas reference other doublings as well, invoking the indigenous and mestizo, rural and urban selves so deeply imbricated in familiar representations of Mexican national identity.

The feminine doublings and disturbing ambiguities of the painting also invoke some of the key iconic representations of Mexican womanhood introduced in the previous chapter, in particular the oft-paired figures of the self-sacrificing Virgin Mary and her dark twin, La Malinche. Taken together, La Virgen and La Malinche represent the possibilities for not only nurturance and self-sacrifice, but also betrayal and destruction intrinsic to the roles of wife and mother. Such feminine representations cannot, of course, be imputed to or imposed upon the experiences of women (or men) as if they had any sort of straightforward determining or explanatory power (Gutmann 1996; Mohanty 1988). Yet these pervasive, polysemic images of Mexican feminine identity do form part of the symbolic idiom of gender in Mexico, operating in complex relation with positionings of class, race, sexuality, region, religion, and age. Working as both cultural resource and constraint, figures like the sainted mujer sufrida and the scorned La Malinche represent ideas about female gender (and race) that may be thrust upon, taken up, resisted, or reworked by individuals in various ways as they negotiate subjectivity and constitute meaning within pervasive relations of inequality (Collier 1986; Martin 1987; Napolitano 2002; Wentzell 2013). And, as we shall see, these iconic images—the values they condense and oppositions they evoke—were critical also in constituting local understandings of living organ donation and the bodies thought most properly available to produce it.

The presence of The Two Fridas haunts not just this chapter, but the physical and imaginative space of the transplant community in Guadalajara as well. A small framed print of the painting was one of the few decorations hung in the IMSS transplant coordinator's office, a space that constituted the social heart of the program, a place through which patients, families, and medical staff endlessly circulated. The head transplant coordinator told me that she had hung it there because it reminds people to think about the suffering and mutual interdependence that mark transplantation. She used the image of The Two Fridas to similar effect in the frequent lectures in support of organ donation and transplantation that she delivered to hospital staff, patients, and their families around the region; indeed, it served as one of her favorite PowerPoint slides. And although her spoken words concentrated on the suffering of the patient in need of an organ in such talks, for me the ambiguity of the doubled Frida provides a whispered counterpoint, evoking also the suffering of the donor whose body is risked.

For the risks of living kidney donation are far from negligible. They include surgical risks related to anesthesia and wound healing, as well as the uncertain risk to donors of developing disease themselves in their remaining kidney. Quantifying these risks is a dicey business and may require questionable translation of statistics generated in one setting (often the United States) into another. The most widely reported U.S. data on kidney donors suggests a risk of surgical death of .031 percent (Segev et al. 2010). Yet even in the United States there has been relatively little detailed tracking of donors over the very long term to study what happens as the kidney-damaging diseases of aging (such as hypertension and diabetes) set in (Ross et al. 2007).[3] And even these data can tell us little about donor risks in other settings with different political economies of transplantation—and of health and well-being more generally (Moazam et al. 2009; Radcliffe-Richards et al. 1998). In Guadalajara at the time of my research there had been no reported kidney donor deaths in either the IMSS or the SSa programs, but there were two known cases of kidney donors who had subsequently developed renal disease themselves and were facing dialysis and/or transplantation. In at least one case, there was general agreement among the horrified transplant staff that an inadequate workup, performed by a harried and inexperienced young doctor, had failed to reveal the heritable nature of the recipient's kidney disease and thus his brother's risk for developing the same disease. Along with the image of *The Two Fridas*, these are the risks that will haunt our exploration of the bodies imagined—and sometimes made—available for living donation.

The Family as National/Natural Resource

> Well of course, if it's possible medically, the mother will usually donate the kidney—it is only *natural* that she should want to be the one . . .
> —Dr. Solano, transplant surgeon, IMSS (emphasis added)

I want to return us briefly to the story of the German mother whose willingness to sacrifice her own flesh (in the form of a donated kidney) to save her son was so recurrently interpreted to me as a sign of her having become *más mexicana*. That story, and the quotation above—a comment frequently echoed by transplant staff as well as patients and family members—call our attention to a powerful local discourse linking together situated notions of gender, family, nation, and nature itself in the service of living organ donation. In part, the frequently recounted German mother's story worked to claim the moral superiority of the self-sacrificial character of Mexican motherhood, illustrated through pointed contrast with the colder, more individualistic ethos of her German relatives, who were horrified that she would risk herself when another option existed. Highlighted here is a sense of cultural identity rooted in the idea that Mexico has retained a set of family-centered moral values that have been lost in the postindustrial world in a blur of money, technology, and self-involvement. Also central to the story—and to the sense of national identity and pride it indexed—was the idea that German physicians sent the family back to Mexico because they judged themselves less skilled at living organ donation than their Mexican counterparts. Mobilized as a sort of cultural technology, iconic notions of la familia mexicana (and that self-sacrificial mother) were thus imagined to enable forms of expertise both clinical and ethical, expertise that rendered Mexican transplant techniques not merely imitative of, but sometimes superior to, other forms of global transplant practice.

Transplant program staff were often explicit about envisioning an idealized notion of "strong" Mexican families as the basic resource that enabled them to carry on the transplant endeavor, despite the considerable resource limitations of the public health-care institutions within which they operated. On the one hand, transplant staff expressed frustration and regret at the lack of cadaveric donors; on the other, the availability of living donors could also engender a certain pride among staff members: "We may not have cadaveric donors, we may not have operating rooms or money or all the medications that we need, but our people will do anything for their families; we can get more live donors than you'll ever see in the United States. That's what keeps us going" (Dr. Fernandez, IMSS). In this way, staff referred matter-of-factly to taken-for-granted understandings of the cohesiveness, size, and collective (rather than individual) orientation of Mexican families as critical advantages in generating living donors.

Both deeply gendered and powerfully heteronormative, we cannot, of course, take this representation of la familia mexicana at face value. Actual families in Mexico, like everywhere, are obviously much more diverse, complicated, and often conflictual than this picture portrays. Indeed, common social formations like la casa chica ("the little house," a second household set up by a married man for his lover and her children),[4] as well as rising rates of migration, separation, divorce, and remarriage in Mexico mean that families are often experienced as complex, many-jointed (also disjointed), and unstable over time (Kelly 2008; Napolitano 2002). Moreover, the possibilities for making family in Mexico are hardly wholly dependent upon the naturalized ties "by blood" foregrounded in local imaginings of living donation. Rather, more expansive notions of familial relatedness also operate through long-standing socioeconomic institutions like *compadrazgo* (godparenthood), as well as more emergent forms of gay sociality (Carrillo 2002; Nutini and Bell 1980). And as later chapters explore, the possibilities for forms of relatedness may open out as well through the experiences of organ donation and transplantation itself, as transplant recipients, donors, and their relatives reimagine new notions of familial bond forged out of shared suffering, need, and bodily substance (see Sharp 2006: 159–205 for a similar dynamic among donor families and transplant recipients in the United States).

But for the moment I want to focus on the way in which such idealized (and ideological) notions of family functioned as rhetorical tools in making sense of how organs circulate in organ transplantation. Transplant professionals, patients, and family members often held up "traditional" values of family cohesiveness and feminine self-sacrifice as allowing Mexico to engage in the transplant endeavor, overcoming the perceived backwardness of both low cadaveric donation rates and limited material resources. Here the representational possibilities and pressures of transplant's iconic status loom large, as transplantation is pressed into the service of national identity-making. Lawrence Cohen has described how notions of "good" and "bad" families are mobilized in relation to asserting Hindu and Muslim identities in the context of the contested category of Alzheimer's disease in India (Cohen 1998). Similarly caught up in complex claims about culture, modernity, and identity, transplantation in Mexico too became a medium for delineating us/them categories through the idiom of family, for differentiating good (organ giving, Mexican) families from bad (organ-selfish, North American/European) families. In this way the iconic Mexican family becomes a kind of *national* resource—both defining Mexico and its values positively against the putative developed world and helping the nation to take its place within that world by enabling it to wield the powerful biotechnical sign of transplantation.

Critically, this national resource of la familia mexicana was also commonly understood as a *natural* resource, as the desire and willingness to donate an organ to a relative was attributed to natural feelings of connect-edness, love, and responsibility. Here, assumptions about the biological roots of both blood kinship and sex/gender roles were often collapsed into one another. As one SSa nephrologist expressed it off-handedly: "Of course, if the mother can donate, she will want to—it's only natural" (Dr. Gomez). Laid bare here is a taken-for-granted expectation among patients, family members, and program staff in Guadalajara that, where possible, mothers, wives, and sisters were the logical first line to be considered as organ donors.

Seamlessly enfolding biological determinism and cultural expectation into one another, this discourse linking women and living donation was so pervasive that it was—literally—a joke in the local transplant commu-nity. In a presentation to a large audience of health-care workers during a national conference on transplantation, an IMSS nephrologist playfully re-marked: "So you tell a family that the patient needs a donor, and what do you think happens? Everyone starts sidling away and looking expectantly at the mother, of course!" (Dr. Mercado). His observation evoked know-ing laughter from the conference crowd, laughter that signaled recognition but that perhaps hinted also at some underlying uneasiness at the power and gender hierarchy thus so nakedly revealed. This presumed feminine "openness" to the wounding of organ donation takes up the symbolic idiom embodied in imagery of the Virgin Mary and the two Fridas, from whose suf-fering bodies flows the stuff of life. Yet at the same time—as the life/death-giving ambiguity of the two Fridas also reminds us—bodies that give life can also withhold, take, or lose it. These darker potentials, as we explore more fully below, are also part of the transplant story in Mexico.

Despite the uneasy laughter occasioned by such jokes, the idea that women's bodies were—and should be—more open than men's to offering up organs seemed to fit so comfortably within naturalized (and idealized) repre-sentations of human biology, gender roles, and family dynamics in Mexico that I rarely saw it explicitly examined, much less challenged.[5] Within the transplant community, physicians and even patients and family members mostly treated as second nature the idea that "of course women donate more often than men," speaking with an off-handed ease that made clear that this was precisely what many people both expected and accepted in a world where the image of the mujer sufrida is an iconic part of the way gen-der is often expressed and experienced. Perhaps more surprisingly, none of the transplant coordinators that I knew—all of whom were female and several of whom self-identified as feminist—responded critically to this discourse of women as "natural" donors. In reference to individual cases I occasionally heard transplant staff criticize an unsupportive husband, or a father who never once appeared at the hospital, leaving the mother to do all of the work, not just of donating but of helping the patient through the lengthy process of being studied and approved for a transplant. Yet such individualized criticisms never quite seemed to blossom into a larger critique of the way gendered expectations were so frequently—even flippantly—bandied about on the transplant wards.

When I asked directly whether the idea that women "ought" to donate seemed at all troubling, transplant staff typically produced a sort of shrug, eye roll, and head nod combination, accompanied by words to the effect that: "Well, of course, it's a problem. People here still have the idea that's how women should be. But it's something that is going to take a long time to change" (Isabel, transplant coordinator, IMSS). Underlying these responses, and the accompanying acknowledging-yet-dismissive shrugs, seemed to be a sense that concerns about such commonplace talk simply paled in comparison to the pressing immediacy of the life-and-death work in which they were engaged. In the face of the desperately ill patients whose physical presence was always before them, the daily (often enormous) challenges involved in getting this patient—right here and right now—transplanted seemed to take precedence over all. And in the evangelical atmosphere of a still-developing transplant program it is perhaps not surprising that such concerns failed to gain much traction—particularly if those concerns, once raised, might call into question the very practices of living organ donation on which that work depended.

Making Symbolic Sense of Women as Donors

If casual assertions that "of course women donate more than men" appeared to signal a set of gendered expectations in living donation, such expectancy was further entrenched by a series of frequently made analogies in Guadalajara that drew deep affinities between the act of offering up a kidney and various aspects of women's bodies and women's work. Exploring three such analogies through a series of representative quotes provides a deeper sense of the symbolic logics within which women as donors came to seem so culturally commonsensical in Guadalajara.

> I gave my son life once, why wouldn't I do it again if I can?
>
> —Elena, preparing to donate to her son, IMSS

As Elena's comment so succinctly evokes, living donation was frequently likened in Mexico to giving birth. By far the most common form of such analogizing, this powerful metaphor evoked the Marian side of the feminine coin, envisioning women's bodies as the source of life, from which both fully formed babies and kidneys can be extracted. Such linkages are not wholly unique to Mexico, of course. The imagery of donation as a "gift of life" has been disseminated globally, and a preference for organ donation from mother to child has emerged in other settings as well. Margaret Lock, for instance, reports that in Japan it is only within the context of the mother-child relationship that receiving an organ is not experienced as incurring an irredeemable and intolerable debt (Lock 2001: 334; see also Simmons et al. 1987 on the United States and Scheper-Hughes 2000 on Brazil). Yet maternal love and sacrifice can also be read to quite different effect. Transplant surgeons from France, for instance, suggest that they are more likely to urge *fathers* to serve as living donors precisely "because mothers have already done their part" (Gauthier 2004). And in Egypt, sacrificing a kidney is sometimes understood as a threat to younger women's childbearing capacities in ways that may actually shield them from the demands of living donation (Crowley-Matoka and Hamdy 2015; Hamdy 2012).

In Mexico, however, the analogy between giving birth and giving a kidney drew force from long-standing ideas about how a child carried within a woman's womb draws its physical materiality from her body, so that taking one more organ from that same source seemed a logical, natural continuation of that already-established bodily intimacy and dependency (Browner 1986). This rendering of reproduction resonates with Carol Delaney's analysis of how women's wombs may be imagined as the "soil" in which babies grow and from which they are harvested, while men provide the "seed" which is the true spark of life (1991). Within such logics, although fathers can also be said to have given life to their children, their bodies are not figured in the same way as the source of fleshy materiality. Mothers, in contrast, can be imagined as having already donated their bodies to the work of gestation—indeed their children have already lived upon the functioning of those selfsame kidneys in utero. Such sharing of material substance between mother and child extends beyond the womb as well, of course, for women's role in reproducing the family and providing the "stuff of life" to children hardly ends at the moment of birth (Morton 1971). And so giving a kidney comes to be seen as just one more link in the chain of shared biological and social substance passed between mother and child, a sacrifice comfortably in keeping with all of the everyday, expected sacrifices that have gone before it.

Intimately connected to this analogizing of living donation with the reproductive labor(s) of women was also the notion that pain and suffering are a "natural" part of both processes, and one that women are intrinsically equipped to bear. Labor pains were often seen as simultaneously acute and insignificant in Mexico—both expected and accepted, they tended to be folded into a larger trajectory of the difficult, wearing work that motherhood was understood to entail (Finkler 1994; Galvez 2011). Like the pain of childbirth, the pain of giving up a kidney could thus be rendered part of women's lot in life, part of their biological (even theological) destiny. Donating a kidney is actually quite painful—more painful in fact than receiving one, due largely to the angle of surgical entry.[6] Yet despite acknowledging this empirical fact, transplant staff also often minimized, even belittled that pain, as in this nurse's speculation: "Well, I think the donors tend to exaggerate the pain, they're not really the center of attention and I think it's a way of getting attention" (Inés, private hospital). Or as a transplant physician emphasized: "Donors are healthy people, they're not the patient—there's nothing wrong with them! They can go right back to work and their normal lives" (Dr. Hernandez, IMSS).[7] Not the "unnatural" or "unfair" pain of illness, the donor's considerable surgical pain is here figured rather as a productive pain, similar to that which must be endured in order to bring forth babies. Thus, living organ donation becomes an act women are assumed to be able to bear, both in terms of bringing it forth and in terms of enduring the bodily toll it takes.

Living Donation as Sex

My sister wanted to donate. But then they told her at the convent that she couldn't take her Orders [to become a nun] if she donated an organ. They told her that she wouldn't be pure anymore, it would be like losing her virginity . . . She didn't want to tell me, she told my mother. But I couldn't let her give up her dream for me.
—Marta, domestic worker, SSa

In a related set of associations, the bodily experience of living donation was also sometimes symbolically linked not only to women's reproductive capacity but to their sexuality as well. The physical act of opening up the body and removing an organ for donation can be imagined as analogous to the (hetero) sex act, as Marta suggests above. In donating, the body is "penetrated" both by the hands and instruments of the surgeon, as well as by the desire and desperate need of the organ recipient. The imagery thus evoked is of the donor body as a passive object, one that is acted upon rather than itself acting, mimicking the supposed sexual passivity of the female body.[8] Also evoked here is an all-too-familiar vision of women's bodies as "open," "unbounded," and vulnerable to wounding, in contrast to the "closed" and "bounded" bodies of men (Grosz 1994). Symbolically, it is this very openness of the female sex that invites penetration, once again naturalizing the link between living donation and women's bodies.

Within this logic, the surgical opening of the donor body can carry with it a symbolic loss of purity, for the body's boundaries have been breached and its wholeness ruptured. For some female donors, it was this logic that animated the above-made connection between the loss of virginity and donating an organ. As we shall see, when men donated (as in fact they did), this loss of purity could be associated with desexualization or feminization, couched in fears about impotency and infertility. These links between living organ donation, sexuality, and loss of purity have emerged elsewhere as well (Cohen 2002; Ikels 1997; Scheper-Hughes 2004). Reports from Moldova, for instance, note that organ-selling there is believed to make men "no better than whores"—a belief that indexes a loss of social value when the body is breached for monetary gain, but which notably couches this loss of purity and value in not just commodified but gendered and sexualized terms as well (Scheper-Hughes 2004: 49). Such associations with sexual impurity in the Mexican setting exemplify how the "open" donor body can be both life-giving and violated—evoking the Marian sacrificial body as well as the polluted body of La Malinche. Reflected here are the complex symbolics and politics of the unbounded, open body with its dual possibilities for pollution, danger, and destruction, but also healing, fertility, and creativity (Bataille [1957] 1986; Douglas 1966; Kristeva 1982). Yet these creative, liberating potentials of the unbounded body come at the price of significant vulnerability—for "boundedness" connotes not only restraint but also protection (Caldeira 2001; Grosz 1994). Haunting these ties between organ donation, sexual labor, and impurity are thus key questions of power and vulnerability, of how risk and protection in the face of transplantation's dire needs are differentially distributed, and of the distinctive regimes of bioavailability thereby produced.

Living Donation as "Housework"

> Women take care of their families, that's what they do. The men go out and earn
> money, but they aren't much good when someone's sick.
> —Vanesa, seamstress and sister of SSa transplant patient

As Vanesa's matter-of-fact explanation of her decision to donate to her sister suggests, a final common form of analogizing in Guadalajara rendered living donation as a form of "women's work" through associations with housework, with the bodily care of families in general, and of the sick in particular. Often naturalized through talk of women's "nurturing instincts," this linkage was also connected to the idea that—in a setting where the sexual division of labor was still commonplace though not unchanging— women's bodies were simply more available for this kind of time-consuming and sometimes contaminating domestic work.[9] In contrast, men's responsibilities for work outside the home frequently shielded them from many of the bodily demands of domestic labor. It has not been uncommon for poor women in Mexico (and elsewhere) to let themselves and even their children go hungry in order to feed the working men of the family and sustain their ability to keep earning money in the outside economy (Gonzalez de la Rocha 1994; Lomnitz 1977). Caught up in a similar calculus of domestic survival, living donation by women could thus be assimilated into already-existing patterns of feminine bodily sacrifice in the service of sustaining the private realm of home and family (though this is not to deny, of course, that men's bodies are also frequently used up in the service of the family). Shaped not just by pragmatic economic concerns, symbolic ideas linking women to pollution, taboo, and danger also inflect this notion of living donation as feminine work (Douglas 1966). Within a cultural logic where women are always already polluted by their associations with the lower regions of the body, with menstruation, with emotion, and in fact with all the body-care work entailed in the domestic labor of the home, it makes a certain (cultural) sense that the task of tending to the sick should fall to them.

Deepening the logical pull of such associations was the fact that most kidney patients in Guadalajara had indeed already required significant amounts of care in the home before the possibility of a transplant arose, and this care had almost certainly fallen to the women of the family. Of all the patients I came to know during my fieldwork, in only two cases were the primary caregivers men (in one case a father, in the other a husband). Similarly, as the family made plans for who would care for the transplanted patient during the extended and labor-intensive recuperation period, it was again virtually always women who took on this role—reflecting a gendered responsibility for family health care that remains dominant in Mexico (DiGirolama and Salgado de Snyder 2008; Kierans 2015). Set within the continuum of such an illness history, the act of living donation could be made to fit all too smoothly into the ongoing care for the sick that women had been performing and would continue to perform for the patient. Firmly positioning the living donor as care*giver* in this way also worked to elide the fact that living donors are, themselves, patients in need of care for the surgical wounds inflicted by the act of donating. Thus symbolically linked with a series of ideas about the home, the division of familial labor, and the care of ailing bodies, living donation was essentially *domesticated*, becoming simply yet another form of nurturing, and thus of "women's work."

Taken together, this range of powerful analogies with giving birth, with sex, and with housework—operating in close articulation with the notion of la familia mexicana as a national/natural resource—produced what we might think of as a pervasive *feminization* and *familialization* of living organ donation in Guadalajara. Within the imaginary thus created, giving a kidney to a family member comes to seem simply culturally commonsensical—just one more circuit in the local circulation of substances through which care is demonstrated and kinship enacted. Such an imaginary was thus consequential, exerting a persuasive pull that worked to enable the transplant endeavor in Mexico, helping to produce the familial donor organs upon which it depended.

From Discursive Expectation to Bodily Enumeration

As the provocative quotes and symbolic connections signaling such deeply gendered expectations in living organ donation accrued in my daily experience and field notes, I began to realize that I too had become expectant—not of the idea that women ought to donate more often, but of the idea that they probably did do so. Yet, when I turned my attention to a different version of the story, to the quantified accounting contained in the patient and donor databases shared with me by the IMSS and SSa transplant programs, I found that the material, bodily reality of organ giving and organ getting was significantly more complex, contradictory, and somewhat resistant to a wholly straightforward analysis of gender inequality than I had initially assumed.

I was given generous access to both the IMSS and the SSa transplant program databases, which together contained information on 745 kidney transplants in total.[10] Despite the occasional inconsistencies and/or missing data that plague all quantitative data sets, these records proved enormously useful in providing at least a broad-stroke picture of transplant activity in the two programs.[11] In the IMSS database, 86 percent of the transplants recorded were performed using living related donors. Another 8 percent used living nonrelated donors, and the remaining 6 percent were done with cadaveric organ donations. In the smaller SSa program, thirteen of the sixty transplants recorded in the database used cadaveric organs. Of the remaining forty-seven live donor transplants, information on the relationship of the donor to the recipient was not available. Extensive observation and conversations over time within that program, however, suggest that the vast majority of living donors in the SSa program were also relatives of the recipient. Of course, identification of potential donors as "related" or not can be a slippery business. Recurring reports from India reveal what has become a routine practice of living donation by organ sellers who pose as "kin with a wink" in order to overcome formal legal obstacles (Cohen 2005, 2011; Marshall and Daar 2000). In contrast, Farhat Moazam describes how the desire in Pakistan to evade the considerable pressure sometimes exerted by transplant staff to provide a kidney for a family member can produce what we might call "not-kin with a wink"—brothers who claim to be only distant cousins, for instance (Moazam 2006). Mindful of how the demands of transplantation can thus remake (and unmake) claims of relatedness (a question I take up in more detail in later chapters), for the moment I want to concentrate on a striking contrast between the dominant discursive representations of living donors in Guadalajara and these readily available numerical accountings.

Because, in fact, despite commonly made (and accepted) assertions that "of course women donate more than men," the numbers of male and female donors were *almost precisely equal* in the two main transplant programs where I worked, as shown in table 1.1. Given the pervasive discourse that so persuasively set women up as the most culturally logical donors, I was

Table 1.1 Donating Organs vs. Receiving Organs by Sex in Both
IMSS and SSa Transplant Programs

	Women	Men	Total*
Living Donors	321	320	641
Transplant Recipients	276	448	724

*The totals for Living Donors and Transplant Recipients will not be equal, as some
living donation cases were missing full data, and because the Transplant Recipients
category includes transplants using cadaveric donations as well.

initially somewhat taken aback by this apparent gender parity. Yet, while
the expected gender difference in who *gives* kidneys was not in evidence in
these bare statistics, there clearly was a gender difference in who *gets* them,
with more than 60 percent of transplants going to men in this sample. Taken
together, these quantified renderings pose a curious question: why are the
numbers for receiving organs so skewed by gender, while the numbers for
giving organs seem not to be skewed in quite the way we would expect?

To begin, the disparity in numbers of men versus women receiving kidney transplants cannot be wholly explained by simple reference to physiological difference: although medical studies have traditionally suggested
a somewhat higher risk of kidney disease for men worldwide, more recent
research has called this into question (Carrero 2010). Nor, from my time in the
transplant programs, did it appear that overt gender biases made it clearly
easier for men to work their way through the lengthy approval process—
although as I explore in chapter 3, there is a gendered dimension to ideas
about the qualities that make for an ideal transplant candidate. I suspect
rather that such disparities may have become entrenched long before
patients ever reached the level of the transplant program, so that fewer
women ever actually arrived at the point where they became candidates
for transplantation. And indeed the fact that the proportion of men being
referred to the IMSS transplant program—about 60 percent—was almost
exactly equal to the proportion of men actually being transplanted seems to
support this supposition.[12]

Barriers that may have kept women from reaching transplant programs
are sure to be multiple, complex, and difficult to weight in terms of importance. One obvious obstacle is the structural reality that women in Guadalajara were simply less likely to have direct access to health-care institutions
like the IMSS because they were less likely to work in the kind of formal sec-

tor jobs that provide such health-care coverage. A related grim irony here is that while a patient must have IMSS coverage to *receive* a transplant in that system, a kidney donor was not required to have such coverage. Rather—similar to the current system in the United States—the costs associated with the necessary testing, surgery, and hospital stay for the donor were subsumed under the transplant recipient's coverage. Thus, it is perhaps not surprising that women were more likely to have access to the role of organ donor than to the role of organ recipient.

Another possibility is that hospital staff in lower-level hospitals and clinics, engaging in informal gatekeeping practices, may have been less likely to send women upward through the referral system—though without direct study this is difficult to know. Family willingness or ability to make major economic (and personal) sacrifices for sick female members could also play a role—as one SSa nurse put it bluntly: "Look, if it's the husband, the wife stays and takes care of him and the whole family supports him and helps pay for the treatment. But if it's the wife who gets sick, he just leaves and the support falls apart" (Anita). And yet another possibility is raised by Kaja Finkler's sensitive ethnographic work on women and chronic illness in Mexico, suggesting that women who understand their bodily and emotional suffering as an expected, unavoidable form of "life's lesions" may be more likely to endure physical problems of the diffuse nature characteristic of kidney disease for far longer than men, before seeking medical treatment (Finkler 1994). Here the figure of the mujer sufrida surfaces once again, similarly conjured up in conversation with a community priest who offered me this explanation for the reluctance of women in his parish to seek health care: "A lot of our women still think that they should suffer in silence, that they should never complain . . . We are trying to change this, but it is a slow process" (Padre Jaime).

Underlying all of these possibilities for why women were less likely to receive transplants may be the same logic animating notions of women as appropriate "ground" for the production of donor organs. As Carol Delaney has pointed out, views of women as the nurturing "soil" (rather than the animating "seed") from which life grows positions them as a means to an end, rather than an end (worthy of investment and sacrifice) in themselves (1991). This is clearly an area that requires more extensive investigation into the levels below and before the transplant programs where I worked, as the gender difference in who gets organs is deeply worrisome. And while the data on live donors do not bear out the kind of straightforward gender

Table 1.2 Living Related Donation by
Relationship Type in IMSS Transplant Program

Relationship to Recipient	Number of Donors
Sibling (Sister/Brother)	328 (168/160)
Child (Daughter/Son)	63 (31/32)
Parent (Mother/Father)	76 (46/30)
Spouse (Wife/Husband)	42 (35/7)
Other Relatives	4*
Total	529

*This includes 2 aunts, 1 uncle, and 1 male cousin.

differences we might have expected, it is clear that in Mexico the apparent "equal opportunity" for women to give kidneys was not coupled with an equal opportunity to get them.

Yet, while the numbers of men and women serving as donors were nearly equal, taking a closer look at living donations by relationship, not just by gender, does reveal some suggestive differences. As table 1.2 shows, by far the largest numbers of donations came from siblings, and in these cases, the gender split was again fairly even. Similarly, among children who donated to their parents there was also virtually no difference by gender. Where the picture does become somewhat skewed by gender, however, is in the case of parents and spouses. In these relationships, women were clearly more likely to serve as donors, with mothers providing some 60 percent of parental donor organs, and—even more markedly, wives providing well over 80 percent of spousal donor organs.

So it seems that women *were* more likely than men to become donors within the context of certain relationships. Here, looking at the gendered political economy of family roles provides one possible reading. In the two relationship categories where gender differences were most marked, parents and spouses, women were more likely to be in a position of greater economic dependence in relation to either the recipient of the organ or to the other possible donor candidate(s). This apparent structural vulnerability to organ donation was borne out ethnographically in those cases where women bluntly explained how economic dependency drove their decision to donate. As Gabriela, an *ama de casa* (housewife) with five young children who had donated to her husband two years previously, explained in her characteristically no-nonsense manner: "Of course I gave him my kidney, he was sick and getting sicker, and if I didn't donate, he would have died. Then how would my kids and I have survived? Who would take care of us?" (IMSS). Similarly, for mothers, it was sometimes simply clear that the family as a whole could afford to risk the mother's time and health more than the father's. Thus for some women in Guadalajara, the decision to donate could be compelled by the everyday, brutal calculus of trying to minimize risk for the family as a whole. This is a calculus to which poorer women are particularly vulnerable of course, and one that has been widely observed elsewhere in the world as well, as dire need drives desperately pragmatic decisions to sacrifice organs (whether to family or to strangers) for economic survival (Cohen 1999, 2002; Marshall and Daar 2000; Scheper-Hughes 2002a, 2004).

Finally, turning back to the apparent gender parity in *sibling* donation, closer examination of the specific configurations of gender, relationship, and giving versus getting an organ is also revealing. In table 1.3, we can see that the majority of sibling donations were between siblings of the same sex (brother to brother and sister to sister). Brothers donating to brothers were the most frequent form of sibling donation overall, with kidneys especially likely to move from unmarried brothers to married ones. We might think of this as a kind of medical mediation of male labor power being mobilized to sustain the continuity of the kin network. In chapter 5, for instance, we will encounter the story of two brothers who successively pooled the resources of salaries, living space, domestic labor, and eventually, a kidney itself in the face of the deteriorating illness of one brother and the collective threat it was felt to pose. Where cross-sex sibling donations *did* take place, however, sisters were more than twice as likely to donate to brothers than brothers to sisters, repeating in the register of sibling relations the earlier noted marital patterns in which female bodies were often sacrificed to sustain male labor in the service of overall family survival. And indeed, for sisters such cross-sex sibling donations were actually more common than same-sex ones. Some of the complex stories underlying those bare statistics are unfolded in greater detail in later chapters—in the story of an unmarried sister giving a kidney to the brother upon whom she depends, for instance (chapter 5), or of a sister willing but unable to donate to her sister under the pressures of her own household demands (chapter 3).

Indeed, while numerical reckonings allow us to track the sometimes surprising patterns in the material realities of organ giving and organ getting, they can only hint at the press of emotion, economics, and familial ex-

Table 1.3 Gender Patterns in Sibling Living
Donations in IMSS Transplant Program

Relationship to Recipient	Number of Donors
Brother to Brother	115
Sister to Sister	74
Sister to Brother	93
Brother to Sister	46
Total	328

pectation involved in producing them. These emerge more movingly in the multitude of stories shared—sometimes eagerly, sometimes haltingly—by those who found themselves suddenly subject to transplantation's call for organs. Many donors described the decision to donate as hardly a decision at all, but rather an automatic, unthinking, but deeply felt response, an immediate desire born out of love upon hearing of a family member's need. As Amparo, a petite pet store owner who fairly bristled with energy and good humor, explained: "She's my sister! What's to think? I learned she needed a kidney and that's it, it's me, of course, of course I'll do it! We've always been close; she is already a piece of me, so right away I just knew I would give her my kidney. I would give her whatever she needed" (IMSS).

Yet familial love and responsibility could sometimes cut the other way, a harsh reality laid bare in the words of Marta, a frail yet quietly forceful young woman who was diagnosed with kidney failure in her early twenties. She described the decision-making process within her own family in frank, unsparing terms: "Well, my parents didn't want anyone in my family to donate. My mother said she would rather have one sick child than two. And all my brothers will have to be responsible for their own families some day, so it wouldn't be fair . . . And I don't have any sisters. So, that's it, I'm on the waiting list" (street vendor, SSa). Given the relative biounavailability of cadaveric donations in Mexico (a condition explored in the following chapter), this was a heart-wrenching decision that was—as she was all too terribly aware—a likely death sentence.

It is a hauntingly stark statement: "my mother said she would rather have one sick child than two." And it was a statement that did, in fact, haunt my fieldwork in terms of both its emotional bleakness and its recurrent nature—for Marta was not the only patient from whom I heard it. In fact, this precise language, of preferring to risk one child rather than two, was rather common—although it was sometimes voiced even more bluntly as "I'd rather have one child *die* than two." And critically, it was almost always couched as the *mother's* prohibition that blocked the movement of an organ from one family member to another. Such statements cannot be taken as a straightforward accounting of the gendered sources of such familial prohibitions—any more than those earlier-examined statements about the gendered sources of organs themselves proved wholly and materially accurate. Just as fathers and brothers sometimes gave organs, surely they also sometimes blocked their donation as well. Yet as we have seen, such discursive representations are themselves a kind of social fact and work to produce certain material effects. In this case, emphasizing maternal prohibitions against donation strikingly renders mothers as both givers and (for the anxious would-be transplant recipient) potential takers (or withholders) of life.[13]

Harking back to the linked figures of the Virgin Mary and La Malinche, the invocation of this maternal calculus reveals the uneasy fact that while family ties and gendered relations may indeed work to produce organs in Mexico, they can also work to withhold them. It is a calculus, moreover, that highlights—in some cases, for some bodies—the life-*risking* potential (for the donor) that lies beneath the commonplace emphasis on familial donation as a loving act of life-*saving*. Such prohibitions thus emphasize—and privilege—the patienthood of some potential donors, moving to protect them from needing care, rather positioning them as a source of care. Here the image of the ambiguous relationship between the two Fridas is useful to recall—reminding us that as the stuff of life flows between two bodies (be they the twinned versions of the artist's body, or the bodies of organ donor and recipient), the relationship thus constituted may be read as symbiotic and/or as vampiric. Such readings, of course, are never innocent. And whether donation is read as life-saving versus life-risking is clearly linked to the relations of power, emotion, and need within which any particular potential donor body is enmeshed. Thus it was that mothers were so commonly understood to "save" their children through donation, while—in contrast—fathers and married brothers could be thought appropriately unable to "risk" themselves.

At stake here is the fetishizing effect of a discourse that focuses on the life-saving effects of living related donation—at least from some bodies—as a biologically and culturally "natural" act. "Fetishization" in Marxist analysis refers to the animating, mystifying effect of commodification, in which the origins of a product (that is, the socioeconomic processes that produce it) are concealed (Marx 1990 [1867]). The fetish thus takes on an uncanny liveliness of its own, seeming to move and embody intrinsic value independent of the complex relations of exploitation and desire that brought it into being. In this way fetishization bears a certain kinship with the way I have been using iconicity here, for reading living organ donation as a "natural" product of female biology and family ties in effect mystifies and conceals the political economic configurations of gender, age, and family structure that often produce such donations. The movement of organs from (some) bodies thus takes on a self-evident quality, a second nature of-courseness that covers over questions about why organs come from living (not cadaveric) donors in Mexico, about who is more likely to give versus get organs, and about the relations of dependency and dominance that often set those specific organs in motion.

In a similar vein, Nancy Scheper-Hughes has written about the fetishizing effect of organ trafficking, in which the life-risking labor of organ sellers is rendered invisible by a focus on the magical, life-saving effect of the mobile organ for buyers (Scheper-Hughes 2002a, 2005). In the context of organ trafficking, this is an effect produced when commodified kidneys are drawn into the voracious maw of the market. Here, however, the fetish is produced instead by a discourse that binds kidneys firmly into a web of "natural" family relations. In this setting, while living donors themselves— who are almost always family members—cannot be said to be rendered invisible in quite the same way, the risk and vulnerability underlying their donations often is made to disappear in the focus on naturalized family ties of love and responsibility. Yet also rendered largely invisible in this story, as we have seen, are the bodies of male donors—while female donor bodies in contrast are made hypervisible.[14]

Such questions of visibility—its exaggeration and its erasure for different sorts of donor bodies and different forms of risk—are precisely what the notion of the iconic helps us to foreground. Thinking iconically brings an aesthetic dimension to the effect of the fetish, drawing attention not just to the question of what is obscured, but to the particular features and qualities and symbolic history of what is instead made to stand in/stand for. And so, drawing deftly on the existing symbolic idiom in Mexico, la mujer sufrida becomes the emblematic source of organs in Mexico, a representation that obscures much about the bodily realities of organ giving and organ getting in Mexico. Yet this image of the (feminized) iconic donor body nonetheless produces real clinical and political effects, rendering organ transplantation culturally intelligible and thus ethically permissible and materially practicable in a way it might not otherwise be. And as the ability to wield transplantation in a distinctively Mexican way becomes a matter of national pride, the recombinant body wrought by transplantation perhaps also shares an eerie echo with that earlier figuring of the nation as a different kind of hybrid body in the image of el mestizo. In the mestizo body, born of that foundational meeting of indigenous woman and male conquistador, there lurks a reproductive logic that conceals the violence of rape. At work in the hybrid body of transplant is perhaps a kindred, but distinctive logic, a logic of celebrated self-sacrifice that conceals what we might call a medicalized violence of stratified survival. Because while organs from familial donors *are* relatively abundant in Mexico, they are not, of course, equally available to all. As we have seen, the ability to access the organs of another, to elicit the sacrifice of a kidney, is unevenly distributed along gradients of gender, age, and economic productivity. And conversely, the ability to shield oneself from the call to self-sacrifice is similarly subject to the pull of power within family relations. Ultimately, such questions of visibility, of iconicity, are fundamentally and critically biopolitical in Foucault's sense, central to how power over extending and also risking life is structured through distinctive local regimes of bioavailability (Foucault 1975, 1976).

So What about the Men?

Thus the gender patterns that emerge in the transplant programs' data do reveal—at least in some partial and more nuanced ways—the kind of gendered hierarchy that the discourse that "of course women donate more than men" led us to expect. Yet it is intriguing that in actual practice the gender inequalities were *not* as pronounced as they were discursively. Casually tossed-off (and just as casually accepted) comments about how "most donors are, of course, women" or "fathers never donate" turn out to exaggerate and even distort existing differences, eliding the fact that half of all donor kidneys came from men. While such disjunctures between what people *say* and what they *do* are not an uncommon feature of social life, this particular disjoint calls for some additional attention: what are we to make of the apparent contradiction between discourse and practice here? There are (at least) two parts to this question. The first relates to the male donors themselves: given the powerful discourse that links living organ donation to

Table 1.4 Age and Gender Patterns in Living Organ Donation in
IMSS Transplant Program

Age Ranges	Male Donors	Female Donors	Total
14–20 years	46	33	79
21–30 years	112	103	215
31–40 years	40	77	117
41–65 years	17	21	38
Total*	215	234	449

*These totals for male and female living donors do not add up to the totals in table 1.1 of 321 women and 320 men for two reasons: (1) these data are drawn only from the IMSS program and do not include the SSa transplant data (which did not include donor age information in a sufficient number of cases); and (2) there were occasional missing data on donor age in the IMSS transplant data base.

women's bodies and women's work, how are we to understand men's decisions to donate, and how did they themselves (as well as others) make sense of their donations? The second asks why the idea that "of course women donate more than men" persisted in the face of easily accessible evidence to the contrary; this is a question taken up in the concluding section below.

Understanding how it is that so many men did in fact come to donate, and what their experiences of donation were like in the face of such pervasive talk about women as "natural" donors, is a task that warrants a separate study all its own, and I do not pretend to offer a definitive accounting here. We can, however, look to the data discussed above for some preliminary insight into men as living donors—providing some clues, for instance, into the differential power dynamics at work in the fact that men were more likely to donate (or not) in more restricted relational contexts, brothers to brothers, for instance, but only rarely husbands to wives. Also, men who donated were clearly most likely to do so in their younger years. In table 1.4, a pattern emerges in which men were far more likely to donate before the age of thirty than after it, while women organ donors in their thirties, forties, and fifties (as well as in their teens and twenties) were not uncommon.[15] This suggests—not surprisingly—that there may be more pronounced changes in positioning for men over the course of their life cycle such that they become more or less willing, more or less able, or more or less vulnerable to pressure to serve as living donors. And it concurs with my ethnographic sense that (among men) it was young, unmarried men who were most likely to be seen as (possibly) appropriate living organ donors.

Manuel, for instance, a soft-spoken mechanic who lived with his parents, described how he came to donate to his older brother in this straightforward way: "There wasn't anyone else really. I'm the only one still at home and my parents are already old. All the others have families of their own, so it came to me to do" (IMSS). Thus, once married and situated within a family of his own, it seems that these nuclear responsibilities came to take precedence over a man's responsibility to his siblings (or other members of his family of origin), as in Tomas's half-wounded, half-apologetic account of why his brother refused to donate to him: "He's married and they have two children, so . . . well, he really just couldn't. My parents agreed that he has to take care of his own family first, and I don't think that his wife wanted him to risk himself anyway" (construction worker, SSa). For women, however, who were more likely to donate organs as wives and mothers than men were as husbands and fathers, establishing a family "of their own" did not seem to shield them from donation in quite the same way.[16]

In trying to make sense of the place of men in a space of donation so heavily feminized in discourse, it is useful also to attend to some of the particularizing ways that transplant staff tended to talk about (at least some) male donors. For men were markedly more likely than women to be described (and to describe themselves) in terms of their emotional attachment to the patients to whom they were donating, and (female) social workers in particular often seemed to take a certain delight in singling out as "special" the cases in which male donors provided organs to female patients. "He just loves her so much, he takes care of her and fusses over her . . . ," reported one social worker, telling me about a brother being studied to donate to a younger sister, "You have to see them together really, it's something very pretty to see" (Lupe, SSa). Isabel, a transplant coordinator in the IMSS program, described her findings from a series of interviews she conducted with male and female living donors for a research class she was taking in similar terms: "Well, wives, you know, they talk about different things, but usually they say it's because they need him, or they say it's because he's always been good to them, so it is their duty. That's how they talk about it. But men, when they donate, they talk about how much they love the patient, for them it's this special thing, it has to do with a special connection and that's why they donate."

Emerging here is a sort of parallel discourse suggesting that when men donate it is "special," a question largely of emotion, in contrast to the already-examined notion that when women donate it is "natural," and often a question of pragmatics. Such emotion-driven male willingness to sacrifice for the family may be marked as noteworthy in the transplant context, but it also enacts a particular, culturally available style of Mexican masculinity, one that is highly sentimental and family-focused in conscious opposition to the iconic image of el macho (Gutmann 1996; Wentzell 2013). Similarly gendered emotional logics distinguishing different acts of living donation emerge in other settings as well. In India, for example, distinctions between "exceptional" male and "expected" female donations can be discerned in the regionalized patterns where kidneys are sold by rural men in times of agricultural crisis, in contrast with urban women for whom kidney sales become simply a routine strategy of everyday survival (Cohen 1999: 138–40). And in the United States, male donors have been described as more likely to judge the experience "momentous" while females tended to regard it as "a simple extension of her usual family obligations" (Simmons et al. 1987: 188).

Intriguingly, scholars working in the United States have not identified the kind of gendered discursive expectations about who should serve as living donors so evident in Guadalajara. This lack of explicit expectation, however, must be coupled with the material fact that more women actually do serve as living donors in the United States. Indeed, gender inequities in living donation in the United States are persistent, with women providing approximately 60 percent of the more than six thousand living donor kidneys provided annually over the past decade or so (UNOS 2014c).[17] Yet this imbalance goes largely unremarked in the U.S. setting, a discursive silencing in which both the moral hegemony of organ donation's portrayal as a "gift of life" (Sharp 2006: 13), and a cherished national self-image of egalitarianism seem likely to play a role. This makes for a provocative contrast between Mexico, where women are assumed to donate more than men, and the United States, where they actually do so.

But while the experiences of male donors certainly need to be accounted for, this disjuncture between discourse and practice, between the notion of women as natural donors and the reality that half of all donors in Guadalajara were men, need not be construed as a troubling contradiction per se. Indeed, such disjoints are a rather common feature of social life, reminding us of the need to tease out the specificities of what people say and what they do with equal care, taking both as important and neither at face value. In the domain of organ transplantation, both Lesley Sharp and

Ruth Richardson point out that discourses about "flat" rates of cadaveric donation in the United States dominate both the medical literature and the popular media, and have persisted in the face of slowly but steadily rising cadaveric donations (Richardson 1996, 2001; Sharp 2001). And in another realm, Margaret Lock has traced the disjuncture in Japan between powerful representations of "lazy" middle-class housewives with excessive complaints of menopausal symptoms and abundant clinical data showing that such women in fact report no more symptoms than women in other class positions (Lock 1993). In each case there is clear ideological work accomplished by these counterfactual understandings of "flat" donation rates or "self-indulgent" middle-class menopausal women. Similarly, I take the persistence of this discourse of women as donors as an example of what we might call the biopolitics of the iconic, as an instrumental imagining through which transplantation in Mexico has come through particular kinds of meaning into particular kinds of being (Butler 1993).

Feminization, Familialization, and Ethical Domesticity in Living Organ Donation

Ultimately, the power of the pervasive, persistent discourse that "of course women donate more than men" is that it so neatly naturalizes not just living donation by women, but living organ donation in general. And in linking living donation so firmly to all of the above-explored ideas about what comes "naturally" to (and from) both women's bodies and families more generally, transplantation itself was rendered both culturally and ethically intelligible. Not just a matter of the needs of transplant, however, this feminization and familialization of living donation seems implicated also in a larger politics of life itself (Rose 2001). For at stake here is perhaps an even more starkly embodied version of what has been widely observed as an increasing resort under neoliberalism to the family as the source of health care, even as a sort of medical agent for the state (Biehl 2005; Garcia 2010). Transplant in Mexico is an endeavor wholly dependent on families offering up not just the time and toil and emotional work of caring for the sick, but the very vital, meaty material of their own bodily organs as well. Indeed, such corporeal sacrifice is the fundamental condition of possibility that has allowed transplantation to become a key site for the staging of biomedical mastery in Mexico. This staging is set, notably, within the public health care system, and thus has come to serve also as a point of considerable state pride and political currency. Thus resonating with broader neoliberal trends in which the family increasingly becomes the resource of ultimate recourse, the discursive feminization and familialization of transplantation in Mexico not only has a deep local history and cultural intelligibility, but also fits rather seamlessly into more contemporary shifts in the Mexican political landscape.

So thoroughly feminized and familialized, the often-contentious practice of transplantation has thus been largely *domesticated* in Mexico, in both senses of the word—made both a private matter of home and family, and a product of national resources. On both counts—as domestic matter, and domestic product—living related donation and the transplantation it enables thus come to seem safe, homey, familiar as well as familial. And they do so in ways that are made to stand in sharp contrast to the associations with the violent, vampiric, market-driven relations between deterritiorialized strangers that the transplant enterprise has so frequently summoned in other settings. On the ground thus discursively laid out, living donation and transplant itself in Mexico come to seem largely tamed—to invoke yet another register of the notion of domestication. Tamed in this way, transplant and the forms of corporeal sacrifice it requires had not been widely taken up in Guadalajara as a question of new ethical problems raised by technological advancement, as they have so often been framed in the United States, Japan, Egypt, and elsewhere (Hamdy 2012; Joralemon 1995; Lock 2001; Sharp 2006). Rather, living donation and the transplant endeavor it enables were made to mesh almost seamlessly with long-standing cultural logics, social hierarchies, and modes of everyday survival. And as such, widespread, sustained local debates over the ethics of using the bodies of some to save the lives of others had simply not emerged in Mexico with the kind of scandal and force seen so vividly in other places in the world (Fox and Swazey 1974, 1992; Hamdy 2012; Lock 2001).

Operating not just at the level of public discourse, what we might think of as the *ethical domesticity* of familial living donation shaped clinical and bureaucratic practice in Guadalajara as well—a matter I take up in greater detail in later chapters. A mother's desire to donate to her daughter, or a brother to his sister, had a cultural and emotional legibility that served largely to soothe the ethical unease—and regulatory urges—so frequently surrounding other forms of organ exchange. To be clear, this is not at all to say that questions were never asked by transplant staff when a family member wanted to donate. Lofty idealizations of la familia mexicana aside, everyone knows all too well that actual families are often messy, conflictual, and shot through with brutally unequal dynamics of power. And yet it was clear that such questions—why do you want to donate, what do you expect to get from your donation?—rarely carried the same urgency or stance of suspicion when family rather than unrelated donors were involved. Indeed, the very domesticity of living related donation can seem to authorize, as Nancy Scheper-Hughes has noted in other settings, a sort of relative silence, an averting of prying professional eyes and ethical debate from the intimate space of familial struggle (Scheper-Hughes 2007). Thus produced is a kind of socially sanctioned privacy, a secluded zone in which the often-painful working out of the questions of bodily risk and redemption at stake in such familial transplant exchanges are largely hidden from public view and collective ethical inquiry. And in enabling particular forms of organ giving and organ receiving, such ethical domestication of transplant yielded powerful effects both biological and social.[18]

All of this, of course, can be framed as primarily a question of pragmatics. And indeed transplant professionals in Guadalajara often did just that, as in frequently heard variations of the following observation: "We simply do not have the luxury of not using living donors. Without cadaveric donations, we *have* to depend on living donors in order to continue" (Dr. Hernandez, IMSS). But it is also, in a deep sense, a question of ethics, a situated working out of the fundamental question of "how to live" that the enactment of transplantation necessarily raises, and to which different regimes of bioavailability provide distinctive answers (Kaufman et al. 2006). In Guadalajara the ethical domesticity of familial organ donation was an effect produced not only by the discursive feminizations and familializations traced out in this chapter. Such domesticity was produced also through explicit contrast with alternate forms of bioavailability, often understood in terms of what may be posed as the alien—perhaps even barbarous—ethical frameworks thought to predominate in "Other" places.

And so the power of the story of the German mother who became *más mexicana* emerges through the doubled contrast not just of her German family's horror at her willingness to sacrifice herself, but of my Mexican interlocutors' horror-at-their-horror as well. Indeed such ethical juxtapositions seem to be a signal—even constitutive—feature of transplantation writ large. Lawrence Cohen has written about the exploitative edge of global attention to India's infamous kidney markets, noting how shocking images of scarred organ sellers are recurrently conjured up, reinforcing a reassuring sense of moral superiority in Western observers—and extracting what we might call a kind of ethical capital in the process (Cohen 1999, 2011). These all-too-familiar extraction patterns from south to north, poor to rich countries, however, were virtually inverted in the ethically domesticated accounts of transplantation so pervasive in Mexico, making claims for both the moral superiority and the material efficacy of the familial forms of bodily sacrifice that have allowed transplant to flourish in that setting.

Such claims in part speak back to a disapproving gaze from the North, to what I described in the introduction as perceptions of transplantation in Mexico as technology-out-of-place, drawing on Mary Douglas's famous formulation of dirt as "matter out of place" (Douglas 1966). Yet as global trends in transplantation increasingly turn to the use of living donors of all sorts worldwide, it seems that "gaze from the North" may be no longer just disapproving, but has perhaps become opportunistically inquisitive as well. The United States, for instance, has seen a profound shift in attitudes toward the use of living donors in the past two decades or so. From the early days of transplantation and into the 1990s ethical unease about the harm done to a healthy person left many U.S. transplant centers reluctant to use living donors at all (Hamdy 2013; Matas et al. 2003). Yet as expansion of the transplant industry has failed to be matched by a concomitant growth in the supply of cadaveric organs, that reluctance has largely given way, and in 2000 the number of living kidney donors in the United States actually surpassed the number of cadaveric donors for the first time (UNOS 2014b).

Indeed, the forms of living donation now considered both medically and ethically acceptable seem to be expanding rapidly in terms of both relationship type (so that not only kin, but friends, neighbors, and outright strangers now routinely donate), and organ type as well (so that living donors can now provide not only kidneys but portions of their liver, lung, intestine, and pancreas—all of which entail considerably higher risk for both donor and recipient) (Crowley-Matoka et al. 2004; Crowley-Matoka and Switzer 2005; Scheper-Hughes 2004). In the face of authoritative projections suggesting that the cadaveric donor supply will never be able to meet the demand for organs (Sheehy et al. 2003), it seems clear that living donors have become the key frontier of opportunity in transplantation in the United States (and in many other settings around the world as well).

This rapidly expanding embrace of the use of living donors surfaced somewhat unexpectedly in the midst of a recent academic presentation I gave on my research in Mexico at a university hospital in the United States.

Toward the end of the talk, a transplant surgeon in the audience stood up and, flushed with enthusiasm, exclaimed: "This is wonderful, 80 percent, 90 percent living donors—you've reset the bar for us! You have given us something to *aspire* to. And I think we can get there, I think we can get *our* families to start donating like this too!" Rather disconcerted that this was the—wholly unintended—message he had gleaned from my talk, in the moment I cobbled together a sort of cautious, cautionary response. In the time since, however, his unsettlingly enthusiastic reaction has come to represent for me something about the densely and unpredictably interconnected routes of global relation and imagining. Both informed and inspired by the new possibilities that my account of transplantation in Guadalajara apparently opened up for him, this transplant surgeon seemed engaged in a sort of reaching out for what struck him as a more useful moral economy of donor bodies.

We might think of this imaginative, instrumental reaching out for "other" cultural technologies and bodily logics as a form of aspiration—one that works in several registers. For aspiration usefully connotes not only hopes and ambitions, but also the drawing in of something from the outside, of air—or more dangerously, food or vomit—into the lungs, for instance. Alternatively, aspiration in a diagnostic mode may signal an extractive process, a drawing out of bodily substance such as fluid or cells in order to assess it. Such moments of reaching out for, drawing in, and/or assessing alternate techniques (ethical, discursive, surgical, or otherwise) work to enable emergent biomedical forms of "making live"—like transplantation. As such, these aspirational moments resonate with recent anthropological work on how differences in ethical frameworks may be imagined, produced, and leveraged—what Adriana Petryna has called "ethical variability" in the context of commercialized global clinical trials (Petryna 2005), and Lawrence Cohen frames as "ethical experimentation" among the for-profit hospital chains proliferating across India (Cohen 2011). This sense of aspiration inflects the small, everyday moments of ethical comparison, imagination, and appropriation within which the domestication of transplantation traced out in this chapter is produced—as a Mexican nurse proudly regales a gringa anthropologist with the tale of a German mother come to Guadalajara to save her son with a kidney, for example. And in such aspirational moments, ethical domesticity may also become productive—as a U.S. transplant surgeon, responding enthusiastically to an academic talk, imagines out loud his hopes for drawing Mexican logics of familial donation more deeply into his own daily practice.

It is hard to know where such moments may lead, of course. In the face of an ever-expanding transplant enterprise and an ever-insufficient supply of organs, will the forms of donor bioavailability in the United States indeed become—like the German mother with whom we began—más mexicana in some sense? If so, what other contours might that iconic donor figure of la mujer sufrida take on when set into interaction with a differently grounded symbolic idiom of gender, family, and nation? And of course, just what it means to be más mexicana (in transplantation and otherwise) will hardly hold still—for the particular entanglements of organ donation, gender, family, and nation described here are situated not just geographically and culturally, but temporally as well. The global demand for organs exerts a relentless pressure to expand existing forms of bioavailability through new techniques of scientific, economic, and ethical practice, inciting new aspirational opportunities in the process. Set into circulation through such moments of global contact, contrast, imagination, and appropriation, these emergent techniques move along pathways akin to the ambiguous circulation of lifeblood in The Two Fridas. Bearing along the forms of biotechnical achievement, bodily sacrifice, and ethical capital they produce, these shifting transplant practices flow in uncertain directions and through articulations that have potentials both life-giving and exploitative.

2. Cadaveric Organ Donation, Biounavailability, and Slippery States

See, this is our problem with brain death here—they think that the dead ones are alive and the live ones are dead.
—Martina, transplant coordinator, IMSS

Death is therefore multiple and dispersed in time: it is not that absolute privileged point at which time stops.
—Michel Foucault, *Discipline and Punish: The Birth of the Prison*, 1975

Biounavailability and Slippery States

Death is a complex matter—biologically, socially, spiritually, and bureaucratically. In the transplant era, determining when it has occurred—and what its occurrence then sets in motion—has been considerably complicated by the introduction of the concept of "brain death," a diagnostic category motivated chiefly by the demand for transplantable organs (Giacomini 1997). In Guadalajara brain-dead donors were relatively scarce, providing organs for fewer than 10 percent of kidney transplants.[1] This dearth of cadaveric donors can be framed—to invert Lawrence Cohen's useful notion of bioavailability (Cohen 2005)—as a form of biounavailability. Such biounavailability of cadaveric donors in Mexico underlaid and critically conditioned the dependence on familial living donations explored in chapter 1. And it was a form of biounavailability shared with many other locations where brain-dead donors are also hard to come by, many—but not all—of them poorer places in the world. Local histories of resistance to brain death and cadaveric organ donation are richly, consequentially diverse, and shape in turn how living donation comes to matter in distinctive ways not always easy to predict. Margaret Lock's exemplary work in Japan, for instance, has revealed how the scarcity of cadaveric organs there emerged, in part, from a generalized mistrust of both local medical professionals and Western biotechnologies in ways that have served to limit local willingness to offer up living donor organs as well (Lock 2001: 170–73). While in Egypt, Sherine Hamdy provides insight into how Muslim understandings of God's authority over the body in death have restricted cadaveric organ donation but do not appear to impede the local dependence on organs from the living—many of them paid, unrelated donors (Hamdy 2012: 209–37).

In Guadalajara, brain death and the cadaveric organs that it produces—despite being only haltingly materialized—loomed large in imaginative terms, frequently dominating both the aspirations of the local transplant community and popular media accounts of transplantation. For despite their considerable pride in the relative abundance of living related donors in Mexico, transplant professionals were all too aware of the lengthy—often deadly—wait that faced patients without a family member either willing or able to provide a kidney. Moreover, while living donation could enable the transplantation of kidneys to take root in Mexico, the lack of cadaveric donors made it difficult to firmly establish transplant programs for other organs, such as hearts, livers, and lungs. On both counts, the biounavailability of cadaveric organ donors limited the full flourishing of transplantation as both clinical practice and iconic sign of advancement in Mexico—and as such, was often keenly felt by transplant professionals as a form of "behindedness" still to be overcome.

This sense of needing to "catch up" with some aspirational Other emerged not just in relation to Mexico's looming neighbor to the north, the United States, where cadaveric organs accounted for more than half of all kidney transplants. Even more sharply felt was comparison with the example of Spain, which ran the most successful cadaveric organ procurement program in the world at the time. A key focus of Mexican aspirations in the transplant realm, what has become known as the "Spanish model" emphasizes the professionalization of transplant coordinators, careful management of the process of asking for organs, and a highly integrated national system for identifying potential donors and distributing their organs (Matesanz and Miranda 1996a; Matesanz et al. 2009). Relations between the Mexican and Spanish transplant communities were close, with transplant professionals circulating often between the two countries in a dynamic based not just on Spain's unparalleled organ procurement successes but also on the dense (and hierarchical) historical, cultural, and linguistic ties between the two countries. Both intimate and fraught, this is a relation whose effects surface throughout this chapter, and to which we will return in more detail in the exploration of the experiential dimensions of working as a transplant professional in Mexico in chapter 6.

In Guadalajara, the biounavailability of cadaveric organ donors was most often publicly framed as a problem of "culture," specifically as a problem of uneducated, frightened family members refusing to donate the organs of their loved ones. Ubiquitous newspaper headlines, often drawn from direct quotes by local transplant professionals, made claims that "Family opposition impedes establishing organ donation" (Rodriguez Gonzalez 2000) and lamented that "We lack a 'culture of donation'" (Bowers and Bonaparte 1999). In this way, both "culture" and "family" were painted as sources of religious superstition and fearful ignorance that served to hold back the transplant endeavor. Such recurrent framings of the problem of cadaveric donation curiously mirrored (in the sense of reflecting but also reversing) the way the success of living donation was often posed in this setting. That is, the natural/national resources of Mexican culture and the iconic familia mexicana that were, as we saw in chapter 1, so vital in generating living organ donations were in this case rendered responsible instead for withholding cadaveric ones. If the last chapter told a gendered story of national pride in the bioavailability of living donors, here the story shifts to one more focused on issues of class, religiosity, and national shame in the biounavailability of cadaveric donors.

Yet, just as discursive accounts of living organ donation did not always reflect material reality—so that women did not, in fact, serve as living donors more than men, for instance—here too, publicly framing the biounavailability of cadaveric donation as a problem of "family refusals" elided a far more complex reality. Indeed, as I tracked the potential cadaveric donation cases that arose over the course of my time in Mexico, it became clear that the media mantra indicting an "ignorant" public for refusing to donate their organs was highly—but intriguingly, tellingly—inaccurate.

Table 2.1 Outcomes in Potential Cadaveric Donation Cases in IMSS and
SSa Hospitals

Outcome of Cases	Number of Cases
Successful donations	21
Patient destabilized before brain death established	10
Hospital staff resistance/interference derailed donation	11
Patient never showed flatline brain activity	11
Family refused	9
Lack of identification, documentation for donor	4
Equipment malfunctions prevented establishing brain death	4
Patient had medical contraindications to donation	3
Family wanted money for donation, donation called off	1
Total	74

Of the seventy-four potential cadaveric donation cases that arose in Guadalajara during my time in the field, twenty-one families consented and
saw the donation successfully carried out (see table 2.1). This translates to
a donation rate of 28 percent—a level of acceptance, by comparison, not
terribly far from rates in many regions of the United States, where donation rates have hovered around 32 percent overall (Sheehy et al. 2003). Such
small-scale statistics from actual potential donation cases in Guadalajara
echoed the numbers seen at a statewide level in a new driver's license program, where 27 percent of applicants listed themselves as willing to serve as
an organ donor (a rate, once again, comparable to similar U.S. programs).[2]
In fact, of the remaining fifty-three cases, only nine were actually lost because the family refused to donate. That is, potential donation cases most
often went awry for a diverse set of reasons having nothing to do with the
attitude or wishes of the family.

Sometimes potential donors simply could not be maintained medically
for long enough to establish brain death and carry out the donation procedure. Or the necessary equipment for testing brain function was broken or
unavailable. Or if the equipment was available, the necessary medical staff
to conduct the tests and interpret the results might not be. Sometimes, in
fact, outright resistance to donation emanated from hospital staff themselves, who might intervene in more or less deliberate and direct ways to

derail a potential donation. Indeed, most of the problems impeding organ donation arose long before the family was ever approached. As in chapter 1, the contrast here between discursive framing (family refusal as the problem) and numerical accounting (only a small proportion of families actually did—or even got to—refuse) invites closer examination.

Two potential donation cases, which occurred in rapid succession about midway through my fieldwork, provide a provocative entry point into some of the anxious, often contentious complexities involved in producing the biounavailability of cadaveric donors in Mexico. In the first of these two cases, Aurelia, the most experienced IMSS transplant coordinator, received a call from a small community IMSS hospital about a young man believed to be brain-dead after being hit by a truck while crossing the street. Jangling with the adrenaline of mixed hope and dread that a possible brain-dead donor always provoked, Aurelia and I jumped into her small car and darted through the congested traffic of the center city, making our way to a quieter, well-established working-class suburb on the edge of the city. Upon arrival at the community hospital, Aurelia immediately swung into action, directing the multitude of clinical tests necessary to establish brain death, alerting the various government authorities, and processing the reams of required paperwork. After several hours of medical and bureaucratic hustle, the diagnosis of brain death was declared official and an ICU doctor broke the news to the anguished parents and young wife. Shortly afterward, Aurelia approached the family to broach the question of organ donation, and—unusually—found them already discussing the topic themselves. The wife, having seen a presentation about organ donation in school, thought it was something her husband would have wanted, and the family quickly came to agreement.

However, just as the final paperwork was being filled out, a frightened ICU nurse rushed into the small office where we were sitting with the family, crying out, "He's still alive!" As the horrified family members leaped to their feet and the other ICU staff quickly gathered round, she reported that the supposedly dead patient had moved, raising his arms briefly and dropping them onto his chest. Mass confusion ensued, with the family becoming alarmed and angry, and the local hospital staff also panicking that such movement meant that the patient was not truly brain-dead—indeed, was perhaps not that close to any kind of death at all. Trying to calm the furor, Aurelia explained again and again that this sort of occasional reflex movement is not uncommon in brain death. It is common enough, in fact, that it has acquired its own term in the transplant literature, where it is frequently referred to as the "Lazarus sign" (in oddly ironic reference to the biblical character whom Jesus raised from the dead) (American Academy of Neurology 2010). Commonplace yet also commonly unnerving, such distraught reactions to the patient's movement cannot be consigned to a technology-out-of-place sort of problem; indeed Lesley Sharp has reported similar responses to the Lazarus sign among organ procurement and ICU staff in the United States (Sharp 2006: 74–75).

Faced with such an uproar, Aurelia patiently, soothingly marshaled all of the biological reasons that this particular kind of movement is not a sign of brain activity, mapping the way such "reflex arcs" are constituted by neural pathways that run solely through the spinal column, never reaching the brain. Her explanations and assertions, however, failed to quell the anguished uncertainties of both the family and the local hospital staff to whom they turned for guidance. The local staff, including the ICU doctor and the medical director of the hospital who had now become involved, were themselves unsure of how far to trust Aurelia's explanations—and Aurelia herself. Frightened of making a deadly mistake, the local staff and the patient's family collectively called off the donation. When it became clear that there was no more she could do to overcome their fears and quell their doubt, Aurelia expressed regretful respect for their decision, and we quietly withdrew. Our car ride back to the IMSS Centro Médico was tense and filled with frustration, as Aurelia went over and over what had been said and done, trying to find a moment when she might have made things go differently. In the end, she said, it was less the loss of this one donor that worried her. Much more troubling was the profound loss of trust—in her, in the IMSS transplant program, and in the very notion of organ donation itself— that she feared both the family and the local hospital staff would surely take away from the experience.

In a contrasting case following closely on the heels of the first one, an ICU physician from another community-level hospital located on the outskirts of the city called into the IMSS transplant office to report what he described as a potential brain-dead donor. The patient had been in a deep coma for several weeks following a gunshot wound to the head and recently had been removed from his ventilator when the scarce equipment was needed for another patient deemed to have a better chance at recovery. Martina, the transplant coordinator on duty at the time, explained that a patient who continues to breathe on his or her own is—by definition—*not* brain-dead and thus not a candidate for organ donation. The local ICU physician, however, was insistent that he had already approached the family about organ donation and that they had readily agreed—and that since they had agreed, the organs should be taken. It seemed to him not only wasteful and embarrassing to refuse the generosity of the patient's family at this point but also somewhat cruel given how eagerly the young man's mother had seized onto the redemptive idea of making something good from such tragedy. Martina held firm, however, reiterating with detailed care the biological—and legal—reasons that an independently breathing patient could not be considered brain-dead and thus could not become an organ donor. To her mounting exasperation, the argument went round and round over the course of several hours and several lengthy telephone calls before she was able to convince the ICU physician that he would have to go back to the family and explain that the donation simply could not take place.

A few days later, in a rare moment of relative calm in the transplant coordinator's office, Martina turned to me to offer her own wry and somewhat chilling commentary on the conjunction of these two cases, uttering the words that opened this chapter: "See, this is our problem with brain death here—they think that the dead ones are alive and the live ones are dead." Condensed in her pithy observation were a whole host of critical uncertainties that haunted brain death in this setting. For surfacing in the pairing of these two cases were profound doubts about the verity of the very concept of brain death itself, as well as about the potential fallibility of its diagnosis. Also emergent in these two incidents were some of the challenges of putting brain death into practice in a setting where a wide range of resources—from ventilators to training to trust—was often scarce. I came to think of these diverse forms of uncertainty in terms of the notion of *slippery states*, a phrase that captures the ways in which brain death was often experienced *as* a slippery state, rife with conceptual ambiguities and practical difficulties. The notion also invokes the difficulties of deploying such a concept *in* a slippery State. For, as raised in the introduction, the iconic figure of the State in Mexico was indeed a slippery, illegible one, responsible for a public health care system that was a lingering ideal of the revolution and also a site of endemic corruption, both deeply necessary and always suspect.

This chapter explores the ways that brain death has proven conceptually, logistically, and politically slippery in Mexico at close range, tracing out some of the causes and effects of such multifarious forms of uncertainty. Doing so will not only provide a more fine-grained view of what underlies the biounavailability of cadaveric donors in Mexico, but also serves to complicate—and explicate—those authoritative, yet inaccurate public claims that "family refusals" constitute the central problem of cadaveric donation. For, as we shall see, such claims about family and culture serve to *frame* the problem of organ donation in both senses of the word—both enclosing it in an interpretive structure and, in the process, strategically assigning blame. Such invocations of culture as explanatory device merit close tracking—as work on the politics of blame by Paul Farmer on AIDS in Haiti and Charles Briggs on cholera in Venezuela has so richly demonstrated (Briggs and Briggs 2004; Farmer 1993; see also Fassin 2001). And so delving into the biounavailability of cadaveric organs will ultimately engage us also in questions about the circulation of blame—of where it is directed, and where deflected—in the politics and practice of transplantation.

Brain Death as a (Conceptually) Slippery State

The concept of brain death was codified in the United States in 1968 by a committee at the Harvard Medical School (Ad Hoc Committee of the Harvard Medical School to Examine the Definition of Death 1968). In their seminal report, published in the authoritative *Journal of the American Medical Association*, the committee made clear that there were two central motivations driving what they saw as the need for this new definition of death. First, the development of ventilator technologies meant that respiration and heartbeat could now be maintained for an indefinite length of time, even in profoundly, irreversibly damaged people. This new technological capacity raised serious concerns about prolonging the suffering of patients and families without any hope of recovery, as well as about the considerable resources that would be consumed in the process. And second, the fledgling transplant enterprise desperately needed a source of organs in order establish itself as a routine medical practice. The Harvard committee proposed that changing the definition of death from a heartbeat/respiration-based definition to one based on brain function would allow some patients previously considered "alive" to be labeled "dead," and hence make it medically, ethically, and legally acceptable to consider these "heart-beating cadavers" as potential sources of viable organs for transplantation. At the time, this frankly utilitarian impetus for redefining death went largely—though not entirely—unremarked and unchallenged in the generally technophilic context of the United States (Giacomini 1997; Lock 2001).

In the ensuing decades the diagnosis of brain death has come to be routinely employed in clinical practice in the United States and many other places around the world, though it has not been so easily accepted everywhere. In Japan, resistance to the notion of brain death as a dangerous importation of Western values provoked a decades-long public controversy charged with the kind of volatility and divisiveness seen in the United States around the issue of abortion (Lock 2001: 143–45). Egypt also has engaged in protracted public debate over whether brain death should be equated with death—medically, legally, or spiritually—with no widely shared resolution yet in sight (Hamdy 2012: 47–80). And even in the United States, despite its relatively seamless adoption into clinical practice, some observers point to the failure of massive public education efforts to substantially increase organ donation rates as suggestive evidence of widespread, tacit rejection of the brain-death concept (Joralemon 1995). Moreover, the concept of brain death continues to generate ongoing clinical, bioethical, and philosophical debate among a wide range of U.S. scholars. Some ask: is it really accurate to call brain death *death itself*, or is this merely a kind of expedient fiction (Shah et al. 2011; Shewmon 1998; Truog 1997)? A fiction, moreover, that reflects—and depends upon—a very Western privileging of consciousness as the source of personhood or meaningful life. Alternatively, others suggest, if we *are* willing to equate total loss of brain function with death, why not go further? Why not decide that there are lesser degrees of brain damage that also result in a loss of meaningful personhood and so could also be called a form of death—and an opportunity for organ donation (Englehardt 1975; Veatch 1993)? Thus, even in a setting like the United States where brain death has been fully incorporated into medical practice, to some degree the concept remains both unsettled and unsettling.

In Mexico, as the story of those two donations-gone-wrong with which I began suggest, the forms of conceptual slipperiness surrounding the very notion of brain death itself were complex, ranging from the biological and experiential to the more spiritual. Publicly, transplant professionals in Mexico stridently insisted on the clear-cut nature of brain death as a diagnosis and a state-of-(not)being. "Brain death is death" was the constant refrain heard in public lectures, media interviews, and private discussions on the transplant floor. As one transplant physician bluntly put it during an educational course being given for regional medical staff: "I insist that we have to erase from our minds the distinction between brain death and death. There are not two deaths of the person . . . A patient in brain death has stopped being a person and *is nothing more than a cadaver*" (Dr. Mercado, IMSS, emphasis added). Though stated somewhat more coldly than was usual, his claim was representative of the unequivocal voice the transplant community strove to maintain in their efforts to educate both other medical personnel and the general public. This insistence on the clarity of brain death, however, seemed to both obscure and introduce some of the multiple uncertainties that often emerged in actual practice, troubling the easy clarity that transplant professionals sought to project.

In on-the-ground practice, there was considerable skepticism among some nontransplant medical staff in Guadalajara about the actual science of brain death and whether it is biologically accurate—and hence ethical—to call this physical state "death." Such doubts echoed in the words of the ICU physician, for example, who told me: "I just don't know where they got this idea about brain death from, as far as I am concerned there is life until the last moment, as long as there is life anywhere in the body" (Dr. García, IMSS). A similar skepticism emerged when another physician stood up to register his disagreement after a hospital lecture on organ donation, asserting: "I would agree with it if they turned the respirator off first and let the heart stop—and then take the organs. Because then the patient really is dead." These objections resonate with the idea posed by Foucault in the epigraph to this chapter, for such concerns resist restricting the location of death to a singular bodily location and temporal moment, suggesting instead that death is indeed "multiple and dispersed in time" (Foucault 1975: 142). In defending the existence of life "as long as there is life anywhere in the body," Dr. García pointed to—and privileged—the fact that the cessation of different biological processes like brain function, heartbeat, respiration, and metabolism does indeed occur not with perfect simultaneity, but rather in somewhat uneven succession.

Such questions about whether the absence of brain function alone should trump all other biological signs in determining death are far from unique to Mexico. Physicians in North America, Japan, Britain, South Africa, and Egypt have also been reported to harbor similar doubts about the scientific validity of the brain-death concept (Hamdy 2012; Lock 2001; Scheper-Hughes 2000; Shewmon 1998). In some cases, clinicians agree that brain death is irreversible but balk at calling it "death itself," while others question even the irreversibility of the diagnosis. Such doubts are not necessarily a product of unfamiliarity or lack of experience with brain death—what might be imagined as a sort of technology-out-of-place problem. Indeed it may be quite the opposite, as Margaret Lock reports from her work in North America: "It is clear that intensivists have few second thoughts about reversibility, but it is also evident that many of them nonetheless harbor some doubts about the condition of a patient recently declared brain-dead, *and it is often those with the longest clinical experience who harbor the most misgivings*" (Lock 2001: 245, emphasis added).

In Mexico, such scientific, biological concerns about whether brain death is *really* death were reinforced by the current state of law which did not permit the removal of a patient from a ventilator—*even a brain-dead patient*—except in the case of organ donation (M. Vega 2000; IMSS 1995).[3] What this created was an uncomfortable contradiction of which at least some hospital staff were acutely aware. In the eyes of the law, brain-dead patients who became organ donors could be "killed" in the name of obtaining organs. But brain-dead patients who did *not* become donors could *not* be removed from the vent until their hearts stopped of their own accord—at least not without risking a criminal murder charge.[4] Not merely a matter of legal—or even conceptual—inconsistency, this contradiction seemed to signal a larger legal and legislative climate in which organ transplantation had only been partially, provisionally accepted. Operating under such equivocal conditions, as Mexican transplant professionals were forced to do, stood in particularly frustrating contrast to the experiences of their Spanish colleagues, who carried out their work with a powerful apparatus of supportive national policy behind them.[5]

If the brain death concept seemed often hard to pin down in either scientific or legal terms in Mexico, this slipperiness was only further compounded by a powerful experiential component. For even when the brain death diagnosis was made and accepted, it was clear that medical staff and family members in Guadalajara did not necessarily experience the brain-dead patient as "dead." Maintained on a ventilator, patients in brain death remain warm to the touch, their chests move up and down as the machine moves air into and out of their lungs, and their heartbeat can be felt and heard by the medical staff who manage them and the family members who mourn them. Such patients may even move, as in the reflexive "Lazarus sign" that derailed the first failed donation case described earlier. These bedside experiences were powerfully embodied, intimately engaging the senses of touch, sound, sight, and smell of those interacting with the brain-dead patient. And, coupled with the need for sometimes very active, invasive medical treatment in order to keep a brain-dead patient stable and the potentially transplantable organs viable, such experiences could make it difficult for all those involved to hold on to the notion of the brain-dead patient as "nothing more than a cadaver."

Such felt contradictions between the formal diagnosis of death and the material signs of life are a common experience in interactions with brain-dead patients worldwide, and often produce a complicated dance of language and affect to accommodate the multiple kinds of death now made possible (Hogle 1995; Lock 2001; Sharp 2006; Youngner 1996). In Guadalajara, transplant and ICU staff could slip easily into talk of keeping a brain-dead patient "alive" long enough for a distant family member to arrive and say his or her goodbye. Or, working desperately to push through all of the necessary medical tests and legal bureaucracy before the brain-dead patient could destabilize into the more traditional cardiopulmonary death, transplant coordinators and ICU staff would frequently find themselves beseeching the patient to "not let go yet" or to "hold on just a little longer."

One such case of a donor "holding on," in fact, became an inspiring, emblematic story told and retold by both SSa transplant program staff and by the donor's mother herself, who later became involved in promoting organ donation. The donor in this case was a charismatic young woman who suffered a sudden brain aneurysm and who was known by her family and friends to have believed passionately in organ donation. Whenever the case was recounted by transplant staff—to medical colleagues, newspaper reporters, transplant patients, or other potential donor families—the young woman was invariably and movingly described as "con tantas ganas de luchar por la donación [with such a will to fight for the donation]." They described the patient as bravely battling to keep her own heart going—despite a complicating heart condition that made sustaining her brain-dead body more difficult—in order to carry out her wish to serve as an organ donor. In these recurrent retellings of her story there was a powerful sense of will, desire, and intentionality ascribed to the donor that seem hard to align with the official insistence on the brain-dead donor as inanimate cadaver.

And even beyond these forms of conceptual slipperiness in biological, legal, and experiential terms, the transplant community's insistence that brain-dead patients are "nothing more than cadavers" was further undermined in Mexico by a set of more religiously inflected uncertainties about the straightforward equation of brain death with death. For many in Guadalajara, spiritual beliefs about the potential for God's direct intervention in everyday human life—typically drawn from Catholicism or evangelical

Christianity—often conflicted with or simply overrode the medical pronouncement of "hopelessness" and "irreversibility" in brain death. Such ideas suffused one anguished father's explanation, for instance, when he refused to donate the organs of his teenage son who had committed suicide. He told the transplant coordinator who had approached him to ask about donation: "Yes, I understand that you believe he is dead, but my faith is my faith. And I believe God can bring him back if He wants to." Reflected in his painful, hopeful words was the fact that for some in Mexico miracles were simply an everyday, ever-present possibility. And in the face of that possibility, people were sometimes unwilling to do anything that could foreshorten God's chances of intervening. Hardly restricted just to laypeople, medical staff also often referred to and drew on these kinds of beliefs as they offered comfort or explanations to the devastated family members of brain-dead patients. The (medically) hopeless diagnosis of brain death was sometimes accompanied by an admission by medical staff that "We have to leave it in God's hands now." And one ICU physician typically defined the limits of medicine's reach in such cases by telling the family "The only way that someone in this state [brain death] could be raised is by Christ himself." For some, this precise possibility, the idea that Christ himself might intervene, was not at all out of the question.

We will return in a moment to the question of miracles and some of the specificities of how they were understood to operate in the Mexican context. For the influence of Catholicism on attitudes about brain death can hardly be taken for granted—as evidenced by the unmatched success of the organ procurement system in deeply Catholic Spain. But first I want to flag how implicit in such invocations of the possibilities for divine intervention was the idea that death is not necessarily determined by the presence or absence of brain function. Making death hinge on brain function alone, as already observed, invokes a very distinctive notion of personhood in which conscious rationality is privileged above all else (Crowley 1998; Englehardt 1975, 1992; Veatch 1993).[6] And indeed, the ethnographic record reveals many other modes for both figuring personhood and marking when death has occurred (Crowley-Matoka 2015; Robben 2004). In Japan, for instance, the death of a person emerges through a social process of family consensus and is neither located solely in the brain nor properly left in the hands of medical authority alone (Lock 2001: 71–72). In Guadalajara and in the presence of ever-possible miracles, personhood was often thought to inhere less in brain function and the thinking mind than in something more akin to the soul or the spirit. And this spirit, this essence of the person could continue to linger undetected (at least by medical equipment) in a brain-dead body, awaiting awakening by God. It could even be summoned back to the body from which it was recently detached—entirely independent of the apparent medical status of brain and other bodily functions.

Such beliefs could certainly work to impede acceptance of brain death— as in the case of that devastated father unable to relinquish the hope of a miracle for his suicidal son. But importantly, belief in the power of the soul and the possibility of divine intervention was also sometimes turned to the task of motivating and making meaning out of the act of donation. In that emblematic case of the young woman who believed so whole-heartedly in donation, for example, her mother invoked a powerful conjunction of both human *and* divine will to account for her daughter's ability to donate despite her precarious medical condition. As she told a local reporter: "There is no doubt that God chose her to give her organs . . . She had a heart attack and it seemed that her heart just wouldn't hold out, but her inner determination to carry out her wish to donate made her resist until the last moment when they could diagnose her with brain death" (Dominguez 2000: 10B).

This somewhat differently grounded logic of personhood—in which both the soul of the person and the will of God may be more vital than medically determined brain function—emerged also in an uneasy debate that took place during a two-day course I attended on organ donation and transplantation, held for regional medical staff in Guadalajara. In the midst of a session on brain death, one of the course participants, a social worker by training, rose to pose what proved to be a challenging question. She asked "At what *precise* moment does the soul leave the body in brain death?" Her interest in the timing of the soul's departure was one often echoed by donor families as well, who would frequently ask for estimates about the timing of the extraction surgery and the final cessation of "life support" so that they could be praying for their loved one at that precise moment. For these families it seems clear that—despite their acceptance of organ donation—brain death did *not* necessarily equate with spiritual death.[7]

In the large auditorium of the professional conference, however, the social worker's question was met first with an awkward silence, followed by some discomfited hemming and hawing on the part of the session panelists, who included two transplant physicians, a transplant coordinator, and a priest. The priest, who was new to work in transplant, ultimately hedged his response, nodding sagely and saying after a long, pondering pause:

"That's a very good question, one I'll have to think about . . ." A few more moments of uncomfortable silence ensued, and then, in apparent frustration, one of the physician panelists took charge and announced assertively that "the soul leaves the body in the moment that brain death occurs . . ."

But the physician's attempt to impose certainty and clarity backfired, for it opened up a lengthy debate among both the panelists and members of the audience about the fact that brain death really cannot be pinned down to "a moment." Rather, the diagnosis of brain death is fundamentally processual; it unfolds over time and is established only through a series of interlocking and confirmatory tests. In Mexico, at the time of my research this testing included two electroencephalograms to test for any sign of brain function, required by law to be spaced at least six hours apart, as well as various other clinical tests commonly used worldwide in the diagnosis of brain death, such as the apnea test to check for respiratory reflexes and the doll's-eye test to check for ocular reflexes. In the progressive unfolding of such tests, death is thus no longer a discrete point that can be easily marked. Instead, the evidence of death accrues slowly, mounting over time until it finally passes the threshold of proof required for its pronouncement. And, as one of the conference attendees astutely pointed out, that threshold of proof is neither scientifically self-evident, nor universal. Indeed, clinical and legal standards and procedures for establishing brain death both vary substantially from place to place and have changed over time, making the uncertain, slippery character of this man-made—and hence malleable—form of death uncomfortably evident.

Religiously inflected debates such as this one about the status of the soul in brain death, as well as beliefs about the possibilities for the intervention of both human and divine will in biological processes, could easily be read as potential barriers to cadaveric organ donation in Mexico. And indeed, the physician panelist who tried—unsuccessfully—to provide a definitive answer to the timing of the soul's departure in brain death seemed to fear just this as he tried to foreclose additional spiritual discussion and move the conversation back to more scientific ground. Similarly, public framings of the problem of cadaveric donation in Mexico also often pointed to "superstitious" or "misguided" religious beliefs as impeding donation, characterizing them as the religious misconceptions of the poor, the uneducated, the rural. Transplant professionals were frequently at pains to distinguish such beliefs from the "correct" interpretation of formal Catholic doctrine, which does, in fact, support cadaveric organ donation as a spiritually permissible and supremely charitable act (John Paul II 2000). Yet—as those families praying for the souls of their loved ones at the precise moment of organ extraction suggest—neither a soul-based understanding of personhood nor a faith in the possibility of divine intervention necessarily predict opposition to cadaveric donation.

Religiosity, as Sherine Hamdy has argued in the context of Muslim Egypt, has often been posed as a sign of the nonmodern, as a mark of irrationality that impedes advancement and the full embrace of science (Hamdy 2012: 68–70). And yet, as her study of Egyptian transplantation so carefully illuminates, this false opposition between science and religion misses much of the complexity and flexibility with which individual people—clinicians, patients, religious leaders, and others—interpret, intermingle, and live out their faith in both God and science in the face of new technological possibilities like transplantation.[8] Analyses of brain death have often explored how this new, man-made form of death in the U.S. context unsettles the fundamental divide between nature and culture understood as central to post-Enlightenment Western thought (Hogle 1995; Lock 2000). Yet, in a Mexican context so deeply infused with both Catholicism and newer forms of evangelical Christianity, debates over brain death and transplantation more generally seemed to reveal an ontologically different order of relations between the categories of "nature" and "culture" themselves.

As we have seen, this is a context where religious beliefs can render the scientific laws of nature as they govern human life simply beside the point—"I know you think he is dead, but my beliefs are my beliefs," as that anguished father of the suicidal son put it. Nature here has a distinctive character; hardly impersonal, inhuman, and immutable, nature instead is imbued with (at least potential) personality, intentionality, morality, and compassion through the will of God. That is, nature in this context does not necessarily proceed according to rational scientific logic—it is not "out there" in Latour's words, separate from human society, politics, and desire—but may be swayed by appeals to God's anthropomorphized will (Latour 1993). And death—brain or otherwise—is thus perhaps never irrevocable, for God can always do what "He" likes. Moreover, not only can human action shape "nature" through such actions as prayers and acts of devotion, but God is imagined to shape the possibilities for "culture" as well. Thus the frequent observations among transplant staff that: "I know that this is God's work we are doing. It's like, I know that organ donation and transplantation are miracles that He has allowed us to have, because if He did not want us to do this, He would not have given us this capability" (Eva, social worker, IMSS).

Critically, the relations among nature, culture, God, and human life in evidence here are deeply reciprocal—God can intervene in human affairs and human biology, but people may invite and shape that intervention through devotion, appeals, and religious promises. This is in many ways a distinctively Mexican version of Catholicism, one that resonates with the long-standing patterns of direct, interpersonal, and reciprocal exchange relations that characterize not just religious but social and political life in Mexico more broadly (Chant 1991; Gonzalez de la Rocha 1994; Lomnitz 1977; Voekel 2002).[9] The unabashed, everyday give-and-take nature of such reciprocal exchanges between God and human, religion and medicine, emerged with particular clarity one day during my fieldwork as I found myself accompanying two IMSS transplant coordinators on a *manda*.[10] This pilgrimage, or religious task of devotion, involved completing a promise they had jointly made to God. The pair of transplant coordinators had agreed that if God permitted a toddler who had recently received a liver transplant to survive the most dangerous posttransplant period, they would travel on foot to visit the venerated image of the Virgin housed in the Basilica de Zapopan outside of Guadalajara. The toddler, a much-adored figure in the program and the first liver transplant patient in that program to survive, had just been discharged home in apparent good health. And so early that Saturday morning, we met at a central city park a few miles from the Basilica to make the pilgrimage and return the favor. The long walk was—as always with these two—a lively time, filled with irreverent banter and much laughter. Completing this task was a solemn, spiritual promise, but also a matter-of-fact part of daily life, fit in among the other errands and plans they had for that day. It was precisely this sort of everyday quality to the give-and-take with God that—along with more scientific, legal, and experiential forms of uncertainty—was so unsettling to the conceptual certitude of brain death in Mexico.

Brain Death as a (Logistically) Slippery State

The transplant community's mantra that brain death does, unequivocally, equal death proved slippery not just in conceptual terms, however, but also in more practical, logistical ones. Advocates of the brain death concept pointed out that brain death always leads irreversibly to (heart) death, *unless* there has been a misdiagnosis. But it was precisely that "unless" about which people in Mexico were often uneasy. In a local world where training is uneven and equipment often fallible, it was difficult for many to have complete confidence in the diagnosis of brain death. The two donations-gone-wrong stories with which we began illustrate the double-edged dangers of such uncertainties—that families and medical staff alike will find it difficult to believe in brain death where it does exist *and* that they may mistakenly diagnose it where it does not.

Yet the potential for diagnostic slipperiness flagged in Martina's wry observation that here "they think the dead ones are alive, and the live ones are dead" cannot just be read as a technology-out-of-place sort of problem, as simply a sign of inadequate training, unreliable equipment, and general backwardness. Even in the United States, the very birthplace of the brain death concept, the possibilities for misdiagnosis have been an ongoing concern. Some two decades after the brain death concept had been put into routine practice in the United States, for instance, a survey of U.S. physicians and nurses likely to be involved in organ procurement revealed that only 35 percent of those involved in making brain death decisions were able to correctly identify the exact medical and legal criteria for determining brain death (Youngner et al. 1989). Even more unsettling were reports of a 2009 case in Syracuse, New York, of a woman mistakenly diagnosed with brain death who woke up as she was being prepared for the procurement surgery (Golgowski 2013). Indeed, putting the brain death concept into actual practice in any setting requires a precise orchestration of human, technical, informational, and political resources. And such logistical complexity itself constitutes yet another way in which brain death can be understood as a slippery state—a state only laboriously established and precariously maintained, which, at any moment, may be disrupted when one of the necessary pieces fails to fall into place.

In Mexico, one of the most basic logistical challenges to organ donation was simply that most brain-dead patients were unlikely ever to be identified as such. Unless a patient ends up at a facility with an available ventilator, diagnosing brain death is simply impossible, as without the technological disentanglement made possible by ventilator support, the cessation of respiration, heartbeat, and brain function simply all occur with apparent simultaneity. And—as suggested by the earlier-told story of the coma patient who was removed from his ventilator in triage-minded fashion in order to make it available for a more viable patient—the availability of such equipment cannot be taken for granted. Yet even if a ventilator were to be available, trying to diagnose a patient with "brain death" specifically (rather than simply identifying her as profoundly, mortally brain injured) might simply never occur to hospital staff. For unless hospital staff were thinking about the possibility of organ donation, there was no real reason to establish a diagnosis of brain death per se. And with transplantation being practiced in only a handful of the most elite specialty hospitals in Mexico, it was hardly surprising that the brain death concept itself had not spread very widely among medical professionals elsewhere.

Moreover, even in the elite hospitals where transplantation did take place, understanding and acceptance of brain death had not always spread much beyond the staff of the transplant programs themselves. As the director of one transplant program put it: "One of our biggest educational needs is here in the hospitals themselves; among health care professionals there is still a lot of ignorance, as well as fear and lack of trust. That's really where we have to start" (Dr. Fernandez, IMSS). Together these problems of technological scarcity, coupled with widespread unfamiliarity with (or even resistance to) the concept of brain death itself among many medical professionals, meant that the only places where the identification of brain death as a potential diagnosis was at all routine were in the handful of hospitals that also housed transplant programs—and which thus housed transplant program staff eager to build the institutional capacity to pursue any potential organ donors.

Even beyond the considerable difficulties of merely identifying a potential brain-dead donor, however, the logistical challenges to establishing the brain death diagnosis and actually seeing an organ donation through to transplantation were also many and daunting. Brain-dead patients are medically unstable, and were particularly difficult to maintain in the Mexican context where resources of all kinds, from equipment to medications to clinical experience with this new form of death, were often scarce. Indeed, of the seventy-four potential donor cases I observed, ten were lost because the patient became unstable and died (in the whole body sense) before the brain death diagnosis could be established. This instability put enormous time pressure on the lengthy series of medical tests and legal procedures required to establish the brain death diagnosis—recall, for instance, that Mexican law required two flatline electroencephalograms, spaced at least six hours apart. And carrying out all of these various tests and procedures required a complex coordination of medical equipment (such as those vital electroencephalograms to measure brain activity) and medical personnel (such as neurologists to interpret the *electros* and ICU staff both trained and willing to engage in the intensive, often invasive management of the brain-dead patient). In overburdened Mexican hospitals, just finding equipment that worked and medical staff with either the time or the inclination or the training to participate in establishing the brain death diagnosis could pose a significant challenge—and potential donations often were lost because of the lack of one or the other.

In addition, government officials from the Ministerio Público (Public Ministry), Servicio Médico Forense (SEMEFO—Forensic Medical Services), and the Procuraduría de Justicia (Attorney General's Office) had to be summoned to verify the legality of the donation and type out reams of paperwork documenting the case and the handling of the donor body. Surgical staff had to be located and operating room space booked, so that if the donation went through, the extraction and transplantation surgeries could actually take place. The patients highest on the wait list who matched the potential donor's blood type had to be tracked down by the transplant coordinator, summoned to the hospital, and usually put through a battery of tests to determine who was in the best physical condition and who would be most compatible with the potential donor.[11] Because cadaveric donations were so rare, and the reliability and completeness of the paper records that constituted patient charts were so often questionable, transplant staff typically summoned a larger number of potential recipients to come to the hospital for review, knowing that some would surely be ruled out for active illness or missing tests or some other problem that would end their hopes of receiving a transplant at that time.[12] Knowing also that there might not be the luxury of time to summon a second round of patients if necessary, this might mean summoning four or even five patients for the two potential donated kidneys, and possibly another two or three patients for the liver as well. Emotionally wrenching and logistically complicated in the always-scarce space of the hospital, this practice of corralling multiple patients together through such a last-minute, high-stakes series of checks could seem shocking to visiting transplant professionals like those from Spain, who were used to a clinical world of up-to-date medical tests and efficiently computerized, nationally networked patient databases.

Thrown together in the close physical spaces of the transplant ward, these potential recipients often already knew one another from the social worlds of the dialysis ward and patient information meetings and waiting rooms they had all come to inhabit during the course of their illness. This was an institutional world in which norms of patient privacy, so dearly held in the United States, were commonly regarded as neither practicable nor particularly pressing. And so, collectively caught up in a poignantly intimate and immediate zero-sum game, these patients and their families would then hang anxiously around on the transplant floor, waiting for hours to hear if the donation would go through and, if so, who among them would be chosen to receive a new organ. The process as a whole could stretch out for hours or even days, with program staff—and potential transplant recipients—remaining in the hospital for as long as thirty-six, forty-eight, or even seventy-two hours at a stretch.[13]

To complicate matters even further, this flurry of activity, phone calls, consultations, and coordinations surrounding the determination of brain death often happened in the middle of the night, and frequently on the weekends as well, because these are the times when the car accidents and gunshot wounds most likely to produce patients with brain death are especially likely to occur. Thus, rousting reluctant public officials and neurologists out of bed to come and participate in the donation process became an additional challenge, and transplant staff became adept at the cajoling, wheedling, and even begging essential to mobilizing the various kinds of support needed to carry through a donation. At every single step, there were multiple opportunities for something to derail the whole process. Problems such as an electroencephalogram out of kilter from having been moved too many times between the different departments that shared it, a government official who simply failed to respond to his pager, or even the lack of a working copy or fax machine in the hospital could put a potential donation in jeopardy. Indeed, of the seventy-four potential donations I was able to observe, eleven were lost due to lack of cooperation from medical staff and/or government officials, another four were lost to equipment malfunctions, and an additional four were lost because the appropriate legal documentation could not be produced. Moreover, in at least half of those ten cases where patients destabilized before the brain death diagnosis could be established, it seemed highly likely that significant delays in the diagnostic processes caused by equipment or staffing problems contributed to the loss of the potential donations.

Critically, all of this frantic activity—along with its potential for problems and derailment—occurred long before the family members of a potential donor were ever approached and asked about their willingness to donate. This meant, as we have already seen, that potential donations were most often lost for reasons having nothing to do with the family's consent. It also meant that there was a tremendous amount of activity and expectation whirling around the "potential donor" long before the family was even aware of the possibility of either brain death or organ donation. Legally and ethically, families could not be asked about organ donation before the diagnosis of brain death was in place. While that diagnosis was being established, however, there was a massive mobilization of resources, people, and hope by transplant staff, so that if the family did agree, the donation could immediately swing into action before the brain-dead patient destabilized entirely. Because donated organs were almost always used within the institution that procured them (a matter I return to later in the chapter), donation and transplant surgeries were usually carefully choreographed to unfold in tightly linked succession, so that the kidneys could spend the least amount of time possible outside of the human body.[14] The considerable logistical challenges of choreographing the donation and transplant procedures, as well as time pressures produced by the medical instability of brain-dead patients, made this massive "behind-the-scenes" mobilization necessary. Yet it also produced some worrisome effects.

One of these effects was the way in which potentially brain-dead patients slipped insidiously from being a "patient" to being a "donor" in the minds, language, and even the clinical actions of medical staff—long before either brain death had been established or the family had consented to donation. Once a patient had been identified as possibly being brain-dead and all the diagnostic and organizational activity was set into motion, it was common practice for the transplant staff to refer constantly to *el donador* (the donor) as they went about their work and communicated with one another. Not merely a niggling question of semantics, this premature usage of the term *donor* both reflected and fostered particular attitudes and actions among staff. And this matters, because the status of donor is radically different from that of patient.

A *patient* is a person who is being treated for his or her own benefit—either to preserve life, or to ease the passing into death. A *donor*, in contrast, is a person who is being medically maintained for the benefit of other patients—all hope for the donor has been abandoned, and the focus of concern is no longer the person as an integrated whole, but the status of the individual organs for transplantation. This slippage of brain-dead people out of the category of patient echoes back to the way living donors too, as we saw in chapter 1, are rendered "not the patient" in the context of the donor/recipient dyad—despite the fact that they undergo major abdominal surgery. One intensive care physician, sympathetic to the transplant program, had developed some expertise in managing potential brain-dead donors and explained it to me this way: "Taking care of a donor is a completely different perspective with a completely different goal. With a patient, you might say things like: 'I can't do that because the patient will retain too much fluid,' but with a donor, that doesn't matter, all that matters is keeping the blood pressure up and the organs perfused" (Dr. Rulfo, IMSS). On multiple occasions I watched this doctor argue with other ICU staff, as he tried to get them to shift gears in this way and "stop thinking about what's for the good of the donor, because that doesn't matter anymore."

Given this kind of language and attitude, it is easy to see why labeling someone a donor prematurely could have real material effects. For instance, ICU staff sometimes engaged in aggressive medical interventions to keep a patient stable and to maintain the organs in usable condition, without necessarily explaining to the patient's family what was being done and why. Of the seventy-four potential donation cases on which I collected data, eleven cases in total were patients who *never* showed flatline brain activity—in other words, these patients died without ever being legally brain-dead. Despite this, all of these patients were referred to, experienced, and treated as donors by hospital staff members up until the moment of their (heartbeat) deaths. In these cases, the sheer momentum of activity often rendered the presence of brain death a virtual certitude for those racing to complete all of the necessary steps. Thus, *not* being able to diagnose a patient with brain death could sometimes be experienced by staff as not just a disappointment but an unfair error of some kind. Speculation and frustration could run rampant as transplant staff complained about equipment problems or the inexperience of the technician running a particular test as ways to explain why a donor failed to conform to their expectations and produce the needed test results.

All of this whirl of activity, as well as the constant reference to the potentially brain-dead patient as "the donor," created a powerful climate of hope and expectation. When the transplant program got wind of a potentially brain-dead patient, the tension on the floor was palpable and mounted steadily as surgeons and nurses passed through the transplant coordinator's office: "¿Hay algo [Is there anything]?" they would ask tersely and obliquely, meaning, "Is there a potential donor?" The transplant coordinator, existing at the center of a maelstrom of activity once a potential donor was identified, tried to field the barrage of questions from clinical staff wanting to know if they should plan to be in the hospital all night. Charged queries came from patients too, who, moving through the tight quarters of the transplant floor, would sometimes overhear just enough to realize what was going on and press for more information, wanting to know if there was a chance that this one might be their chance at a new organ. Information was parsed out carefully, depending on the questioner, about the potential donor's status, the apparent family situation, and the amount of progress made in the lengthy process. All of this tense attention and collective effort created a sort of forward momentum that makes the idea of derailment such an apt way to describe what happened when a potential donation went awry—like a train hurtling downhill, the activity and emotion surrounding a potential donation continued to pick up speed and force as it went forward.

Once all the testing had been done, the operating rooms booked, the surgical staff put on alert, and the patients next on the wait list assembled anxiously around the program offices, there was a tremendous amount riding on the family's decision to accept or refuse donation. For deeply committed transplant staff, the experience of fighting so hard at every step along the way to make the donation go through could be gut-wrenching, exhilarating, and exhausting in turn. As transplant staff hustled through the hospital corridors, working the phones and coordinating reams of paperwork, they had constantly before them (both figuratively and in the flesh) the haunting faces of the desperately ill patients waiting balanced on a knife's edge of hope and fear for word about the donation. The emotional pressure thus created was enormous. Indeed, one transplant coordinator confessed that she nearly always vomited from anxiety before approaching the family of a potential donor, torn between the anguish she felt at their loss and the urgent need of those patients awaiting a transplant.

Driven by this punishing momentum, transplant staff usually tried—covertly—to learn as much as possible about the family during the hours of testing before they could be approached for the actual "petition" for donation. This could be a delicate and daunting task, as the complicated and sometimes conflictual combinations of people and relationships glossed under the term *family* might include spouses, lovers, children, parents, stepparents, aunts, uncles, siblings, half-siblings, nieces, nephews, grandchildren, grandparents, ex-relations, and friends. The complex (and not always congenial) dynamics of emotion and power entailed in such groupings were thrown into stark relief by the tension and grief surrounding the kind of sudden, catastrophic event that usually precipitated brain death—as well as by the pressing need to make a decision about donation. During the time that elapsed while ICU and neurology staff established the formal brain death diagnosis, family members were often kept under virtual surveillance by transplant staff, as efforts were made to discern their level of distress, their attitude toward the hospital itself, and the dynamics among the various family members present. Information about the family's apparent socioeconomic status, education level, and area of origin (with urban/rural distinctions often carrying particular weight) were also observed and discussed among program staff, as they tried to gauge the likely response to a petition and to strategize how best to approach the family when the time came.

Maintaining a formal separation between transplant staff and those caring for and diagnosing the brain-dead patient (a separation regarded as a standard of ethical practice in transplant medicine worldwide), transplant coordinators were scrupulous about avoiding direct contact with the potential donors or their families before the formal diagnosis had been established and delivered by the ICU team. At the same time, they often joked about doing "reconnaissance" on the families of potential donors, even changing their hairstyle or their eyeglasses in order to observe the family at close range without later being recognized when the time came to introduce themselves and raise the possibility of organ donation. One described how she "hid behind doors, or under partitions so that I can get a look at them first. It's very important that they not see me though, not before they've been told about the brain death and been given time to process the news. Otherwise we seem like vultures, hanging around" (Lupe, SSa). Indeed, that haunting image of transplant professional as vulture was a common one, to which I return in chapter 6 to take up in greater depth. Viewed as a matter of both strategy and ethics, these efforts to conceal the flurry of donation-related activity from the family of a potential donor before the actual petition had been made were regarded by transplant program staff less as a "concealment from" than a "protection of" the family.

The atmosphere of expectation and intense backstage activity that surrounded the potentially brain-dead patient occasionally backfired, however, when the curtain between what was going on behind the scenes and what the family actually knew was breached. In some instances, such a breach may have been the accidental result of the way excitement (and sometimes consternation) over a potential donor case could spread quickly even among nontransplant staff. For these were hospital work spaces markedly smaller and more intimate than the large medical centers in the United States, where donation activity is both more routine and more easily cloaked in privacy. In one such case, for instance, a completely unwitting family was addressed by a security guard in an offhand manner as *la familia del donador* (the organ donor's family). The family, not surprisingly, was shocked to hear themselves referred to this way, since as far as they knew their relative might still be saved. They became furious with the hospital staff, and in the face of their anger, all question of the potential donation had to be dropped. This kind of incident projected exactly the kind of image transplant staff were always on guard to prevent—namely, that they cared more about the organs than the patient/donor and that their eagerness to obtain organs might lead them to hover prematurely over the bodies of helpless and (potentially) hopeless patients.

In other cases, nontransplant hospital staff sometimes seemed *intentionally* to breach the web of silence surrounding a potential donor's family. Indeed, several of the cases tracked during my fieldwork were derailed because of seeming direct resistance or interference from hospital staff, which could include not just physicians or nurses, but administrators, security, and housekeeping staff as well. In all, I recorded eleven such cases. In some of these cases, resistance took the form of simply refusing to inform the transplant program of a potentially brain-dead patient in a timely manner or to provide the necessary equipment or personnel support in order to establish a diagnosis of brain death. This sort of opposition most commonly emanated from either the intensive care unit or from the neurology department, and seemed rooted in a combination of skepticism about the very concept of brain death and resentment about the diversion of scarce institutional resources to the transplant endeavor. In the angry words of one ICU director: "Look, I don't really agree with this brain-death idea. And I don't have enough beds for the patients we *can* save. I don't need you people pressuring me about the ones who don't have a chance" (Dr. Fuentes, IMSS).

And in yet other (even more emotionally wrenching) cases, hospital staff intervened directly with the potential donor's family to give them conflicting information about brain death and the status of their patient. In one such case, an ICU doctor approached a family who had just been told that their son was brain-dead, with no hope of recovery, took the parents aside and quietly told them "As long as there is life, there is hope. We have to leave it in God's hands now." In the context of this renewed hope offered by a physician, the family—not surprisingly—became unwilling to consider organ donation. In other such cases, nurses also offered families a form of hope, telling them that their patient was "doing better" after a diagnosis of brain death, or that they were going to try "using an ice pack to bring the swelling down in his brain." Often the lines between merely offering commonplace words of comfort to families, or giving deliberate expression to an alternate understanding of death, or even actively trying to undermine the diagnosis of brain death could be difficult to discern. At times, however, the conviction among at least some hospital staff that brain death was *not* the same as death seemed clear. And ultimately, the very complexity of the entire process—with its exacting choreography of people and resources and time—thus created multiple opportunities for such uncertainties about the *conceptual* slipperiness of brain death to contribute, in turn, to its *logistical* slipperiness as well.

Brain Death *in* a Slippery State

Finally, although much of the uncertainty and resistance surrounding brain death in Mexico centered on perceptions of brain death *as* a slippery state in both conceptual and logistical terms, there was also an element of uncertainty, mistrust, and fear generated by the prospect of putting brain death into practice *in* a slippery State. That is, in a setting where the iconic figure of the State—in its myriad institutions and incarnations of governance—was widely understood to be at once a source of vital resources (such as health care) *and* profoundly corrupt. This is an enduring model of governance with roots that stretch back to the era of Spanish colonial rule, as keen observers of the Mexican political scene have noted, one in which political power routinely operates as an opportunity to (mis)appropriate resources (Friedrich 1987; Lomnitz 1995). Such seizing of public resources serves not just as a matter of personal greed and gain, but also as a means for the strategic redistribution of benefits of all kinds to various constituencies—benefits that then help to further consolidate political support. Indeed, this is very much the political logic of Mexico's long history of single-party rule under the overwhelmingly dominant Partido Revolucionario Institucional (PRI). Emerging from the chaos that followed the end of the Mexican Revolution in the 1920s, the PRI was enormously successful not only at consolidating power centrally at the level of the national government but at extending that power in capillary fashion through the co-optation of local governments, labor unions, and community organizations that filtered down to the level of regional city, hardscrabble *colonia*, and rural *pueblo* (Gutmann 2002; Helms 1982; Wilkie 1967). During its eight decades of hegemonic rule, the PRI built an enormous network of government bureaucracy, institutional structures, and political alliances in which the intricate, ongoing exchange of favors was a primary mode of enlisting loyalty and maintaining power.[15] In this way, the State under the PRI was consolidated as a deeply biopolitical source both of widespread corruption and insecurity *and* of practical, everyday benefits.

It is within this wider political context that the publicly funded healthcare system was simultaneously depended upon and mistrusted by many in Mexico. Seen as one of the last remnants of the ideals of the Revolution, the public hospitals were a site of both fragile hope and frequent disappointment. Such disappointment was regularly deepened by the recurring newspaper exposés of medical scandals involving malpractice, profiteering, and institutional corruption in Mexico (see, for example, Amaral 2000; Atilano 2000; García Partida 2000; Orozco García 2000; I. Vega 2000). And amid the ubiquitous stories of tainted blood supplies and hospital pharmaceuticals diverted to the black market, neither the integrity nor the benevolence of medical professionals was likely to be taken for granted. As many scholars of transplantation have noted, public trust in the medical profession and its institutions is vital to the successful enactment of brain death and cadaveric organ donation. Margaret Lock, for instance, has documented how long-standing skepticism toward the motives of medical professionals was a key element in the deep resistance to brain death in Japan (Lock 2001: 135–36). And Sherine Hamdy has explored how the controversy over brain death in Egypt was both a product of and a contributor to the profound crisis in medical authority in that country (Hamdy 2012: 47–80). Similarly, in Mexico, unease about the slippery State within which publicly employed transplant professionals were enmeshed became yet another barrier to putting the brain death concept into practice.

Indeed, such unease emerged with particular explosiveness in an incident that occurred in the SSa hospital shortly before my fieldwork began, and whose repercussions could still be felt in that hospital when I first arrived. A physician in the government-funded hospital was publicly denounced for removing the corneas of deceased patients in the hospital without family permission and using them for transplantation. As rumors spread throughout the hospital and the wider city, it became common practice over the course of the next several months for families to refuse to leave their patients—alive or dead—alone in the SSa hospital. Family members took to sleeping on the floor beside their patients, keeping guard over them during the night out of fear that their corneas, kidneys, or other bodily resources might be stolen if left unattended. SSa hospital staff recounted the palpable anger and tension of that period, as one social worker described it: "It was terrible, everyone was so suspicious. They were scared of us, people didn't want to be in the hospital, they didn't want to tell us anything or trust us at all. It made it so hard to do our work. For them and us the hospital felt like a dangerous place" (Magda, SSa). A dangerous, yet also deeply necessary place: even at the height of the scandal, the hospital's beds nonetheless remained filled to—and even beyond—capacity.

Eventually the fever pitch of fear subsided, and the practice of keeping constant watch over patients slackened, but it seemed clear that the profound mistrust ignited by this case remained simmering just beneath the surface for many in Guadalajara. Scandals such as this one have erupted elsewhere as well, including in the United States, where a Los Angeles County morgue was similarly accused of removing the corneas of cadavers without family knowledge or consent (Frammolino 1997; see also Hamdy 2012 on Egypt, and Sanal 2011 on Turkey). In Mexico, this scandal was perceived as shocking but also all too predictable, a grimly expected product of the generalized climate of vulnerability and insecurity within which so many experienced their daily lives (Partida 2000a, 2000b).

This pervasive climate of mistrust circulated not only among the general public but permeated relations within and among health-care professionals and government officials as well. Suspicions of corrupt self-interest and potential criminality emanated from all sides, so that physicians mistrusted other physicians, as well as the officials from the Ministerio Público, SEMEFO, and the Procuraduría de Justicia with whom they had to work on donation cases—while in turn, those government officials often seemed to mistrust both their own colleagues and the health-care professionals with whom they interacted. The doubts and reluctance noted above among some ICU and neurology staff to participate in brain-death diagnoses and organ procurement reflected not just jealousy over the distribution of institutional resources or uncertainty about the validity of the brain-death concept. In at least some cases, hospital staff resisted getting involved in organ transplant work because they suspected corruption and feared being tainted by association. Such fears seemed to color the local hospital staff hesitation in the face of the potential donor's unexpected movement in the first donation-gone-awry with which I began this chapter, as suddenly the transplant coordinator's motives, as well as her scientific claims about brain death, came to be suspect. Animating the power of such widely circulating suspicions and unease in the transplant sphere was also the long-standing role of rumor in Mexican political life more generally, where it has often been regarded as a more legitimate source of information than the official version of the way things stand (Lomnitz 1995).

In some cases, the very iconic status of transplantation—so useful in attracting both public interest and material resources—contributed to the problem as well, as nontransplant staff sometimes looked askance at the new medical equipment or media attention being garnered by a transplant program, skeptical about what was "really" behind them. Emanating not just from medical professionals outside the transplant world, however, transplant staff in one program sometimes cast aspersions on other transplant programs: "To them, it's a business, what they care about is the money," I was told by staff in one program, while staff in the program to which they referred would cast oblique accusations in return, with comments such as: "They say bad things about us, but I wouldn't trust how they run their wait list." Such suspicions were only strengthened by the insular and somewhat opaque nature of the local transplant economy in the absence of an effective national or even regional program for organ distribution—for organs were almost always used in the institution that procured them, going to patients selected from their own, internally maintained wait list. Not surprisingly, operating under such widespread—often mutual—uncertainties had profound personal and political effects on the professionals engaged in the work of transplantation, a matter taken up in more detail in chapter 6.

For their part, government officials from the Ministerio Público, SEMEFO, and the Procuraduría de Justicia often resented being pulled into the process of establishing a brain-death diagnosis and authorizing organ procurement. As I was told by one disdainful official during a drawn-out, middle-of-the-night case: "We hate working these donor cases. It's not the hours. It's this brain-death thing, it's just an excuse they use to justify killing people to be able to use their organs—it's not really death. I don't trust the whole thing and I don't like being involved with it" (Licenciado Muñoz). Reflected in his comments was the way that resistance to brain death was often a compound phenomenon, braiding together doubts about conceptual slipperiness ("it's not really death") with political unease about the always-suspect motives of others. Such suspicion and discomfort was mutual, however, and transplant staff often commented on how much they disliked dealing with government officials in the course of organ donor cases: "They are all corrupt, those officials. They like having the power, but they don't want to work, all they want to do is make money. They can't believe that that's not what *we* are trying to do here, so they treat us like criminals," complained one transplant coordinator (Isabel, IMSS).

Throughout, as all of this mutual suspicion swirled around and among those involved in transplantation, there was a self-protective element to these circulations of blame, to the endemic mistrust and the always-vague finger-pointing. It was as if the transplant endeavor was felt to be so fraught with the potential for corruption that both hospital staff and government officials involved with it sought to disassociate themselves from this potential by casting suspicion on others instead. Haunting such interactions was the slippery State illegibility of the figure who might be physician, profiteer, politician, and/or traficante, and whose motives, allegiances, and potential for doling out life-saving resources or life-threatening harm remained ever uncertain.

This aura of suspicion and of (at least the possibilities for) corruption seemed to have led the Catholic Church in Mexico to largely distance itself from the transplant endeavor. The relationship between Church and State in Mexico is historically and politically complex, marked by both deep interdependence and profound ambivalence (ambivalence that has, at various historical points, flared into violent conflict) (Becker 1995; Schwaller 2011). For our purposes, it is important to note that the Catholic Church remains an extremely powerful voice in Mexico in terms of both public policy and private life. It has, as we have seen, provided some of the most central icons of Mexican national identity, with that ubiquitous figure of the *Virgen de Guadalupe*, for example, indexing a form of national pride often posed in explicit contrast to the more secular character of Mexico's neighbor to the north (Napolitano 2009; Wolf 1958). Given the ongoing political and poetic resonance of Catholicism in Mexico, members of the transplant community in Guadalajara frequently lamented the fact that they had been able to garner little public support from the Church.

In fact, local Catholic leadership had issued a variety of conflicting messages on the issues of brain death and organ transplantation. Although Pope John Paul II has made formal statements in support of organ donation and transplantation, affirming that the Catholic Church does view clinical brain death as death (John Paul II 2000), members of the Church "on the ground" in Mexico have made very different statements on brain death both publicly and privately. Despite issuing a few formal statements of general support for organ donation (see, for example, Martinez 2000; Sandoval Iñiguez 1997, 1999), one Catholic bishop from Mexico City, in a widely heard radio address delivered during my fieldwork, both condoned organ donation and in the same breath said, "I don't know where they got this idea of brain death from though, it is perfectly clear to the Church that there is always a chance of recovery from coma." This comment confused the very different medical states of brain death and coma.[16] And it threw the local transplant community into a furor, causing transplant coordinators who had spent so much time convincing the family members of organ donors that their patients *were* dead a great deal of anguish. As one particularly distraught transplant coordinator worried aloud to me the morning after the address: "What if my donor families heard that, and now they think that I talked them into *killing* their patients? People here take the word of the Church as authority, people will believe him!" (Lupe, SSa).

This kind of confusion (or perhaps intentionally ambiguous support) on the part of the Church for the concept of brain death and the practices of donation and transplantation emerged at a variety of institutional levels. During an interview with the bishop of the main cathedral in Guadalajara, for instance, I was told that living donation is "the ultimate act of Christian love and charity, giving of one's own body to save another's life." Yet the bishop was also emphatic that the brain-death concept is wrong because "as far as I know, if a patient is still being treated in a hospital, there is still life and there is still a chance for recovery." This same bishop also told me unequivocally that he believed there was no role for the Church in the public promotion of organ donation—although he declined to elaborate much on why this was so. Other parish-level priests were less reticent about the Church's hesitation, however. In an interview with one of the community priests from my own neighborhood in Guadalajara I was told:

The government here is very corrupt, and everyone knows this. So the institutions, the hospitals, and so on are also filled with corruption. There is too much risk for the Church, if we were to publicly support organ donation now, without knowing for sure that it will be run in the proper way. Right now there is too much uncertainty in our institutions, in the system, to have this confidence. The Church must hold itself separate from association with government corruption, or we will lose our voice and our credibility with the people. (Parish priest from a middle-class Guadalajara neighborhood)

Such comments indexed widespread perceptions of the Mexican government as a slippery State, and affirmed the Church's own interests in maintaining an identity separate from that State. Mixed messages emanating from the Church about the permissibility of cadaveric donation operated at more personal levels as well. I was told of several potential cadaveric donation cases in which the advice of the family's parish priest resulted in the refusal of donation. Yet a handful of priests—like the one who served on the conference panel that became embroiled in controversy over the soul's departure in brain death—had become personally involved in promoting cadaveric organ donation. Nonetheless, transplant staff remained generally wary of the potential pitfalls of involving priests in the donation process. As one transplant coordinator put it: "You just never know what you might get; some priests would come in here and talk the family right out of donating and convince them against the idea of brain death. That is not what we need at that point, so we try to only call in priests that we know are with us" (Aurelia, IMSS). Given the Church's equivocal position—embedded within and inflected by the larger context of political corruption and mutual mistrust—this task of knowing which "are with us" (and which are not) was itself a slippery proposition for transplant staff.

The degree to which Church, State, and the slippery status of brain death were enmeshed with one another emerged powerfully in one particularly agonizing potential donor case I observed in the SSa hospital. At the center of this story was the brain-dead body of a young woman, Maria, shot in the head, an apparent suicide (although her distraught mother suspected the nefarious involvement of an estranged husband). Maria lay in a bed at the end of a long echoing ward, her space partially partitioned off by torn curtains, her breathing maintained by a rhythmically wheezing ventilator. Because there was no heart monitor available on the ward, nurses stepped in at intervals to measure her heart rate and other vital signs by hand. Found bleeding and unconscious in a dismal rented room, she had been admitted to the SSa hospital in the afternoon and promptly shuttled off to the neurology ward when no bed could be found in the intensive care unit. A resident overseeing her case contacted the hospital's transplant coordinator and reported the admission of a potentially brain-dead patient. Various medical tests and bureaucratic processes were set into motion, and eventually the official diagnosis of brain death was established. A physician informed the family of the diagnosis, and a short time later the transplant coordinator approached them to raise the possibility of organ donation.

Over the course of the next several hours, the transplant coordinator spent time with Maria's family in various permutations—present at different times in different combinations were the mother, several siblings, an uncle, the estranged husband, and her two young children. They talked through the circumstances of Maria's "accident" endlessly and with sometimes bitter re-crimination, trying to make sense of her condition and their own feelings of responsibility for what had happened. There was considerable dissension among them on the issue of donation. Maria's husband expressed his willingness to accept donation, further inflaming her mother's suspicions as she continued to insist: "She's still warm, she still *feels* alive. Isn't there any hope?" The transplant coordinator, who at this point had been in the hospital for more than thirty-six hours straight, divided her time between meetings with the family and phone calls to various patients on the waiting list for a transplant, alerting them to the possibility of an organ donation.

Then, suddenly, just as the family appeared to be reaching a fragile consensus to accept donation, a friend of Maria's arrived at the hospital, and taking aside the transplant coordinator and one of the sisters, related her suspicion that the young woman might be two months pregnant. Everything changed. After ascertaining that the hospital was out of the reactive agent necessary to perform a pregnancy test on Maria (so there was no way to be sure about the pregnancy), the transplant coordinator put in a frantic call to the surgeon who was the transplant director. The possibility of trying to maintain the patient in brain death long enough to allow the (possible) fetus to reach viability—something that is sometimes done successfully elsewhere in the world (Feldman et al. 2000)—never arose. Focused wholly on the organ donation question, the transplant coordinator and transplant surgeon debated back and forth but eventually agreed reluctantly that the potential donation had to be called off. In the director's words: "We can't take the organs now. Now it is two lives, not just one. There's nothing we can do" (Dr. Paredes, transplant surgeon, SSa). When another staff member pointed out that a fetus would be nowhere near viable at this early stage, the coordinator countered regretfully but firmly that it didn't matter: "To the Church, it is life from the very first moment. This is too sensitive a subject here. Abortion is illegal, you know" (Lupe, SSa). Laying special emphasis on the potential fetus as not just a spiritual but a legal issue, the coordinator went on with a dark reminder to her colleague about the dangers of giving suspicious and self-interested government officials any opportunity to make trouble for the transplant program. And so the family was summoned again and informed that because of the possible pregnancy (something of which both mother and husband were unaware), the donation could not take place. Stunned by this additional blow, they filed back to the bedside in numb silence and then—somewhat to the surprise of hospital staff—simply left the hospital. Several hours later, Maria's heart stopped, and she was declared dead.

Painfully revealed in this case were layer upon layer of grim tragedy—it was a case that haunted those of us who were there that night, one that surfaced again in collective reflection over the next days and weeks as we tried to make some bearable sense of it. It was a story in which the contingent, contested possibilities for defining death, the scarcity of basic resources, and the paucity of trust all played a critical role. The life and death of the brain versus that of the body, of the woman versus that of the (possible) fetus—these shifted uneasily in meaning and import throughout the course of the case. Indeed, in framing the case as involving two lives now in question, the transplant surgeon himself produced precisely the kind of linguistic cracks through which the manifold uncertainties about whether brain death is "really death" so often slipped, for it posed the brain-dead young woman herself as someone with a life left to lose. And while resource limitations shaped the ultimate outcome, they clearly did not, by themselves, determine it. For while the material inability to perform a pregnancy test foreclosed the possibility of donation here, it was only within the context of a complex set of religious beliefs, political struggles, and legal codes surrounding maternal and (even potential) fetal life and death that the lack of this test signified in the first place. And that signification, of course, became only further fraught in a local world where the potential corruption of government officials must always be taken into account.

Ultimately, condensed in the compelling figure of this brain-dead and possibly pregnant young woman were the multiple forms of slipperiness—conceptual, logistical, and political—integral in producing the biounavailability of cadaveric organ donors in Mexico. Against this backdrop of the manifold complexities of materializing brain death as in a slippery state, I now return to the public framing—and strategic blaming—involved in identifying culture and family refusals as the key barriers to organ donation in Mexico.

Legislating a "Culture of Donation":
Domesticating Bio*un*availability

In April 2000 the Mexican government passed a surprising new initiative aimed at increasing organ donation from brain-dead donors (Jimenez 2000). Part of a larger amendment to the previous legal framework established in the Ley General de Salud or General Law on Health (IMSS 1995; Ley General de Salud 2000: Artículo 3: XXVIII),[17] the new initiative established a system of "presumed consent" for cadaveric organ donation in Mexico. Previously, Mexico relied on a "contracting in" system in which organs for donation could only be taken from a brain-dead person after seeking consent from the family; this is similar to the current legal system governing organ donation in the United States. In contrast, "presumed consent" operates on a reverse "contracting out" logic, in which all citizens are presumed to be willing organ donors, unless they have documented their desire *not* to serve as a donor. Thus, the new presumed consent legislation essentially established the bodies of the Mexican citizenry—at least in death—as a kind of commons to which society as a whole has a right.

Versions of the presumed consent system have been implemented in many countries around the world, most notably in Spain, the country that serves in Mexico as such a powerfully aspirational model for organ procurement success. Yet Spanish transplant professionals routinely report that they do not, in fact, "presume" consent, but rather *always* seek family consent for organ donation. This is a stance upheld in the medical literature on the "Spanish model" of organ procurement, and repeated in the formal workshops and more informal, collegial conversations I observed when Spanish transplant professionals came to Guadalajara to provide training to the local transplant community (Matesanz and Miranda 1996a; Morales and Camposol 1999). Framed as a largely strategic decision, Spanish transplant professionals explain that the costs of the negative backlash that even one disgruntled family could provoke in the media would far outweigh the gain of any individual donation (Matesanz 1996). The benefit of the presumed consent framework, they argue, is simply in creating a general climate of social consensus and expectation regarding donation, which thus works to lighten the burden of responsibility family members feel in making the decision. In other European countries, however, including Austria and Belgium, the presumed consent model has been put into what is often called "hard practice," such that organs may be taken even in the face of family opposition (Michielsen 1996; Rithalia et al. 2009).

In a country where transplantation was still a relatively fledgling enterprise, the legislative move to presumed consent was a bold and somewhat shocking one. It provoked a virtual firestorm of media attention both lauding the initiative and issuing dire warnings about the consequences of obtaining organ donations *a fuerzas* (by force) (for examples, see Barajas 2000; Diaz 2000; Jimenez 2000; Notimex 2000a, 2000b; Villa Herrejon 2000). Indeed, the new law, put forward by then Secretary of Health Jose Antonio Gonzalez Fernandez, caught many members of the transplant community in Guadalajara by surprise. Local transplant professionals found themselves in an uneasy position, for many were convinced that the new law was ill conceived and likely to produce significant public resentment and opposition to organ donation: "We are just not ready for a law like this, there is not enough education about organ donation for people to accept it. It will just scare them and make more people refuse," worried one of the most seasoned transplant coordinators (Aurelia, IMSS). Indeed, other settings where similar legislation has been precipitously introduced have seen precisely this response, reportedly driving panicked citizens (particularly among the poor) to flock to register their frightened rejection of organ donation (see Scheper-Hughes 2000: 209–10, on Brazil).

Yet despite their misgivings, publicly criticizing the proposed law would have put local transplant professionals in a contradictory and untenable position, seeming to pit themselves against organ donation and lending apparent credence to public fears about corruption in organ donation and transplantation. "What can we do, how will it look if the people who work in this seem worried, seem like we don't trust the system? If *we* don't have trust, then no one will," lamented a transplant surgeon (Dr. Gomez, SSa). Members of the local transplant community were frustrated by their perception that the secretary of health had forged ahead on this legislation, seemingly without much consultation with the community of transplant professionals. Such consultation, they argued, would have developed more incremental changes to the law, better attuned both to their own needs and to the current climate of public opinion. To many in the local transplant community, the initiative seemed to appear out of nowhere, ushered with suspicious rapidity through the legislative process—news stories about it first began appearing in early March 2000, and by the end of April the law had been approved. The uncustomary alacrity with which the new law was ratified seemed to many to confirm speculations that this was a profoundly political move, calculated to garner media attention for both the ambitious secretary of health and for his political party, the PRI.

While fully untangling the particular history of this new legislation merits its own separate study, the motivations for taking such a bold step seem likely to have been at least twofold. At one level, this move to promote transplantation can be read as a (perhaps somewhat desperate) political bid for alignment with "modernity." The political climate of spring 2000 in Mexico was a particularly volatile one, with the presidential race that would eventually lead to the defeat of the PRI party (for the first time in over seventy years) and the election of Vicente Fox of the Partido Acción Nacional (National Action Party), heating up in earnest. Questions of change, globalization, and modernity were especially key to this presidential campaign, with the charismatic Fox wielding his excellent English and his close ties to the U.S. business community (he worked as an executive for Coca-Cola in the United States for some years) as signs of his ability to forge a new direction and a prosperous future for Mexico. Central to his campaign's logic was the claim that only by breaking with the stagnant and corrupt past (represented by the monolithic PRI party) would Mexico fully join the ranks of the developed world.

Given this political context, it seems plausible that latching onto some of the modern cachet of organ transplantation could have had considerable political appeal for the foundering PRI. Public officials issued statements making this link between transplantation, modernity, and Mexico's place in the global order explicit, as in Sub-Secretary of Health Manuel Urbina Fuentes's comment: "With this new visionary legislation on organ transplantation, Mexico has taken on a new leadership position at the world level" ("México establece liderazgo en materia de legislación sobre trasplantes de organos." El Informador, April 28, 2000). By leveraging the iconic power of transplantation, the legislative initiative provided a stage on which to play out progress narratives about Mexico's self-identity as a nation finally emerging into full-fledged modernity.[18] It was in this sense that local transplant professionals would sometimes refer to the new presumed consent law as little more than an electoral stunt.

Yet, at another level, the new legislation on organ donation not only mimicked the successful example of Spain (despite that country's disavowal of ever truly presuming consent) but also responded directly to the way that transplant professionals had been publicly (and inaccurately) framing the problem of organ donation all along as one of family refusals and culture. Those mantra-like headlines claiming that "Family opposition impedes organ donation" (Rodriguez Gonzalez 2000) and calling for creation of a "culture of donation" (Bowers and Bonaparte 1999; Paredes 1999) clearly worked to establish family consent and public attitudes as the chief barrier to organ donation in Mexico. Such accounts elided the diverse forms of uncertainty—conceptual, logistical, and political—that, as we have seen, most often derailed potential organ donations. Indeed, transplant professionals themselves often deliberately downplayed the question of limitations in resources and training, as in one quote-turned-headline claiming that: "We have the infrastructure, what we lack are the donors" ("Afirman que 'Hay infraestructura; faltan donadores.' " *Mural*, March 11, 2000). With the problem of organ donation framed in this way, the PRI government's move to establish presumed consent seems in many ways a logical—if heavy-handedly authoritarian—response.

In the time since the legislation was first passed, it is not clear that the presumed consent law has made much change in the actual practices of those involved in organ donation work in Mexico. Taking their cue from their Spanish colleagues, transplant professionals in Guadalajara were generally emphatic that they too would never force a donation through against a family's wishes. And return visits to Mexico, as well as subsequent communications with members of the local transplant community, suggest that family consent does continue to be actively sought—neither simply presumed nor disregarded. Public furor over the issue of being forced to donate a fuerzas eventually died down, and transplant staff saw little of the negative backlash they had feared—people did not seem to refuse donation in greater numbers, nor did they appear to be flocking to notary publics to pay to record their desire to preserve their organs in brain death.

Yet whether or not presumed consent is eventually put into "hard practice" is not the only way in which this legislative move—and the public framing of the problem of organ donation that motivated it—may be understood as coming to matter in Mexico. For even if donations are never obtained a fuerzas in Mexico, public discourse and political action have been effectively consolidated around the issue of consent. That is, around a moment which, as we have seen, *the majority of potential brain-dead donors never even reach*. And in the process, public engagement with the considerable and messy uncertainties entailed in the biounavailabiliy of cadaveric donors in Mexico is neatly sidestepped. In focusing on the issue of consent, the problem of cadaveric donation is essentially individualized, reduced to an issue of personal decisions, willingness, and knowledge—rather than a matter of the larger structural and political conditions that shape the very (im)possibilities of putting brain death into practice in Mexico. Such reductions are not uncommon, of course. After all, the complex story of conceptual ambiguities, ever-scarce and always-contested resources, and abiding political mistrust traced out here offers neither easily condensed and catchy headlines nor simple solutions. Serious examination of the failures of cadaveric donation leads perilously into a larger set of anxieties over both the uncertainties of science and the failures of the State. And so it is perhaps not surprising that a public discourse about ignorant families and an inadequate culture of donation might seem more palatable, more media-savvy, and more politically expedient. Simpler representations, like icons themselves, offer powerful advantages in the ease and stability with which they can circulate and establish a particular story of the way things stand (Dumit 2004; Latour 1987).

But it is not just a simplified set of representations that are set into circulation here. For attributing the biounavailability of cadaveric donors to a problem of family refusals also works to apportion blame, conjuring images of an uneducated, superstitious, and backward public responsible for holding back the transplant endeavor (and hence, the nation itself). Such images map on to familiar social and spatial geographies, such that the poor, the rural, the indigenous, and the "magically" religious were those most commonly indicted as obstacles to the growth of transplantation—and progress more generally—in Mexico. There is an all-too-familiar resonance here with the way that African American resistance to organ donation in the United States has also often been portrayed in public discussion as a problem whose primary solution is similarly one of culture and education (Boulware et al. 2002; Callender et al. 1991, 2004; Siminoff et al. 2003). In both the Mexican and the U.S. cases, posing problem and solution in this way shifts much of the blame onto marginalized shoulders and elides the question of whether resistance to cadaveric organ donation in fact points to problems not with the resisters, but rather with the system and practices of donation and transplantation.

In the United States, for instance, education and promotion efforts directed toward the African American community fail to ensure that the distribution of organs actually is racially equitable. Nor do these efforts do anything to prevent the all-too-common African American experiences of discrimination in the emergency rooms and intensive care units where potential organ donors are treated. Similarly in Mexico, legislating presumed consent or holding conferences and staging media events in order to educate the public does little to tackle the generalized experience of living in a slippery State that seems to underlie much of the suspicion surrounding brain death and organ donation in that setting. Nor does it address the uneasy questions posed by perceptions (among medical professionals as well as the lay public) of brain death *as* a slippery state in both conceptual and logistical terms. Evident here are the biopolitics of the iconic once again. For if the iconic figure of living donation is the endlessly giving mujer sufrida, the iconic image of (failed) cadaveric donation is the poor and probably rural family, steeped in superstition and ignorance. And that is an image with consequences, an image that focuses political will and clinical action in certain directions—and deflects them from others.

There is a cruel irony to all of this, to what Didier Fassin has described as the victim-blaming so often at work in "cultural" explanations of public health problems (Fassin 2001): those least likely to benefit from the transplant endeavor are held, simultaneously, most responsible for its failures. Operating here is perhaps an internal version of the distancing displacement work accomplished by the technology-out-of-place story more generally, a sort of instrumental finger-pointing that allows the problems and potential dangers that lurk within transplantation to be located always "out-there"— whether the out-there is conceived of by complacent North Americans as "third world" organ bazaars, or by urban Mexican medical professionals as ignorant, rural indios, inappropriately mistrustful of the transplant endeavor. This displacement work is also a form of containment, of course, for it tames the unruly uncertainties entailed in materializing brain death by condensing them down to an easily identifiable and all-too-familiar— even iconic—scapegoat. And tamed in this way, the problem of the biounavailability of cadaveric donors in Mexico was essentially rendered merely a matter of family and culture, rather than of conceptual ambiguity, resource limitations, and political corruption. That is, like the bioavailability of living donors, we might say that the problem of biounavailability too was largely— and effectively—*domesticated*.

PART II

GETTING KIDNEYS (OR NOT)

3. Being Worthy of Transplant, Embodying Transplant's Worth

I think of the transplant patients sometimes like the babies of women who had trouble conceiving—they are *productos valiosos* [valuable goods, products].
—Dr. Ramirez, psychiatrist, IMSS

How Transplant Patients Come to Matter

The notions of bioavailability and biounavailability foreground the question of what kinds of bodies are made available to the fleshy demands of transplant for organs—and what kinds, conversely, are rendered unavailable. As we have seen, this is a question that requires close attention to bodies both iconic and material. Organ transplantation, however, requires not just bodies to give organs, but bodies to receive them. And while this seems simple, even obvious, the need for an organ transplant is not a self-evident biological fact. Rather, this need must be produced, both by medical staff motivated and trained and funded to offer transplantation, as well as by patients who come to believe that receiving a transplant is both feasible and desirable. Both sides of this equation—the offering of transplantation and the willingness to receive it—must be carefully cultivated.

The epigraph describing transplant recipients as productos valiosos was offered during the course of a conversation with Dr. Ramirez, the psychiatrist assigned to the IMSS transplant program. A dapper, self-assured man, he was clearly delighted to have landed a position at the most prestigious hospital within the regional IMSS system. The psychiatrist's role on the transplant team consisted primarily of evaluating potential transplant recipients and their potential living donors to assess whether there were any underlying psychiatric or psychological issues that might cause problems with either giving or receiving an organ. Over a leisurely cup of coffee one day, Dr. Ramirez was telling me about the differences in family support he had noted between dialysis patients and transplant patients. In particular, he was struck by how often he saw dialysis patients come to the hospital alone, whereas pre- and posttransplant patients were almost always *acompañado* (accompanied).

The notion of acompañado is at once a straightforward term meaning simply accompanied by someone else, and a culturally resonant index of a commonplace sense in Mexico that people should not move through daily life *a solitas* (meaning alone, but also lonely), but should have, as much as possible, the protective, enfolding company of family and friends. For the psychiatrist, this distinction between patients who were (and were not) acompañado registered as a difference in value. Interpreted through the analogy with hard-to-conceive babies, this was a form of value produced by the level of investment, effortfulness, difficulty, and desire associated with making possible that particular life. And it was through the density and visibility of a social network in which the patient was (or was not) patently enmeshed that this form of value was most clearly indexed. It was not precisely a question, he went on to clarify, of people getting transplanted because they necessarily were more valuable, but perhaps of people becoming more valued through the arduous processes of transplantation itself.

This identification of transplant patients as productos valiosos provokes the question—how and why do some patients become valuable goods, and others do not? What precisely are they products *of*—and what are they produced *for*? And just what kind of good (in both senses of the term) might they come to represent? Attuned to the representational powers and pressures of transplant's iconic status, it seems important to ask not just what patients come to mean in this context, but what the transplant enterprise needs them to mean in order to justify its own existence in not just medical, but in economic, political, and ethical terms? And in the process, how are particular kinds of patients themselves rendered iconic? This chapter takes up these questions by following the footsteps of patients at close range through the processes that lead (for some) to becoming a candidate for kidney transplantation. This will require attending to interactions among patients, family members, and hospital staff; listening to the discursive shape of statements made in patient charts, staff meetings, and hallway conversation; and watching the effects of actions taken (and not taken) in the course of clinical and bureaucratic process.

For these are the capillary processes by which patients are *materialized* in Judith Butler's sense, as bodies are called upon and named in certain ways (and not others) and, through the repetition and stabilization of this meaning-making, thus come to matter in particular ways, and in particular places and times (Butler 1993; see also Foucault 1975 and Mol 2003). Coming to matter here carries the sense of both producing "an effect of boundary, fixity of surface" (that is, of "real" materiality), *and* of becoming important (Butler 1993: 9).[1] It was through the cumulative effect of these small, everyday moments in the hospital hallway and the clinic exam room that individual patients were produced as particular kinds of subjects, as someone who should—or should not—receive a transplant. It was also in the midst of such moments that transplantation itself was produced as a particular kind of clinical and moral enterprise—for decisions about who should be transplanted were also, critically, decisions about what transplant itself should be. And, in turn, transplant was consequentially caught up in debates about what larger institutions—medicine, the family, the nation—are, and should be.

Kidney Interpellations

A primary reason that the need for a kidney transplant cannot be regarded as self-evident biological fact is simply the complex and contingent array of things that must happen before a patient can even be recognized (and can recognize him- or herself) as a possible subject of transplantation. Bodily dis-ease must be constituted as *kidney* disease. Kidney disease must be constituted as *treatable* disease. One form of treatment (transplantation) must be constituted as superior to other forms of treatment (dialysis, homeopathy, prayer). And each of these points require both health-care institutions and personnel to proffer particular kinds of care, as well as patients able and willing to reach out for that care. In Mexico (as elsewhere) neither side of this equation could be taken for granted, as not only biomedical resources but also willing patients were all too often in short supply.

In fact, as I explore in both this chapter and chapter 4, transplant professionals in Mexico often had to work quite hard not only to find potential patients in a setting where many simply went undiagnosed, but actually to recruit them into believing that transplantation was both within reach and worth reaching out for. Such recruitment efforts in the transplant endeavor are sharply, importantly, distinctive from other domains of health care in Mexico, where overburdened and underresourced public sector clinicians so often hope that fewer—not more—patients will find their way to them. Matthew Gutmann, for example, describes how the head of an IMSS HIV clinic in southern Mexico shared his somewhat guilty but utterly pragmatic hope that patients with HIV would simply never hear of his clinic, because he had so very little to offer them (Gutmann 2007: 75).[2] Clearly there are many differences—regionally, clinically, and otherwise—between the settings of that southern HIV clinic and the northwestern transplant programs where I worked. Yet the iconic status of transplantation—its ability to stand for something larger than itself and to embody the aspirations of both medicine and the nation itself—seems an important undercurrent in the drive to materialize transplant patients, and through them, the transplant enterprise itself.

Tracking those efforts to build transplantation by courting new patients requires close-to-the-ground attention to the complex processes by which some patients came to be identified—and to identify themselves—as candidates for transplant. Here Althusser's concept of interpellation, with which Butler's work is deeply in conversation, helps to further specify some of the ideological and intersubjective dimensions at work in materializing transplant patients. For Althusser, interpellation is the process by which an institution hails an individual and, in recognizing herself as being addressed and responding to that hailing, the individual is constituted as a particular kind of subject (Althusser 1984 [1970]). In the classic example, a police officer calls out, "hey, you there!" and in the moment of turning around you have already recognized yourself as subject to the laws of the state, indeed as a potential criminal. Such institutional hailing is always ideological, it summons individuals to conform to a particular worldview and a specific structuring of power—and in responding to that summons, individual subjectivity is thus shaped in profound ways.

The concept of interpellation has most often been used in analyses of contexts where institutional power is highly consolidated, even hegemonic, as it reaches out to hail people in the voice of the police or the judge or the physician. Yet the situation in Mexico, where the transplant enterprise was itself still in formation, offers a more uncertain set of relations. This was a setting where institutional power was considerable but not yet wholly consolidated, where the voice of the transplant endeavor had authority, yet sometimes faltered or simply went unheard. Understanding the spaces of the village clinic, the local hospital, and the regional transplant program as key sites where biomedicine tried—but sometimes failed—to hail individuals, this section explores two key moments of interpellation that operated as preconditions for transplantation becoming a possibility. For we cannot understand how some people come to matter as candidates for transplant (and others do not) without first examining how bodily distress comes to be recognized as kidney disease and how kidney disease, in turn, comes to be recognized as amenable to biomedical intervention.

Indeed, constituting bodily ailments as kidney disease in Mexico was no mean feat. Merely being diagnosed with kidney disease was vastly complicated by the clinical features of the disease itself, by the political economy of health care in general (and the specific social history of kidney care in particular), as well as by the culturally inflected ways that failing kidneys were experienced by patients in Mexico. Kidney failure first presents through a series of diffuse, vague symptoms such as fatigue, nausea, and headache—ailments easily attributable to a wide range of physiological as well as more emotional or social ills. In the early stages of kidney failure the remaining functioning portion of the kidneys can largely compensate for the lost function, such that patients are often largely unaware that anything is seriously wrong until the kidney disease is quite advanced.

Intriguingly, this compensatory ability of the kidneys was often characterized by Mexican kidney specialists in terms of a certain "nobility," constituting the kidney as a hard-working, self-sacrificing sort of organ, one that exerts itself heroically to cover its losses until it simply can no longer do so. As one IMSS nephrologist was wont to put it, "Es noble, el riñon . . ." ("It's noble, the kidney . . ."), going on to say: "it works and works and we never know it, we never even think about it. And even when it gets sick, it just keeps working even harder until finally, it just can't anymore and it gives out" (Dr. Mercado). Rendered here was a rather proletarian image of the kidney as the unseen, unappreciated workhorse whose importance to the whole bodily system was understood only in its absence, whose nobility was revealed only in failure. This image of an organ that literally works itself to death constituted the kidney in ways deeply resonant with how many poor and working-class people in Mexico experienced the using-up of their bodies more generally in the constant toil and turmoil of daily survival (Finkler 1991, 1994). In a local world where "work" (as figured in both bodily organs and life histories) was often more likely to be degenerative than productive, the inevitable progression of this process into total failure seemed perhaps all too familiar to many of those patients who did, eventually, come to identify their suffering in terms of kidney disease.

Indeed, as deterioration of the kidneys continues over time, waste builds up in the blood, excess fluid accumulates in the body, and blood pressure soars out of control, all of which not only cause increasing discomfort that grows over time into a relentless all-over pain but eventually damage virtually all major organ systems. Without diagnosis and treatment, this process leads inexorably to death. And critically, unlike the heart or lungs or even the liver, the kidneys cannot be felt or heard through the surface of the body. Thus inaccessible to direct observation, the kidneys seem silent, elusive, legible only through invasive and abstract diagnostic technologies, for only a chemical analysis of waste products in the blood or a direct biopsy of the renal tissue can definitively identify the developing kidney disease. For many in Mexico, both the medical expertise and the technical resources necessary to produce such analyses were simply unavailable.

In part this unavailability was reflective of the larger, long-term political economy of health care in Mexico, with resources highly concentrated in urban centers, supplies for diagnostic testing often scarce, and overcrowded public institutions and costly private ones requiring a prohibitive investment of time and money on the part of patients seeking answers to their unexplained suffering (Gutmann 2007; Hunt 1995; Mesa-Lago 1978; Nigenda 1997). Yet the problem was more specifically complicated in Mexico by a marked and historically rooted dearth of expertise about the kidneys in particular (García García et al. 2010). Many clinicians recounted how for decades there had been no hope at all for those with kidney disease in Mexico—diagnosing the disease was possible but futile, because there was no available treatment. As I heard it put many times, kidney patients simply "se murieron como moscas" (died like flies).

Although replacement therapies for kidney failure (such as dialysis) had been available in the United States since the 1970s, the ongoing costs of these therapies are exorbitant—in fact, in the United States it had required a unique act of Congress authorizing federal funding for renal disease to make them widely available (Rothman 1997). In Mexico, particularly in the context of the national "belt-tightening" that followed the debt crisis of the 1980s and the resultant structural adjustment policies imposed by the World Bank and others, such astronomically expensive therapies were simply unthinkable.[3] Given this context, most Mexican physicians found nephrology (the medical specialty devoted to the kidney) far too depressing to contemplate as a career, and kidney disease was given little emphasis in medical school training. Indeed, a long-standing joke was that they might as well change the name from *nefrología* (nephrology) to *necrología* (necrology), since all you could do was watch your patients die. At least in part as a result of this history, Mexico still had relatively few trained nephrologists and few general practitioners with much kidney expertise at the time of this research, and many physicians believed that the majority of patients with kidney disease in Mexico continued to die undiagnosed and untreated. Not surprisingly, given the high costs of treatment for kidney disease, this is a story whose general lineaments are repeated in many other nations on the economic periphery as well (Ikels 1997; Kher 2002).

Coupled with this lack of biomedical kidney expertise was the simple fact that the kidney bore little cultural weight in Mexico. Unlike China, where the kidney has traditionally been read as central to bodily vitality and balance (Ikels 1997), the kidneys have not played a major role in long-standing health beliefs in Mexico. Nor do they figure in a rich cultural symbolics of emotion, like those described for the uterus in the United States or the heart in Iran (Good 1977; Martin 1987; Oakley 1984). Though expressive associations were often made with hearts, livers, and bowels, Mexicans rarely spoke of their kidneys at all, except for the occasional reference to back pain as *dolor de los riñones* (pain in the kidneys). Mexican kidneys, one might say, were most decidedly *not* iconic. Reinforcing this relative cultural invisibility was the lack of direct, experiential access to these organs. Inaccessible both to the clinician from the exterior of the body and to the patient himself from within its felt interior, the kidney remained, for most patients, simply unknown. And being unknown meant also unsuspected; increasingly ill patients suffering from a bewildering array of symptoms were thus highly unlikely to imagine the kidney as the cause of their illness and to seek out specialized treatment.

Together these clinical, political economic, and cultural features of kidney disease in Mexico meant that considerable time, resources, and energy were frequently consumed simply in trying to put a name to the suffering, to obtain a diagnosis. Ailing patients in search of an answer were often driven in desperation from physician to physician and from homeopath to *curandero* (folk healer), receiving a wide variety of diagnoses and treatments, none of which alleviated their increasingly dire symptoms. Roberto, for instance, whose deteriorating health cost him his job as a farm laborer, was variously diagnosed with hypertension, tuberculosis, a heart condition, and *nervios* (nerves) by several different biomedical physicians as well as a village herbalist, before his kidney disease was identified at the SSa hospital in Guadalajara. Such clinical odysseys in the face of kidney disease have seen little improvement over time, as reflected in Ciara Kieran's recent account of a young girl in Guadalajara who went through three clinic physicians and two hospitals—receiving along the way two separate diagnoses of a throat infection—before her kidney disease was properly diagnosed (Kierans 2015). It was this situation of generalized unfamiliarity with kidney disease—among both laypeople and many clinicians—that drove transplant professionals into the role of public educator and evangelist. Thus, for instance, did the IMSS transplant coordinator Aurelia feel it necessary to make her impassioned rounds on a regional lecture circuit in support of transplantation, where she so often used that powerful image of *The Two Fridas* encountered in chapter 1. So useful in evoking moving themes of the human frailty and mutual dependence entailed in transplantation, it seems telling that it was Kahlo's image of those symbolically charged hearts—rather than some depiction of the far less visible kidney—that was so readily culturally available to assist Aurelia in her education work.

We might think of the contingency and difficulty of this process of merely identifying kidney disease as a sort of "interpellation interruptus," a series of failed connections and misrecognitions that could impede or even thwart entirely the process of coming to matter not just as a sick person but as a kidney patient. Perhaps the lab lacks the correct reagents to run a patient's blood work on the day she manages to get a ride to make the long trip to the clinic. Or, disillusioned with the failure of biomedicine to produce any answers, a patient turns his hopes and attention from clinic to church, and goes searching for a miracle through the completion of a complex *manda*, a pilgrimage of devotion like the one described in chapter 2. Or, worn out from the exhaustion of his disease and the time and expense of traveling from place to place in search of an answer, another patient subsides into suffering, deciding his remaining energy is better spent in making his peace with his estranged family. The opportunities for patients in

Mexico to die from kidney failure without ever knowing what killed them were heartbreakingly legion.

Yet even for those who did manage to be recognized—and to recognize themselves—as kidney patients, constituting their disease as *treatable* also often posed further daunting, sometimes insurmountable, challenges. Currently there are three standard options for renal replacement therapy: peritoneal dialysis, hemodialysis, and kidney transplantation. Although transplantation is generally regarded worldwide as the optimal treatment, none of the three therapies is a cure for kidney failure—the underlying disease remains, and each therapy (including transplantation) offers only an imperfect proxy for native kidney function. And while clinicians in the United States often prefer to avoid dialysis entirely and proceed directly to transplantation if at all possible, in Mexico the common lengthy delays in diagnosing kidney failure meant that dialysis was an almost obligatory passage point to transplantation: most patients were simply too sick by the time they were diagnosed to be able to avoid dialysis. Yet, as with the difficulties in diagnosis, key clinical, political economic, and cultural features of these treatment possibilities meant that identifying kidney disease did not always proceed seamlessly to treating kidney disease.

In Mexico, home-based peritoneal dialysis was by far the most common treatment for chronic renal failure (García García et al. 2005). In the early 2000s, for instance, the IMSS system in the state of Jalisco supported approximately 1,300 peritoneal dialysis patients, as compared to 222 hemodialysis patients and 170 active transplant patients.[4] A low-tech (though costly) therapy, peritoneal dialysis involves using a permanently placed abdominal catheter to fill the peritoneal cavity with a chemically balanced fluid that draws out excess fluid and waste products. The process—referred to by patients as *cambios* (changes)—relies on a simple system of tubing and gravity, takes about an hour to complete, and must be repeated an onerous three to five times per day. The supplies for peritoneal dialysis are both physically bulky and enormously expensive, in a single week a patient could go through four or five 25-lb. cases of dialysate fluid, representing a cost of about 2,250 pesos (approximately $240—an astronomical sum in a setting where average monthly salaries hovered around $150). Particularly for poor, rural patients who might have to travel long distances by bus each week to pick up their supplies, finding the required room to accommodate dialysis in overburdened schedules, cramped homes, and strained budgets could prove simply impossible. Dialysis costs were perilously high for the stretched-thin health-care institutions as well, as reflected in the IMSS medical director's observation that kidney patients "make up about 1 percent of our patient population, but consume about 20 percent of our institutional resources, because dialysis is so expensive" (Dr. Paredes).

Given these economic and logistical burdens, the difficulties of sustaining dialysis over time were so severe that some clinicians in community clinics and hospitals simply refused to offer it to patients, believing it both more realistic and more merciful to them and their families simply to let them die. For those patients who were told about dialysis, however, treatment could not be started until they had proven to medical staff that they could provide the minimal living conditions necessary for dialysis, which included having an entire separate room dedicated just to dialysis, with a covered floor, roof, and windows, and nearby running water. Given the densely crowded and frequently makeshift living conditions of the *autoconstrucción* (self-made) homes of many working-class and marginalized poor in Mexico, these material requirements could be difficult to meet.

Patients also had to prove that they could bear the social and economic costs of the treatment—staff had to be convinced that they would have both the money to purchase the needed supplies over the long term and family members willing to commit to helping them with their dialysis for the rest of their lives. And when these conditions failed to materialize, medical staff were faced with the grim task of denying a patient the therapy, knowing full well that this was a certain death sentence. This was a decision that weighed heavily, and hospital staff sometimes resented being put in the role of arbiter of life and death. As one frustrated, heartsick social worker confided after rendering her judgment in one such wrenching case: "Sometimes I just get tired of feeling like the wicked witch. I don't want this kind of power, I don't want to make these kinds of decisions. But I *can't* put him on dialysis when there's no chance of supporting it—he would still die and just suffer more along the way" (Magda, SSa).

Yet if peritoneal dialysis was frequently unobtainable for kidney patients in Mexico, hemodialysis was even more so. Though generally preferred over peritoneal dialysis in more resource-rich countries like the United States and Japan, hemodialysis was an extremely scarce treatment in Mexico.[5] The process uses a dialysis machine that acts as an artificial kidney to filter waste products and excess fluid directly from the patient's blood, using a surgically implanted shunt that allows a large and rapid flow of blood between patient and dialysis machine. In Mexico, hemodialysis machines were located almost exclusively in hospitals—and usually only in elite tertiary level hospitals—rendering the therapy highly inaccessible to most patients from rural areas (and many in urban settings as well). This contrasts sharply with the United States, where federally funded chronic hemodialysis is typically provided through a prolific number of local, stand-alone (and often for-profit) dialysis centers.

Echoing the larger story of scarce expertise and resources described above, the perpetually weary head of nephrology in the SSa hospital told me a rueful story about starting the hemodialysis program there in the 1980s (as the hospital's sole nephrologist) with a single donated hemodialysis machine that had only narrowly escaped discard after languishing in the hospital cellar for two years. Prior to his arrival, apparently no one had known what it was. That same hemodialysis machine was still in use in the program some two decades later, along with four others subsequently donated to the hospital. With access to machines so scarce, patients usually received only two hemodialysis sessions a week (rather than the three sessions per week generally regarded as optimal in U.S. centers). Moreover, hemodialysis was generally reserved only for those patients no longer able to perform peritoneal dialysis at home (because of repeated infections or other medical problems) and patients sometimes died simply waiting for a slot in the hemodialysis schedule to become available. Although both the IMSS and SSa hospitals ran their machines around the clock, seven days a week, there was never enough capacity to meet patient need.[6]

Both forms of dialysis exact a heavy toll from patients in various ways. Because neither therapy can fully replace kidney function, dialysis patients must maintain an extremely strict diet, cutting out all salt and drastically limiting their liquid intake. Patients often lose significant amounts of weight on dialysis but also struggle with painful swelling of their feet and legs due to excess fluid. This excess fluid, if it continues to build up, can cause significant damage to the heart and lungs over time. Life-threatening infections are also a serious risk for patients on dialysis, due to the constant exchange of blood and fluids through their catheter or shunt site.

Such relentlessly repeated fluid exchanges registered as particularly problematic in a setting where blood has long had deep cultural resonance as a central source of strength and homeostasis.[7] Many long-standing local healing practices revolve around replenishing "weakened" blood or allowing diseased blood to drain properly, and *consultando la sangre* (consulting the blood) by "reading" or "listening" to its circulation at the wrist is a common diagnostic technique in such practices, thought to reveal much about the gravity of a patient's condition (Rubel, O'Nell, and Collado Ardón 1984). With embodied experiences often framed by such beliefs, many patients understood their bodies as being dangerously depleted by the inexorable cycles of dialysis, "Se acaban muy rápido en dialisís" ("They get used up quickly in dialysis"), explained Jose M., "it takes too much from the body" (janitor, SSa). The more technologically mediated and inhuman nature of hemodialysis was particularly feared in this regard, a fear only intensified by a walk through the hushed hemodialysis unit, where desperately ill patients lay half-propped-up next to hulking machines, partially covered by hospital gowns often blood-spattered from the imperfect connection between machine and human vein. As another patient put it: "Me da asco (It disgusts me) . . . With hemodialysis you live only through a machine, you can never escape the machine" (Sara, student, IMSS).[8]

And in fact, dialysis often does render patients deeply exhausted and progressively weakened, and many struggle with serious depression as the physical and temporal demands of carrying out the cambios can come to dominate their daily lives and curtail their social interactions. In addition, their bodily habitus is often dramatically altered, with a characteristic dark yellowish cast to the skin, dry, lifeless, and matted-looking hair, a sometimes unsteady gait from dizziness and exhaustion, and a distinctive and unpleasant odor produced by the build-up of bodily toxins. Added to these general effects of all dialysis, hemodialysis patients in Guadalajara were also at high risk for contracting hepatitis and other blood-borne illnesses due to the constant exchange of blood through the hemodialysis machines, as well as the common accompanying need for blood transfusions. This particular risk was so acute that one IMSS social worker grimly dubbed them maquinas infectuosas (infection machines). Moreover, many patients in Guadalajara were already so deteriorated by the time they went on hemodialysis that they often did not survive long on the therapy. Observing these outcomes, Mexican kidney patients sometimes fearfully resisted hemodialysis, having come to believe that it was more likely to hasten death than to prolong life.

Indeed, although some patients can live for quite a long time on dialysis (one young man I knew had been on peritoneal dialysis at home for more than eight years), in general the mortality rates for both forms of dialysis were grim. In one study of more than seven hundred peritoneal dialysis patients in western Mexico, only 30 percent survived after two years on the treatment (Ortiz et al. 2000; Romero Diaz 2000; see also García García et al.

2007).[9] Nor do these statistics look to be improving over time; in 2010 researchers in Jalisco reported that approximately half of those patients who were diagnosed with kidney failure died within six months of initiating dialysis or first visiting a nephrologist (Guiterrez-Padilla et al. 2010). To put these bleak survival statistics in comparative perspective, two-year survival rates on peritoneal dialysis in the United States have been reported at 77 percent, and five-year survival at 74 percent (Fried et al. 1996; Ohashi et al. 1999, respectively). These (lack of) survival rates produced a profoundly demoralizing environment in the dialysis programs. As Martita, an indomitable young woman who had been in peritoneal dialysis for four years, once commented to me, "Practically everyone who was in dialysis when I came in is dead . . . so now I'm the 'old-timer' around here" (student, IMSS). Such disheartening realities meant that coming to matter as a dialysis patient in Mexico—despite the arduous process of complex interpellations it required—rarely registered as triumphal success, as a biomedical "happy ending" to the story of suffering that preceded and produced it.

Yet for some patients, of course, dialysis was not the end of the story. Some patients went on to be hailed as candidates for transplantation, a prospect which—as we shall explore first in the following sections and more fully in chapter 4—did hold out heady promises for a more happily-ever-after ending. In turning now to track how some patients—but not others—came to matter as potential transplant patients, the story of one surprising patient who did so despite disadvantages of geography and class offers some important clues along the way. Arturo was a slight, dark-skinned young man from a small, mountainous village a few hours from Guadalajara. A carpenter by trade, Arturo had first become ill about three years before I met him, and spent nearly a year shuttling frantically from doctor to doctor to curandero to naturalista, trying to find an answer to his mounting array of symptoms of exhaustion, dizziness, and swollen extremities. Arturo knew nothing about kidneys or their functioning at the time. Nor, it seemed, were many of the various health practitioners he consulted much better informed, as he received a variety of diagnoses ranging from heart trouble to emphysema to susto (a folk illness induced by receiving a terrible shock or a fright) (Rubel, O'Nell, and Collado Ardón 1984).

Finally, he was diagnosed with kidney failure in a small IMSS hospital near his village. With the sponsorship of his family's patron, for whom his father had worked for many years and who promised to help support the burdens of the therapy, Arturo was enrolled in a regional peritoneal dialysis program and learned the time-consuming process of dialyzing himself at home three times a day. After about a year on this form of dialysis, Arturo heard about the IMSS transplant program in Guadalajara by chance from another patient in his rural clinic—no one else had ever raised the possibility of transplantation with him. After many conversations with this fellow patient (who knew about the program from a cousin who lived in the city) he approached his local physician about a referral to the transplant program. But Arturo was brusquely told that it "wasn't for him" and that there was no point in even thinking about it. He went on raising the possibility of transplant at each of his frequent clinic appointments over the ensuing months, but each time his request for a referral was ignored.

Giving up on the official channels, Arturo drew on his extended family network to cobble together the money for bus fare and came to Guadalajara on his own, where he showed up in person on the transplant floor. Dressed in clothes both conspicuously worn and spotlessly clean, he bore carefully organized copies of his complete medical chart from his local clinic.[10] Polite, friendly, and persistent, Arturo was indefatigably patient as he waited around the program floor for hours at a time over a several-day period, telling and retelling his story to various people. Each time he was told that he needed a referral from his local doctor for admittance into the program, he would nod his head in understanding, then inquire with gentle insistence if, after all, there weren't some other way to move things along, some other person he might be able to speak with to plead his case. Staff began to note his persistence and level of motivation to one another in tones of nearly equal irritation and admiration, and eventually, his strategic self-presentation and resolve paid off. Circumventing the usual referral requirements, arrangements were made by one of the staff nephrologists to admit him directly into the transplant program for evaluation.

At work in Arturo's case and others in which both likely and unlikely patients gained access to transplant candidacy was often a certain quality related to the culturally resonant notion of *agilizar* (to speed up, to make more flexible). Agilizar, a verb, was used frequently by both patients and staff in Guadalajara to refer to the ability to facilitate things, to move with agility through the bureaucratic system of health care, smoothing the process and negotiating its politics and pitfalls with a certain savvy and sense of initiative. It connotes the idea of motivation, effort, and movement that exceeds the boundaries and timelines of the formal system. It is an action that one can request others to perform on your behalf, or, with the addition of a reflexive article (*agilizarse*), it becomes something done for oneself, leveraging social relationships of various kinds in order to move oneself through a series of bureaucratic barriers. In getting on a bus and coming directly to Guadalajara to plead his case and enlist the support of the staff members he came to see every day, Arturo was *agilizando* the process of seeking a transplant by going around (and above) the local doctor who stood in his way. This sort of motivation and nimble proactivity bespeaks a social confidence often fostered by a certain level of economic and educational attainment—but that may exist, as in Arturo's case, as a form of socially attuned savvy separate from the benefit of socioeconomic privilege.

I came to think of the notion of agilizar as useful for capturing a certain cultural style to how things get done in daily life in Mexico, for the way in which institutions of all kinds are assumed to be labyrinthine, obstructive, and often corrupt bureaucracies, best navigated by circumventing the official processes and rules through a combination of favors, personal connections, winsome appeals, and the politically astute application of pressure. This is a widely observed feature of social life in Mexico, evident in studies of patronage relationships and the strategic mobilization of favors across both hierarchical and horizontal relations (see, for example, Chant 1991; Gonzalez de la Rocha 1994; Lomnitz 1977; Lomnitz-Adler 1992; Lomnitz and Pérez-Lizaur 1987; Nutini 1995). This is a form of social relationship that has been shown to be central to survival for people at all levels of privilege and privation in this setting. From my own fieldwork, the importance of agilizar comes back to me in a series of mental snapshots. Watching transplant social workers place their daily series of strategic calls to friends in other hospital services in order to wheedle—as a personal favor—earlier appointment times for their patients in perpetually overcrowded specialty clinics. Listening to desperate dialysis patients strategize about any connections to powerful players in the local government they might muster as a way to pressure for help with the overwhelming costs of the dialysis supplies upon which their lives depended. And in my own daily life, being frustrated but naively accepting when told at the window of the migration office that obtaining the visa I needed to leave and reenter the country to deliver a conference paper was absolutely impossible. Impossible, that is, until friends stepped in and found someone who knew someone who got me an introduction to a high-level local official, who obligingly and casually produced the visa in a matter of minutes over a cup of coffee.

Contained within the concept of agilizar is the idea both that one must get around the way things are usually done in order to accomplish anything and that getting around the formal rules is precisely how things are usually done. In effect, one must work (in the sense of finesse) the system in order for the system to work (in the sense of function).[11] Indeed, as one of the most experienced transplant coordinators wryly observed to me on more than one occasion: "Ya ves? Aqui, todo de favor . . ." ("You see? Here, everything runs on favors . . .") (Aurelia, IMSS). At the heart of this dynamic of agilizar is precisely the kind of reciprocal relationality that suffuses social, political, and religious life in Mexico more generally. This is the fundamental logic of everyday give-and-take, of ongoing affiliation and obligation, out of which the fabric of daily survival and social connection is woven. It is a cultural style, moreover, that both emerges from and contributes to the pervasive sense of living in a slippery State.

Within the transplant programs themselves, there is a resonance between this notion of agilizar and the informal transaction system of "the underlife of the hospital" that Veena Das has observed in the way that transplantation (and health care more generally) works in India (Das 2000: 275). She describes how lower-level hospital staff there receive payments from patients and their families for help in bending the rules, while higher-level medical staff traffic more in personal favors and political pressure in providing ways around bureaucratic barriers. Das's analysis reveals the way that institutional rules can thus pose an obstacle to patients, while offering hospital staff a form of resource by which they can wring additional benefit from their institutional role. While official rules in many ways pose similar obstacles and opportunities for the trading of favors in Mexico, the notion of agilizar also captures an additional dimension here, for it helps to illuminate how rules-as-obstacles also become a medium through which patients may prove their worthiness of receiving a transplant. That is, the necessity of working around the rules becomes not just a feature of institutional functioning, but an opportunity to demonstrate a certain socially valued form of "agility" that comes to constitute patients in very particular and powerful ways.

The following sections build on this insight to explore the locally specific set of meanings and values through which potential transplant patients in Mexico came to matter in diverse ways by exploring individual cases in which patients were alternatively hailed as "agile," "ungainly," and "worth agitating (for)." Like the powerful images in operation on the donation side—la mujer sufrida and the superstitious, ignorant family—we can think of these patient representations also as iconic figures. Figures, that is, in which ideas about transplant's meanings and value were condensed in ways that proved consequential both for the lived bodies of individual patients and the collective, imagined body of the nation.

....

THE "AGILE" PATIENT: *JAVIER*

> For me, it has gone very well. Everyone always asks me how did I get to my transplant so fast. Other patients are always asking me that. I think they are looking for advice, but also wondering why me and not them. And I just tell them that it is because I took such good care of myself. I was in good conditions, and the doctors could see that. They could see that I would do well with my transplant, and when a chance came, I was ready.

Javier was a wiry man in his early thirties whose boyish face was half-obscured by an exuberant mustache. A little over a year before I met him, he arrived at the SSa transplant program with a diagnosis of kidney failure already in hand and the goal of a transplant firmly in mind. He had been working in the United States as a cook for several years when he fell ill. Upon receiving his diagnosis from a U.S. doctor, he was advised that a transplant was the best treatment for his illness. Without firm health insurance, however, he was unsure of his chances for getting a transplant or any kind of ongoing care in the United States. He was also frightened by the idea of being sick in the States by himself, and was eager to return to the support of his family still in Mexico. When he arrived in Guadalajara, Javier started talking to everyone he knew and quickly learned of the transplant program at the SSa hospital from a neighbor who had a cousin in dialysis there.

Javier presented himself and his carefully maintained U.S. medical records to the transplant program and was started almost immediately on dialysis. Tests were begun to determine his medical eligibility for a transplant and the nephrologist managing his case set up appointments for the usual series of exams by cardiology, ophthalmology, dentistry, urology, proctology, psychiatry, and several other specialties. Often accompanied by his sister, Javier was generally prompt for his appointments, with test results and other paperwork in order. He was courteous, well spoken, and seemed to understand things the first time they were explained to him. He asked questions, especially about the next steps that needed to be taken in the protocol for establishing whether or not he could receive a transplant.

As Javier progressed through the series of exams, transplant program staff called in a few personal favors to get appointments with other services scheduled more quickly than usual. They were motivated to do so in part by Javier's own proactivity and by the fact that they felt confident he would keep the appointments and not waste the favor spent on him. In a few instances, tests were required for which the hospital lacked the necessary equipment or material. Javier pressed staff for ways around the delays, and drew on his savings to go to a private clinic to have his electrocardiogram and some X-rays done. Throughout the testing process, he did well on dialysis and never contracted one of the peritoneal infections that so often plague dialysis patients. Staff complimented him often on how well he seemed to be taking care of himself, and held him up as an example to other patients faring less well in their own dialysis.

Within three months, the transplant protocol testing was complete and Javier's name was placed on the waiting list for a cadaveric donation, as no family members had come forward who were either willing or able to serve as a living donor. Within two months after that, Javier was called in for a potential donation and received a transplant. He explains his apparently rapid progression through the wait list by virtue of his "good condition"—there were other patients who had been on the list longer, he says, but none who were compatible with the donor *and* in good enough health to receive a transplant at the time of the donation.[12] The transplant was a success and Javier returned to work at a brother-in-law's machinery shop and began planning a wedding with a woman he had met at the hospital. Although he missed the United States and the money he was able to earn there, he doubted he would return because he was afraid to risk going without his transplant medications or follow-up care.

....

Javier's story exemplifies some of the key qualities characteristic of patients considered to be good candidates for transplantation in the programs I studied. This case study (and those that follow) is based on close observation of the patient's engagement with the transplant program and process as it unfolded over the course of several months during my fieldwork. In trying to understand the trajectory and character of this case and others, I draw on interviews with the patients and the staff involved in their cases, as well as ongoing observations of their interactions with one another, with other patients, and with other hospital staff. It was clear from the start that Javier entered the transplant program with several distinct advantages. He was initially hailed as a kidney patient under the very different interpellative conditions of a U.S. health-care system that has uniquely incentivized the development of resources and expertise for treating kidney disease. Javier thus returned to Mexico with a diagnosis made fairly early in his disease process. Once there, his relatively high level of education and intelligence, his social confidence in interacting with hospital staff, and the economic means and family support to help the process along when necessary all placed him several steps ahead of the game in comparison with many of the other patients at the SSa hospital. But these advantages do not tell the whole story. Rather, what emerged in Javier's story was a mutually constituting process in which such advantages helped Javier come to matter as what we might term an "agile" patient—one with the agilizando skills and motivation to produce a successful transplant and thus become a producto valioso of (and for) the transplant endeavor itself. We might imagine the dynamics at work here as a form of reciprocal relationality in a clinical register, as care is proffered to the patient who can offer some sort of justifying return on that investment. Hailed as a patient who mattered in this way, a variety of discursive, bureaucratic, and clinical practices began to work in Javier's favor in order to make this a self-fulfilling prophecy.

At the discursive level, Javier was quickly understood by hospital staff as a committed, highly motivated, and hard-working person. Javier's ability and willingness to agilizarse in the process of seeking a transplant—to pay for outside tests in order to move things along more quickly, for instance—was taken as evidence both of his desire for the transplant and of his capacity to care for it properly once obtained. In language that stressed Javier's motivation and willingness to work for a transplant, staff often commented approvingly on Javier's good health on dialysis, using resonant, recurrent phrases such as "he takes very good care of himself" and "he is very careful with his dialysis" over and over again. Such comments spoke in part to the familiar issue of compliance, to the idea that Javier was willing to follow the rules of biomedical practice as laid down by his physicians. Compliance, of course, is an issue of near-obsessional dimensions in biomedicine writ large, and several scholars have explored its particular importance in shaping decisions about who is worthy of receiving a transplant in the United States (Fox and Swazey 1992; Trostle 1997). In this setting, however, staff comments indexed not just his willingness to work within the system, but to *work* (finesse) the system in pursuit of his goal. Thus, while transplant staff members' confidence that Javier would comply with his posttransplant regimen was important, the bureaucratic realities and cultural style of local health care (and daily life more generally) added an additional dimension to the image of the ideal transplant patient. In this setting, particular value was placed not just on obedience to the rules of the system, but on the ability to move creatively around within them as well—to agilizar as well as comply with his health care.

Intimately connected with the images of motivation and working for the transplant evoked in the notion of Javier's "agility" were impressions circulated among the staff about his potential productivity as well. Remarks reflecting on how "he has such a will to work again" and "he's so young, all he wants to do is go back to work" became stock accompaniments to any discussion of Javier's case. Staff members would trade stories with one another about how many jobs he had held simultaneously while working in the States (he often juggled kitchen jobs in several restaurants at a time), and about his efforts to keep working from home during his illness by helping his mother do piecework while on dialysis. Javier's will to work, his youth, and his apparently supportive family relationships (in both emotional and economic terms) were all used to speak to the more generalized social utility of transplanting someone like Javier in language that justified the investment of precious societal resources both in transplanting Javier *and* in transplantation more generally.

The story being woven together, passed along, and stabilized in these interactions was that this was a patient who would *produce value* through his ability and desire to return to working life, and who thus would be a *valuable product* of transplantation, a demonstration and justification (in both economic and moral registers) of this iconic biotechnology's place and purpose in Mexico. This was a story with a strong gender dimension, for the image of an agile and valuable patient emphasizes stereotypically masculine qualities of independence, self-assertion, and mobile movement through the circuits of both institutional bureaucracy and local/global labor markets. In the Mexican context, this resonates with a long-standing racialized imagery as well, indexing iconic images of the modern mestizo on the move who stands in opposition to the inert and passive "land-bound Indian" (Knight 1990; Stepan 1991).

Once established among themselves, program staff began to circulate these images of Javier as an "agile" patient more widely, both in justifying favors asked of hospital staff in other services on his behalf and in holding him up to other patients as an example of how to succeed in getting a transplant. And as Javier himself became a sort of icon of what transplantation was meant to achieve (both to transplant program staff themselves and to the wider community of patients and hospital staff) it became critical to ensure that he did, in fact, succeed. Illustrated in part here is one of the ways that transplantation's iconic status as both sign of and vehicle for modernity comes to matter. For program staff deeply invested in proving that transplantation does work in Mexico, Javier was one of the patients who should make it—and in sometimes more, sometimes less subtle ways, their actions began to assure that he would. At work here was not some sort of orchestrated campaign to push one patient through the process at the expense of others. Rather, through the repetition of small, largely unexamined, and commonsensical actions, individual staff members shaped reality such that it came to conform to their narrative expectations.

At the level of bureaucratic practice, for instance, Javier was both more capable of navigating the labyrinthine complexities of forms, test results, and validations from diverse administrative offices and medical services and more likely to have someone walk down to an office with him or take the time to help him fill out a necessary form. As mentioned above, physicians and social workers sometimes expedited appointments for Javier, circumventing the often months-long process of waiting to get into one of the more overburdened specialty clinics. When snags were hit, such as the hospital's electrocardiogram equipment going on the fritz, staff came up with alternate strategies for keeping the process going, and Javier was sent to a private clinic for the necessary tests (albeit at his own expense). At each of these moments, the action taken did not represent any overarching or agreed-upon plan to help Javier more than other patients. Rather, individual staff members responded to each particular situation as it arose and in accordance with their own (largely unexamined) hopes for and expectations of Javier; that is, perceiving Javier as an "agile" patient motivated staff to agilizar the process on his behalf. And as Javier progressed through the protocol process fairly rapidly, this progression itself became further evidence of Javier's ability to agilizarse.

Javier's status as a patient who *should* be able to attain a transplant also came to shape clinical practice. Being perceived as someone who did not get infections and who "took good care of himself" was central here. As a result of this perception, and of staff members' related trust in his ability to understand and act on information, Javier was sometimes given more detailed and more thorough advice on maintaining his diet and his dialysis. If he expressed concern about something, nurses and physicians were likely to take him seriously right away and examine his catheter site or his dialysate fluid. They had come to trust Javier's judgment and to feel that he shared their orientation and motivation toward the transplant. During clinical consults, physicians were more likely to look at Javier directly and to listen to his comments and questions—over time, Javier had come to be viewed as more of a partner in the clinical endeavor, rather than an inert (or even resistant) object of the physicians' ministrations.

Ultimately the tacit agreement evident in Javier's case that he was an "agile" patient likely to do well with a transplant set into motion practices that stabilized and materialized him as such. For transplant staff invested in particular understandings of transplantation's role in Mexico, Javier promised a happy ending to the story, and so he came to matter to transplant staff as a patient who *should* be transplanted in order to fulfill that expected conclusion. The mediation of clinical practice by narrative expectation here recalls Brigitte Jordan's concept of "moral requiredness" (Jordan 1980). In her classic cross-cultural analysis of birthing practices, Jordan argues that medical models of all kinds are characterized by a sense of not only technical but moral superiority that enables any given medical model to function by allowing its practitioners to maintain faith and confidence in their own actions. Such moral requiredness, however, is also what makes it very difficult for practitioners to allow for alternative approaches or possibilities, for it defines any deviation from the norm of a given model as "unethical" or "dangerous." Javier's case came to represent for program staff an iconic vision of the way they believed transplantation should work, and so ensuring a good outcome became instrumental in maintaining their own belief in the transplant endeavor. As we shall see in the following sections, however, staff beliefs about how transplantation should function could work to the opposite effect, so that other kinds of patients came to be seen as endangering the hoped-for happy ending and thus, the transplant endeavor itself.

I don't know. My sister and I came and in the beginning we were very
excited for the transplant. She wanted to donate to me, even though her
husband was worried. So we came to the hospital and we started doing
all those tests. But they were so far apart, and sometimes we would come
and something would go wrong and they would send us home without
the test. All those papers all the time and people sending us up and down,
all over the hospital—we spent whole days in the hospital sometimes. It
was really hard. And my sister was missing work and her husband was
mad at her, and my mother too didn't want her to donate. Everything
was taking so long, and I started feeling worse, I was so tired all the time
from coming to the hospital on the bus every week. . . . Then the last
time the doctor told me some of my tests were lost or weren't any good
anymore. I don't know, we haven't done any tests for a while, and I don't
really know what will happen . . .

Lidia was a short, round woman in her midforties, with a slightly hunched posture and the sallow, drawn skin of a long-term dialysis patient. Although separated from her husband for more than a decade, she continued to have access
to the IMSS system through him and his job as a night janitor in a factory. Lidia
was childless and, after her separation, returned to live with her mother, an
aunt, and an unmarried brother in their two-room apartment. When she was
able to work, which was less and less often after she went on dialysis, Lidia
helped her mother run a small taco stand on a nearby street corner.

When Lidia was first diagnosed with kidney failure nearly two years before I met her, she had already been feeling ill for several months. The doctor in her local clinic kept telling her that she just needed to get more rest
and watch her blood pressure—just one example among many of how the
diagnostic process for kidney disease in Mexico was so often plagued by
such failures of recognition, by a form of "interpellation interruptus." Eventually, however, Lidia went to a homeopath, who told her he thought she
had something wrong with her kidneys. Her mother, having grown increasingly worried, borrowed money from a brother working in the United States
to have tests done at a private clinic, where she was diagnosed with kidney
failure. The private doctor, who also had an IMSS appointment, referred
her to the IMSS transplant program.

When Lidia arrived at the program she knew virtually nothing about dialysis or transplantation and found the large hospital in an unfamiliar part of the city confusing and frightening. She was put on dialysis soon after arriving at the program, and although program staff had raised the idea of a transplant with her, she was unsure what it meant when she was told to find herself a donor. As a result, she did nothing about looking for a donor for several months, and never even mentioned the idea to her family. As she settled into dialysis, however, and began talking to other patients, she started to develop a better idea of what a transplant might mean for her. Eventually, she talked to her family about donation, and a younger sister to whom she had always been close volunteered to give her one of her kidneys.

Lidia brought her sister to the hospital and the social workers set up the first few in a series of appointments for them to be tested for eligibility and compatibility. As time went on, however, Lidia and her sister started to run into problems. They were often confused about the protocol process and missed several appointments because they went to the wrong place at the wrong time, or because—dependent on multiple city buses to reach the hospital—they arrived late and the physician refused to see them. About halfway through the series of appointments, several sets of test results went missing from their files (a common occurrence in the overburdened hospital bureaucracy), and as they did not have copies themselves, the tests had to be rescheduled. Lidia had an especially hard time managing all of the paperwork because she had difficulty reading—this problem was complicated by the fact that she was ashamed of her inability to make sense of the paperwork she was given and tried to hide it, a self-defeating effort eventually recognized by one of the program social workers.

Program staff became frustrated with Lidia and her sister as they found themselves having to reschedule appointments for them on multiple occasions. Lidia's reticence in dealing with staff members often came across as sullenness and, as she was afraid or reluctant to ask many questions, they often took her silence as either tacit agreement or lack of interest. When Lidia's sister began to miss more appointments because of pressure from both her employer and her husband about all the time away from work and home, staff members took this as a sign of lack of seriousness on her part about the donation. During this period, Lidia contracted a painful peritoneal infection as a result of her dialysis and was hospitalized at her small community hospital for more than a week. After being released from the hospital, she did not return to the IMSS transplant program because at the time she did not have any appointments pending and she and her family were simply worn out by the seemingly never-ending process of testing. She thought she and her sister would take a break and go back in a few months.

Six months later, Lidia did return to the transplant program, only to find that she and her sister would have to start the process over again nearly from scratch—most of their tests, they were told, were now too out of date to be of any use. As this new round of testing was begun, it was discovered that Lidia had been infected with hepatitis, probably from a transfusion she received while hospitalized for her peritonitis. Plans for a transplant were derailed and she was sent to receive treatments for the hepatitis. Depending on the outcome of those treatments (which would last at least several months), she was told she might or might not be eligible for a transplant at a later date.

Lidia's case offers a window onto how certain patients came to matter not as an "agile" producto valioso of (and for) transplantation, but rather in terms of a certain "ungainliness." Although not drawn directly from local parlance like agilizar, the notion of "ungainliness"—signifying both awkward movement and failure to produce gain—captures a conceptually useful opposition to the image of the nimble, value-producing patient. Just as Javier entered the transplant program with several clear advantages, Lidia's relative lack of education, economic resources, and social confidence surely played a role in her (stalled) movement through the transplant program. But identifying class differences is not sufficient to explain the local meanings (and effects) that eventually condensed around those differences. It is true, of course, that class often played a role in how staff viewed particular patients and in how they were able to communicate and, perhaps most importantly, empathize with them. And it is also true that transplant staff in Mexico (as elsewhere) had to grapple with very real issues of medical and ethical responsibility as they considered which patients to transplant. Transplanting a patient who was unlikely to have long-term access to medication and care was not only probably pointless, but also potentially cruel, as the physical process of rejecting an organ can be ferocious. Yet, as we saw earlier in Arturo's politely persistent case, some patients did gain access to transplantation from unlikely positions of socioeconomic disadvantage. So how are we to make sense of Lidia's awkward engagement with the IMSS program here, of her experience of being hailed by a transplant endeavor that then—in a sense—turned away from her? As in Javier's case, following some of the on-the-ground discursive, bureaucratic, and clinical practices that coalesced around Lidia is revealing.

In Lidia's case, a perception of her as "ungainly" began with uneasy comments traded between staff members on her demeanor and her seeming difficulty in understanding much of what she was told. "I think she's slow," a physician would comment as he passed through the office, shaking his head in a worried manner, and the transplant coordinator would counter with a story about the latest difficulty in getting her to fill out a form or show up for an appointment on time. Closely coupled in this imagery of slowness was a sense both of a cumbersome physical body, swollen and painful with the fluid retention of her advanced disease, and of a clumsy intellect, awkward and ineffectual in clinical interactions.[13] Such forms of physical and intellectual "ungainliness" were surely shaped by the material conditions of Lidia's hardscrabble life, yet often took on a sense of biological and even moral innateness in staff discussions. As stories and observations about Lidia's "slowness" accrued over time, an image of her as fundamentally inert, as "difficult to move" began to emerge in staff expressions of frustration. In a setting where the ability to nimbly navigate the obstructions of bureaucracy was considered essential not just to success in transplantation, but in social life more generally, this was an image that mattered a great deal—raising the question of whether Lidia would be able to successfully maintain a transplant if she received one. As with the masculine valuation of the "agile" patient, there are gender (and racial) dimensions evoked by this particular image, with its emphasis on the passivity, inertia, and inadequate intellectual capacity often associated with both women and the indigenous in long-familiar local stereotypes (Knight 1990). This is not to say, of course, that women (or indigenous people) may only come to matter as "ungainly" in transplantation, any more than (only) men necessarily come to matter as "agile," but rather that these are materializations that map on to familiar and long-entrenched grids of difference and hierarchy.

Adding another dimension to concerns about the possibilities for success in Lidia's case, a second discursive theme emerged that further stabilized perceptions of Lidia as "ungainly" by raising the specter that—even if she were to receive a transplant—she might be a patient of questionable social value. Over time, and particularly as Lidia's sister began to miss more appointments due to pressures at work (her boss threatened to fire her if she took more time off), staff began to talk worriedly about whether there was sufficient family support in place for Lidia. These discussions took up the question not just of her sister's support but of the rest of the family as well, none of whom had put in an appearance at the hospital. Compliance, of course, was part of the issue here, as patients who cannot count on family support (emotional, economic, and logistical) during their recovery and over the long term are less likely to maintain the difficult posttransplant regimen and to do well. However, recalling the psychiatrist's observations that opened this chapter, the fact that Lidia was not acompañada, that she had not materialized a visible social network within which she was clearly encradled, also raised questions about whether her own family thought that she was worth the time and trouble. This apparent familial abandonment of the childless Lidia suggested not only that she would be unlikely to produce a "good" transplant, but that perhaps relatively little social good would be wrought by transplanting her, offering not even the iconic happy ending of a family preserved. Of note here are the gendered dimensions of Lidia's value being read, primarily, as a function of her perceived family (dis)connectedness. In contrast to Javier, the issue of her potential (or lack thereof) for productive posttransplant employment seemed less often at issue.

As a discursive picture of Lidia began to take shape among staff members, the bureaucratic evidence of her "ungainliness" also began to mount. Staff, alerted to the fact that she was considered a problem patient, kept a close eye on her paperwork and careful track of appointments missed. Interactions between Lidia and staff sometimes took on the form of unspoken efforts to test her—sending her off to retrieve test results in another part of the hospital, or to schedule an appointment somewhere else, in part to see if she could and would do it. Because she was perceived as needing to prove herself in ways that an "agile" patient like Javier was not, she was rarely offered the kind of extra help from which he benefited. Over time, this began to condense into a material record of her inability or (as it was sometimes read) unwillingness to navigate the protocol process successfully. Her patient file amassed notations from doctors, nurses, and social workers attesting to the various problems encountered in the bureaucratic process, and in this way the emerging, shared understanding of Lidia as "ungainly" moved from the spoken discursive realm to the "objective" written record.

Accruing even greater fixity and surface, this materialization of Lidia as an "ungainly" patient eventually took on a physical, bodily form as well, as the repeated naming of her as a problem patient came to color not just bureaucratic but also clinical practice. In keeping with the idea that Lidia had to prove herself, she was given very little leeway by physicians and nurses. If she arrived late for an appointment, she might be sent away with a stern lecture about the importance of being on time. In the case of her peritonitis, she was in fact sent home the first time she came in complaining of abdominal pain, and it was only after the infection had advanced significantly that she was examined and then hospitalized. This peritonitis was itself then taken as further evidence of her carelessness, slowness, and lack of motivation, and she was often admonished about the need to "take better care of herself." These admonishments, however, did nothing to address (or even recognize) the likely effect of her living conditions on her ability to dialyze herself according to instructions. With at least four and often more people living in a two-room apartment, keeping a dedicated space separate just for dialysis and maintaining the kind of disinfection regimen recommended was virtually impossible. Thus, staff expectations about Lidia's inability to take care of herself and her actual embodied experiences with illness and dialysis became mutually constituting, as staff expectations fostered attitudes and actions that rendered Lidia more vulnerable to problems with her dialysis and this in turn reinforced those expectations of failure.

Unlike the productive, valuable outcome staff came to anticipate in Javier's case, Lidia's "ungainliness" posed a threat to the iconic promise of transplantation—revealing the flip side of the moral requiredness engendered by staff commitment to transplantation. Just as Javier came to represent how transplantation should work, Lidia came to embody how it might fail. Particularly insidious in the inequality materialized in a case like Lidia's was the informal and largely unexamined nature of the processes at work. In the hectic and overburdened daily life of the transplant programs, no one need take a particular action against a particular patient in order to render a transplant unattainable. Rather, simply by not making the extra effort (the agilizando) often required to get patients through the protocol process, certain cases, like Lidia's, could be effectively derailed. At no point in this whole process did anyone necessarily need to say, either to themselves or to the patient, that this particular person should not and will not have a transplant. Thus, transplant staff were rarely forced to articulate and confront the professional, ethical, and personal responsibility for making a firm decision that a patient would or would not receive a transplant. Instead, the whole process could simply be allowed to drag on interminably until the patient had deteriorated so much on dialysis that a transplant was no longer a medically viable option. In Lidia's case, receiving a diagnosis of hepatitis most likely spelled the end of her hopes for a transplant.

One IMSS transplant coordinator, Isabel, described this process of simply "allowing the system to work" (without exerting the effort of "working" the system) in terms of a sort of "natural selection."[14] She believed that transplant staff operated on an implicit justifying belief in such cases: if a patient does not have sufficient economic, intellectual, and social resources to wend his or her way through the protocol process, goes the logic, then he or she is unlikely to be able to maintain a transplant anyway. This particular transplant coordinator, a self-identified feminist with Marxist leanings, was critical of what she saw as a variant of social Darwinism—for her it was a reflection of the increasingly neoliberal logic of medicine in Mexico more broadly and represented a betrayal of the revolutionary foundations of the IMSS health-care system. Profoundly troubled by what she perceived as acquiescence to this imagined and unjust "natural" order, this transplant coordinator would sometimes intervene in such patient materializations, interrupting the condensation of one "truth" about a particular patient and attempting to insert alternate understandings of both individual patients and the purpose of transplantation more generally. In the third case study below, we will track what happens in the event of such interventions, interruptions, and reinventions of how particular patients come to matter.

THE PATIENT WORTH AGITATING (FOR): *ALICIA*

> The transplant coordinator has supported me a lot, more than my own family. I think sometimes some of the doctors don't want me to have a transplant, but [the transplant coordinator] keeps telling me not to worry, I have my donor and that's what matters . . . It's all been so confusing.

Alicia was a frail young woman from one of the mushrooming and desperately poor squatter settlement areas that surround Guadalajara in ever-widening rings. At twenty years old, Alicia had been on dialysis for a year and a half and had been diagnosed with kidney failure soon after the birth of her first baby. She and her husband, with whom she had run away when she was fifteen, had a tempestuous relationship, and her elopement with him had left her estranged from her family for some time. Alicia's father was an active and sometimes violent alcoholic, and her mother was worn down by the demands of child care and multiple back-to-back pregnancies; she was, in fact, pregnant again during this period.

When I first met her, Alicia was in a sort of limbo with regard to getting a transplant. She had access to the IMSS system through her husband's job and had been referred to the transplant program shortly after being diagnosed with kidney disease in her local hospital. An older brother was willing to donate, and the protocol process had been initiated. After completing about half of the required exams, however, she and her brother started missing appointments, and eventually it seemed that the protocol process had stalled or perhaps halted altogether. A few months later, one of the transplant coordinators, Isabel, happened to look through Alicia's chart and realized that it had been nearly a year since she initiated the protocol process. She tracked Alicia down and after talking to her and her brother, ascertained that they did in fact want to pursue the transplant but had become confused, discouraged, and economically drained by the protocol process and the constant travel back and forth to the hospital.

Isabel decided to take Alicia's case in hand and usher her through the protocol herself, explicitly conceiving of this project as a way to counteract the disadvantages of education and income that had hampered Alicia's ability to complete the process. The transplant coordinator was aggressive in agilizando Alicia's case, pushing to get rapid appointments for her and arranging for her transportation to and from the hospital, even to the point of driving out to the hardscrabble colonia where Alicia was staying to pick her up herself and get her to the hospital for her appointments. She made it clear to other staff that she saw this as a test case for proving that poor patients could—and should—be transplanted.

As Alicia neared completion of the protocol, numerous problems began to erupt, including active opposition from other program staff. Some began to complain that Isabel was forcing the case through with dangerous disregard for Alicia's ability to maintain a transplant afterward. As the time for her transplant approached, this opposition became more heated and more open, and Alicia found herself caught in the midst of a power struggle within the program. A physician would refuse to see her for a necessary appointment, saying that he was too busy or that she was too late to be seen, and the transplant coordinator would charge in and demand that she be taken care of at once. A resident would try to send Alicia home after she had been hospitalized for a necessary exam, saying that she had an infection that precluded doing the test, and the transplant coordinator would get another physician to examine her and contradict the resident, authorizing the completion of the exam. At this point Alicia's physical state had deteriorated so much on dialysis that often she was too fatigued and mentally cloudy to follow much of what was going on—a fact that some staff used in support of their contention that she was simply not intelligent or educated enough to maintain a transplant safely.

In addition to all of this, problems arose with the family support Alicia would need for the three-month recuperation period after the surgery. During this period she had separated from her husband, who had become physically abusive and had even threatened to quit his job just so that she would no longer have IMSS coverage. Her parents, with whom relations had long been tense, were saying that she could not come back home to stay with them for her recuperation. Her father vehemently opposed her brother donating and her mother said that she was already too exhausted and too thinly stretched financially to take on one more burden. The transplant coordinator (who had by now enlisted several other staff members in her campaign) dealt with these family problems equally forcefully. She made repeated visits to Alicia's parents' home to talk to the parents (in particular the mother), asking again and again why they didn't care if their daughter died and stating bluntly that they had to take Alicia in, that it was their responsibility as parents. She found a benefactor in a wealthy former patient, who agreed to pay for Alicia's food and other supplies during her recuperation period and fund the construction work needed to prepare an appropriate room for her in her parents' still makeshift home. In the end, the mother acquiesced and agreed to allow Alicia to recuperate there.

Alicia was eventually transplanted successfully, although her case continued to be a point of contention and some rancor among different members of the transplant program staff. Isabel, the transplant coordinator who had pushed her case through felt a great (and somewhat proprietary) satisfaction at seeing Alicia transplanted, although over time she acknowledged that the personal and political costs of taking such a stand within the program had been high. When last seen, Alicia was doing well with the transplant but had begun distancing herself from the transplant coordinator and expressing her desire to be more independent now that she was healthy.

....

In Alicia's case, all of the various processes outlined in the two earlier cases were similarly in play. When I first met her, she was clearly an "ungainly" patient well on her way to foundering hopelessly in the protocol process. But in her case, these processes were consciously interrupted, as one program staff member went (often quite literally) to battle in order to agilizar Alicia's case herself. For the transplant coordinator Isabel, Alicia became a patient worth "agitating," worth deliberately stirring up in order to get her moving again through the protocol process, *and* a patient worth agitating *for* among resistant transplant program staff. Her decision to disrupt the "natural" course of events threw the processes by which patients came to matter as valuable "agile" patients or risky "ungainly" ones into high relief, as program staff began to take sides in the struggle over this patient, countering particular stories about Alicia with retellings (and rereadings) of the same stories. Alicia's intelligence (or lack thereof) in particular became the site of some of the most intense wrangling, with some pointing to Alicia's deteriorating state and multiple infections as signs of an inborn slowness while others held that it was the illness and suffering itself that made it hard for her to concentrate and think clearly. In part, contention over Alicia's case became so bitter precisely because in challenging the labeling of Alicia as "ungainly," the transplant coordinator forced the narrative expectations and tacit assumptions with which program staff typically operated to "slip from the unseen to the seen" (Merry 1995: 53). And once "seen," staff members were forced more explicitly to articulate and defend their own visions of what transplantation should mean, and for whom it should be reserved.

One important dimension of Alicia's case is what it reveals about fault lines among the transplant program staff themselves. Although staff were usually able to reach and maintain an unspoken consensus about both individual patients and the meaning and (larger) purpose of transplantation, contentious differences could and did erupt. In the hospitals where I worked, one key axis of such difference was between physicians and transplant coordinators (all of whom were social workers by training); thus, it is not surprising that in Alicia's case it was a transplant coordinator who decided to take her in hand and change the course of events. Social workers in Mexico are virtually all women and tend to be well educated and solidly middle class. Hospital social workers, particularly in the transplant programs, often served as the primary liaison between physicians and patients (and their families), helping them to manage much of the complicated logistics of institutional health care and answering the questions and assuaging the concerns that people were sometimes reluctant to put to the doctors directly. As such, both their socioeconomic location and their structural position within the hierarchy of the transplant programs often rendered them socially and emotionally closer to patients than many physicians. Transplant coordinators, like many patients, also experienced on a daily basis their lack of power relative to the (largely male) physicians. Given this, it is not surprising that they sometimes empathized with particular patients to a greater degree, and might rebel against what they sometimes saw as injustice and insensitivity on the part of physicians.

The question remains, however: why were some cases, like Alicia's, taken up and championed, while others were left to run their "natural" course? The transplant coordinator who led the battle to get Alicia transplanted was quite candid about why Alicia's case appealed to her so poignantly: her youth and her recent motherhood. Alicia was a pretty, delicate young woman with a soft-spoken manner—she had an air about her that invited protectiveness. These personal qualities were used strategically by Isabel to motivate others to help her as well, as Alicia's status as both young and a woman was deployed in order to engage cultural values about the need to protect and care for someone in this doubly vulnerable position. In highlighting Alicia's vulnerability, the social worker would often articulate a specific vision about what the purpose of transplantation in Mexico ought to be, arguing that if transplantation was to be offered, it must be for the poor and unprotected, as well as for the privileged. It was an argument often accompanied by explicit reference to the status of the IMSS system as "the only thing we have left from the Revolution." Embedded in Isabel's vision was a critique and a reworking of the iconic notion of transplantation as a sign of and vehicle for modernity; she was pleading for a form of advancement not driven by capitalist, neoliberal logics, but made to fit with both local conditions and imagined national ideals. For Isabel, Alicia thus became—if transplanted successfully—a producto valioso not just of transplantation, but of an institution and a society still imbued with a set of more communal-minded, revolutionary ideals as well. Thus Alicia came to embody, for this transplant coordinator, an alternative set of hopes for what both transplant and the nation itself could, and should, be.

In talking about the case (to practically anyone who would listen) Isabel would sometimes show a touching, talismanic picture of Alicia with her daughter and speak ardently about the need to save not just Alicia, but this baby as well. Here, the discursive practices of telling stories about patients were redeployed to reverse earlier narrative versions of Alicia and her story. In these stories, Alicia was no longer imagined as one of the multitude of irresponsible poor indiscriminately having babies for whom they are unable to care. Rather, Isabel would tell stories about watching how tenderly Alicia cared for her baby and with what joyful gurgles the baby would respond to her mother. She would talk about how hard Alicia had worked to support her baby until she had fallen ill, and would make it clear that with such an undependable father, the baby's fate rested in Alicia's frail hands. And while her husband's desertion revealed the fragility of that iconic vision of la familia mexicana, Alicia's brother's loving commitment to giving her a kidney provided a narrative counterpoint that served to reinforce the values of family cohesiveness and mutual support. Foregrounding such ties of motherhood and sisterhood, Alicia's case was thus rendered an issue of saving not just an individual life but a wider family.

In the end, of course, Isabel's efforts to intervene in this particular patient materialization were successful: Alicia did receive the transplant and when last I saw her, was doing well. Aware, at least to some degree, of the contention surrounding her case, she had since distanced herself somewhat from Isabel, commenting tersely that "I just want to be normal now." When the topic of Alicia's case arose, Isabel expressed a complex mixture of vindication, exhilaration, and disappointment. Alicia's subsequent good health was triumphant proof that she was not "reckless" in pushing the case through, as other staff had charged. Yet she was disappointed in Alicia's unwillingness to continue to serve as her poster child for transplanting the poor. For Isabel at least, Alicia's distancing felt like a failure of the clinical reciprocity for which she had hoped, as Alicia declined the role of iconic producto valioso of/for transplantation. This sense of symbolic failure even in the face of clinical success was compounded at a national conference on organ donation and transplantation, where Isabel presented a case study on Alicia, filled with enthusiasm for the social justice statement she felt the case so powerfully made. Over lunch after the presentation, however, she was deflated and downcast, sharing with me how disillusioned she was by what she took to be the condescending response of the audience (an audience made up chiefly of physicians and other social workers): "They think I am foolish, naïve; they were laughing at me, I could see. They're content to just do their few transplants to say that they do them—and who cares about the poor." Her disappointment with the presentation seemed to heighten her growing sense that neoliberal logics increasingly trumped revolutionary ideals in the medical community and Mexican society more generally.

Alicia's case makes clear that coming to matter as either "agile" or "ungainly" is a process far from irreversible or inexorable. As Judith Butler points out, it is only through repetition and reenactment that the "mattering" of bodies is condensed and stabilized into particular meanings and specific subjectivities (Butler 1993). And as Marilyn Strathern has noted, repetition creates opportunities also for interruption, reinvention, and disturbances both small and large (cf. Franklin 1997: 2). In Alicia's case, the repetitious work of telling stories that initially named her unsuitable for transplantation also created opportunities for intervention, for retelling those stories to different ends. Yet it is important to note that while doing so did change the course of Alicia's particular case and forced some tacit assumptions into greater visibility, it really did not challenge existing understandings of which sorts of patients appropriately embody transplantation's purpose and value. In the end, Alicia's story was retold in ways that largely conformed to existing ideas about what transplantation is for and what kinds of bodies are its worthwhile goods. These ideas were essentially reinscribed by arguments that focused on preserving a family by transplanting Alicia, or that positioned that her slowness as merely a transient consequence of her illness rather than an innate quality.

Alicia's was not the only such case I observed. During my fieldwork I encountered several patients in both transplant programs whose courses took similar shifts from mattering in one way to another. Such shifts can head in either direction, of course, carrying patients closer to or further from a transplant as the meanings produced around and through them are altered and restabilized. Engineering such shifts was not the exclusive purview of hospital staff, as Arturo's earlier-recounted agile escape from confinement in his village dialysis program reminds us—although enlisting the help of hospital staff was eventually necessary to his story as well. A frequent feature in such cases was the promise of a particularly dramatic transformation or redemption. In Alicia's case, the idea of producing a stable young family from a situation of chaotic desperation promised one such transformative effect.

In another such case, a young indigenous man struggling with drug and alcohol addictions became the focus of a doctor's hopes for the redemptive powers of transplantation (Ernesto, occasional construction worker, SSa). Dr. Montero, a young physician recently returned from a stint of training in England, was convinced that receiving a kidney from his long-suffering and devoted mother would be the second chance that would not only give Ernesto life itself, but the motivation to stay clean and sober and begin working to support his doting, aging parents. By most other staff members he was judged a poor risk, but the doctor's enthusiasm and conviction eventually wore their initial resistance down, and he was transplanted. Within six months Ernesto had gone back to drinking, stopped taking his medications regularly, and his body was beginning to reject the kidney. Dr. Montero's disillusionment in this case was intense, although when the topic of the case arose among staff she would often offer a defensive shrug and the observation that "at least we gave him a chance, that's all we can do." Ultimately, however, the perceived failure in this case produced an effect similar to Alicia's success, serving to reinforce the values and logic underlying already dominant understandings of what constitutes a life worth transplanting.

Productos Valiosos and Patient Devaluations

In the end there is much here that resonates with other recountings from other places about the social values embedded in how patients are selected or rejected for transplantation and other scarce life-saving therapies (see Fox and Swazey 1974, 1992 for the classic work from the United States). Yet understandings of what sorts of bodies and lives are worth saving through transplantation are attuned to local imaginaries and conditions of possibility and marked by specific hierarchies, including those of gender, class, and race/ethnicity. Particular arrangements of institutional bureaucracy, economic production, family relations, revolutionary idealism, and regimes of value shape how local meanings are condensed in the bodies of individual patients. In tracing out the ways in which some patients came to matter as valuable products of transplantation (and others did not), it becomes possible to see both how inequalities are (re)produced in transplantation, and also how those inequitable effects are often the unintended result of people going about their daily work with the best of commonsense intentions. The three key materializations explored in this chapter, of patients as "agile," "ungainly," or worth agitating (for), are reflective of common sets of relations and imaginative possibilities in this setting. Yet these iconic figurings of patient possibility are not, of course, the only ways in which patients could come to matter through transplantation. The cases offered here in a certain sense represent ideal types, heightened versions that mark out a continuum of possibility along which the meaning and clinical trajectory of individual patients emerge. Just as what Judith Butler (1993) has called "the girling of the girl" does not produce subjects who materialize every aspect of feminine possibility in the same way, we should not imagine all patients who attain transplants as thoroughly "agile," nor all those who do not as unrelievedly "ungainly."

I want to return, finally, to the notion of transplant patients as productos valiosos. Ideas about the production of meaning and value and the ways in which bodies become entangled with and are made differently meaningful by them will continue to occupy the chapters that follow. The cases above traced how ideas about what constitutes a valuable product of and for transplantation can shape how individual patients come to matter in the course of seeking a transplant. Before turning to chapter 4, however, I want to foreshadow the fact that transplanted patients do not always hold their value once the transplant is achieved. The case of Ernesto, whose return to drinking jeopardized his transplant, offers one such example—although his story can be (and by many staff was) read as a reversion to or a revelation of his true state of "ungainliness."

The particular ways in which transplanted patients are made to embody meaning and value for the transplant endeavor—or risk exclusion—were highlighted even more poignantly for me in the story of Beto (student, IMSS). Beto was a young man who had been transplanted about three years before I met him and who subsequently lost his kidney to rejection. Beto was very active in the social network of IMSS transplant patients and continued to attend the transplanted patient monthly meetings even after he was forced to go back on dialysis. During one of these meetings, he angrily recounted how he had not been allowed to participate in the previous year's national Transplant Games—an athletic event designed to showcase the success of transplanted patients, modeled on the Olympics and the Special Olympics and now celebrated at local, national, and international levels. He was told that he could not compete in the Games because he traía la *bolsa* (carried the bag)—meaning that he was back on dialysis and had an abdominal catheter. A devoted athlete, Beto was crushed by this rejection and noted with pointed resentment: "But I am *still* a transplant patient, even if I am on dialysis now." To the event organizers—as well as to some of the patients in the room with still-functioning transplants—the decision to forbid his participation seemed obvious, a straightforward matter of simple definition. Yet Beto's assertion challenged the idea that only "successful" transplants should count, making a claim that he still mattered as a product of transplantation. Indeed, laid bare in Beto's experience is the exclusionary force exerted by a transplant endeavor driven to prove itself a valuable good, an endeavor for which rejected transplants cannot be permitted to form part of an iconic public face.[15]

Taking a cue from Beto's painful story, in the next chapter we turn to the complex story of posttransplant life, to explore the embodied experiences, the forms of success and value, and the risks for rejections of various kinds that were produced when (some) patients did finally receive a transplanted kidney.

4. The Unsung Story of Posttransplant Life

It's like we get the transplant and then nobody cares what happens next. We get sent off to our local clinics and that's it . . . I don't think I was really prepared for what living with my transplant would be like. I thought everything would change, once I got my kidney. And it has—but not always like I thought it would.
—Felipe M., traveling salesman, IMSS

The Romance of Transplant

Like the story of Beto's exclusion from the Transplant Games for "carrying the bag" of dialysis, Felipe's poignant observation above pushes us to ask, what happens to patients once they actually receive the deeply desired transplant? The iconic vision of transplantation is typically triumphal, salvational, a vision in which receiving a transplant is posed as the narrative climax to the dramatic arc of a patient's suffering and struggle. But what happens next? The critical and all-too-often unasked nature of this particular question emerged for me with particular power in the story of another transplanted patient I encountered a few months into my fieldwork. He was a patient whose posttransplant course, like Beto's, proved unable to uphold the biotechnical promises it was meant to embody. I came into the IMSS transplant program one morning to find one of the transplant coordinators, Isabel, just on her way out the door to an appointment. She pulled me aside and asked if I would mind sitting with a patient who was having a hard time and, as she put it: "just needs someone to listen." As listening was one of the few useful skills I had to offer on the transplant wards I of course agreed, and she took me back to a small conference room adjoining some of the patient rooms that was often used for staff or family meetings. Isabel introduced me to Jose, a tall, lanky man in his midthirties who was sitting slumped sadly by himself at a small round table, a picture of palpable dejection. She told him that I was a researcher who had been spending time with them and that he could talk to me if he liked, and then with an encouraging pat on his shoulder, she bustled back out of the room leaving the two of us alone. Feeling rather awkward, I asked if it was okay to sit and just keep him company for a bit; we could talk or not as he liked. He agreed with a shrug, and after a moment of silence, asked what she had told me about him. I told him Isabel had just said that he was having a hard time, to which he nodded, heaved a deep, shuddering sigh, and responded that indeed, he was having a *very* hard time. And over the next couple of hours he poured out a story that has troubled me ever since.

Jose told me that he had received a transplant, using a kidney from his younger brother, about a year before and that, like Felipe above, he too "thought everything would change, once I got my kidney." He had been in renal failure and on dialysis for about three years, and described the experience as brutal and terrifying: "I suffered, a lot, a lot, a lot on dialysis . . . there were so many times I thought I wasn't going to endure. Those *cambios* [dialysis exchanges] just finish you, leave you exhausted and sick, like empty." But he had a wife and three young children to support, and so throughout that time he kept working at his job as a mechanic in an auto shop as much as he possibly could. After about a year and a half on dialysis his family could see he was getting worse and worse, and his youngest brother offered to donate—it seemed like a miracle, he said, an answer to his prayers. So he and his brother worked their way through all of the testing—it took a long time, but little by little, they did it. Throughout it all, he told me, "my wife and I were closer than ever, fighting together to get me to the transplant— that's what gave us *ánimo* [spirit, energy]." And then, he got it, he finally got the longed-for transplant: "I thought—we all thought—that was it, problems solved, no? But, well, it hasn't been exactly like that. . . ."

He went on to explain that he was, of course, grateful to be alive, and deeply grateful to his brother. But Jose had a lot of problems with rejection of his transplant right in the beginning and found himself in and out of the hospital for the first few months, enduring wretched regimens of high-dose immunosuppression. And then he lost his job—his old boss wouldn't take him back, and he found that he couldn't secure another steady job. He told me that people seemed to be scared of him—scared that he would never be healthy enough to be reliable, but also, perhaps, just scared of him in a more diffuse, fear-of-the-unknown sort of way. He told me: "Now I just go from door to door, asking people if they have anything they need fixed, because I'm good with my hands and machines and things. I don't make very much, and it's tiring. Sometimes people look at me like I'm a beggar, but all I'm trying to do is work."

At this point, he broke down, and beginning to weep quietly, he told me the last part of his story, the part that seemed in danger of breaking him entirely. Because on top of everything else, his wife—his champion and partner throughout the whole process of trying to get the transplant—had left him a few weeks ago. She told him that she "just couldn't cope with being around a sick man anymore." The fact that she left *after* he'd received the transplant made it a doubly cruel blow. He told me: "I keep thinking, this isn't what I imagined it would be like, once I got the transplant. I thought things would get easier in my life, but they haven't . . . I'm getting tired of just fighting so hard all the time just to get by, and I don't know how much more I can stand."

As we sat there that afternoon I felt overwhelmed and saddened and utterly useless, unable to offer much beyond time, company, and a sympathetic ear. And I also felt something akin to Jose's own shock about the course of his posttransplant life. Though I certainly knew that living with a transplant was not always smooth sailing, this was just not the way the story was supposed to go. Jose's story struck me with particular force in part because of the gut-wrenchingness of that experience of sitting with him over that long afternoon. It has stayed with me too because of the way his story made me more acutely, specifically aware not just of how challenging posttransplant life can be for many patients, but also of how those difficulties run so counter to the narrative expectations we often bring to transplant. Indeed, his story foregrounded for me how utterly absent those challenges usually are from transplant's iconic salvational story line.

As many have noted, a great deal of media and even scholarly attention to transplant—both in Mexico and elsewhere in the world—has focused on the drama of *getting* to the transplant, while the realities of posttransplant life have garnered far less interest in both popular media portrayals and scientific literatures worldwide (Hogle 1999; Joralemon and Fujinaga 1996; Lock 2001; Scheper-Hughes 2000). The imagery of organ donation as "the gift of life" circulates globally, yet rarely is much depth offered about just what sort of life is actually made possible through this particular gift. Similar to trends reported for media attention in the United States, for example, popular news stories in Guadalajara have made the suffering of patients in need of a transplant (and the heroics involved in getting transplants for as many of them as possible) a relatively familiar story, while the realities of not just receiving a transplant but of living with one over time went largely untold (see, for example, Bareño Martinez 2000a, 2000b; Notimex 2000c; Salinas Galvan 2000). There is an air here of the formulaic Hollywood romance, where the movie ends with the hero and heroine getting married and riding off into the sunset together. Receiving the transplant, like marriage, is an end point, and beyond that point, narrative conventions imply that all simply live happily ever after.

Yet the voices of transplanted patients like Jose and Felipe and Beto alert us to the precarity of posttransplant health, work, love, and even of the very status of counting as a transplanted person at all. They demand that we not be romanced by the iconic vision of transplantation as death-defying triumph of science over sickness, imploring us to track their progress not just to the point of receiving a transplant, but beyond it as well. For the lived experiences of the transplanted patients I came to know in Guadalajara revealed a much more contingent and often deeply vexed version of the "gift of life." And so, this chapter will trace the trajectory of transplanted patients' experiences through three key phases: learning to desire a transplant, finally receiving one, and learning to live with a transplant over the long term. As the embodied productos valiosos of transplantation leave the hospital and are set into wider social circulation, what constitutes a "successful" transplant? In what ways do these transplanted patients produce and retain particular kinds of meaning and value—and in what ways are they at risk (and do they pose risk) through their ongoing articulation with the transplant endeavor? Of central interest as we trace out how particular forms of desire, risk, and responsibility are constituted in this setting will be the slipperiness of the categories, identities, and valuations to which transplant patients are subject. For as we shall see, the promises of transplantation often turned out to be elusive, and the dream of restored health all too frequently seemed to slip away in the months and years that followed transplantation.

Cultivating Desire: The Promise of Transplantation

> At first, I didn't even want a transplant. I didn't even want to hear anything about it, because it just seemed too ridiculous, too strange, to have anything to do with me. At that time, I was doing fine on dialysis at home, and so it seemed crazy to . . . to think about something so outside of my world.
>
> —Lupe, housewife, SSa

The desire for a transplant was hardly an immediate or automatic one for most patients in Guadalajara. On first hearing that they might need a new organ, most reported being taken aback, a bit confused, and even frightened by the prospect, as was Lupe above. Even beyond the considerable challenges of access and expertise described in the previous chapter, transplantation retained a science-fictional quality for many, seeming to pertain to some temporally or geographically distant world, not to their own everyday reality, and certainly not to their own bodies (Brodwin 2000). As such, many patients hesitated when initially hailed by the transplant endeavor, uncertain that they recognized themselves in its call. One such patient described how she hung back, disturbed and somewhat alienated by the idea of transplantation: "My doctor mentioned the idea of a transplant to me when I was first diagnosed, but I thought, that's not for me. I was frightened, I didn't really know much about it. It didn't seem real. I suppose it seemed like something for rich people, movie stars, people who can go up there [to the United States]—not for me" (Berta, telephone operator, IMSS).

Compounding this reluctance for many were the effects of living under a slippery State, with cynicism about the politicization of health care in Mexico widespread and perhaps deepening in recent decades (Gutmann 2002, 2007; Laurell 2011; Mercado Martinez 1996; Wilson 1995). As privatization pressures made increasing inroads on the public health-care system, and as scandal after disheartening scandal continued to erupt in newspaper headlines, trust in medical professionals and the institutions they worked in could hardly be taken for granted. This atmosphere of mistrust had consequences not just for people's willingness to give organs for transplant (as seen in chapter 2), but for their willingness to receive them as well.[1] Some patients were wary of program staff claims that transplantation offered their best option—although most were careful to hedge their bets and conceal these reservations in order to maintain a "good patient" image. As one such patient, Jose M., described his strategy: "I am getting the tests done, so that if it turns out I need a transplant, I can get one. But I am not sure I really need one. I've been doing really well on dialysis . . . And I think there is a chance that my kidneys might be coming back . . . So I think maybe I'm getting better and I won't even need one. I don't really want a transplant right now. But *I don't tell that to the doctors, I go along with the tests, just in case*" (Jose M., janitor, SSa; emphasis added).

As Jose M. suggests, another element contributing to the lack of urgent desire for a transplant among some patients was the somewhat paradoxical truth that those patients most eligible for transplantation in Guadalajara were also those who had done relatively well and achieved some measure of stability on dialysis. Having seen so many die so quickly in dialysis, these patients could be reluctant to relinquish the treatment they knew for the treatment they did not. And an additional dimension to this initial hesitance toward transplantation was the local dependence on living donors, for—all glorification of the iconic *familia mexicana* aside—at least some patients found the prospect of asking family members for a kidney simply unbearable. Given the biounavailability of cadaveric organ donations, patients were generally told that they could not initiate the process of being considered for a transplant without a potential living donor—and so unwillingness to approach family members became an additional barrier for some.

All of this, combined with the wider political economy of kidney disease where, as described in chapter 3, the majority of kidney patients in Mexico simply go undiagnosed and untreated, created a context sharply distinctive from the familiar logic of scarcity in North America, where ever-increasing numbers of patients clamor for an always-insufficient number of organs.[2] Given the general bioavailability of living related donors in Mexico, kidney transplant programs in Guadalajara were not primarily limited by a shortage of available organs (although for those without a living donor, the situation was obviously desperate). Rather, the volume of transplants performed in these programs was more directly limited by a lack of available candidates ready for transplantation.[3] This meant that the "demand" for transplants had to be created in Guadalajara, and staff worked with great deliberation and dedication to draw patients into the transplant endeavor, to coax them into recognizing themselves in transplantation's call. Patients had to be convinced that transplantation was not only feasible but desirable as well, in order to motivate them to persevere through the demanding set of tests, appointments, and paperwork required to be medically approved for transplant.

The IMSS transplant program, for instance, held monthly meetings for patients and families where the mechanics of transplantation and the bureaucratic processes surrounding it were explained, and the benefits of transplantation were extolled by transplant coordinators, physicians, and transplanted patients brought in to give ritualized *testimonios* (testimonials) about their own lived experiences with transplant. Patient testimonials are also used in instrumental ways in U.S. transplant programs to provide information in a powerfully personal, embodied mode, and indeed draw more generally from traditions of "witnessing" as a form of religious—particularly evangelical Christian—expression often turned to the purpose of proselytizing (Sharp 2006: 110–15). Frequently invoking issues of faith, hope, and the need to persevere in the face of despair, such patient testimonios in Mexico both acknowledged the considerable local challenges of achieving transplant and positioned success as a matter of attitude and effort both pragmatic and spiritual. Less often a tale of personal triumph over illness, the stories patients had to tell were rich with a sense of the reciprocal relations—the give-and-take between family, friends, God, and members of the transplant team—that had carried them through the transplant process, often agilizando various obstacles of biology, bureaucracy, and scarce resources along the way.

Beyond such formal education and recruitment efforts, however, it was in the more informal interpersonal interactions that staff in both hospitals often exerted the most persuasive pressure. Staff remained alert to cases where patients and/or family members were reluctant and uncertain about transplantation's promise, and these were the people sure to be hailed from the transplant coordinator's office as they passed by, called in for a figurative "pulse-taking" as staff probed for the sources of resistance or doubt in order to counter them. As one transplant coordinator explained: "This isn't something natural for most patients, you have to help them understand it, you have to show them why they should want a transplant. You *have* to motivate them or they will never get through it and we won't have any patients" (Magda, SSa). Thus the first task that lay before transplant program staff in Guadalajara was that of enrolling patients into the project of transplantation, of fostering a new form of desire and identification among their patients, one centered on the hope for a transplant.

Many staff members maintained a stock repertoire of inspirational patient stories that they drew on in such situations, calling, for instance, on the story of a desperately poor man who was transplanted and had since found a job and moved his aging grandmother into a comfortable new home, or of a young woman who had married and started a family since her transplant. Staff members might pull out photographs of other patients, showing dramatic "before" and "after" transplant pictures, or heart-warming photos of transplanted patient gatherings such as the annual program Christmas party. Such photographs were often treated by staff members with a tender reverence: they were motivational not only for the patients they were used to sway but also for staff members themselves as treasured talismans of the purpose and value of their work. Staff members often orchestrated meetings between these hesitant patients and successfully transplanted patients—calling transplanted patients to join them as they passed by in order to provide their testimonio as to the wonders of transplantation and the changes it had wrought in their own bodies and lives. The notion of the testimonio aptly suggests not just religious witnessing but also sales pitch, capturing the way these transplanted patients were prompted to go through the paces of their story for the benefit of the reluctant or fearful patient: "Tell him, Don Jaime, how frightened you were . . . tell him how sick you were . . . tell him how you felt the day after your transplant . . . tell him what your life is like now" (Carmela, transplant coordinator, IMSS). Often even more important than the story itself, though, was the physical presence of the transplanted patient—the embodied proof that transplanted patients walk and talk and look (almost) just like anyone else.[4]

At the heart of these efforts to incite desire and mobilize motivation for a transplant was a powerful discourse about the ability of transplantation to restore patients to a "normal" health and life. Ideas about what constitutes the normal cannot be taken for granted, of course, shaped as they are by historically and culturally specific expectations (Poovey 1998). Reflecting one such set of locally situated expectations, the transplant coordinator who ran the IMSS informational meetings often told patients: "With a transplant, you get your kidney and it starts working in your body, and you can have a normal life again. You can work, have a family, be just like any other person again" (Aurelia). Or in showing those inspirational pictures of transplanted patients, staff members would ask: "Tell me, do they look like sick people to you? What do they look like to you? Like healthy, happy, normal people, right?" (Carmela, transplant coordinator, SSa). Powerfully at work in such exhortations was what others have termed an "ethics of normalcy," such that patients were called to strive for health through transplant as a moral imperative, while succumbing to illness (particularly in the face of a therapeutic option) was implied—and often felt—to be a form of moral failing (Kaufman et al. 2006; Rose 2001).

Yet it was not merely biological well-being that was being exhorted here. Indeed, a set of very particular, socially saturated images proved central to the life promises proffered and the ethical obligations extended through transplantation. These were culturally potent and highly gendered images related to physical strength and activity, to the ability to work, and most especially to the ability to have a family. Thus, the transplanted patient who has since become a marathon runner was one emblematic symbol of the normal (and even *beyond* normal) physical capacity to be regained through transplantation. And images and stories of transplanted patients in their places of work also became central to the discourse and promise of normality, such as an often-used photograph that showed the IMSS program's first transplanted patient standing proudly behind the bar of the small restaurant he now owns. But perhaps most powerful of all were the images and ideas related to the iconic notion of la familia mexicana, and the promise that transplantation could restore to patients the "normal" (and "natural") ability to establish (or maintain) romantic relationships, to get married, and—critically—to have children. Staff members told stories of transplanted patients, both men and women, who had started families since their transplants, proudly displaying pictures of these hallowed families made possible by transplantation: "Look at her beautiful baby, look how happy she and her husband are. Just two years before she hardly got out of bed she was so exhausted all the time from dialysis. And now look at her, she looks just like any other proud mother, doesn't she?" Such proffered promises about the possibilities for single-kidneyed pregnancy stand in particularly sharp contrast to the way female transplant patients in Egypt are sharply rebuked for indulging their reproductive desires (Crowley-Matoka and Hamdy 2015), as well as to the common *requirement* in India that women undergo sterilization before being allowed to give up a kidney (Cohen 1999).

The call to normality exhorted in Guadalajara was thus a very particular one, in which powerfully gendered, heteronormative, and pronatalist notions of family were central—specifically the ability to support a family (through employment) and to make a family (through marriage and reproduction). In a setting where the social value of bodies was so heavily invested in familial (re)productivity, the success of a transplant thus came to require a great deal more than just biological survival, more than what Giorgio Agamben has called "bare life" (Agamben 1998). It was a fully social, participatory form of survival—one that was engaged but also constrained—that was at stake here. And as we shall see, constituting desire for (and expectations of) transplantation in this particular way had profound—and sometimes pernicious—consequences for patients living with transplantation in Guadalajara.

Transplant program staff members were matter-of-fact about throwing their full persuasive weight behind transplantation in order to motivate patients. They knew all too well that transplantation is better understood as the substitution of one kind of chronic illness for another, rather than as a miraculous restoration of normal health and life possibilities. However, given the grim mortality rates for kidney failure patients in Mexico, most felt justified in representing transplantation in somewhat over-exuberant terms to patients, convinced that it was the best chance they had to offer patients. As one surgeon explained to me, with a deep sigh and an accompanying resigned shrug: "Look, a transplant patient will always be a patient. They can never just forget about being sick and go on with their lives. But a transplant is the best quality of life and the longest survival that I can give them. So whatever we can do to convince them that this is their best chance is what we have to do. That's it, that's what I have, what else is there to do?" (Dr. Martinez, IMSS).

Transplant staff also pointed out that the process of going through the transplant protocol is so arduous that patients must be motivated (and often remotivated) to keep going through the complicated series of tests and bureaucratic procedures without giving in to frustration and despair. As one transplant coordinator explained: "It's a fight here to get every single patient transplanted. So patients need to feel that the transplant is worth fighting for" (Aurelia, IMSS). Many transplant team members justified the promises proffered in the name of transplantation in terms of what they perceived as the therapeutic benefits of hope. In the words of another IMSS transplant coordinator: "Patients need hope or they just give up. But if you start them in the protocol process or put them on the wait list—even if there's not really much chance that they will get a transplant—they often do better just because now they have hope and something to work toward. I've seen it over and over" (Isabel).

Patients responded in a variety of ways to the narratives of hope, desire, and normality woven around transplantation. Not all were seduced by the promises: some pulled back, dropped out of the transplant programs, or deliberately allowed themselves to slip through the cracks by missing appointments or misplacing test results. Such instances of turning away from the call of transplantation, such moments of "interpellation interruptus," were often motivated by fear, skepticism, or a desire to pursue what they believed were other viable alternatives first, such as herbal treatments or religious cures. In one such instance, a devout mother refused to allow her teenage daughter to be considered for transplantation because she was confident that, through the concerted entreaties of her evangelical church's prayer circle, she could convince God to bring the girl's kidneys back to life. The patient had been very ill before being put on dialysis, and the mother took her rapid improvement once she was being dialyzed as proof that her kidneys were beginning to work again. She regarded any attempt by the physicians to interfere with this miraculous process as an affront to God and a demonstration of a profound lack of faith. Scolding the staff members for their skepticism, she asked: "Don't you remember? God can move mountains; He can certainly bring my girl's kidneys back if He wants to" (Doña Althea, IMSS).[5]

Other patients, like Jose M. above, who believed that his continued ability to urinate while on dialysis might signal a reversal of his kidney failure, hedged their bets, continuing along in the protocol process "just in case," while maintaining private reservations and quiet hopes of another sort. And a few patients were so convinced by the dazzling promises of transplantation that they held out hope for an even more wondrous technological innovation soon to come, as Evangelia confided: "I don't want my family to risk themselves to donate to me. I think soon they will be able to use pigs for transplants, I think they already do it all the time up North. So I want to wait for that. I offered the doctors to bring in one of my husband's pigs, but so far they say no" (housewife, SSa). Her porcine hopes were at once steeped in the rural conditions of her own daily life and cannily attuned to the promissory outer edges of transplant science, where animals—pigs in particular—do indeed hold out enticing but still elusive possibilities as an abundant future source of transplantable organs (Sharp 2013: 52).

Over time, however, the repetition of messages about transplantation and the moral weight of the promise of resuming a culturally normal (re)productive life eventually overcame, for many patients, the initial uncertainties about transplantation. As patients' own hopes and sense of imaginative possibility increasingly came to be shaped by this narrative of promised normality, many patients found themselves responding to the call of transplantation and stepping forward to enter actively into the lengthy process of medical and psychological evaluation required for a transplant. It was at this stage that an interpellative set of social and institutional processes was set into motion that committed such patients even more firmly to the transplant goal—and to a sense of self deeply bound up with that goal. In part, simply the social experience of the transplant programs worked toward this end. For patients chained to a grueling dialysis schedule and often profoundly isolated in the sick role to which their illness consigned them, becoming part of a community of staff members and other patients intimately acquainted with their illness was an enormously seductive experience. As Marta noted: "I feel embraced here. People understand me. The people I see here every day have become like my family . . . I guess it feels like home in a way" (domestic worker, SSa). Admission into this "family," of course, was based on sharing the goal of a transplant, for that was the vision that bound the community together and provided a shared language and set of expectations through which to relate.

In addition to this persuasive feeling of identification and belonging, a motivating sense of accomplishment was also created through the process of working through the complex protocol of medical exams and bureaucratic requirements to qualify for a transplant. Patients sometimes entered the protocol on a tentative, contingent basis, as did Felipe R.: "I started this thinking I didn't know if I even wanted a transplant. But I thought, I'll start it and see what happens" (mechanic, SSa). But over time, the experience of working one's way through the protocol could serve to increase the desirability of the ultimate goal. Each test completed, each form successfully finished, could come to feel like a hurdle successfully vaulted—and with each success, patients often began to feel more invested in the process and its eventual goal. Mago described her experience in this way: "I was unsure at first. But you take each test and you think, maybe this will be the one where they tell me no. And then when they don't and you go on to the next one, you start to have a little hope . . . Until toward the end, waiting for the results of those last tests I could barely stand it. I was so scared that something would go wrong after everything we had been through. That's when I knew how much I wanted a transplant" (housewife, IMSS).

Thus the very process of seeking a transplant created a momentum that served to reinforce the preciousness of the ultimate goal. As the IMSS psychiatrist in chapter 3 observed in the connection he drew between the productos valiosos of both assisted conception and transplantation, it is in part through the effortfulness involved in producing a particular life (be it baby or trans-

plant patient) that commitment, desire, and value are so powerfully constituted (see Franklin 1997 and Roberts 2012 on similar processes in IVF). Thus,
in responding to the call of transplantation, patients found themselves inexorably enmeshed in a set of institutional processes and a distinctive regime of
value that reshaped their imaginative horizons and even their sense of self.

And so, over time, many patients came to narrate their own hopes, possibilities, and identity through the stories offered up by program staff about
the promise of transplantation, becoming single-minded in pursuing a new
kidney to restore the disrupted life expectations stolen from them by
illness. "I can't wait for my transplant" confided one eager patient, "I am
like broken cup now, without a handle. And with a transplant I will be
whole again and healthy. I will be able to work and take care of my family"
(Jaime, waiter, IMSS). Another patient, Juan, imagined the transplant as a
means of erasing the "nightmare" of his sudden and unexpected illness:
"My dream is to go back to my normal life; I want to be like I was before
all this happened. My dream is that a transplant will make this come true
and it will be like it never happened at all. I would give anything for that"
(day laborer, SSa). Similarly, Maria, recently married and newly diagnosed,
focused on the hope that she would be able to give children to her husband
through a transplant: "I just want to be a normal woman. I want to be a
mother and a real wife. And that's what a transplant can give me, so that is
why we are going through all this now, so that we can be a family" (salesclerk,
IMSS). Driven by such hopes, these patients pressed on, working their way
through the protocol process, maintaining before them the vision of the
normal/natural family life they hoped transplantation would restore.

Waking Up Different: The (Possibly) Transformative Moment

I woke up after the surgery and I thought I was *dead*, because there was
no pain. I hadn't been without pain for years at that point. On dialysis,
everything hurt, even my hair hurt. When I was sick, I learned to love that
split second just before waking up, because I wasn't aware of the pain
yet. And there I was, with no pain at all. I couldn't believe it. I just lay
there for a minute and then I thought, maybe I'll try moving one toe, and
see if that hurts. And so I did. And I went like that moving each toe, each
foot, up my legs, testing every part of my body, my fingers, my arms, everything. And then I got to my head. And there was still no pain. At that moment a nurse walked into the room, and I burst into tears, because at that

moment I realized that I wasn't dead, and that the surgery had worked, I had my transplant. (Ana, dental hygienist, IMSS)

For those patients who actually received a transplant, this moment represented a profound break with the previous stage of working and waiting and hoping for the transplant. In jumping from the hope-filled phase of seeking the transplant to this moment of postsurgical awakening I am, of course, eliding the experience of the actual surgery itself. This is deliberate, for it mirrors the experience of patients themselves for whom the surgery did indeed represent a blank, a gap in time and consciousness. I return to the space of the surgery in chapter 6, as part of a story more focused on the experiences of the clinicians for whom the operating room is a central site of vividly aware experience. Remaining with those newly awakened patients for now, however, this moment was—at least for some patients—a break with the experience of illness itself. Like Ana, the patient whose eloquent account of awakening from her transplant surgery is quoted above, some patients reported an immediate and joyous difference, sensed as soon as they emerged from unconsciousness. Just as the effects of kidney disease are so diffuse and so multiple, causing high blood pressure, nausea, dizziness, exhaustion, severe swelling of the limbs, dull, scaly skin, and lank, lifeless hair in many patients, so too are the reversals that receiving a new, functioning kidney can set into motion. Patients were often amazed at immediate feelings of energy and well-being, and their family members were stunned at the rapid change in their appearance, with eyes that sparkled, renewed complexions, and swollen limbs deflating back to their former shape as if by magic. "I felt different right away," reported Luis. "I knew as soon as I woke up that it worked. I felt more like my old self than I had in years, I felt like I could jump up and do whatever I wanted to now. Even my incision didn't hurt. And my family, they couldn't believe how good I looked" (retired engineer, SSa).

Patients who experienced this kind of success immediately following the surgery spent the first few days rejoicing in their reclaimed bodies, reveling in the freedom to move without pain and relishing the resumption of long-lost bodily rhythms. When I visited Antonio the day after his cadaveric transplant, he drew my attention to the bag of urine attached to his catheter and slowly filling on the floor beneath his chair, exclaiming with great glee (and a smile nearly too big for his face to contain): "Look, I'm peeing! I haven't peed in eight years and I had forgotten how *wonderful* it is!" (piece worker, SSa).

In sad contrast to these moving stories of immediate transformation, for other patients the transplant represented a break of a different kind—a break with their hopes for the seamless restoration of a healthy body and a normal life. While "success" in transplantation is a slippery designation that will require careful consideration below, in general the majority of kidney transplants in Mexico were surgically successful, and transplant surgeons in Guadalajara reported a five-year graft survival rate in the low 80 percent range, roughly comparable with those of kidney patients in the United States (Monteon 2000). There were, however, some patients in whom the transplanted kidney never began to function, or whose bodies rejected the new organ so immediately and so violently that no amount of immunosuppressive therapy could save the kidney. In both cases, the effect on the patients was emotionally devastating—for what had been held out as their best hope, the goal toward which all their efforts and dreams had been directed, had failed. In cases of rejection, the physical effects were also brutal. Not simply left with the same problems and pain as before, these patients could find themselves in a battle for their very lives as their bodies attacked the transplanted organ.

As Carmen recounted, recalling her experience with immediate posttransplant rejection: "It was so terrible I just wanted to die and not feel that way anymore. I had put up with so much for so long, but that was worse than anything. Not only did the transplant not work, it almost killed me" (housewife, IMSS). And even after such patients got through the immediate physical repercussions of a failed transplant, the experience often resulted in such severe depression that they could deteriorate even further. This is the flip side of the "therapeutic hope" generated by the possibility of a transplant. Somewhat paradoxically, some patients found their way out of this depression only through learning to have hope in transplantation once again. Despite lower success rates for each subsequent retransplantation,[6] over time patients were usually gently urged by program staff to start thinking about the possibility of trying again, for they believed it was the only hope they had to offer them. Luz, a vivacious young woman whose body rejected her first kidney within days of the transplant surgery, describes how she came to accept the idea of a second transplant:

When I lost the first kidney, I thought I would die. I said I would never go through that again, I didn't want to hear anyone talk about transplants to me. Better to live on dialysis forever than suffer like that, I thought.

But then, as I got stronger again, I started to change my mind. I talked a lot to other patients and to my family. I decided that I couldn't give up. I'm young, and they don't know why my father's kidney didn't take to me, but maybe the next time it will. I am on the waiting list now; it took a long time for me to work up to that. But now I am ready to try again. I have to have faith I guess, and hope. If not, what else is there? (student, IMSS)

Not surprisingly, for many patients the immediate experience of being transplanted occupied a middle ground between these two extremes of unmitigated joy and devastating failure. Many patients struggled with low-grade rejection reactions in the first days after surgery, which can be controlled with aggressive (but often extremely unpleasant) immunosuppression therapies. Others had to wait for a heart-stopping day or two before the transplanted kidney began functioning normally, and so they existed suspended in an uncertain limbo, trying to maintain a sense of hope in the face of their rising panic. Berta described these mixed and uncertain emotions in her early days as a transplanted patient: "I felt worse, physically, than before. I had a lot of pain and my body was rejecting it, so they had me on all kinds of medicines. But still, I wasn't waiting for it anymore. My transplant was finally here, and so I tried to just stay focused on that and leave the rest up to God" (telephone operator, IMSS). Some of these patients perceived that the transplant had brought them, not a return to normal life, but a new kind of state, suspended part-way between health and illness, with which to contend. Others continued to hold out hope that these initial problems would be resolved and that the early promise of transplantation could still be borne out. As Ricardo put it: "Some of the guys are surprised or mad when it isn't perfect. They keep hoping it will still turn out that way. I guess I figured out fast to hope that it would be better than before, but not like my old life and my old body. And that's more or less what I got" (street vendor, SSa).

The classic notion of liminality seems useful here for thinking about this in-between state in which many patients found themselves upon receiving a transplant (Turner 1969; Van Gennep 1906). Understood as the "betwixt and between" state through which individuals must pass as they exit the normal structure of society in order to reenter it in a new social role, liminality is usually associated with isolation, with the absence (or reversal) of social hierarchy, and with symbols of death and rebirth. Steeped in the promises of normality-through-transplantation, patients underwent the transplant surgery eager to shed the role of dependent patient to which they had been confined and emerge transformed into a healthy person. The immediate postsurgical period was an anticipated space/time apart from the organization and activities of daily life, a period when patients expected that they would be isolated from social contact, confined to a solitary room at home for a three-month period in order to minimize the risk of infection to their compromised immune systems. Throughout this period, the patient was dependent on others for managing the tasks of daily living, such as food preparation and the frequent and meticulous cleanings of the room and bathroom that he or she was using. For many patients this anticipated "betwixt and between" phase was a curious period characterized by helpless waiting but also by a form of sometimes unaccustomed social power, in which much of the family resources and energy were devoted to meeting the needs of the transplanted patient. As Alicia, the patient worth "agitating for," described in chapter 3, noted: "It's sort of a strange feeling. For a long time I didn't have much support from my family, but now here they are taking care of me. Whatever I want to eat or want them to bring me, they do, and I just sit in my room waiting to be strong and ready to start my life again" (single mother, IMSS).

Consistent with the classic conception of liminality, patients initially anticipated that this was to be a finite period, a state through which they expected to pass as they shed the identity of sick patient in order to reclaim that of normal (re)productive family member. As we shall see in the following section, however, such expectations were not always borne out. With a body/self marked by difference and the threat of returning illness always imminent, many transplanted patients found themselves forced to linger betwixt and between the states of health and illness, patient (who depends on others) and normal person (who participates in and contributes to a family).

Liminality That Lingers: Posttransplant Life

As transplanted patients ended the anticipated period of postsurgical isolation and began to reenter normal life, they often found that the reality of living with transplantation was not quite what they had expected (or dreamed). Rather, it seemed that for many transplant recipients the liminal period remained indefinite and open-ended, while the new social identity they had hoped to claim remained always precarious and contingent. A similar sense of lingering uncertainty has been identified in other settings as well where the exuberant promises of biomedicine fail to fully deliver, as patients living with cancer or with chronic pain have also been described as existing in a state of "persistent liminality" (see, for example, Jackson 2000; Little et al. 1998; Navon and Morag 2004).[7] This notion of liminality that lingers, liminality that becomes not a mode of transformation but a modality of living, seems helpful for capturing the uncertainty and instability that often suffused patients' posttransplant experiences. The following three subsections explore this notion of lingering liminality in terms of the three key elements of the promise for normality held out to pretransplant patients: health, productivity, and reproductivity.[8]

Transplanted Health

Transplant recipients in Guadalajara quickly discovered that having a new kidney was not quite like regaining their former pre-illness self. To start, the immunosuppressive medications on which they depended carry a host of side effects ranging from merely bothersome to medically serious. Effects such as swollen "moon" faces, hirsutism, and shaking hands could be accompanied by more dangerous effects like soaring cholesterol levels, heart disease, and cancer. Many patients also found that the transplant medications (particularly steroids) could alter their personalities somewhat, making them more volatile and prone to quick flashes of anger, as Jorge reported: "That's been one of the hardest things we have had to get used to, my wife and I. I am much more irritable and will get angry without control, which isn't like my old self at all. Along with all the other things the medications do that we have to deal with, that is one of the hardest" (restaurant owner, IMSS).[9] Recipients soon learned that a delicate balance must be struck with their medications—taking enough to counter the rejection reaction, but not so much as to risk *quemando* (burning out) the precious kidney. As a result, recipients had to undergo careful monitoring of medication levels and kidney function over time, for this is a balance that must be struck and restruck as the body adjusts to the medications and the new organ.

In addition to these immediate effects of the transplant and medications (many of which do subside over time), recipients had to learn to live with the realization that the transplant had not restored them to normal physical health. Transplant recipients, in fact, remained lifelong patients, a reality reinforced on a daily basis as they managed their battery of medications and kept up with regular doctor's visits and tests to monitor the transplanted kidney.[10] Emphasizing their persistent "patienthood," the medications and monitoring served as a constant reminder of the precariousness of their new state of (relative) health. Recipients were under constant threat of losing the transplant and had to adjust to that ever-present possibility. In Ana's words: "You always know, on some level that you can lose it and end up back on dialysis. But you can't live fearing it all the time, you have to try to live as if that won't happen" (IMSS, dental hygienist). Here too a delicate balance had to be struck. If transplanted people lived in constant fear of losing the transplant, then it was hardly worth it after all. If, however, they became too confident or complacent about the transplant, they risked becoming careless and thus losing it, as did Victor:

> I had my kidney for about five years, and I was doing really well, felt great, no problems. Then I started thinking, I'm normal now, everything's good. So I started smoking a little again, and drinking sometimes too. And nothing happened . . . I started thinking, my kidney's taken to me now, it's mine. I don't need all those pills every day anymore. I stopped taking my medicines. First I would just skip a day or two. Nothing would happen, and after a while, I just stopped taking them at all. I was tired of them, they made me feel like a sick person when I didn't think I was one anymore. Then, of course, I went into rejection and lost the kidney. (IMSS, factory foreman)

It was in part this inescapable precariousness that kept transplant recipients suspended in a liminal state, unable entirely to shed the role of patient for that of a healthy person. It also put them in the paradoxical position of being able to maintain whatever normality they were able to achieve through transplantation only by remaining constantly alert to the fact that they were most decidedly not normal.

While the challenges of learning to live with medication side effects and the constant threat of rejection are common to transplanted people generally, the political economy of transplantation in Guadalajara rendered the health of these patients even more precarious in several ways. In particular, the difficulties of maintaining ongoing access to both specialized medical care and the necessary immunosuppressive drugs posed serious challenges for many patients. For wealthy recipients, of course, access to specialized care could be obtained by paying for follow-up care in transplant physicians' private clinics, while transplant medications could simply be paid for outright or covered through private insurance. However, for the majority of transplant recipients whose resources limited them to staying within one of the government-run systems, the situation was quite different—and substantially more uncertain. Thus, the constant risk of losing the transplanted organ (and the fear of that risk) was heightened for many patients by the trajectory of their posttransplant movement through the health-care system. For most recipients maintaining (or, in the case of SSa patients, gaining) rights to the IMSS system with its prescription drug coverage was the most common and effective strategy for ensuring access to medications. Yet, because access to the IMSS system was tied to paying into the system on an ongoing basis (usually through an employer), having drug coverage today was no guarantee of having coverage tomorrow. Given the difficulty of maintaining steady, full-time employment for many transplanted patients (an issue explored more fully below), the threat of losing coverage, losing access to the medication, and thus losing the transplant itself was very real for many patients.

However, even for patients with rights to the IMSS system, the growing number of transplanted patients meant that it was no longer feasible for all of the posttransplant patients to continue to be seen by the physicians in the transplant program itself—maintaining the momentum and growth of the transplant program required that those physicians had to move on to new patients and new transplants. As a result, after a period of six months to a year, many transplanted patients were *mandado a la clínica* (sent down to the clinic) to be managed by physicians in their local hospitals and clinics. Depending upon where patients were from, this could mean having their care managed by someone not only unfamiliar with transplantation (for virtually none of the physicians in the lower-level facilities had this expertise), but inexpert in kidney disease more broadly.

The potentially disastrous—even deadly—effects of this practice were beginning to be seen in the IMSS transplant program, as a trickle of patients were returning to the program in search of a second transplant, having lost the first one due to apparent medical mismanagement. Patients returned with stories of physicians who refused to change their medication levels over time because they did not know how to do it (cyclosporine in particular must be gradually reduced over time in order to avoid toxicity). In other cases, patients were told that they no longer needed the medications, and their prescriptions were cut off, as in Vicente's case: "After a couple of years my doctor told me, 'The kidney is yours now. It's stuck to you and gotten used to you, so you don't need these drugs anymore.' I was worried, but what could I do? He wouldn't listen to me, and after all, he's the doctor" (day laborer, IMSS). This notion that the transplant would eventually *pegarse* (stick to) the patient and no longer require immunosuppression was not uncommon, and Vicente, like several other patients I met during my field-work with similar stories, lost the transplant shortly afterward.

Some of the patients transplanted during the earlier days of the program never had to contend with this problem. The talismanic quality of those early cases for the transplant program staff meant that they were originally regarded as too precious to send down to the lower clinic levels, and over time these patients developed personal relationships with their physicians that made it unthinkable to send them away.[11] Berta, for instance, a telephone operator who received her kidney transplant nearly fourteen years ago, continued to be seen at the tertiary level transplant program, where staff often joked about what a *chiqueada* (pampered favorite) she was of the IMSS program director.

Other transplanted patients, alert to the problems they saw unfolding for those "sent down" to the lower levels of the health-care system, adopted a variety of strategies for trying to *agilizar* the usual processes and stay under the care of the physicians at the transplant program itself, strategies that ranged from personal appeals to individual physicians, to formal, legal petitions made to the hospital director. Manuel, for instance, a portly, middle-aged Jehovah's Witness who received his first transplant six years ago, lost the kidney three years later when a lower-level physician dramatically *increased* his cyclosporine dosage (accountant, IMSS). Upon being retransplanted a second time, Manuel had a lawyer friend help him draw up a formal letter petitioning the hospital administration to be able to keep coming to the transplant program for his care: "I refused to go back to that doctor. She had no idea what she was doing, and because of her my brother's kidney was wasted and I had to go through rejection and dialysis all over again. I forced them to keep me here, whether they wanted to or not." It is worth noting here that Manuel already had considerable practice (and success) in pushing hospital staff and administrators to transgress usual policy, as with each transplant he had to convince the reluctant transplant team to commit to performing the surgery without the use of blood products (in accordance with his religious beliefs).[12] Highlighted in these cases are thus the advantages of being an "agile" patient not just in *receiving* a transplant, as we saw in chapter 3, but in being able to *retain* one as well. But of course not all patients have the ability or the opportunities to agilizar their post-transplant care in these ways.

In the SSa transplant program, the situation was somewhat different. There, the significantly smaller size of the program meant that staff had not yet reached a point where they could no longer handle the logistics of caring for all the "old" transplanted patients, as well as the new incoming patients. Despite this, however, many transplanted patients found themselves driven away from the SSa program for a very different set of reasons. Because the charity mandate of the SSa did not include coverage for outpatient medications, patients in the SSa program were not provided ongoing access to the medications necessary to maintain their transplants—unlike patients in the IMSS system who received these medications as part of their health-care coverage. This inability to guarantee patients' access to the necessary medications was a major limiting factor in the SSa program's ability to perform transplants, for the kidney program director was reluctant to transplant anyone without a firm plan for obtaining the posttransplant medications in place.

For a time the SSa hospital was able to provide partial support to patients for the first few months after the transplant, selling them the medications at drastically reduced prices. Within six months, however, patients were expected to have found some other solution. In most cases, this solution took the form of getting coverage under the IMSS system (usually through a new job) in order to gain access to the system's prescription coverage plan. The official nature of this policy of sending their transplanted patients to the IMSS system was reflected in the language of a memo that was distributed to staff and patients and posted prominently on the nephrology floor during my time in Guadalajara: "I wish to inform you that the distribution of cyclosporine to kidney transplant patients, according to our limited means, will be restricted to the first six months. After this period, patients should look for work with social security benefits, in order to be accepted into the IMSS system and receive treatment over the long term" (memo from SSa Kidney Transplant Program director, May 2000).

Many SSa patients found switching programs a somewhat unsettling experience, having become so comfortable with the staff and all of the institutional idiosyncrasies of the SSa transplant program. Not only were both the IMSS system and the personnel new to these SSa patients, they could also be somewhat antagonistic, for there were mixed feelings among both the administration and medical staff in the IMSS system about supporting the extremely expensive medication needs of these patients transplanted elsewhere. Although some IMSS staff were sympathetic and saw this as a pragmatic solution to the SSa hospital's economically dire straits, others regarded it as an unfair and irresponsible "dumping" of patients who should not have been transplanted if they could not be supported. As one IMSS transplant coordinator explained it: "I think we should support them, because they have just as much right to a transplant and to life as anyone else. And the SSa hospital does charitable work for all of us, it supports our society, so we should support it. But there is some resentment over the cost, and that we have to take on their patients, that's true" (Aurelia). In a few cases, however, even this somewhat controversial solution failed, and some transplanted patients were unable to find either a way to access the IMSS system or the money to buy the extremely costly medications outright. Caught in an impossible bind, these patients eventually went off their medications and ended up rejecting the hard-won organ.

Transplant patients who lost access to their medications, whether because they lost IMSS coverage after the loss of a job or were never able to gain it after being transplanted in the SSa hospital, attempted a variety of responses to the medical crisis this precipitated. Some formed informal collectives to try to pool medication and monetary resources, sharing medications among themselves so that all got some, even if none got enough.[13] Other patients attempted to establish more formal patients' advocacy groups that sought to organize fundraising and awareness campaigns around their medication needs. During the period of my research, however, the medication-garnering efforts of these groups had little success—although, as we shall see below, such groups also produced other possibilities for political action and self-formation.

Importantly, these challenges of gaining and maintaining access to specialized care and medication are not unique to Mexico but have been reported among transplanted patients in other settings as well. Informal patient collectives organized to pool medications and eke out transplant survival have been reported in both India and the United States, for instance (Cohen 1999; Sharp 1999). In the United States, such medication crises were often precipitated by the fact that—until very recently—federal funding for the treatment of kidney disease provided coverage for the transplant surgery, but cut off payment for transplant medications after three years (Chakkera et al. 2005; Fox and Swazey 1992; Levinsky and Rettig 1991; Yen et al. 2004).

Similar to the SSa transplant program strategy of shifting transplanted patients onto the IMSS system through posttransplant employment, the U.S. policy assumed that transplant patients should be gainfully employed and privately insured within three years posttransplant—an assumption reflective of the powerful motivating discourses of normality characteristic of the transplant world writ large, but not always congruent with the realities of posttransplant health (Sharp 1999).

Like their counterparts elsewhere in the world, transplant professionals in Guadalajara were well aware of these problems with the posttransplant management and support of patients. For some professionals, narratives similar to those that explained the failure of some patients to reach a transplant also helped to make sense of the failure of others to maintain one. Patients who lost their transplants sometimes were understood as having been insufficiently *agile*—as having failed to finagle a job with IMSS access or to ask for extra help when it was needed. Responsibility for the failed transplant thus could be shifted from the organization and political economy of transplantation itself (or of health care more generally), and on to the individual patient, as in this transplant coordinator's comment: "It's a shame, such a waste that he's rejected his mother's kidney. But he never came to us, he never let anyone know that he was having difficulty, so what could we do? If they won't help themselves, well . . ." (Aurelia, IMSS). Similarly, one of the SSa nephrologists commented: "Look, it's a problem that sometimes they aren't motivated to get a job, and then they can't get their medications—but what can *we* do? It's a question of motivation more than anything . . ." (Dr. Montero).

Indeed, we might understand Isabel's decision to send *me* in to sit with the distraught Jose in similar terms. For Isabel, his suffering was of personal nature—tragic, but not really related to the transplant per se and hardly a responsibility of the transplant program—and so all they could really offer him was my sympathetic (but essentially unskilled and powerless) ear. As we shall see below, these individualizing, privatizing—perhaps even *domesticating*—responses ignore the structural challenges many transplanted patients experienced in finding and keeping employment. Reflecting not just the locally specific values embedded in the notion of agilizar, such responses were also inflected by wider neoliberal trends evident in Mexico and elsewhere in the world, as the (moral) responsibility for illness and misfortune more broadly is increasingly shifted to a question of individual behavior and blame (Ewald 2001; Lupton 1999; Rose 2001).

As pressures to privatize health care in Mexico (and the accompanying logics of risk and insurance) were on the rise—perhaps only intensifying the long-standing logics of a system that must always be agilizado, that must be worked in order to work—it is perhaps hardly surprising that such domesticating explanations would focus on personal rather than system failures.

Other transplant professionals gestured toward their own limitations of reach and responsibility in a health-care system where patient care is increasingly fragmented along lines of specialty care and institutional politics. One IMSS nephrologist, for example, offered this explanation:

> There are problems, of course. There is a lack of experience among some of our colleagues, because for them a transplant isn't something they see every day, so they don't keep that knowledge right in their minds all the time. But we have to be very careful here, because there is already tension and jealousy and we have to be sensitive to not just tell them what to do and act like the big power. I have had patients come to me that want me to change something another doctor has done, change a prescription or something, and I have to tell them that I can't do that. Once they leave here, they aren't my patients anymore, and I cannot just take over another doctor's patient and contradict him. We have to learn how to work with the doctors at lower levels, but in a way that doesn't make them feel threatened. (Dr. Mercado)

Reflected here in part is the multiply fragmented perspective characteristic of the general biomedical approach to health, in which a physician's responsibility extends to what are defined as the biological—but not social, economic, or institutional—problems of his or her patient. Further fracturing is the effect of the increasing specialization within biomedicine writ large, such that physicians feel individually responsible for ever-smaller portions of their patients (hearts, kidneys, ear-nose-and-throats) and thus become highly invested both in defending their own specialized territory and, in return, in respecting that of their colleagues. Such familiar characteristics of global biomedical knowledge and practice are clearly in evidence in Mexico, and, as Dr. Mercado's quote suggests, interact with the local politics of health-care institutions to shape when a physician feels able (or willing) to claim a patient as his/her "own" and thus to intervene in posttransplant care. Thus organizing risk and responsibility for patients' posttransplant trajectories in powerful ways, such attitudes combined with the bodily experiences, institutional organization, and political economy of maintaining a kidney transplant such that many patients could never feel firmly ensconced in a healthy state. Rather, transplant patients often seemed to occupy a more nebulous and slippery border zone between health and illness, coming to inhabit what we might call a form of "perpetual patienthood."

Transplanted Productivity

If transplant recipients found that the promise of health was not always fulfilled by the realities of transplanted life, many also discovered that the goal of economic productivity, of "being able to take care of their families" was similarly difficult to attain. Some recipients found that they were not really reliably healthy enough to hold down a regular job. The demands of frequent doctor's appointments and occasional hospitalizations for rejection rarely endeared them to employers. Compounding the problem, many common laborers' jobs were closed to transplant recipients who could not risk exposure to the kidney-toxic chemicals often used in factories, machine shops, and agricultural settings. In addition to coming face to face with the reality of their own limitations, many transplanted patients were forced to confront others' (usually even more pessimistic) perceptions about what those limitations might be. Numerous people reported that they were turned down by potential employers once their status as a transplanted person was revealed, as in Ramon's case: "The minute they find out you have a transplant, forget about it. They don't want anything to do with you. They think you're going to be sick all the time, no matter what you tell them. They think you won't be able to do the work" (farm laborer, SSa).

This reluctance to hire transplant recipients has been reported in other countries as well and was likely related in part to the unfamiliarity of transplantation in wider society, as well as to the ongoing hardscrabble economic situation for the working class in Mexico, where applicants often far outnumbered jobs (Scheper-Hughes 2006; see also Sharp 2006, for the United States). Under such conditions, employers perhaps felt little need to take on the unknown risk of a transplant recipient—especially (but not only) when the job required physical labor. Multiple such experiences drove some patients to hide their transplanted status—a tactic sometimes successful as long as there was no requirement for a physical exam where the tell-tale surgical scar would have to be revealed. Another strategy employed by some transplanted patients was to develop a network of referrals and support for one another, and once a sympathetic or open-minded employer was identified, his or her name would be passed along to other transplanted patients in search of work. As Ana explained:

I have a friend who is a jeweler, and since he knows me, he isn't scared of transplants. He needs a lot of workers to do small, meticulous work and it's perfect for us because it's light, there are no chemicals and the schedule is very flexible. So I've sent him a lot of friends. We joke that it's like a branch of the transplant program over there now. It's good, because it's hard for a lot of us to find work, there can be a lot of prejudice and ignorance because people just don't know about it. (dental hygienist, IMSS)

An additional strategy for dealing with the problems of employability and economic hardship that faced many transplanted patients emerged from one of the transplanted patient support groups organized by IMSS patients. This particular group took the form of an *asociación civil*, which is one of the established mechanisms of social organizing in Mexico, providing organizational legitimacy to civil society groups, often so as to facilitate relations with both State and private industry. In this case, the transplanted patients' group was organized to promote organ donation and transplantation and to garner support for the needs of transplanted patients. These goals sometimes proved to be at odds, however, as drawing attention to problems such as precarious access to medication or the difficulty of finding employment sometimes provoked concern among patients (as well as transplant program staff) about undermining the claim that transplantation can (and should) be done in Mexico.

This tension was evident in the controversy that emerged around the group's discussion about whether to seek special "disability status" from the state government for transplanted patients. This status could be used to obtain cards that would give transplanted people special support for finding appropriate employment, as well as free access to public transportation, potential discounts on medications, and possibly other benefits as well. The suggestion, which was greeted with great enthusiasm by some transplanted patients, sparked intense debate over the implications of labeling transplanted people as "disabled." Some transplanted people resented the label and saw the move as accepting the limitations that others (such as employers) often tried to impose on them. As one of the leaders of the group, the burly, self-assured Luis, put it: "How will we ever get people to see us as normal and whole if with the other hand we are asking for special treatment?" (retired engineer, IMSS).

Not surprisingly, many transplant professionals were also vehemently opposed to the idea of disability status for transplanted people, for it would undermine the most exuberant claims for transplantation, revealing all too painfully the inadequacy of the iconic happily-ever-after story of transplantation. Similar to the reading of posttransplant failures as a failure in patient *agility*, staff members interpreted the discussion of disability status as further evidence that (at least some) transplanted patients simply lacked *ánimo* (will or spirit) and were unwilling to exert themselves to agilizar the process of finding employment: "There are some who want everything given to them, they don't think they should have to work—it's an attitude of laziness, of always being the victim. It happens sometimes with people who have been sick for a long time" (Dr. Martinez, transplant surgeon, IMSS).

Ultimately, as the story of Jose's posttransplant sufferings with which this chapter began has already alerted us, these difficulties in finding work imposed real economic hardship on some transplanted patients, putting at risk their ability to support themselves and their families—as well as their ability to support the transplant. Struggling to (re)enter the workforce for many patients could be disastrous both in terms of basic survival and in terms of a self-image in which becoming a productive, working person again played a central role. These posttransplant effects (in terms of both social identity and economic survival) were often strongly gendered in the Mexican context where cultural expectations and political economic structures place the majority of the burden (and opportunity) for formal wage earning upon men. Although women in Mexico are working outside the home in ever-increasing numbers, they were still most often employed in the informal sector (including the infamous and exploitative *maquiladoras*), rather than the formal sector with its access to higher wages and social security benefits (Gaspar de Alba 2010; Townsend et al. 1999; World Development Report 2012). Given the structure of health care in Mexico, this meant that women were more likely to depend upon a male family member's employment for rights to the IMSS system, while men were more likely to depend upon finding employment for themselves to gain such rights. Thus, within a context where losing rights to the IMSS system (and thereby losing access to specialized care and medications) could be disastrous, male recipients could be placed at particular risk by the difficulties of maintaining steady employment as a transplanted person. As we shall see in the following section on reproductivity, however, other dimensions of the promises and realities of living with transplantation were more likely to place women at particular risk.

Caught between expectations that they *should* work and employers' doubts about whether they *could*, transplanted patients endured a lingering liminality that was reinforced by their relationship to economic life. Transplanted patients were under great pressure to obtain work—not only to fulfill their vision of normal posttransplant life, but to meet their material needs for ongoing access to medication and specialized care as well. Yet rather than being granted full reentry into the world of the productive workforce, many found that they were held back, forced to scrabble around the edges of economic life, relying on favors or government help or even lies about their transplanted status in order to try to make a living. Like all entities that elude clear social categorization, these transplanted patients often found themselves tinged with a hint of danger and suspicion—both in the eyes of dubious potential employers and in the eyes of transplant program staff who sometimes suspected laziness rather than discrimination when employment failed.

Transplantation could thus produce an unexpected stigmatizing effect— becoming a mark that must be hidden or minimized in order to "pass" in the eyes of employers. However, the stigma of transplantation—like many stigmas—here produced not only exclusion, but also possibilities for forming a new, validated and collective identity around the source of stigma itself (Goffman 1963). Thus groups such as the transplanted patients' asociación civil held fragile opportunities for forging a new form of biological identity not held hostage to the expectations of normality engendered in the process of seeking a transplant. They held out hope, that is, for imagining a self no longer trapped betwixt and between (unemployable) sick and (employable) healthy. Such efforts evoke work by Rayna Rapp and Deborah Heath on the biosociality of deeply felt ties, social inclusion, and political activism forged among people stigmatized by the same genetic disease (Heath 1998; Rapp et al. 2001; see also Rabinow 1996 on biosociality). Yet as the contentious debates over disability status for transplant patients make clear, defining the ground, content, and political goals of such a reclaimed and revalorized bioidentity could be a slippery business, subject to competing needs and pressures from different quarters.

For all the difficulty of being accepted as a "full person" in the economic world, many transplanted people found acceptance in their day-to-day social worlds even more difficult to come by as they reported a variety of stigmatizing social experiences in both public interactions and intimate relationships. Many transplant patients in Guadalajara, especially during the first year posttransplant, wore surgical masks when outside of their own homes, in order to protect against infection. This practice (not one common among transplant patients in the United States) was encouraged by some transplant physicians in Guadalajara and discouraged by others, and was likely related at least in part to long-standing identifications in local culture of "the street" as dangerous and polluting, in contrast to the protected and protective interior of the home (Napolitano 2002). Due to this practice, transplanted people were often visibly marked by their surgical masks as they circulated in public spaces, and many described the fear, curiosity, and even hostility elicited by this marking. With varying degrees of ironic humor and hurt frustration, patients described strangers sidling away from them on buses, or even crossing the street to avoid passing too close by: "They move away from me like I have a disease and they are scared I will make them sick. And really it's *them* who are a danger to *me!*" (Jaime, waiter, IMSS). Francisco, a tall young man with an easy-going sense of humor, described being followed in a department store by a store manager, who, when confronted, confessed that he thought the mask made Francisco look "suspicious" (computer programmer, IMSS).

Transplanted people also described more positive reactions from people who learned of their transplanted status—but sometimes lamented that even these reactions set them apart in ways they would have preferred to avoid. Eríc, a high-school-age boy who was transplanted about a year previously, related that he stopped playing his beloved game of *fútbol* because as soon as anyone he played with learned about his transplant, they treated him with such careful respect that it was no longer like a real game: "They go easy on me, try to protect me. I know they mean well, but it ruins the game for me, and I think for them too. I don't want to be treated like something delicate and precious. So I just don't play anymore." Padre Tomás admitted somewhat sheepishly that some of the members of his congregation refer to him fondly as their "Miracle Priest" because of his transplant (priest, private hospital). He too was made uncomfortable by this attention, and tried to downplay his transplanted status, taking care never to make reference to it from the pulpit.

Experiencing others' reactions to them could become even more painful for many transplant recipients when it came to forming and/or maintaining romantic relationships. For added to the difficulties of maintaining the productive role for many transplant recipients were difficulties for many of fulfilling the reproductive role within the family. The experience of illness and transplantation can put great strain on existing relationships, and while some marriages were strengthened by the shared experience, others came apart under the pressure. Thus, Jose's earlier-recounted (and devastating) experience of being left by his wife *after* the transplant was not entirely uncommon. As Jorge explained: "It happens a lot, actually. People think everything will be great with the transplant. And then it turns out that everything isn't solved. Sometimes they just wear out from struggling" (restaurant owner, IMSS). In addition, the irritability and short-temperedness often associated with transplant medications (steroids in particular) compounded the strain on intimate relationships for some transplanted patients. Clearly the perpetual patienthood of transplantation can take its toll not just on recipients, but on those around them as well.

The situation was equally (if not more) difficult for people seeking to establish new romantic relationships after the transplant, for many found that nontransplanted people were unable or unwilling to see them as whole, normal people. "I can't tell you the number of times girls tell me they 'just want to be friends' as soon as they find out that I have a transplant," lamented Guillermo, who joked publicly about being a ladies' man, but privately confessed that people see him with so many different girls because they never lasted once they learned that he was transplanted (university student, IMSS). Echoing the dilemma of whether or not to hide one's transplanted status from employers, Leticia noted: "I never know when to tell people—especially men. If I say it too soon, I might not get a chance for them to get to know me. If I tell them too late, it seems like something to be ashamed of, because I'm hiding it" (secretary, SSa).

Others discovered that even if they found a partner who accepted their transplanted status, finding a whole family who did so as well could be even more difficult. Patí, for example, found her relationship severely strained by her boyfriend's parents' resistance: "They always ask him why he can't find someone healthy. They are worried that I won't give them grandchildren" (domestic worker, IMSS). Similar to many recipients' experiences with employers, the unfamiliarity of transplantation and its stigmatizing mark of difference was likely at least partly responsible for this discomfort among potential romantic partners (and/or their families). Some recipients resolved this problem by looking for love among other transplanted people—indeed, two such couples were engaged during my time in Guadalajara.

In fact, this problem of establishing romantic relationships was significant enough that transplant program staff themselves were acutely aware of it—even to the point of discussing sponsoring a "Lonely Hearts" dance in order to help transplant recipients meet romantic partners. Tellingly, however, this idea provoked considerable debate among program staff themselves about whether it was appropriate to invite "normal" people as well as transplant recipients—thus revealing the ambiguous status of transplanted people, even among those most invested in the transformative, restorative narratives of transplantation. Like the debates surrounding the question of whether transplant patients ought to be considered disabled, this question of whom to invite to a transplant recipient match-making event thus also illuminates the tensions between promoting transplantation as a life-saving technological miracle and grappling with the ongoing life struggles that transplantation produces for many patients.

Whether seeking to establish or to maintain a relationship, some transplant recipients also commented on the way transplantation affected perceptions of their sexuality—both how it was perceived by others, and how they themselves experienced it. Some patients reported feeling asexual and unattractive after transplantation, in part because of some of the side effects of the medications, like weight gain and hirsutism. Others found themselves and their partners sexually paralyzed by the perceived fragility of their transplanted bodies: "My husband and I just keep wondering if it's really safe to have sex yet," confessed a woman in her midthirties. "I think we're just scared to trust my body after everything it's been through and everything it's put us through" (Maria, salesclerk, IMSS). One particularly explicit evocation of the effect of being transplanted on one's sexual and gendered self came from a somewhat surprising source, a Catholic priest: "It's like this. I grew up around horses. And here is the difference before I got my sister's kidney and now that I am transplanted. Before I used to love to sing and drink and go out with my friends all night long. Now, I am quieter, calmer. I lead a more tranquil life. *It's like the difference between a stallion and a gelding*, that's really the difference in me now" (Padre Tomás, priest, private hospital).[14]

Posttransplant sexual identity could also become tangled up with how the commingling of donor and recipient selves was imagined in transplantation, and sexual ambiguity and unease could be particularly acute when those selves were differently gendered. Padre Tomás—who we will encounter again in chapter 5—also noted that several of his friends in the priesthood liked to tease him about the effects of having received a woman's kidney, asking: "Do you like men now, now that you're half woman?" And so questions of sexuality and gender identity for transplanted patients could become yet another way in which people found themselves marked as different and relegated to a persistently liminal space unmoored from clear social roles such as "husband," "wife," "parent," and "lover," and even "masculine" and "feminine."

Questions of sexuality are often connected not just to issues of identity and desire, of course, but to issues of reproductive potential as well. As Patí's above-described difficulties with her boyfriend's family suggests, the importance of childbearing often placed particular strain on relationships for transplant recipients. For male recipients, the challenges to reproductivity were primarily those described above of finding a romantic partner willing to be with a transplanted person. Given the difficulties of maintaining steady employment with a transplant and thus meeting powerful culturally defined expectations for men, however, this challenge could be considerable. Nonetheless, once such a relationship was established, a man's transplanted status had no particular impact on his ability to conceive children. For female transplant recipients, however, the situation was somewhat more complex. While women's ability to hold down a formal sector job was less likely to be considered a factor in marital suitability, their ability (both perceived and real) to bear children was typically more socially salient. Fears that transplantation had rendered a woman unable to have children could make male partners unwilling to establish or maintain a relationship, particularly under pressure from family members who saw no need to risk tying one's familial future to the fate of someone of uncertain health. In addition, given that women were more likely to be dependent on a relationship with a man for access to the IMSS system, the difficulty of establishing romantic relationships for a female transplant recipient could jeopardize her access to health-care coverage as well.

However, even when they did achieve a romantic relationship, female recipients were vulnerable to the failure of these reproductive hopes in yet another way, due to the medical risks of pregnancy for transplanted women. Although successful pregnancies are not uncommon for transplant recipients in the United States and other high-resource settings, childbearing puts added strain on the transplanted kidney that must be monitored carefully. In Mexico, where kidney disease (and hence patient deterioration) was often significantly more advanced before diagnosis and transplant, and where access to both ongoing medications and expert monitoring could be difficult to maintain, posttransplant pregnancies could be risky. I knew of several patients in Guadalajara who had lost their kidney transplants in just this way, including one woman who subsequently gave up the child she had so desperately wanted because she was too sick to care for her. Gendered cultural expectations could thus place transplanted women at risk not only for failing in the hoped-for normal social role, but for actually losing the transplant itself as a result of trying to meet those expectations. Recalling the operation of that powerful image of the self-sacrificial mother, la mujer sufrida, in the work of living donation, here we have a sacrifice made not just as a mother, but in order to become one. Staff reactions to such cases typically turned once again on the question of individual (ir)responsibility, pointing to the failure of patients to obtain proper medical monitoring before (and during) pregnancy. Such reactions elided both the real economic constraints experienced by many patients, as well as the way in which expectations for normal reproductivity were constituted by staff's own representations of transplantation as they sought to leverage the therapeutics of hope. Ultimately, this complex combination of sociocultural norms and political economic conditions could thus render male and (particularly) female transplant recipients persistently and unexpectedly liminal in their relationship to reproduction and familial expectations as well.

Defining Success in Posttransplant Life

Having traced out some of the complexities and contingencies of posttransplant life, it perhaps becomes more possible to see why popular (and even medical) stories of transplantation so often end at the moment of transplant. The trajectory of posttransplant life is messy. For many patients it provides no clean narrative arc and satisfying culmination, but rather an ongoing and equivocal movement between joy and despair, health and illness, success and failure. In fact, the very notions of health and success (as well as their dark twins) become hard to pin down in the context of transplantation, for they turn out to look somewhat different when seen from different points in the organ transfer process and through the eyes of individuals articulated with transplantation in distinct ways. In its most exaggerated version, this meant that a transplant surgeon, focused on the technical challenges of a new procedure, could speak of a *transplant* having been a success (because the liver or kidney functioned), even though the patient died. Meanwhile, for a transplant social worker, simply getting one more patient out of the deadly dialysis ward might well be seen as a success worth celebrating. While for a patient, the joys of finally receiving a transplant could be hard to hold onto over time in the context of inaccessible medication, elusive employment, and hard-to-meet familial expectations. Veena Das has parsed such differently positioned meanings of success and failure along the lines of a tension between the experimental and the therapeutic, such that a functioning organ might mark the mastery of a surgical technique even when it fails to save the patient (Das 2000: 277; see also Fox and Swazey 1974). The complex stories of posttransplant life unfolded in this chapter reveal yet other axes of meaning around which other versions of success and failure may also register: in frequently dashed patient hopes for not just biological but social restoration, for instance, or in the flawed policy presumption that transplanted patients will return to self-supporting (and health insurance–generating) employment.

Not just a matter of individual assessments, accountings of success and failure could also prove hard to hold steady at the institutional level, particularly when framed in the seemingly straightforward terms of economics. In Mexico, as elsewhere, kidney transplantation was often posed as the most *pragmatic* response to kidney disease through accountings that laid out compelling comparative columns of numbers demonstrating higher annual costs for dialysis versus transplantation. After the expensive first year of the transplant surgery itself, for example, the IMSS medical director estimated the relative costs as approximately 45,000 pesos per year for transplant patients versus 160,000 pesos for peritoneal dialysis and 220,000 pesos for hemodialysis.[15] Calculated in this way, each transplant achieved could easily be read as an economic win—and it was this cost-saving logic that led the medical director to describe the transplant program as the IMSS hospital's "number one priority." Yet accounting is a slippery business, and needs, once constituted, have a habit of multiplying in sometimes unpredictable ways. How, for instance, might one calculate the financial implications of the longer survival of transplant patients compared to those on dialysis? Or how to account for the way the existence of a transplant program provided a new motivation for hailing a wider population of kidney patients than ever before—patients who would never have even been identified (much less treated) in the grim era when *nefrología* might as well as have been *necrología*? On both counts, it was already becoming clear that transplantation might well do more to produce new costs rather than contain old ones, with ever-larger numbers of patients living longer (and hence more costly) lives. And, as a result, the success of getting a patient to transplant could—when followed out over time—shape-shift all too often into a cascade of subsequent failures: of institutions unable or unwilling to cover the long-term costs of immunosuppressive medications, of transplants lost to the rejection reactions that predictably followed, and of patients returned to the deadly, costly dialysis wards from which transplantation had freed them.

Set among such shape-shifting possibilities for success and failure, expectations for the transformative potential of transplantation nonetheless ran high on all sides in Guadalajara. For patients, the dream of regaining a normal (re)productive life could be both a motivating promise in the process of seeking a transplant, and a demoralizing mirage in the realities of living with one. In the end, transplant recipients came to different accommodations with the lived experience of transplantation. Some grappled with significant depression, which in a few of the most severe cases even led to suicide, an act so profoundly antithetical to the long battle for life that achieving a transplant represented for most patients. Others found ways to get (relatively) comfortable in the liminal spaces of perpetual patienthood carved out for them by transplantation, coming to terms with instability (in health, in employment, in love) as a way of life. And still others, through mediums like the asociación civil, had begun to at least explore the possibilities for forging a new form of biological identity for themselves, a place of belonging and political action organized around the experiences of living with transplantation in which they might be able to shed both the role of patient and the pressures of passing as normal. It remains to be seen where these efforts will lead, buffeted as they are by competing pressures both to bolster support for (and thus reinforce the value of) transplantation *and* to grapple with the daily challenges it poses for those who receive this particular form of medical salvation.

For their part, transplant program staff not only incited expectations and desire in transplantation, but partook of them as well. As we have seen, transplant professionals themselves were often deeply invested in representations of the transformative potentials of transplantation, and their own responses to the instabilities of posttransplant life reveal disappointments in a different register. Transplant clinicians and social workers often shared with me their belief that receiving a transplant should make patients "better people," both more grateful and more generous to others—indeed, such hopes for redemptive patient transformations have a long-standing history in transplant medicine (Fox and Swazey 1974). By becoming "better," recipients would justify not just the sacrifice of the donor (whether living or cadaveric), but the more general economic, political, and emotional investments required to materialize transplantation in Mexico as well. As one physician explained this thinking (and the disappointment to which it could lead):

> I feel disillusioned sometimes. We work so hard to help these patients and they are given life, the most profound gift of all. And I want to see them use that gift well. They should go out and want to help others, teach people to read, or donate their time to charity, or even just come and help support other patients who are still waiting for a transplant. But most of them just stay selfish and in their own world, full of their own problems. Sometimes it makes me feel like I should go and do something else, like this is all just a waste. (Dr. Hernandez, IMSS)

This notion of transplant recipients as sometimes disappointingly flawed resonates with the tendency explored above for transplant professionals to read posttransplant failures through the lens of individual patient (ir)responsibility. Viewed through this lens, patients unable to maintain steady employment were suspected of laziness, and those who lost access to their medications and rejected the transplant were simply insufficiently "agile" in negotiating the politics and bureaucracy of health care. In this move, such posttransplant stories are no longer stories about transplantation (and its failures) in Guadalajara, but rather are rendered stories about the flaws in individual patients' character, quality, and value. Like Beto, excluded from the Transplant Games because of his failed transplant, such posttransplant realities are thus largely written out of the story of transplantation. And at the same time, the stories of productos valiosos of and for transplantation—stories of the marathon runner or the proud restaurant owner and father—are made to embody transplantation as both desirable and achievable.

Taken on their own, the situated challenges of posttransplant life examined in this chapter may seem to resonate with a technology-out-of-place vision of transplantation in Mexico, embedded as they are in local hardships of health care, employment, and gender relations. Yet, as I noted at the beginning of the chapter, the fraught story of posttransplant life does not go largely unspoken just in Guadalajara, and transplanted patients in many other places—including the United States—have faced similar challenges in gaining and maintaining access to the medications and specialized care they require to support their transplants over time. In considering these more general patterns—this tendency to focus on *receiving* a transplant rather than on the realities of *living* with one over time—insights from science and technology studies again remind us that there is perhaps an instrumental dimension to this elision of the thorny complexities of posttransplant life.

After all, iconic representations of transplantation as a relatively straightforward solution, one whose conclusion is clear, predictable, and generally salvational, provide a much neater, simplified—and therefore more easily circulated and stabilized—story to tell (Dumit 2004; Latour 1987; Latour and Woolgar 1979). Thus, patients who lose their transplants due to difficulties with medication access or employment status can be simply written out as individual, "ungainly" inadequacies, essentially erased from the public story of transplantation. Simplicity, after all, has considerable representational and political advantages, and the slippery realities of posttransplant life traced out in this chapter make for neither pithy sound bites nor unequivocal answers about the meaning and value of transplantation for either individual bodies or wider society. Ultimately at work here is perhaps yet another form of ethical domestication: for rendering the problems of posttransplant life a matter of individual failings—rather than of institutional, structural inequalities—quite neatly contains the difficult questions about the place and purpose of transplantation in Mexico and in medicine more broadly that might otherwise be posed.

PART III

FRAMING TRANSPLANTATION

5. Gifts, Commodities, and Analytic Icons in the Anthropological Lives of Organs

A pound of that same merchant's flesh is thine.
The court awards it and the law doth give it.

. . .

Tarry a little, there is something else.
This bond doth give thee here no jot of blood;
The words expressly are a "pound of flesh."
Take then, thy bond, take then thy pound of flesh;
But in the cutting if thou dost shed
One drop of Christian blood, thy lands and goods
Are by the laws of Venice confiscate
Unto the state of Venice.
—Portia, from *The Merchant of Venice*

The human kidney weighs in at not quite a full pound of flesh. And it too cannot be extracted without the shedding of blood: as previous chapters have explored, the act of organ donation entails suffering and risks both biological and existential. Portia's words, penned by a sixteenth-century English playwright as he unfolds a Venetian drama of love, money, and animosities simultaneously entrepreneurial and religious in nature, come from a place so very distant from our ethnographic ground of millennial Mexico. And yet, already at play in this canonical play—the only one of Shakespeare's to mention Mexico, as it happens[1]—are some of the thorny tensions still so deeply at stake in how transplant has come to matter in our present day. Antonio's pound of flesh, which Portia so deftly defends from extraction in repayment of his debt to the merchant Shylock, usefully flags for us the terribly long history of anxieties about the relationship between flesh and money. Part and parcel of this history, contemporary kidneys raise similar anxious, ancient questions about bodies and markets as they are caught up in the desperate demand for ever-more organs to feed the expanding transplant endeavor. Indeed, transplantation has become a central site within anthropology for exploring precisely these kinds of concerns about how people draw (and redraw) the lines of both sharp distinction and dense articulation among persons, things, and money (Sharp 2000: 305).[2] Bringing these insistent questions about bodily commodification to the ethnographic ground of Mexico, this chapter (and the following) also takes up a set of wider questions about how transplant has come to matter in anthropology and how anthropology, in turn, comes to matter through transplant.

Recall those initial, almost eager technology-out-of-place reactions to my research from anthropological colleagues and friends: "Organ transplantation in Mexico, interesting . . . So you're studying black market stuff, organ selling, that kind of thing?" Bodily commodification is clearly one of the central frames through which anthropology apprehends the transplant endeavor, wherever it may take place. And rightly so, as the growing global market in human organs demands urgent analytical and activist attention. Yet the commodification frame in transplantation is also always already neatly paired with its implied analytic opposite: the gift. Inescapably invoked in those technology-out-of-place assumptions, after all, is also the notion of a transplant medicine more properly "in place" in both geographic and moral terms—producing, for instance, those very differently charged expectations provoked by mention of my work on transplant in the United States and Spain, as compared to Mexico. If the implicitly proper geographic place in such exchanges is clearly the Western, postindustrial world, this geographic space maps onto a moral terrain as well, in which the organ as altruistic gift, rather than bought-and-sold commodity, holds powerful sway.

There is an entrenched moral politics of the market and the gift at work in all of this, one that runs throughout the anthropological scholarship of transplantation in consequential ways. Portia's speech above offers a provocative point of departure here.[3] In her speech to the court, Portia thwarts the moneylender Shylock, who seeks to wreak revenge on his enemy Antonio by exacting the pound of flesh he is owed for the merchant's failure to repay the money he owes. Portia offers an argument that hinges on the idea that you cannot get a pound of flesh "by itself"—and reminds us that the body and its parts come entangled in a thoroughly interpenetrated web of substances and meanings that can never be fully disengaged and "purified" from one another (to borrow from Latour's useful naming of the fertile but futile work of modernity) (Latour 1993).[4] This is to say, notwithstanding all the mechanistic biomedical discourse in the world, a pound of flesh is never "just" a pound of flesh.

Furthermore, the imagined (but never consummated) exchange of flesh for money in Shakespeare's play evokes the terribly long history of the mixing up of bodies and markets—commodifying the human body, after all, is hardly a recent invention (Sharp 2000: 292). Moreover, the play suggests that the relationships engendered by such commodifying claims are not necessarily just impersonal relations mediated by the market. Rather, these may be complex social relationships that can exist before and extend beyond the moment of the market transaction. Indeed, it is precisely the personal, emotional quality of the long-standing animosity between Shylock and Antonio that produces the pound of flesh bargain. And that animosity is not merely personal, of course, but structural as well. For both Antonio's careless disdain for repaying his debts and Shylock's thwarted, poisonous resentment are born too of their relative insider/outsider status in the anti-Semitic social order in which the play takes place. Despite the frequent fears that bodily commodification must inevitably entail the *objectification* of human beings, in this case it is in fact precisely the richly contextualized *subjecthood* (and inter-subjectivity) of Antonio and Shylock that animates the market transaction and invests it with particular value.

Ultimately, Portia's cunning legal analysis offers some useful guideposts for the task I take up in this chapter: exploring—and then reaching beyond—the moral and affective politics, as well as the analytic effects, of the gift/commodity frame in the anthropology of transplantation. In doing so, I take seriously the contention that you simply cannot get a kidney "by itself," as well as the observation that market relations may be shaped by and productive of highly charged relations of social connection, hierarchy, and emotion. In the sections that follow, I first sketch out the central place of the concepts of gift and commodity in anthropology writ large, and in analyses of transplant specifically, before returning to the ethnographic ground of Mexico to explore the analytic possibilities of employing a wider temporal and relational frame.

Anthropological Icons

Gifts and commodities have long been key analytic icons in anthropology. Flowing from foundational work by Marcel Mauss on the gift ([1924] 1976), and Karl Marx on the commodity ([1867] 1990), a great deal of anthropological labor has gone into distinguishing gifts and commodities from one another. Central to the contrasts commonly drawn between gifts and commodities has been tracing out the different kinds of relations between persons and things they entail, as well as the different forms of sociality they thus foster. Anthropological analyses of gift exchange have, across a wide swath of settings and times, explored the way that reciprocal obligations to give, to receive, and to return the gift work to weave social ties. Animating this power of the gift to make sociality is the way some portion of the identity or spirit of the giver—what Mauss called the *hau*, drawing on the Maori term—lingers in the thing given and thus impels its return in a reciprocal offering. In contrast to these socializing and personalizing effects of the gift, impersonality has long been a central characteristic—and consequence—of the commodity form in anthropological analyses. There is the sense of impersonal, fleeting social relations created as buyer and seller are imagined to meet in the anonymity of the market, exchange money for goods, and go their separate ways. And there is the impersonality of the commodity-thing itself, seen as uniform, utterly interchangeable with others of its kind and shorn, as Marx would say, of the human conditions of its production.

Thus imagined as radically different—even opposing—forms of exchange, gifts, and commodities have also long been associated in anthropological work with different forms and scales of society. Gifts were classically seen as the defining mode of exchange in small-scale, intimately face-to-face societies, while commodity exchange characterized the alienatingly large-scale, "modern" societies to which anthropologists themselves tended to belong (Appadurai 1986; Frow 1997). And, as such notions of primordial intimacy and modern alienation suggest, there is an important temporal and affective dimension to all this as well, with the gift (and its characteristic societies) often suffused with a nostalgic, romanticized sense of altruism and generosity, and the commodity (and its attendant social worlds) colored in a colder, more individualistic, self-interested, and future-oriented light. Thus embedded within the gift/commodity distinction was also an implicit them/us distinction, an identification of the ethnographic Other with the gift—and thus, of the anthropological Self with the commodity. Indeed, the very convention of referring to this web of ideas and associations and affects in terms of "the gift" and "the commodity" hints at the iconic status of these concepts: symbolically powerful, they are representational nodes in which a whole host of anthropological models and beliefs and commitments have come to be condensed.

Yet running alongside this deep vein of anthropological work exploring and establishing such distinctions between gift and commodity is also a long history of critiquing such polarized representations of these two reified forms (Appadurai 1986; Callon 1998; Frow 1997; Rus 2008; Weiner 1992). On the one hand, for instance, gifts have been recurrently revealed to have a frankly calculative, self-interested dimension—one that may work to produce not just social bonds, but social binds of hierarchy and inequality as well. While on the other, commodities too have been shown to have sometimes curiously gift-like dimensions as they move along the course of complicated social lives. Indeed, both the magic of marketing and the identity-making powers of consumption may imbue commodities with precisely the kind of lively, person-like qualities more typically associated with Mauss's hau-laden gift. And not only do stark delineations between gift and commodity prove hard to hold, so, too, do the associations of each with distinctive forms and scales of society. Indeed, it turns out that both forms of exchange seem persistently, promiscuously present across the wide range of societal possibility subject to anthropological scrutiny.

Organ transplantation has fallen firmly within the grip of this long history of invoking—and critiquing—the iconic gift/commodity frame. There is often, in anthropology, a recurrent association of certain places with particular topics or theoretical problems, so that India comes to seem a classic place to study kinship, for example, while Melanesia seems a site for the investigation of both gender and exchange (Gupta and Ferguson 1997). Such associations can become so ingrained as to have an almost sensorial relationship, so that one might say, for instance, that the notion of hybridity has the flavor of South Asian postcolonial and subaltern studies, while the kindred concept of mestizaje tastes more strongly of Latin America

(Alonso 2004; see also Bakhtin 1981). In a similar way, transplant has an unmistakable, inescapable whiff of gift/commodity debates in anthropological work.

Indeed, from the very first ethnographic investigations of transplant—present at the very beginnings of the modern transplant endeavor itself—the obligatory back-and-forth dynamics of the gift exchange have provided a central theoretical framing. In this vein, Fox and Swazey's classic work identifying the tyrannical potentials of an unmatchable gift that can never be returned continues to carry considerable analytic force (Fox 1978: 1168; Fox and Swazey 1992). Lesley Sharp's work, in turn, has delved deeply into the possibilities of organs-as-gifts for forging new kinds of social ties and even fictive kinship through the bond of shared body parts (2006: 159–205). Such gift-driven analyses have focused insightfully and usefully on the social bonds and binds created through the medium of transplantation—that is, on the personalizing, socializing possibilities of such organ exchanges. At the same time, transplantation as a rapidly expanding and deeply worrying site of new forms of bodily commodification has also drawn intensive anthropological analysis, particularly in the work of Nancy Scheper-Hughes (2000, 2004, 2005; see also Cohen 1999, 2002, 2005; Moniruzzaman 2012). Here we often see reflected the impersonalizing, even dehumanizing, potentials of the commodity form in anthropological critique, as alarm is sounded about how both human bodies and human relations are increasingly devoured in the voracious maw of the global organs market.

And while much of this work has tended to focus on one side or the other of the iconic gift/commodity divide, also repeated in the transplant context is the anthropological impulse both to distinguish gift/commodity forms from one another, and to complicate and critique those distinctions at the same time. Thus Lesley Sharp's research on the altruistic cadaveric donor system in the United States, for instance, reveals how beneath the formal, sacralizing language of the organ-as-ultimate-gift lies a highly commodified system of profitable transplant programs, organ price lists, and big-budget organ procurement organizations (Sharp 2006: 50–51; see also Sharp 2007). While in turn, Lawrence Cohen's tracking of the global flows of organ buyers and organ sellers discerns a powerful impulse toward social identification as a form of market differentiation, as nonresident Indians return to India and overseas Chinese to China in order to seek out organ sellers imagined to offer more desirable affinities of affect and biology

(Cohen 2011). Thus it seems that transplantation has offered a new—and richly productive—terrain on which to deploy these iconic frames of gift and commodity along well-honed lines of anthropological inquiry.

Yet there is one curious form of reversal here. And that is the way that associations of gifts with the ethnographic Other "out there" and of commodities with the anthropological Self "here at home" have largely traded places in anthropological accounts of organ transplantation. Those gift-centered accounts of transplantation have focused largely on high-income EuroAmerican settings, while anthropological analyses more concerned with commodification are highly concentrated, instead, on areas of the world known variously as the global south, the developing world, or simply the poorest and most peripheral countries in the current world order.[5] Thus the anthropological gaze that so often has imputed something of a nostalgic moral high ground to its ethnographic Others (not unproblematically, mind you) seems, in the context of transplantation, to be producing something quite the opposite. Indeed, we might say that in organ transplant, the ethnographic Other has increasingly become a site not of longing for a romanticized past, but rather of anxiety about dystopic possible futures.

This too, of course, is a simplification. As just noted, Lesley Sharp's work on organ transfers in the United States does indeed engage the commodified aspects of the booming transplant industry (2006). And Nancy Scheper-Hughes's globe-trotting hunt after organ traffickers has taken her not just to Brazil and Moldova and South Africa but to her very own birthplace of Brooklyn as well (2011). And yet these broader paradigm patterns of organ-as-gift here at home, and organ-as-commodity "out there" in the unruly wider world, seem unmistakable. Such patterns seem unmistakable not only across the general swath of the scholarly literature on transplant, that is, but also in those intimate, daily exchanges of scholarship and friendship encountered in the course of my own work in different places in the world.

Ultimately, I am interested in the way these patterned deployments of the iconic analytics of gift and commodity in the transplant realm have produced particular condensations of anthropological attention and affect. That is, in making organs-as-gifts more visible in some settings and organs-as-commodities more visible in others, what might we thus become less able to see? These are the very questions that a focus on the iconic—in biomedicine, in transplantation, and in anthropology—helps us to pose. And so, in what follows, I want to draw on the ethnographic material from Mexico to suggest that what these condensations around the iconic figures of gift and commodity in the anthropology of transplant may lead us to miss may be (at least) twofold.

First is the way that the gift/commodity frame produces a temporal focus on the moment of exchange, on that proverbial passing from one (presumably rational) subject to another of the gift, the good, the money, the kidney itself. And in bringing that transactional moment so sharply into focus, the far longer duration of relations and conditions that extend both before and beyond that movement of an organ from one body into another may run the risk of being left more blurry and indistinct—or even largely outside of the analytic frame (see also Cohen [1999: 148] on the "transactional frame" in ethical analyses of transplant). In seeking here to widen the temporal angle of inquiry there is a kinship with the approach I have taken in earlier chapters, with attending to the way, for instance, that the iconic narratives of transplantation as medical salvation also encourage a restricted temporal focus. A focus, that is, on *getting to* the transplant that works to elide the more complicated, long-term story of what comes next in the realities of actually living with that much-desired transplant over time.

And second, alongside this question of temporality is one of relationality, and the way that the gift/commodity analytic encourages thinking primarily in terms of the dyad of giver and receiver, seller and buyer, organ donor and organ recipient (see also Ben-David 2005; Kierans 2011; Sharp 2006). Yet there are, of course, *never* just two people involved in the movement of an organ from one body into another. Such movements necessarily require—at minimum—a complicated choreography of transplant professionals to plan and execute the array of medical procedures that mediate the actual bodily exchange, as well as family caregivers to provide essential emotional and economic and bodily support (and sometimes pressure) both before and after the surgical moment of transfer. These other forms of relation, in which that hard-to-look-away-from dyad of organ giver and receiver are inextricably enmeshed, also entail a complex set of exchanges that are not merely tangential to the one of the kidney itself. For it is the very payment of medical costs, the profitable and prestigious possibilities of transplant for the professionals who proffer it, as well as the complicated back-and-forth reciprocal dance of familial love, dependency, and obligation that condition—indeed that make possible—that fleshy exchange in the first place. And yet, as the gift/commodity frame so compellingly trains our focus on the dyadic relation of organ donor and organ recipient, this wider web of potentiating relations and exchanges may also tend to slip from focused view.

With this sense of both the illuminating powers and the limiting parameters of the gift/commodity analytic thus in mind, here I want to explore the possibility that employing a longer temporal view and a wider relational field might open up what we are able to see in transplantation, might produce a somewhat different, more processual sense of what happens when human organs are set into circulation. Tracking the social life of individual kidneys over the course of their distinctive biographies, in the spirit of the classic works by Appadurai (1986) and Kopytoff (1986), may enable us to expand beyond critiques that point out how gift-like commodified organs and how commodity-like gifted organs often are—for such critiques nonetheless retain the underlying gift/commodity frame. Doing so may also help to unsettle both the moral and the geographic expectations that so often converge around the notions of gift and commodity in the anthropology of transplant. To this end, the specificities of the Mexican case are particularly useful, for here we have a setting where—despite the "Other-ing" context of highly constrained resources—organs most often pass between emotionally connected family members, rather than economically driven strangers. And yet, employing an expanded temporal and relational view makes clear that neither the social effects nor the moral tenor of such gift-like exchanges between family members necessarily held steady when tracked out over time and across a wider social circle. No more necessarily steady, as we shall see, were the social and moral consequences of the more commodity-like exchanges that also sometimes occurred in Mexico.

Kidney Interpellations, Extended

> So, you need to find someone who can give you a kidney. Who in your family do you think might donate to you? Do you have brothers and sisters, do you think any of them would? Why not? And what about your mother? Your father? What about their brothers and sisters? Are you married—do you think your wife would donate . . . ? You need to go home to your family and talk to them *very seriously*; you need to tell them that you need a kidney. Then, anyone who is willing to donate you should bring to see me.
> —Aurelia, Transplant Coordinator, IMSS

Such conversations were the day-to-day reality of a transplant program that depended almost entirely on living donors.[6] The scene is the cramped and hectic transplant coordinator's office on the transplant floor, with two or three other conversations going on simultaneously and people waiting anxiously in the doorway for a chance to inch their way into the tiny space. The patient is perched uncomfortably on the edge of a narrow plastic chair, while the transplant coordinator leans forward over her desk, her posture communicating both intimacy and urgency as she works her way through the all-too-familiar (and familial) list of possible donors. The patient speaks softly, with downcast eyes, as he tries to come up with a response to the barrage of questions. After mentioning each family member, the transplant coordinator pauses, waiting to extract an uncomfortable yes, no, or maybe from the patient. Uncertainty or refusal provokes more questions, why wouldn't this person or that person be willing to donate, do they have health problems of their own, or are they too scared, too busy, or just not very close to the patient? For an observer, the interrogation can be agonizing to watch as the patient is forced to define and defend his or her various relationships with family members. The questions that lie at the root of all this are basic and brutal. Who loves you enough to give you a kidney? On whom can you really depend? To whom can you turn to make such a request? These are difficult questions to face in the privacy of one's own heart, much less in the crowded confines of a transplant coordinator's office.

These are also the questions that amplify the kidney interpellations explored in chapter 3, extending transplant's call beyond the faltering kidneys of the sick patient to the healthy kidneys of those who might save him. In this interpellative moment the kidneys of others—especially of those in the patient's family—are hailed in a manner that imbues them with new meaning, new character, and new potential. The patient's own kidneys have gone from being an unseen, unfelt, and unknown entity to being the failing center of the lived experience of illness. And suddenly, in raising the possibility of living organ donation, the kidneys of family members are transformed as well. No longer an anonymous and undifferentiated part of another person, others' kidneys can now be imagined as detachable, as an "extra" resource to be given or withheld at will. Newly conjured in this way, the kidneys of others could become an object of intense—but sometimes guilty—desire. As one young woman described: "I couldn't say anything to my family about donating. I wanted a new kidney so much that I felt overwhelmed, like I couldn't show that to them, that I couldn't pressure them with how badly I needed it. I felt like it would change everything if they knew" (Marta, domestic worker, SSa). Another middle-aged man, less reticent about pressuring family members, baldly expressed the frustration and anger wrought by his thwarted desire for a kidney: "I try to understand why they're scared to donate, but it's hard. It just seems so selfish when they don't really need it [the kidney] and I do. To them, it means nothing, and to me, everything" (Jaime, waiter, IMSS).

In this first key stage in the social life of a potentially transplantable organ, the very possibility of donation thus profoundly changes the meaning and value of other people's bodies for patients, for medical staff, and for family members (now rendered "potential donors") themselves. And once hailed in this way as potential donors, there was no going back to the time before when one's kidneys were simply one's own in an unexamined and undifferentiated way. Whether someone decides to donate or not, the "extra" kidney cannot revert to being wholly "self" again in the same way that it once was, for the potential for separation and the possibility of another's claim to it lingers. As one man who refused to donate to a nephew put it to me: "I decided I couldn't donate to him because what if my, what if one of my own children needed one of my kidneys some day and I had already given it away to someone else? Well, I couldn't risk wasting my extra kidney on someone else" (Francisco, uncle of IMSS patient). Here, although the kidney is not donated and remains (for now) part of his body, its meaning has fundamentally shifted: it has become "extra." The kidney now represents a detachable but finite resource that must be "spent" wisely.

Tellingly, this was a common form of refusal—a refusal staked not on the right to protect one's own body and retain its wholeness, but rather on the rights of one's children to claim those bodily resources if necessary.[7] That is, it was a form of refusal that nonetheless cedes the logic and ethics of living donation—a vivid example of how merely being hailed by transplantation can shape subjectivity, altering the way people experience their bodies and imagine the kinds of claims to which they may be subject. For sure, fear of bodily fragmentation and a desire for self-protection may also lie beneath such refusals of living donation. Yet it seems clear that these were apparently not the reasons that felt socially—or morally—acceptable to offer up in the face of a donation request. The very potential for donation has structured the terms of possible refusal. Ultimately these are interpellative effects unique to neither Mexico nor transplantation, of course, but characteristic of many forms of biotechnology that need only be imaginatively available (and not actually accessed), to change embodiment, realign subjectivity, and as Sharon Kaufman has put it, "expand the field of moral action" (Kaufman et al. 2006: 83; see also Franklin 1997; Rapp 1999).

Once family members were called to donate, their kidneys often became objects of contention within the dense web of familial relations of power, emotion, and imagination. In some cases, as we saw in chapter 1, a donor might be summoned forth immediately by the emotional reflex of familial love and obligation. Thus Dorotea described her reaction upon learning that her sister needed a kidney in the familiar language of the lovingly offered, altruistic gift: "I didn't even think about it, I just offered. If she needs something and I can give it to her, of course I'll do it. We've always been close; we've always supported each other" (accountant, sister of SSa patient). When there was no such obvious candidate, however, a sometimes-lengthy period of debate and even conflict could ensue, as various family members assessed and sometimes openly asserted their own and one another's suitability or unsuitability as candidates for donation.

As explored in chapter 1's examination of the local shape of living donor bioavailability in Mexico, axes of gender, age, and marital and employment status often came into play at this point, in ways that could render women and/or younger, unmarried family members more vulnerable. Contention among family members over who should donate might take the form of open conflict or, perhaps more often, of a sort of silent, unbearably tense game of "chicken" in which each person held back, hoping that someone else would break from the emotional pressure and offer him- or herself up as a donor first. Rico described the months leading up to his own decision to donate to his older brother in this way: "He just kept getting worse, and no one said anything. I was scared, I didn't really want to, but I saw that he was going to die and no one else was going to. I didn't feel like I had a choice. My wife kept saying, 'Why does it have to be you?' But after waiting and waiting, I could see finally there was no one else" (brother of IMSS patient). The benign language of the gift seems, somehow, not quite adequate to capturing the constrained and emotionally fraught nature of the decision here.

As such weighty debates and decisions played out among family members, the next key stage in the social life of these potentially transplantable organs began to unfold. For it was at this point that an initial narrative began to be woven together to make sense of both what might motivate and what might flow from any particular offering up of a kidney. Critically, this was a narrative constituted not only between potential donor and potential recipient, but among the various family, friends, employers, transplant professionals, and even visiting anthropologist with whom they were engaged as well. Much like the way the stories of individual patients as "agile" or "ungainly" were built up in the process of seeking a transplant (see chapter 3), donation stories also came to matter over the course of the everyday interactions of happenstance hallway conversations, hushed late night conclaves in the kitchen, tense family meetings with transplant staff, and the mundane filling out of bureaucratic forms. And in the process, meaning was made out of the movement of a kidney from one body into another, offering a narrative sense of both what precipitated that movement and what consequences it might weave in its wake.

For some donors, this was primarily a story of love and guilt, one in which allowing the patient to die of kidney disease when there was a chance to help was simply impossible, emotionally, psychologically, and within the social relations of the family. In the words of one middle-aged shopkeeper: "She's my mother, she gave me life. How could I not do the same for her if I can? How would I face myself or my father . . . *or my own children* . . . if I just let her die?" (Nancí, daughter of IMSS patient). Emerging from her words is a powerful inversion of the idea that mothers who have given life through birth ought easily to do so again through organ donation, for here the mother who has given life instead is owed it in return. For other donors, the story of a donation's meaning was a more pragmatic one, folded into a larger story about the everyday demands of survival: "Well, my husband couldn't take the time from work, his boss would never permit it, and my son, we needed him to keep earning too, you know? But with me, my sister could come in and help with the little ones, and well, that's what made sense, for it to come from me. And they've always supported us, helped us when we were struggling . . . it's just, it's just what you do." (María, daughter-in-law of IMSS patient). For still other donors, the story that initially set the kidney into motion was more explicitly transactional, imagined as a fairly straightforward exchange of a kidney in return for a promised car, a house, or the money to travel to the United States: "My uncle was going to buy me a house if I gave him my kidney. And I would have done it, why not? That way, we both get something, we're both happy. But the doctors said I wasn't compatible" (Manuel, nephew of private hospital patient).[8] Here again, the language of gift and commodity seems hardly adequate to the extended family complexities of Maria's pragmatically calculated decision to donate to her mother-in-law or Manuel's eager anticipation of how he might have profited from giving a kidney to a favorite uncle.

As with Manuel, such transactional imaginings were not uncommon within the bounds of the family. But, not surprisingly, they were even more characteristic of the small minority of cases where a kidney was offered up by someone outside the family—a friend, a neighbor, a coworker, or even, in a few cases, a stranger.[9] Such nonfamilial living donation typically falls into two broad categories, those cases in which the donor and recipient are considered "emotionally related"[10] through friendship or shared community membership in a church or a workplace, and those in which the donor and recipient seem to have been mere acquaintances or even unknown to one another prior to the donation. In some "emotionally related" cases, where the connection between donor and recipient was long-standing, that crucial moment in which the potential donor kidney shifted from being an undifferentiated part of "self" to a possibly detachable object mirrored the kind of emotional reflex that often occurred within families. As Lupe, who offered to donate to her childhood friend, described it: "As soon as I knew she was sick, I said, 'I'll do it. If you need a kidney, take mine.' I didn't even think about it; we've always been so close, and this was something I didn't need that could help her" (friend of IMSS patient).

In other such cases, however, it was not just the *patient*'s need that caused the kidney to be reimagined as separable but also some need of the potential *donor* that might be met through the newly perceived fungibility of the kidney. A person who hears an ad on the radio, for instance, asking for a kidney and offering some sort of undefined help in return, starts to imagine what he or she might ask in return for a kidney, what might be gained for the sacrifice of this body part that had previously gone unnoticed and unvalued. There is a curious play here between Marx's classic distinction of use-value and exchange-value (Marx [1867] 1990). The relative cultural silence around kidneys in Mexico often meant that the moment in which the kidney itself first became visible to a potential donor was often the same moment in which its use-value (to self) was also represented as negligible at best. That is, donors often became aware of their kidney only upon being told that it was "extra," upon learning that it was something without which they could do. And in the same moment that the kidney's use-value (to the donor) was perceived as minimal, its *exchange*-value took on previously unguessed potential, as speculation arose about what that same kidney might be worth to a desperately ill patient awaiting transplantation.

Such speculations about the possibilities opened up by the newly "extra" kidney were not confined to stranger-donors with visions of money dancing in their heads, of course. Familial donors too might imagine not just the material rewards of house or car, but more intangible forms of benefit made possible by a donated kidney—a closer relationship, for instance, or the loving gratitude and approval of a long-distant parent. Yet whether within or without the bounds of family, whether framed at first as more gift-like or commodity-like, these initial narrative understandings—of both what motivated and what might result from the offering up of a kidney—were hardly the end of the story. For both the social life of the organ itself and the relations between donor and recipient (as well as the wider social networks within which they were entangled) continued far beyond the moment when the kidney was set into either imaginative or material circulation. And so the meanings and consequences of that circulation continued to evolve over time and across a wide range of relationships as well.

Once through the longed-for transplant surgery, recipients had to find some way to accommodate this new kidney within both self and social relations. For some, the organ was unequivocally integrated into their sense of self, becoming simply "my body," shorn of any identity as a separate entity or a part of someone else. Tere, for instance, emphatically insisted: "I don't think of my kidney as separate from me in any way. It's just mine. It's *not* my sister's anymore, it's part of me just like all the rest of me" (street vendor, SSa). But more commonly for the patients I met in Mexico, the transplanted organ seemed always to retain some sense of both the identity and the claims of the donor. As Luz described her own feelings: "*It's my mother, a part of her that she gave to me.* So of course I must take very good care of her kidney always" (student, IMSS). Such frequently expressed sentiments highlight the way transplantation's successful hailing of kidneys as expendable and hence extractable does *not* necessarily render those organs wholly objectified and mechanistic, emptied of the self of the donor from whom they came.[11] As Portia might remind us, a pound of flesh is never *just* a pound of flesh.

In some such cases, the identity-laden organ could draw the two parties closer over time, forging a more deeply intimate relationship and a more profound investment in and identification with one another's lives and well-being. As Magda described her relationship to her donor brother: "We're even closer now. For him, *me* doing well is like *him* doing well too. He's so proud of anything I do—it's because of him that I can do it. And for me, whatever I can do for him, however I can help him and support him, I want to give back" (accountant, IMSS). The symbiotic relationship she describes here might recall one possible reading of those interconnected, twinned bodies depicted in The Two Fridas from chapter 2. Yet Magda also went on to describe how this deep identification with her donor-brother both delighted and distanced her other siblings, who rejoiced in her survival but sometimes felt left out of the newly intense nature of their relationship.

For other organ recipients, however, this intimacy could become overwhelming, or even suffocating. As first explored decades ago in the classic notion of the "tyranny of the gift," receiving an organ could clearly make some patients feel so irredeemably indebted to their donors that it bred resentment and a desperate desire to be free of their deep entanglement (Fox 1978: 1168; Fox and Swazey 1992). This resentment sometimes flowed from the other direction as well, as donors could come to second-guess their own sacrifice, or to feel disappointed in their transformative expectations of the donation. In one such tyrannical case that I watched unfold over time, Luís, a hard-partying young university student, received a kidney from the older sister who had practically raised him due to their mother's failing health (IMSS). After the transplant, Luís found himself increasingly and unbearably burdened by his obligation to her. As he told me one afternoon over a shared plate of fresh mango with chile, "Really it's gotten so I can barely stand to be around her, to look her in the eye even. It's like this weight, what she wants from me, what she wants to control. I suppose it was always like that with us a little, but now, with this [the kidney] it's much harder, it weighs more . . . the kidney, it just, *weighs more*." Over time, Luís gradually isolated himself from his sister and even from the rest of the family as well, feeling himself marked even more indelibly as the unrepentant black sheep of the family. His sister, for her part, was candid about her disappointment that her donation did not "make him turn his life around, with this new chance." When last I saw them, their once-close relationship seemed to have deteriorated almost completely under the strain.

Clearly the social lives of organs can take many twists and sometimes saddening turns. Yet tracking the what-happens-next in the story is critical not just in those cases where kidneys actually were made to move. For just as the potentially extractable kidney, once hailed, cannot subside into being wholly self once again, so too those kidneys *not* donated turn out to have social lives and social effects that also deserve to be part of the story here. Sometimes a refusal to donate further frayed already fragile family bonds, as it did for Lulu, who reported feeling profoundly abandoned by her family when no one came forward to offer her a kidney (SSa, domestic worker). Or imagine, for instance, what the customary Sunday family meal might be like in those cases described in chapter 1, after a mother blocks a sibling donation, announcing that she would "rather have one child die than two."

Yet other possibilities exist as well. In Omar's family, his rapidly deteriorating kidney failure rallied his extended family around him in a way none of them would have expected after several years of estrangement. When Omar, a soft-spoken university student with a wickedly wry sense of humor, fell catastrophically ill, the imminent threat to the acknowledged family favorite swiftly shifted the family dynamic. Not only his father and brother came forward to donate but also two cousins and an uncle, all of whom insisted on showing up to his every appointment at the IMSS Centro Médico where they proceeded to jockey jocularly among themselves for the privilege of giving up a kidney. Yet despite this embarrassment of potential donor riches, one by one each candidate was ruled out—hypertension in one, anomalous renal vasculature in another, and so it went until none were left standing, and Omar was consigned to the slim chances of the cadaveric wait list. Though hopes for a living donation had withered, those renewed bonds within the wider family circle decidedly did not, and the circle of would-be-donors shifted gears to become his dedicated *compadres de dialisís* (dialysis comrades) instead, making sure he was always acompañado for his daily regimen of dialysis cambios and the endless round of clinic appointments. In all of these cases where kidneys *not* given had profound effects— for good or for ill—we can begin to see yet another way in which the focus of the gift/commodity frame on the moment of exchange may cause us to miss other important social dynamics set into motion by just the possibility of organ giving and getting—even when such an exchange never actually occurs.

Ultimately revealed here is a range of possibility entailed in transplantation's hailing of human bodies: for kidneys that move between bodies and those that stay put, for kidneys drawn forth by the pull of social connection or by the lure of economic benefit, for kidneys that do—and do not—retain the identity of the donor. And in that interpellative moment, when kidneys are rendered at least potentially separable and exchangeable, human relations of various kinds may be strengthened, woven together more densely and tightly over time. Or, alternatively, they may be weakened, loosened, or even unraveled entirely in the wake of the movement of a kidney from one body to another. Or both—in different ways, at different times, and across different modes of relation. While the language of gift and commodity is often indispensable—indeed, inescapable—in trying to analyze these complex social processes, it seems not quite sufficient. In the following section I follow two contrasting cases at close range in order to more thickly explore what might be gained by a more processual approach, one that aims to attend to a wider temporal and relational field in the realm of organ transfer.

On the Ground, Over Time

MAGO

Mago was a plump, extraordinarily warm woman in her midforties with gracious manners and an infectious laugh. She was diagnosed with kidney failure as a result of her diabetes about three years before I first met her. She had lived in Guadalajara all her life and came from a large, close-knit family of ten brothers and sisters, most of whom had also stayed in the city to marry and start families of their own. When Mago's kidneys finally failed and she was told that a transplant was her best hope for long-term survival, she was terrified but grateful that she had so many relatives to turn to for help. And yet, when she informed her eldest sister of her situation and asked her to share her plight with the rest of the family—the usual mode of passing along information and requests in the family—she was deeply shocked and distressed to hear nothing back from any of them for several months. Mago's everyday interactions with her extended family became unbearably strained with the weight of all that went unsaid about her need and their implicit refusal. She became depressed and withdrawn, relying only on the company of her teenage daughter and her doting, increasingly frantic husband who would gladly have given her a kidney if he had been a match.

And then, one day, a call came from out of the blue. Her sister Rosa, who had been living in the United States for several decades and had become little more than a distant memory and an occasional voice on the telephone to most of the family, was calling to say that she wanted to donate, that she wanted to be the one to save Mago. As Mago described it: "She was the last person I *ever* would have dreamed of doing this for me . . . just because she had been so far away for so long." Rosa, however, was adamant about her desire to donate, and rapidly made arrangements to leave her American husband and teenage children at home in order to return to Mexico for several months-long stretches of testing, maintaining all the while the patiently persistent pressure necessary to keep the process moving.

During these lengthy visits she lived with Mago and her family in their spacious apartment in a quiet, middle-class neighborhood in the city, periods during which she and Mago spent nearly every waking moment together. During the intimacy of the long hours required to work their way through the lengthy protocol of testing and approvals at the hospital, they relived for one another the years during which they had been separated, coming to know one another's families and day-to-day, year-to-year histories as they had not since Rosa's departure from Mexico nearly three decades earlier. Rosa told Mago that she had become increasingly saddened by how much she had drifted apart from her Mexican family over the years, and when she finally, belatedly, learned of Mago's problem during one of her infrequent phone calls to another sibling, she "just knew immediately that it should be me—it was like I felt it in my bones."

There were a seemingly endless string of obstacles—both medical and bureaucratic—to Mago's transplant in the IMSS program, from lost tests, to doubts among some staff about whether transplant was a good idea at all given Mago's advanced diabetes. But Rosa was dogged in her determination to move the case forward and fierce in her insistence that her sister be transplanted. Recounting her sister's unflagging commitment, Mago joked that: "¡Tenía tantas ganas a donar—a veces más ganas que yo para el trasplante!" (She had such a desire to donate, at times more desire than I had for the transplant!). There is a sense here of the compelling way that familial webs of obligation and emotion can work to pull patients along on the path to transplant even when the promise of restored health begins to wane—this is an effect about which both Sharon Kaufman (Kaufman et al. 2006) and Laura Heinemann (2014) have written beautifully in the context of U.S. transplantation. For her part, Rosa recounted her role in agilizando Mago's transplant with a certain relish—there were frustrations, to be sure, but also a satisfying sense of regaining a set of culturally central survival skills that had atrophied during her time in the United States.

After about six months of bureaucratic battle and multiple trips for Rosa back and forth from the United States, the transplant finally took place, and was a relative success. Rosa's kidney began functioning almost immediately in Mago, though she did experience several significant bouts of rejection requiring hospitalization and brutal amounts of immunosuppressives during the first days and weeks after the transplant. Rosa's own recovery from the donation surgery was relatively easy, and the sisters recuperated together back in Mago's apartment, with Mago's husband and daughter happily waiting on the pair hand and foot. During this period the rest of the family also began to come around again, bringing food and magazines, staying for long chatty visits and slowly rebuilding the ties that had become so strained under the pressure of Mago's desperate need for a kidney.

After her recuperation, Rosa returned to the States with not just a renewed, but a fundamentally altered, set of relationships with her family in Mexico. The intensity and intimacy of her relationship with Mago, forged during the all-consuming process of getting to the donation and transplant, deepened in the months and years after the transplant in ways that neither of them could have anticipated. The sisters described their relationship in terms of a new spiritual, psychic, and deeply embodied connection that they attributed to the fact that Mago now carried a piece of Rosa within her. The first time she told me her story, Mago described how she had taken on some of Rosa's attributes since the transplant: "My hair, which was always totally straight, is curly now, like hers. And I'm stronger, assertive like her too. My daughter stopped me the other day as I was telling a story and said, 'Mamá, you sound just like Tía Rosa, you even use your hands like her when you talk!' " Not just a question of altering Mago's sense of identity, the shared kidney had changed Rosa as well. As she described to me on one of her now-frequent visits to Guadalajara several months after I first met Mago, Rosa felt that she and her sister now had direct access to one another's emotions and physical state as well. As Rosa told me: "I can be at home in Oregon and I wake up and know when she's sad. I get on the phone and I'm right, she needed to talk to someone . . . I woke up last month with a terrible pain in my foot, and a couple days later learned that was when Mago fell and tore something in her foot." This was a form of profound and cherished connection far beyond what either sister had imagined possible, one that rendered the donation and transplant deeply, movingly meaningful to them.

In the years that followed the transplant, however, it was not just relations between Mago and Rosa that were altered but ties between Rosa and the rest of her family in Mexico as well. Rosa continued to return to Mexico several times a year, often bringing her children and husband with her. As her children grew older she began to send them on their own for extended visits, rotating among the various siblings so that they came to know the entire extended family well over time. Similarly, Rosa's home in Oregon became a family resource—a base of operations in the United States—for many members of the family in Mexico in a way that it never had been during the previous decades of her time there. For the other siblings in the family, the donation and transplant not only saved the life of one sister, but restored to them another sister whom they thought they had lost to el Norte.

For her part, Mago was gladdened by these renewed bonds between Rosa and the rest of the family, but retained a sense of quiet distance from her other siblings that she didn't think would ever change. She told me: "I understand it, of course, to donate a kidney is a great thing, a big thing to ask. But before I got sick I understood my family in one way, and now I see them differently. Now I have seen how far they would go for me, and, well, I don't blame them, but it made me see that our family is not what I thought it was. We still have the dinners, the fiestas together, we talk all the time, they accompany me when I need to go out, all of that—but in my heart I will always know . . . well, I will always know that they would have let me die."

Contained in Mago's clear-eyed, painful assessment that "I will always know that they would have let me die" is just one of the forms of relational complexity that emerge from a more expansive view of the social dynamics of organ transfer. In many ways, Rosa's giving of her kidney to Mago fits neatly, comfortably—even ideally—into the gift model. Motivated by emotional ties and embedded in the ongoing back-and-forth reciprocity of familial relations—but given with no expectation of material compensation—this is precisely the sort of organ exchange one might hold up as an exemplary illustration of how "the gift of life" can heal not just bodies, but social relations as well. And yet, while some ties have indeed been renewed and strengthened, others—between Mago and the rest of her family—were clearly called into question, and even profoundly harmed. Casting an even wider relational view, it is worth noting the strain in her marriage that Rosa privately confided her decision to donate had caused. Though she never said anything to Mago about it, her Anglo husband worried about the risks she was taking to donate and began to resent the time away from her own family that all of the travel to Mexico had required. Such uneasy feelings on his part did not entirely abate over time either, for Rosa told me that the regaining of her Mexican family has sometimes seemed to him like a loosening of her ties to their life together in the United States.

Such relational ripple effects could be traced out even farther of course— what did Rosa's own children make of her decision to donate? In light of that earlier discussed and commonly offered form of refusal—"I can't donate to him, because what if my own children need my kidney one day?"—might their mother's sacrifice for her sister have felt like a lack of care for them?

And what of those siblings whom Mago could never quite see in the same way again? Just as Mago must now live with knowing that they would have let her die, those siblings too must live with that uneasy self-knowledge as well. And their children—including Mago's own child—share this terrible life-and-death knowledge of familial limits as well. Such widespread effects are also part of the social life of this particular organ exchange, and they are, moreover, effects that will surely not stay stable over time, but will continue to shift and evolve long past the point that I can track them here.

And moving beyond the bounds of the family itself, what of the transplant staff who worked with Rosa and Mago? The sisters were open not just with me, but with several members of the transplant team as well, about the ways in which they experienced the donated kidney as a sort of two-way conduit for emotions, communication, and connection. Their stories of being able to sense one another's physical and psychic pain across the great distance between Oregon and Guadalajara resonated powerfully for some of these transplant staff, producing a shiver of motivating mystery and pleasure that lay at the heart of the grueling, often grim work in which they were engaged—an embodied experience on the part of professionals that I take up more directly in the following chapter. Indeed, I was first introduced to Mago by one of the IMSS transplant coordinators who thought I should hear her story precisely because "it's so beautiful, how they are connected now— it's something you should see, this other side of the ugly work that we do, this is the mystery, the beauty that keeps us going" (Aurelia, IMSS). And so, among the effects spooling out from the movement of Rosa's kidney into Mago were these, too: transplant staff who found themselves captivated— and inspired—by the possibilities for new forms of bodily and psychic connection wrought by transplantation, as well as an anthropologist who knew from her first conversation with Mago that this was one of the stories she would surely write about here. And such writing itself, one might imagine, could feed back into the shifting shape of the ongoing story as well, for perhaps one day Mago or Rosa or others involved in their case may hold this book in their hands and decide how my version of the story aligns with, departs from, or alters their own sense of things.

Ultimately, framing Rosa's kidney as a gift to Mago does indeed capture some important things about the nature and terms of what happened here—drawing attention to the social relationships that drew forth the kidney and that were, in turn, themselves subsequently structured by the organ exchange. Yet to focus too tightly on the moment and terms of exchange and on the relationship between Mago and Rosa runs the risk of eliding the rich and decades-long history of varying closeness and estrangement among the wider sibling circle that preceded and conditioned Rosa's donation. It could miss the complexity of the far-reaching social (and bodily) ties remade and profoundly deepened but also, in some cases, irrevocably damaged in the process. Perhaps even more powerfully, in focusing on the gift given by Rosa, we might also overlook the effects of the gifts *not* given by Mago's other siblings, from whom she had expected such embodied support to be more easily forthcoming.

The relational complexity and change over time so vividly evident in Mago's case was not, of course, unique to her particular story but characterized many of the stories I encountered during my time in Mexico. In Felipe's case, too, for instance, none of his eight siblings—most of whom were then living in the United States—initially offered him a kidney (SSa, mechanic). Indeed, his parents, who had joined the rest of the family up north, had expressly forbidden it out of that familiar fear of losing two children instead of just one. Only his brother, Oscar, the only one still living in Guadalajara and thus privy to his deterioration at painfully close range, became willing—eventually—to risk both surgery and parental wrath to try to save his brother. But it was a pressured, reluctant decision reached out of desperation and steeped in resentment of the distant family who had absented themselves from living face-to-face with the grim consequences of their refusal. For Oscar, these consequences included not just losing his brother but also gaining the weighty, unwanted responsibility for supporting Felipe's wife and young son if he died.

The two brothers drew closer during the intense period of the donation and transplant itself, even living together with their families for a period of time—had I met them only then, their story would surely have seemed one of social bonds made only more dense and resilient through transplant.[12] Yet in the months and years that followed, Felipe and Oscar pulled sharply away from one another, each for his own reasons. For Oscar, whose wife had been terrified of and angered by the risks both physical and financial that he took to donate, it was important to rededicate himself to his own family and to repair his marriage by proving that his brother would not always come first. For his part, Felipe was well aware of the strain his need for a kidney had caused and felt compelled both to shield Oscar and his wife from the sight of the body that had asked so much of them, as well as to shield his new kidney from their resentful gaze. And for both brothers, the painful feeling of having been abandoned by the rest of the family remained strong, even years later.

Other such stories revealed similar complexities of emotion, obligation, calculation, and change over time across a far wider range of actors than just organ giver and organ receiver. Antonia, for instance, a young housewife made desperate when no one in her family was medically able to donate, reluctantly accepted a kidney from a long-unrequited admirer, José. Though his offering was couched in the admirable language of the altruistic gift, it seemed clear to Antonia, to her husband, indeed to her entire family circle that, as her cousin so succinctly put it, "he was trying to trade his kidney for her heart." Yet instead of winning her heart, the donation instead produced a complex mixture of guilt and resentment not only in Antonia, but in her husband and her wider family, to whom José had always been close as well. After she was successfully transplanted in the IMSS program, the sense lingered—and only grew—that both his act of sacrifice and their own relationships with him had been tainted by the imposed intimacy created by a form of giving that could not be refused yet asked too much. In the context of José's emotional attachment, accepting his flesh into her body carried a sexual charge of penetration that the married Antonia found increasingly difficult to bear.[13] Aware of their intensifying discomfort in his presence, José—broken-hearted and now single-kidneyed—gradually drifted away from the close-knit family network of which he had been a part for years.

In other cases, a donated kidney seemed not to change—for better or for worse—existing social arrangements so much as solidify, harden, or further entrench them. Such was the case with Padre Tomás, the priest we encountered in chapter 4 whose transplant with a kidney from his sister so memorably transformed him from a "stallion to a gelding." A member of the old-money, land-owning oligarchy in Guadalajara, Padre Tomás had originally hoped to receive a kidney from one of his younger nephews, whom he intended to reward with a car or some travel in return. Yet when none of his nephews proved compatible, he reluctantly accepted the "less fresh" kidney of the middle-aged, unmarried sister who had cared for their aging parents until their deaths, and now kept house for him. For his sister, so simultaneously devoted to and dependent upon him, Padre Tomás saw little need to reward her for her kidney. As he put it: "I could have sent her on a trip or something, but she doesn't really like that sort of thing. For her, there wasn't really anything like that to give her. I already take care of all her needs, and she likes a simple life." Seeming to accept her kidney as little more than his due—and reflecting the degree to which he had wholly integrated the new kidney into his sense of self—he joked about the ease of her recovery with the quip: "She never even missed this kidney of *mine!*" (emphasis added). In their case, the passing of a kidney from sister to brother was made to seem rather unremarkable, simply part and parcel of the way their lives were already entwined and shaped by long-standing relations of gendered expectation and hierarchy.

In all of these cases, in the stories of Mago, Felipe, Antonia, Padre Tomás, and so many others, the analytic figure of the gift helps to tell part of the story, but also hones our attention in particular ways. Shifting the analytic gaze to include, but also exceed, that iconic framing helps to open up more complex possibilities by attending more carefully to the multiple and ever-shifting ways that social relations of various kinds may be—over time—thickened or thinned, loosened or tightened, sweetened or embittered in the face of transplantation.

DON JAIME

Don Jaime was a soft-spoken man whose weathered face, after years of farming, made him appear older than his fifty years. The eldest among his close-knit eight siblings, and father to four children of his own, Don Jaime had long been the stalwart patriarch of his family and a respected figure in his small village several hours north of Guadalajara. With a devastating family history of diabetes, to which he had already lost three siblings, the kidney disease that developed after many years of managing his own diabetes was all too familiar to Don Jaime. As his health declined and dialysis became necessary, Don Jaime left off farming and set up a small streetside *hamburguesa* stand in his village, which he ran with his wife and one of his sons. When dialysis finally became necessary, Don Jaime enrolled in a program in his small regional hospital, and after some difficult early months, was able to achieve some relative stability dialyzing himself at home and helping out at the food stand when he could. Yet, when he heard about the SSa transplant program from a neighbor who had relatives in the city he was immediately intrigued. Having watched his siblings succumb so quickly before him, Don Jaime decided that the risks of the unknown were worth taking.

Calling in various favors to marshal the resources necessary for the trip, Don Jaime and his wife traveled to Guadalajara to throw themselves on the mercy of the SSa transplant program. Once there, they spent several long days waiting to be able to get in for an initial appointment so that they could learn about the transplant process and whether he might be eligible. Finally scoring a few rushed moments with one of the resident doctors training at the SSa hospital, Don Jaime learned that a living donor was his only realistic chance of getting a transplant—without at least the possibility of one, the program would not enroll him or be willing to list him for a cadaveric transplant. Yet, for Don Jaime, who had watched kidney disease run so rampant and deadly throughout his family, asking one of his siblings—or worse, one of his children—to risk their own kidneys was simply out of the question. When his wife proved incompatible as a potential donor, he returned home to his village sadly convinced that a transplant was simply out of his reach.

A few weeks after his return, however, as news filtered throughout the village network about his plight, he was approached by the nephew of a close friend. The nephew, an enthusiastic frequenter of the one local Internet café, told Don Jaime that he should think about asking someone outside of his family, maybe even a stranger, to give him a kidney. He told him that he had read about people in other parts of the world doing it that way and so why not here, too? Don Jaime felt uncertain and slightly uneasy about the idea, but also felt he lacked other options, and so decided to at least try circulating such a request to see what would happen. Unwilling to directly approach any of his many friends and acquaintances in his small village, Don Jaime placed a small ad in a local newsletter. The ad described his situation and asked for help in simple, straightforward terms, describing himself as a humble family man with a sickness in his kidneys from which he would die if he could not find someone to give him a new kidney. Although the ad made no direct mention of a payment or reward of some kind, Don Jaime told me later that he had expected he would need to offer something in return for something so precious as another person's kidney—but he found it hard to imagine just what that might be until he could meet the actual person who might be willing to do this. At work in his hesitation to define a form of compensation before meeting the person to whom it might go seemed to be a deep sense of this exchange as something inherently relational, something that could take firm form only within the back-and-forth dynamic between two specific people.

A week or two after the newsletter went out, a farmer from the next village over contacted Don Jaime. Though they were strangers to one another, Pablo and Don Jaime knew several people in common, and Don Jaime described how over the course of several meetings Pablo quickly came to seem very familiar to him: "He's a *campesino* [farmer], like me, younger, still building his family, but like me, like I was those years ago. It was easy, really, to talk, to understand each other—we were, well it felt like it happened almost right away, *somos simpáticos* [we are in sympathy]." The two met several times, usually in Don Jaime's village, although Pablo invited him to his home as well, to meet his wife and children. They spent the time getting to know one another and talking about what giving a kidney would mean for Pablo, and what getting one would mean for Don Jaime.

Over the course of their conversations, an agreement was reached that if Pablo would give his kidney, Don Jaime would turn over to him the use of a plot of land he had inherited from his uncle—one that he could no longer farm himself, and which his sons could not take on either. Together the two had visited the land that Pablo was already farming, where they talked about planting strategies and tired soil, and Don Jaime told him how much he still missed working the land, for all its frustrations and frequent disappointments. Pablo was candid that he and his family were struggling, the land to which he had access was too small to support them and they felt they were running out of options to stay in the village that they loved. When they first saw the ad it was his wife who urged him to explore what it might mean. She told him: "Maybe you help someone and there is help for us in it too—how can we know unless we go and ask?"

Having reached an agreement, as well as some level of familiarity and comfort with one another, Don Jaime and Pablo returned to the SSa program together, where they were quite open about their arrangement—it didn't seem to occur to them that anyone would see anything wrong with it. As Don Jaime put it: "It was normal for us, we are both campesinos, we've had similar lives, we both know what it is to struggle. I needed his help, but I could help him too." Although one doctor did advise them that they might want to be a bit more discreet about it, for the most part no one ever said anything to them about the agreed-upon exchange. The two men worked their way through the testing protocol with relative rapidity as the SSa program had been having trouble getting transplant cases lined up and so were eager to move them through the process. Within three months the donation and transplant surgeries were scheduled and took place without any major obstacles or complications. Don Jaime felt the change as soon as he woke up from surgery and reveled in regaining his strength and energy. Pablo found the surgical incision more painful than he'd expected, but felt largely recovered within several weeks—although he did note a new feeling of nagging, persistent hunger that he attributed to "the hole, the new space I now have inside of me—I want to eat all the time, all the time, to fill it."[14] After the transplant, Don Jaime was able to get coverage in the IMSS system through the influence of a friend, which provided access—at least for now—to the lifelong immunosuppressive medications his transplant required.

In their own small communities, a number of rumors about the organ exchange eventually circulated, including one that Pablo had received five thousand U.S. dollars in return for the kidney. In relating this rumor to me, Pablo laughed disbelievingly at the idea of what seemed to him such an extraordinary sum, saying—"Do you think if I had $5,000 I would still be living in that dump? I would have started building a decent place for my family by now. And, anyway, that man didn't have anything like $5,000 to pay me, it's just crazy to think that." For his part, Don Jaime was troubled by the rumors but also thought that time, and seeing the relationship that had grown between the two men and their families, would eventually quell the disapproving talk, for the two men stayed in contact after the donation, in part because of the land that Pablo was farming and to which Don Jaime still felt some attachment. Their wives and children became friendly, and the two families fell into a habit of visiting one another every few weeks for long days of shared meals and advice and village gossip. When last I saw them, Don Jaime told me that Pablo had increasingly become "like a son" to him and related how glad he was to help when Pablo turned to him for "fatherly" advice. This sense of kin-like attachment seemed to extend beyond the two men as well into the wider family, and Don Jaime's wife Maria had begun to advise Pablo's wife, Teresita, on how she too might set up a small food stand in their own village.

....

Set against Mago's story told above, there are distinctive features of Don Jaime's transplant experience for which the term commodity does indeed seem useful—for this was a transaction between strangers, animated by mutual need rather than emotional ties, and clearly marked by the exchange of kidney for economic benefit. And yet, the impersonality so often imagined to both produce and flow from more market-like exchanges here seems a poor fit. Like the flesh-for-money bargain between Shylock and Antonio, this was an exchange conditioned by the structured social identities of the two participants—although in this case it was not animosity but rather a form of sympathy, of strong social identification between the two campesinos, that seemed to make it possible for Pablo to offer and for Don Jaime to receive the precious kidney. Not just a matter of comparable class positions, gender too seems to have played a role here—with familiar circulations of male labor power in Mexico helping to normalize both the offer of a kidney from Pablo (notably, not from his wife), as well as Don Jaime's ability to solicit it in exchange for the valuable land resource over which he had control. Like a mirrored version of the story of the German mother made *más mexicana* (in which the possibility of the father donating to save their son seemed never to arise), here the possibility of Pablo's wife offering up her kidney in order to bring in outside resources for the family seemed similarly never at issue.[15]

Indeed, Don Jaime's observation about how very "normal" it seemed that he and Pablo—so similarly situated in so many ways—would help one another in this way references precisely this sense of familiarity and mutual identification. Also familiar was the way that the exchange between the two, though clearly in some sense "marketized," fit quite comfortably within the long-standing norms of relationality, of the everyday back-and-forth of favors and goods that have been so thickly described as a fundamental part of social relations and basic survival in Mexico (Chant 1991; Gonzalez de la Rocha 1994; Lomnitz 1987; Lomnitz and Adler 1977; Selby, et al. 1990).[16] Here, the exchange of kidney for land use was folded into an ongoing series of mutual exchanges and interdependencies that came to bind the people involved together ever more tightly over time. And this ongoing social elaboration of the original biological tie of the transferred kidney worked, eventually, to produce a new form of imagined biological connection in those naturalizing claims of being like father/like son to one another. These are not the depersonalizing—even dehumanizing—effects of the one-time economic exchange assumed in the usual renderings of bodily commodification. Rather, in Don Jaime's case, the initial kidney transaction became the starting point for ramifying social connections between not just organ-giver and organ-receiver but beyond them as well. From that initial interpellative moment when Pablo (and his wife) first imagined his kidney as detachable and exchangeable, the meaning and effects—both social and economic—of this particular kidney exchange have continued to evolve and change over time, and no doubt are continuing to do so beyond the point where I have been able to track them.

Like other organ exchanges, the effects of Don Jaime's story can also be traced out far beyond that donor-recipient dyad. The two men's families, of course, were clearly drawn into a new set of relations by the flesh-for-land-use bargain between them. Yet also drawn into the story of this exchange were the neighbors of both men, observing them at a distance, speculating about the terms of the transaction, and circulating uneasy, titillated rumors about what might have passed between them. It is hard to say what the effect on these other observers over time might be. Will they, as Don Jaime hoped, come to see the exchange in a different, more benevolent light as they observe their relationship over time? Or will local suspicions about their case feed fears about the ease of organ selling, further solidifying some people's sense of living under an unsettlingly slippery State? Or both, in turn, at different times and for different people?

And what of the transplant program staff who were privy to the pair's candid accounting of the terms of their kidney-for-land-use exchange? Most staff I knew who had come into contact with them reacted with a sort of wry embarrassment over the case, embarrassment that seemed to operate in (at least) two registers. In one register, there was a slightly sheepish sense that this was clearly different—and more morally questionable—from the idealized, iconic form of familial (and presumptively altruistic) living donation on which the local transplant endeavor depended. Yet neither did the case quite conform to the horror-story images of black market kidney bazaars from other parts of the world. Just as the you-help-me, I'll-help-you reciprocal dynamic felt familiar to Don Jaime and Pablo, so too—for at least some staff—did their transaction seem most like a new variation on long-standing patterns of survival strategies in Mexico. Hence the sense of a reaction more mild than shock or outright condemnation—yet nonetheless not wholly comfortable—that mention of their case so often seemed to provoke.

And in another register, transplant staff sometimes remarked with a certain bemusement on the simplicity of the two men's apparent lack of awareness that their arrangement might be deemed inappropriate, even, perhaps, illegal. For some of the urban professionals who worked in the transplant program, the two men's lack of guile about their exchange seemed further evidence of the deep divide between urban and rural worlds in Mexico. The apparent naiveté of the two campesinos in this regard could thus be read as a sign of their innocence in both senses of the word, rendering them as guiltless, but also childlike. This was a reading heavily charged—perhaps particularly in the presence of a gringa anthropologist—with the ambivalent mixture of nostalgic admiration and condescension so often characteristic of urban/rural relations writ large in that setting. Theirs was a complex response in which awareness of global ethical standards about organ selling mingled with a sense of local norms of rural custom and reciprocal relationality. Though this complexity produced some moral ambivalence about the case, it did not, notably, provoke any official attempt to block the donation.

The deeply personalizing and socializing effects of Don Jaime's organ exchange are, of course, just one version of how such stories might go. And while no one would argue that Don Jaime's story is the norm for what happens when kidneys are commodified, neither was it wholly unique. During the course of my fieldwork, I also met a woman, Maria, who was in the process of being studied to donate as a nonrelated living donor to Faustina, a younger woman from her neighborhood. The two women were distant acquaintances (as was almost everyone in their small colonia) but Maria hadn't known that Faustina was sick until she ran into her on the street one day and commented on how terrible she looked. When she learned of her illness and of her need for a kidney, she told me that she started thinking about the possibility of donating herself—she said it occurred to her immediately because she had a distant relative who had donated to a sibling several years ago and was fine. Maria recounted how the two began to talk more intimately after that first meeting, and as she learned about how Faustina and her husband had only been able to have one child because of her illness, her heart simply went out to her. She said: "I began to compare her life to my own, I've already had all my children, I've had a good life, full life, so why shouldn't I try to help her have the same?"

Both women were open about their agreement that Maria would receive help for rent and food during the time she was recuperating from the surgery. As in Don Jaime's case, the two families were of roughly equivalent socioeconomic status, both struggling among the hardscrabble working class of Mexico. And also, as in Don Jaime's case, gender seems significant here as well: Maria was estranged from her husband and was thus supporting herself and her now nearly grown children—she had no male recourse for bringing in outside resources. Yet providing her kidney to another woman, someone she knew, at least slightly, and whose own life struggles as a wife and mother were deeply resonant for her, helped to fold the organ transfer into the pattern of other familiar—even familial—forms of exchange. Indeed, when interviewed separately, both women spoke warmly about one another: "They treat me just like family," said the donor. "They visit my house sometimes; they have gotten to know my children." Faustina, for her part, was touched by Maria's empathy and concern: "She really worries about me. She even brought me *caldo* [broth] when I was sick and tells me all the time to take care of myself. We've become close, going through all this, like sisters."

Upon first meeting them, Faustina and Maria's case thus seemed much like Don Jaime's, a story of the possibilities for a sort of fictive kinship to emerge from what began as a more commodity-like exchange.[17] Yet here too, the importance of tracking their story out over a wider range of time and relationships emerged when I encountered the donor, Maria, again on a return trip to Guadalajara. Passing her by chance in the hospital court-yard one day, I learned during a hastily snatched conversation that Maria was still in regular touch with Faustina a year or so after the donation and transplant surgeries, and that both seemed to be doing well. I also learned that Maria's estranged husband now was planning to donate a kidney as well, also to a stranger and also in exchange for some unspecified form of help. She told me: "He saw how well it went with me, and I guess it made him think. He gets desperate, with the drinking and the trouble with his work, and so now he's going to try this with his kidney. Who knows if they'll accept him, with everything he has, who knows—but he says he's going to try." There was little time to learn much more about Maria's husband as she hurried off to an appointment, but even just these scant lineaments of his story suggest how the interpellative hailing of transplant can reverber-ate along paths both predictable and unsettling. Thus we can see how the story of Maria's kidney exchange did indeed expand the field of moral (and economic) action, touching off possibilities for another potential organ transaction, one that will follow its own path over time and across different gradients of need, power, and social connection.

Alongside these complex stories of kidney exchanges that were both commodity-like and deeply embedded in—and productive of—social re-lations, there were, of course, other more explicitly, starkly marketized stories to tell as well. Josefina, for example, was a well coifed and well-to-do matron from one of the wealthy suburban enclaves just outside the city. She had been cared for primarily in a private clinic during the course of her developing kidney disease, and her nephrologist shifted her briefly to the IMSS program (where he also held an appointment) to carry out the transplant surgery. She arrived at the IMSS hospital with her donor, a young man described rather tersely to one and all as "a family friend," in tow, and all of her protocol testing complete. The donor, Juan, was a young man in his early twenties whose inexpensive clothing, style of speech, and slightly wary attitude suggested a social class well beneath Josefina's.

During the few days that the pair was hospitalized for their surgeries and recovery, Juan told several nurses that he was leaving for the United States as soon as he was fully recovered in order to study to become an engineer. This led most staff members to assume (quietly and among themselves) that Josefina was paying for him to go to the United States in return for his kidney. Although a number of staff were clearly disturbed by the case and continued to gossip about it guardedly for months afterward, no one moved to prevent the "donation" from taking place. After being released from the hospital, Josefina returned to seeing her physician in his private clinic. Juan, who did not have rights to the IMSS system on his own, was not seen or heard from again by anyone in the IMSS transplant program.

In Josefina's case, the power of the privileged to access the organs of the poor seems clearly in evidence, and though I was not able to track their relationship over time, the possibilities for an emerging fictive kinship to grow from their exchange certainly seem vanishingly slim. Indeed, the general outlines of this case feel perhaps all too familiar from the richly rendered accountings we now have of organ selling worldwide. Yet here too, tracking what happens next in their story—over time and across relationships— seems vital. How did Josefina account for her new kidney to family, friends, and acquaintances? Was her choice to use Juan's kidney driven by a desire to protect willing potential donors from her own family circle (as Lawrence Cohen and Sherine Hamdy have reported is often the case in India and Egypt, respectively; Cohen 1999, 2002, 2005; Hamdy 2013)? Or was this a decision driven by the desperation of having no other choice of donor? And in either case, what happened to those motivating relational circumstances over time in the aftermath of her transplant surgery? Similarly for Juan, we would want to know both about what drove his choice to enter into this exchange relation with Josefina, and about how that decision was situated within and subsequently affected his own network of relationships and responsibilities and life possibilities.

The fact that I cannot answer these questions here is also, itself, part of the story of the wider relational effects of this particular organ exchange.

For their case was marked, during their brief stay in the IMSS hospital, by an unusual reticence among staff, a reticence both to talk *to* them, and to talk much *about* them. In a setting where the vast majority of donor/ recipient pairs were related, Josefina and Juan made many of the transplant program staff uncomfortable, and while no one moved to block the donation, interactions with both seemed more limited and markedly less warm than with most other patients in the program. At work in this relative distancing seemed to be a deliberate will not to know—not to know more about the precise circumstances of their case and thus be compelled, perhaps, to action. This produced what we might call a deliberately unknowing complicity that seems related to Stanley Cavell's notion of the critical difference between a failure of knowledge (as a piece of ignorance) and a failure to acknowledge (as an avoidance, a denial of the Other) (Cavell 1976). In *choosing* not to know more about them—not, as Cavell might have it, to acknowledge them—staff were aided by the aloofness that Josefina in particular adopted with one and all. This was an aloofness that may have simply been part of her character or her class position, but could also have been (and by some, was) read as a measure of her guilt. In this way, Josefina's standoffishness and relative silence stands in stark contrast with the perceived "innocent" openness of Don Jaime and Pablo. The deliberate avoidance exercised by staff seemed to extend not just to the patients themselves but to the physician who engineered their admittance into the hospital as well, for during the time of their case his appearances on the wards were brief and far chillier than was the norm for day-to-day interactions among the generally close-knit staff.

All of this produced an atmosphere of silence around the case that, coupled with Josefina and Juan's own refusals to speak with me, made it difficult to penetrate more deeply into the situation, much less to follow the story out of the hospital doors and into their subsequent lives. It seemed to me at the time that to push too hard to follow more closely the contours of this particular story would risk rupturing the relationships I had so carefully built among program staff and jeopardize being able to follow all of the other stories that now make up this book. Yet whether my own form of deliberate unknowing in this case was a question of ethnographic instinct or a failure of courage, I now find hard to say. The work of some of those who have chosen to follow the trail of organ selling suggests that there are costs and compromises and tough choices to be made in delving into that world, and Nancy Scheper-Hughes in particular has written eloquently about this in her accounts of the "undercover ethnography" that her work has required (2004). In my own field setting, where Josefina's case stood out precisely because it was such a departure from the everyday life of the local transplant wards, the potential costs of pursuit seemed too high. Yet this severing of the story, as well as the chilling effect on staff interactions both with the admitting doctor and among themselves, also form part of the relational effects rippling out from this particular case.

In the months that followed, staff, particularly female social workers, would sometimes make oblique but disapproving reference to Josefina's case—and to the physician who had brought them into the program. Though day-to-day interactions with Josefina's physician gradually returned to the normal tenor of alternating formality and jocularity that was typical among program staff, Aurelia, for instance, quietly commented to me one day with a darkly meaningful nod toward his departing back: "Well, there he goes, all jokes and compliments today, yes? But he's not the one I would trust with my mother, my son, is he? Not after what we've seen. . . ." And with a shake of her head, she turned back to the eager line of patients perpetually pressing to get through her door.

Some months after Josefina's case a conversation arose in the winding down moments of the late afternoon in the transplant coordinator's office about another, earlier case where the relationship between donor and recipient was also nonfamilial and, to many, suspicious. All agreed that such cases were rare, but unsettling. Yet when I asked whether any such cases had ever been halted, the group of social workers also agreed that the answer was no, each of those few cases had gone through—with discomfort, but without dispute. Responding to the implicit critique embedded in my question, several social workers went on to say that they felt somewhat helpless in the face of the impossibility of knowing the truth of the relationship between two people. As one put it, referring to a case in which a father brought in someone he claimed was a coworker to donate to his son: "It's not fair to stop it if we don't know for sure—and the reality is, we *can't* know for sure. And anyway, it's still saving a young boy's life." A nurse, referring back to Josefina's case chimed in: "Look, if that kid gets a chance to go to the U.S. and make a good life for himself, who am I to say that it wasn't worth it? How do I know what it's worth to him to give a kidney? Should I have the power to say he can't take that opportunity if he wants it?"

Their replies neatly captured the double-edged difficulty of how one could know the truth of such an exchange, as well as how one might judge that truth, even if it were known. At work here was in part what legal scholar Margaret Radin has called the double-bind of prohibiting organ selling: it does nothing to address the inequality and desperation which make some people willing to sell their organs, and perhaps does more to protect those of us who can afford to debate ethical principles and indulge our moral squeamishness (Radin 1987, 1996). Yet bound up with the complex moral economies explored in previous chapters of those deemed worthy to receive organs and those under pressure to provide them, such responses also invoked the paralyzing effects of what Lawrence Cohen has called the "transcendent ethics" of the justifying appeal to transplantation's life-saving properties (2005). Out of the opacity of recipient/donor relations, such salvational possibilities were made to stand out and justify inaction, while the life-risking possibilities for the donor receded, rendered invisible, unremarked, and illegitimate as a basis for stopping a questionable organ transfer.

In the end, as with the gift analytic, the figure of the commodity does indeed illuminate critical aspects of these still-unfinished stories of Don Jaime and Faustina and Josefina and others like them, bringing the marketized terms of bodily exchange and the possibilities for exploitation into analytic focus. Yet here too, it seems worth attending carefully in these cases to the wide-ranging and complicated ripple effects over a more expansive range of time and relationality, attending, that is, to the possibilities for violence and silence, for new forms of fictive kinship and embodied subjectivity, as well as for the reinscription of long-standing patterns of sociality and hierarchy that transplantation may produce. Tracking such effects across not just those who give and those who get organs, but across the extended family, friends, neighbors, transplant professionals, and even observing anthropologists who come into contact with them, provides additional dimension and depth to our understanding of the social, material, and ethical consequences of such flesh-for-money bargains.

Everything Is More Complex . . . So What?

Ultimately, why might it matter to try to open up the iconic gift/commodity analytic? Why bother—as I have here—with the painstaking building of this more processual picture of complexity and ongoing change over time? Perhaps all of this storytelling, compelling though the human details may be, is just a complementary analytic move, part of an all-too-familiar intellectual back-and-forth: with one hand we scholars strip down and condense into tight, useful generalizations, while with the other we protest that, of course, all of this is far more complicated than such generalizations suggest.[18] And yet, in the particular stripping down that the gift/commodity analytic provides, it is not just a loss of complexity that is at stake. For those iconic figures of gift and commodity are not merely condensed representations: they are representations heavily charged with moral and spatial associations as well. Such associations work to produce powerful effects of recognition and rejection, of identification and distancing, so that in transplantation the much-feared depersonalizing, even dehumanizing effects of the commodity become a problem run most rampant "out there" in the poorest regions of the world. While in turn, the socializing, personalizing, enmeshing effects of the gift become something to explore primarily in the more privileged spaces of EuroAmerican transplantation. And in the process, some modes and spaces of organ exchange are reassuringly exoticized, while others, in turn, are comfortably, comfortingly domesticated.

Crucial here are the ways that not just particular—usually more gift-like—forms of organ exchange are domesticated in the process, but so too the entire transplant endeavor itself. In chapter 1 we saw how the iconic image of *la mujer sufrida* worked to produce the ethical domesticity not just of living donation by women, but of living donation in general. This rendering of living organ donation as so seemingly familiar and familial, so simultaneously natural and national in character, has been central to materializing transplant in Mexico. I want to suggest that the iconic notions of gift and commodity, like that image of la mujer sufrida, may accomplish similar important work, focusing attention in ways that also serve—perhaps paradoxically—to enable the transplant endeavor as a whole. And so clinicians and politicians and bioethicists and even we anthropologists delve into the terms of organ exchange, debating passionately over what sorts of equivalencies of bodies and social relations and value can—and ought to—be made, while other, perhaps more fundamental questions may go largely unasked. Too tight a focus on the issue of organs as gifts or commodities elides a more basic set of issues: not just does trading a kidney for cash create injustice and threaten human dignity, but does trading the health of one person (the donor) for that of another (the recipient) always already threaten the same? Like the reluctant donor who declines to offer up a kidney in case his own child needs it someday, in focusing our attention too tightly on the question of organs as gifts or commodities we perhaps already cede the terms of debate.

And so, in the end, I love these messy, on the ground, over time and always-incomplete ethnographic stories for themselves. But I love them also for the way that telling them works against the powerful pull and politics of the icon. Rendered in rich (though inescapably insufficient) detail, such transplant tales become harder both to exoticize *and* to domesticate. These stories seem to me to be both deeply, familiarly human and strikingly strange and unsettling, all at once. And in the realm of transplantation, this seems intellectually, politically, and ethically useful if it helps us to remain alert to that pull to demonize and exoticize and, equally so, to the impulse to heroize and domesticate. For these are impulses to frame, to contain, and to apportion blame that anthropology may well, at times, participate in, but which it is also—perhaps uniquely, ethnographically—positioned to disrupt.

6. Scientists, Saints, and Monsters in Transplant Medicine

He was a familiar figure in and around the hospitals where I worked in Guadalajara. El Niño Doctor de los Enfermos (Baby Jesus, Doctor of the Sick) appeared on small prayer cards bought from street vendors outside the hospital entrances (as in the version reproduced in figure 6.1) or in larger paintings or statues as the centerpiece of small shrines sometimes set up in hospital hallways or the waiting areas of the intensive care units. The image of El Niño Doctor depicts an infant Jesus, dressed in a doctor's whites with a crown of glory over his head. In the versions I collected in Guadalajara, the words Dr. Jesus were usually embroidered on the white coat, often in the style particular to the SSa public charity hospital system in the city.[1] Not just modern-day healer, however, Jesus here is also, himself, a patient, as signaled by the old-fashioned wheelchair upon which the son of God sits in many of these images. In a study centrally concerned with the question of icons, here at last is an icon in the classically religious sense, one that serves as a vivid touchstone for the task I take up in this chapter: exploring how notions of science and the supernatural, hope and horror, self and other operate not only in imaginings of transplantation itself, but in the self-fashionings of the clinicians who enact it, as well as the scholars who seek to analyze it.

Figure 6.1 *El Niño Doctor de los Enfermos* (Baby Jesus, Doctor of the Sick).
Photo by Taylor England.

To the largely secular eyes of a gringa anthropologist, El Niño Doctor seemed at first an intriguingly odd bricolage—putting the baby Jesus in contemporary doctor's garb was something impossible to imagine in the suburban, East Coast Catholic Church of my own childhood. Equally hard to imagine was the idea of such an image, surrounded by an unruly accretion of votives, flowers, and small handwritten notes and drawings, being allowed to linger in the stark, antiseptic halls of the intensive care units where I have spent time in the United States. Indeed, the image initially tugged at me because of the way it seemed to transgress what felt like boundaries between the sacred and the profane, with those everyday trappings of the medical profession appearing not just incongruous but something bordering on sacrilegious when draped around the son of God. Not just a matter of transgressive *content* however, the *context* of the image too—showing up in those ICU hallways—seemed also to transgress the same set of boundaries, but in the opposite direction. That is, the presence of El Niño Doctor in the hallowed halls of high-tech medicine felt—to me, at first—almost like another sort of sacrilege, a somewhat startling intrusion of religion in a space wholly dedicated to an endeavor of a different kind.

That experience of strangeness in my own first encounters with El Niño Doctor recapitulated a long colonial and anthropological history of imagining self against other through the categories of science and religion, categories that also evoke ideas about the sacred and the profane, about salvation and corruption. Like the concepts of gift and commodity explored in chapter 5, these too can be seen as analytic icons in anthropology, forming other key axes along which ideas about difference and affinity, rationality and irrationality, past and future have long been explored and asserted (Durkheim [1915] 1964; Malinowski 1948; Tambiah 1990). In the transplant context, both Margaret Lock in Japan and Sherine Hamdy in Egypt have explored the effect of spiritual beliefs on the local shape of transplantation but have also attended carefully to the problematic ways in which religion is so often marshaled as a politically expedient explanatory device, a readily available label that works to establish distance and apportion blame (Hamdy 2012; Lock 2001). And so here I approach El Niño Doctor (and the complex of relations and values and possibilities he entails) with caution, intrigued by his hospital presence as ethnographic fact but also alert to the problematic presumption that *of course* Catholic saints would make an appearance in a study of organ transfer in Mexico.

My own initial, almost knee-jerk response to the figure as an intriguingly anachronistic intrusion of sedimented tradition into the high modern space of transplant medicine was quickly unsettled by learning some of the (very recent) history of El Niño Doctor. Hardly a harbinger from some hoary, belief-bound past, El Niño Doctor proved to be emblematic instead of the dynamic and unruly nature of present-day popular Catholicism in Mexico. For El Niño Doctor is very much a contemporary—and sometimes controversial—phenomenon, a modern-day twist on the biblical stories from the Gospels of Jesus as healer of the sick. A key site of religious innovation operating at the margins of officially sanctioned Catholicism, the cult of El Niño Doctor is one of the fastest growing in Mexico in recent years (Hughes 2012). Both wildly popular and deeply populist, El Niño Doctor also bears a kinship with another, even more provocative, emergent Catholic icon in Mexico, the "narco-saint" La Santa Muerte (Saint Death).[2] Patron saint of both narcotraficantes and police officers, La Santa Muerte symbolizes the threat of violent death that surrounds both of these figures in contemporary Mexican society. And, as such, La Santa Muerte underscores the frequent illegibility of the line between them in the current slippery State conditions of the brutal drug war. In a different register, El Niño Doctor also indexes a shifting, uncertain politics of life in a local world where access to both medicine and miracles must be agilizado—that is, where salvation in both biological and spiritual registers is experienced as deeply contingent on the skilled mobilization of personal relationships and the savvy exchange of favors.

Like many of the figures upon which I have drawn throughout this book—The Two Fridas, La Guadalupe/La Malinche, and indeed the bodies of both organ donors and organ recipients themselves—El Niño Doctor is a productively ambivalent image. A whole host of seeming oppositions are commingled and condensed here, not just between science and religion, sacred and profane, modernity and tradition, but between healer and patient, savior and supplicant, as well. Moreover, as both wheelchair-enthroned infant and the medically trained Son of God, this is an image from which emanates an uncanny conjunction of vulnerable frailty and transcendent power. Not just simultaneously fragile and potent, it is worth noting that Jesus in his infant form is also, sometimes, downright dangerous. For there is a long tradition of so-called lost gospel stories, such as the one in which a mischievous baby Jesus crawls up into the clouds, leaving his eager but all-too-earthly playmates to follow behind and tumble to their deaths.[3] Also contained within the tender, venerated body of the infant Jesus is, always, the seed of suffering and sacrifice that await Him. Offering the salvation of eternal life through his own broken body, the Christ figure resonates powerfully with the logics of transplantation and the suffering bodies of organ donors both living and dead. And so—like transplant itself—El Niño Doctor seems to signal potentials for both life-saving and life-taking. Thus densely indexed in this haunting image are both the sacrificial demands and the salvational promises of medicine and religion alike.

Such complex interminglings between the received categories of science and religion, as well as between the promise of life and the threat of death, have already surfaced in many of the stories encountered in previous chapters: as transplant coordinators set off on a *manda* to give thanks for a beloved toddler surviving his liver transplant, for example, or as clinicians engaged in thoughtful debate over the precise moment when the soul leaves the body in brain death. Indeed, as we have seen, transplantation's successes in Mexico were often regarded not just as modernist triumph of scientific mastery but as equally powerful evidence of the efficacy of carefully cultivated divine intervention. Across such stories, the everyday interpenetration of biomedical technology, spiritual faith, and sometimes inexplicable mystery was pervasive during my time in Guadalajara, both suffusing and sustaining the transplant endeavor not only for patients and family members but often for professionals as well.

Yet transplantation was not merely sacralized. Transplantation in Mexico (as elsewhere) was also, always, haunted by darker potentials, by the specter of back alley butchery and occult body snatchings. Such potentials surfaced in public panics like the scandal noted in chapter 2 over accusations of stealing the corneas from corpses in the SSa hospital. They surfaced too in more private insinuations like those that flowed between transplant professionals and government officials in their uneasy dealings around brain-dead donors. Such widely floating fears about the spectral face of transplantation were clearly attuned to and precipitated by the grim realities of the contemporary global market in human organs, and only compounded by the day-to-day experience of life in a slippery State. But these specters drew as well on a deep local history of popular fears about the plundering of bodily vitality to meet others' (often foreigners') need/greed. This is a history marked by centuries of regional storytelling, populated by images of spookily pale conquistadors coveting the vigor of Indian blood, of twentieth-century American airplane pilots in search of blood and fat to fuel their engines, and—most recently—of body-snatching grin-gos in search of organs for transplantation (Adams 1999; Ayora-Diaz 2000; Campion-Vincent 1997; Wachtel 1994).[4]

Emergent here is a tense oscillation between sacralization and a sort of demonization that seems a constituent dimension of transplant's iconic pull, one that we find echoed virtually everywhere it is practiced. Both life-giving and death-ridden, transplant medicine has, since its earliest days, invited awe and horror in nearly equal measure (Fox and Swazey 1974, 1992; Lock 2001; Sharp 2006; Youngner 1990). As such, transplant seems to carry with it always a deep moral duality, one that recalls the notion of the icon in its religious form, as a saintly image that can both incite fervent devotion and invite suspicion of being an idol, a false god.

Poised precariously on the knife's edge of this moral duality is the transplant professional, a figure I take up in this chapter as a focal point for exploring the intermingling of exuberant celebration and anxious con-demnation (in both secular and sacred registers) that surrounds the trans-plant endeavor. Respected, remunerated, even, on occasion, lionized for the life-saving work in which they were engaged, transplant professionals also figured frequently as the source of danger in those widely circulating horror-story visions of transplant as well—as the corrupt, greedy surgeon willing to steal the organs of the unwitting, unwilling poor, for instance. Thus posed as dangerous by (and to) others, transplant professionals in Guadalajara often felt themselves endangered by such public fears, tainted by suspicion and the ever-present threat of scandal that seemed always ready to erupt in the slippery State conditions in which they lived and worked. Having devoted much attention in previous chapters to the way transplan-tation offered possibilities both redemptive and endangering for those who give up organs as well as those who receive them, in this final chapter I turn more explicitly to those who worked to enact such organ transfers. In doing so, I draw on the term *professional* in part for its pragmatic inclusiveness, for its ability to mark the sense of common purpose and commitment that pulled together the diverse range of experts (from social worker to surgeon, from nurse to nutritionist) who worked together to make transplantation come to matter in Mexico. But also useful to the work of this chapter is the way that *professional* invokes ideas not only about cultivated expertise and a shared moral code of conduct but also—harking back to its roots in the verb *to profess*—a provocative sense of doubleness in its possibilities for both faith and falsity, for affirming belief *and* for asserting a dubious claim. Pursuing such questions of duality and morality, as well as of expert knowledge and belief-based faith, will offer yet another angle of inquiry into the notion of the iconic in transplantation, and in anthropology itself.

A Liver Jumps with Joy

One slow, sticky afternoon in the SSa intensive care unit, about six months into my fieldwork, Lupe told me the story of the first time she had successfully convinced a family to donate the organs of a brain-dead patient. Lupe was a trained social worker who had taken up work with the transplant program out of a sense of personal destiny: she had lost an adored young niece to kidney disease and afterward felt called to help build the transplant program in her own hospital. The work was difficult at first—voluntary, lonely, and subject to the criticism and suspicion of many of her colleagues, friends, and family, who wondered why she would want to get mixed up in something so *feo* (ugly). It was also nerve-wracking—it was Lupe who confessed that she nearly always vomited from fear and anxiety before approaching the families of potential donors, at least in the early days. But she persisted, buoyed by the commitment of a charismatic transplant surgeon, recently returned to the SSa from training in the United States, who was eager to initiate a liver transplant program for which he desperately needed cadaveric donors.[5] The first few families she approached all vehemently rejected—sometimes sorrowfully, sometimes angrily—the idea of organ donation.

And so it was with a sense of mounting frustration and undermined confidence that Lupe learned that Alma, a liver patient to whom she had grown very close during her increasingly frequent hospitalizations, had just been readmitted to the hospital in terminal liver failure. Without a new liver, Alma would surely die within days or even hours. Shortly after hearing the news about Alma, Lupe learned that a patient had just come into the ICU after sustaining a massive head wound in a car accident. Talking with ICU staff, she learned that they considered the young man's case to be a hopeless one and, with the help of the transplant surgeon, Lupe entreated them to carry out the still-unfamiliar additional testing necessary to formally establish a diagnosis of brain death.

Having carefully shepherded the diagnostic process to completion, Lupe at last approached the brain-dead young man's family, a bundle of nerves, fear, and hope. And she was immediately, furiously, rejected. The devastated family members—the patient's young wife, several siblings, and his elderly mother—were adamant that they wanted nothing to do with the idea of organ donation. Lupe, however, made desperate and bold by her awareness of Alma's dying presence just upstairs, pressed the point as she had never done before. She literally begged them just to let her talk to them: "Please just let me tell you about this, it is so beautiful, I promise you," she pleaded, "please just let me talk to you and I know you will see that it is not what you think." They grudgingly agreed to let her stay, and there ensued a several-hour-long session in which Lupe kept the family company in their heartbroken vigil, sometimes just letting them talk, and sometimes returning to her own agenda, trying to get them to see how urgent and how transcendent she understood organ donation to be.

She told me that during those hours with the young man's family she listened intently to their disjointed, distraught conversation, remaining constantly alert to clues as to how to appeal to them, how best to pitch the idea of donation. At one point, the mother of the potential donor bemoaned the many things that would be left undone by her son's untimely death, among them, the tragedy that he had never been able to fulfill a lifelong dream of going to Tijuana. As Lupe described it, a flash of intuition went off like a light in her head at the mention of Tijuana, and seizing on this opportunity, she asked them: "What if he could still fulfill that dream? What if he could go to Tijuana?" The family, not surprisingly, was momentarily bewildered by a sense of wild hope at her words, not yet understanding that she meant he could fulfill his dream through organ donation. Lupe went on to explain that her liver patient so desperately in need of this donation was, herself, from Tijuana; if she received a liver, she would eventually return there to live with her family. In this way, Lupe reiterated, he could truly "live out" his dream in the body of another person. Such an opportunity, she suggested, was nothing short of a miracle. This miraculous conjunction of donor dreams and recipient residence proved to be a crucial turning point, and after some additional uncertain, but also awe-struck back-and-forth, the family finally consented to donation.

During the hours Lupe had spent with the family, the rest of the transplant staff had been frantically engaged in all of the necessary backstage tasks, running tests, calling in surgical staff, and booking operating rooms. Once consent was received, the donation and transplant procedures quickly swung into action. As she was wheeled into the operating room the patient Alma was hopeful but also terrified, scarcely able to believe that a liver had finally come through for her. On his way to scrub in, the surgeon, Dr. Paredes, stopped by her gurney and took her hands in his, telling her to be calm, to have faith because, as he put it: "These are God's hands in there, not mine." The grueling ten-hour surgery that ensued was a success, and Alma's new liver started functioning immediately.

Several days into her recovery, Alma was told about her donor's lifelong desire to see Tijuana, and the pivotal role her own connection to that city had played in the family's consent.[6] For Alma, in those anxious early days of the posttransplant period, it was a story that reassuringly conferred a sense of destiny and durability to her unlikely survival—a sense that this particular liver was meant for her, and that it would *want* to stay with her. It was a feeling confirmed by her experience upon returning home for the first time with her new liver. When she first caught sight of Tijuana from the car window, Alma told me, "I literally felt the liver jump inside me and fill with joy."

This arresting image, of her transplanted liver jumping for joy, is one that Alma not only shared with me but also frequently recounted in public *testimonios* that she later was invited to give as part of various public education efforts staged by the local transplant community. In many such settings Alma told her story with gusto and reverence but also with astute awareness of its power in counteracting the gruesome imagery that transplantation so often conjured in the popular imagination. Here, instead, was a profoundly human, socializing, and also spiritualizing vision of this iconic biotechnology. Clearly more than just an objectified, extractable "pound of flesh," the leaping, joy-filled liver in this story carried the emotions and extended the experience of the much-mourned donor from whom it came. And in feeling and sharing in that joy, Alma entered into not just a new phase of her own restored life but into a curious ongoing relation with her donor as well, whose liver both sustained her own body and seemingly retained some sense of independent liveliness, animation, even emotion.

Like Alma, the transplant coordinator Lupe also told her version of the story as both a source of private wonder and a tool for public teaching. For Lupe, Alma's survival, rapid recovery, and joyfully leaping liver deeply affirmed her own sense of spiritual rightness in the wrenching work of asking for organs. She regarded the serendipity of Alma's case, quite simply, as miraculous. After hearing the story for the first time in private conversation that slow, sticky afternoon, I went on to hear it many more times. For Lupe told Alma's story frequently, compellingly in the training sessions she had begun to organize to teach other social workers how to ask for organs in their own hospitals. In such settings it was a story of salvation *and* of strategy, of trusting in the divine authorization of the transplant endeavor and of remaining calculatingly alert for just the right angle to persuade a reluctant family. And rather than creating contradiction, for Lupe, it was precisely this intermingling of spirituality and instrumentality that gave the story such power.

It seems significant that this was a tale that took time to share, a story offered up to me only after many months of spending time with Lupe, after a wide range of experiences together, ranging from the tedium of stagnant, slow afternoons in the hospital to the tense, hectic middle-of-the-night pace of a possible donation. There seems a telling contrast here with the story of the German mother who became *más mexicana* by donating a kidney to her son, that story with which I was greeted so enthusiastically, so insistently, immediately upon entering the field. Though the story of Alma's liver jumping for joy was hardly a clandestine one, it was also not the first one with which to regale a newly arrived gringa anthropologist (who might well be full of those familiar technology-out-of-place assumptions, after all). And while both Alma and Lupe told and retold the story in various public venues, there were other venues in which it was markedly not voiced, venues in which transplant was given a very different kind of public face. When giving interviews to the press, or advocating for support from government officials, transplant professionals generally offered up—not surprisingly—a vision of transplantation carefully stripped of such dimensions of mystery and spirituality, one in which scientific rigor, economic rationality, and a high modern technological gloss were instead made central. Evident here is the way that more scientific and more spiritual facets of transplant's iconic face are brought to the fore at different moments, for different interlocutors, and to sometimes dramatically different purpose and effect.

Perhaps even more striking in the story of that leaping, joy-filled liver— as in the figure of El Niño Doctor himself—is the somewhat different set of relations that emerge among those iconic analytic categories of science and the supernatural. This is clearly not a local world in which religion seems to wither away in the face of science, nor where science has been undermined by religious irrationality. So often in accounts both anthropological and popular, science and religion have been rendered as oppositional—if not outright antagonistic—systems of belief, enacting a familiar co-constitution of categories through contrast. Yet here transplant professional and transplant patient together describe a world in which the technological achievements of transplant and God's miraculous power instead become proofs of one another, that is, a world in which we have transplant because it is God's will, and transplant is, itself, evidence of God's will in the world.

This was a vision voiced not just by patients and their families but, as the leaping liver story highlights, by transplant professionals themselves. Though this occurred, of course, in particular performative settings—in teaching both strategy and a certain reverent structure of feeling to new initiates to transplant work, for instance—but *not* in international professional meetings, or national debates over how to spend health-care pesos. Attending carefully to the spaces and relations within which a more spiritually infused understanding of transplant is made to show its face—as well as to those where it decidedly does not—is clearly necessary. Yet I want to take seriously matters of subjectivity as well as strategy, to attend to the ways in which it was not only patients who were acted upon and altered through the medium of transplant (a dynamic by now familiar from many settings where transplant is practiced). Rather, in Lupe's spiritual call to the difficult, tainting work of organ donation, as well as in Dr. Paredes's invocation of his own surgical hands of God, we hear hints of the way not just those who give and receive organs, but also the professionals who enact such transfers, may experience their involvement with transplantation in transformative, transcendent ways that merit tracking as well.

"Frankenstein Syndrome": Who's the Monster?

There is an intriguing diagnostic label in transplant medicine, used to refer to patients who have failed to fully integrate a transplanted organ into their sense of self: "Frankenstein syndrome" (Beidel 1987; Sharp 2006, 2007; Youngner 1996). It is a label sometimes invoked when a patient is deemed unhealthily preoccupied with her organ donor's identity and its potential for impact on her own tastes, personality, emotions, and abilities. Despite this pathologizing label, the experience of being altered—beyond the biological—by the introduction of another person's organ has been widely reported for transplant recipients worldwide (Fox and Swazey 1974, 1992; Lock 2001; Sharp 2006). As just one example, recall Rosa's account, from chapter 5, of the more assertive personality and newly curly hair acquired—unexpectedly—as aspects of her sister Mago along with the donated kidney.

Other transplant recipients report changes such as a newfound love for fried chicken, a sudden craving to douse everything in outrageously spicy hot sauce, or an inexplicable attraction to a certain shade of blue (tastes, in each case, subsequently revealed to mirror those of their donors).[7]

Though the medicalized label of Frankenstein imputes a sense of monstrosity, transplant recipients in Guadalajara were by no means always—or even usually—distressed by such experiences.[8] Like Alma's experience of her leaping liver, many transplant recipients found the sense of connection with not just the material body but the self, the person, the spirit, of the donor a rich source for making meaning out of the uncanny experience of incorporating another's organ. To be sure, some patients could be disquieted by such possibilities for connection beyond the purely biological, and differences in gender, or large gaps in age between donor and recipient, were sometimes a particular source of uneasiness. Padre Tomas's reflection on his transformation "from stallion to gelding" with the receipt of his sister's kidney, described in chapter 4, offers one example of this. And still other patients rejected such ideas entirely, firmly asserting their own sense of uncompromised identity and of a machine-like body "fixed" by transplantation with comments like: "It's my kidney now, it's just a part of me and I don't even think about it. It's simple, like getting your car fixed. I had a broken part, and now it's fixed. But it hasn't changed *me*, the real *me*" (Luis Carlos, SSa, day laborer). Yet for many patients, the lived experience of receiving a transplant—whether from a living, known donor or an unknown, cadaveric one—often complicated biomedicine's familiar claims for a clean, mechanistic separation between body and self.

Despite their own occasional use of the pathologizing label of "Frankenstein syndrome," Mexican transplant professionals too—as we have seen—found themselves in sometimes shifting relation with such foundational scientific claims about the body/self, subject/object divide. On one level, the entire practice of transplantation can seem to rest on a vision of objectified body as machine, made up of interchangeable parts that carry biological function, but not personality or spirit, between one person and another. It is in this way that transplantation can serve as such a powerful icon of science in all of its rational, objectifying, modernizing glory. Indeed, one might say that transplant represents an ultimate extension of the Cartesian logics of biomedicine that anthropologists and others have so often critiqued.[9] And in certain contexts, this pinnacle-of-science vision was indeed the face of transplantation that professionals and politicians foregrounded and celebrated—in proud public pronouncements, for instance, about successful transplantation as the mark of a modern nation. Yet, as has emerged in various places throughout this book, there were also many moments when transplant professionals not only embraced but felt themselves fundamentally sustained in their own work by a more mysterious, spiritual vision of transplantation.

Just one such example emerged in the transplant coordinator Aurelia's reaction to the experiences of uncanny connection shared by the sisters Mago and Rosa, when she said: "it's so beautiful, how they are connected now . . . this is the mystery, the beauty that keeps us going" (Aurelia, IMSS). A similar sense of beyond-the-biological connection was also evident in a commonplace observation sometimes made by transplant staff that "love makes a difference" in how a transplanted organ fares in its new corporeal home. As one transplant coordinator put it: "When the donor really loves her husband, the kidney just wants to work and the transplant goes well" (Isabel, transplant coordinator, IMSS). And so it seems that Alma's leaping liver was hardly alone in embodying, transporting, and transmitting the emotions and intentionality of the donor from which it came.

Still other possibilities for deeper meaning beyond the strictly scientific emerged in a variety of cases that staff experienced as touched by the inexplicable, the ineffable, even the miraculous. A nurse tells the story of her patient who simply knew, with unshakeable certainty, in the moment just before the phone rang that a kidney had finally come for her—indeed, when she picked up the phone she calmly told the transplant coordinator that she was on her way, before a single word had been spoken. And in telling the story, the nurse shares how the memory never fails to raise the hairs on the back of her own neck (Ana, nurse, IMSS). Or ICU staff are awed by a young brain-dead woman (encountered in chapter 2), whose body—amazingly, unaccountably—withstands multiple and seemingly insurmountable medical crises so that her fierce desire to donate her organs can be carried out. Or, for the social worker Lupe, the timing of Alma's liver donor's fatal accident—just when Alma needed him most—combined with the serendipity of his longing for Tijuana to form an impossibly perfect conjunction, one that she regarded as unmistakably miraculous. For Lupe, and for other transplant professionals I encountered, it was precisely this deeply mysterious and moving quality that sacralized her work in transplant and enabled her to withstand the doubts and disapproval of her family at being "mixed up in something so ugly." And for many transplant staff, though these decidedly were *not* the stories strategically shared with the press or rationally reported to hospital administrators, they were the stories they often loved to tell to—and among—themselves.

Not surprisingly, a sense of the miraculous was not the only explicitly religious framing brought to the range of unsettling experiences produced by the moving of body parts from one person to another. In a context where the imagery and logics of Catholicism and evangelical Christianity carry such considerable cultural force, ideas about resurrection and redemption in particular also often had deep resonance for patients and donor families—as well as for transplant staff themselves.[10] The notion of rising from death to live a new life (albeit in the body of another) in cadaveric donation bears such compelling resemblance to the central drama and promise of Christianity: Christ's own resurrection as proof of the life-after-death that would be granted to His followers. Indeed, in the complex dance of life and death, sacrifice and salvation that transplant requires, possibilities emerge for a sort of doubled resurrection—for the recipient to live on by means of another's body *and* for the donor him- or herself to live on in that body as well. In this way, the organ donor can be made to powerfully symbolize both Christ the Savior and the saved all at once. Or, as the visual idiom of El Niño Doctor might have it: both healer and patient, all at once. Not just a matter of renewed, resurrected life, ideas about redemption, about the conversion of sin and suffering into a kind of spiritual grace, also operated powerfully in notions of how organ donation might make transcendent good come from terrible tragedy.

And even beyond such clearly Christian narratives, a set of long-standing popular traditions in Mexico that bring death deeply into daily life and impart it with a kind of liveliness—traditions like the ubiquitous folk art images of *calaveras* (skeletons) engaged in the trappings and activities of everyday life, and the vibrant *ofrendas* (offerings, altars) set up in honor of the Día de los Muertos (Day of the Dead)—could impart a certain cultural legibility to the very idea of making life possible through death via the medium of transplantation.[11] It was precisely these sorts of uncanny life/death interpenetrations that animated one elderly campesino's bemused, laughing observation to me, on seeing an X-ray of his own skeleton for the first time, "Look, I really *do* have death inside of me!" (Don Oscar, farmer, SSa). For him, the image of a skeleton was one he had only ever seen externalized, in those iconic folk art images of calaveras playing mariachi music, getting married, and offering wry commentary in the political cartoons in which they frequently appear in Mexico. Both familiar and unfamiliar at once, that skeletal image contained on his X-ray film was a medically mediated proof of the deeply embedded nature of death-in-life with which he was already so familiar.

Scholars of transplantation have traced the way narratives of resurrection and redemption emerge across a variety of settings, often emphasizing the instrumental way such narratives are wielded by transplant professionals as a means to ease the way for grieving families to agree to donation (see Sharp 2006 for the United States and Ben-David 2005 for Israel, for example). And, to be sure, transplant professionals in Mexico also recognized and made strategic use of these powerful spiritual resonances in their everyday work, deploying them in a variety of ways that pulled on the possibilities for life-after-death and the redemption of tragedy through the medium of organ donation. And so the families of potential donors were often told, for instance, about how the patients who receive organs pray for their organ donors every single day for the rest of their lives: "Just imagine how quickly someone gets to heaven on all those prayers!" as one transplant coordinator frequently put it (Martina, transplant coordinator, IMSS).[12] Particularly in cases where the cause of death was perceived as shameful, even (literally) damning by families—criminal violence or suicide, for instance—such redemptive promises could, understandably, carry enormous persuasive power.[13] Similarly, the deepest desire of grieving family members to see death reversed and life restored was also often consciously, strategically activated by transplant staff. Recall, for instance, Lupe's question to the family of Alma's liver donor: "What if he could still fulfill that dream? What if he could go to Tijuana?" That unsettling question was utterly pivotal, forming the turning point that led the donor's family to begin to forge a new form of hope and meaning from death.

Strategic, however, does not necessarily mean cynical. Transplant staff often acknowledged the matter-of-fact productivity of such narrative framings in making meaning for families that enabled donation and thus the transplant endeavor itself. But we have also seen how such spiritualizing frames could be profoundly meaningful in enabling transplant professionals' own work and sense of self as well; making sacred (rather than gruesome) meaning out of Lupe's engagement in the grim work of organ donation, for instance. In another register, many transplant staff found meaning in the way that such narratives of redemption and resurrection served not just as an effective tool to extract needed organs, but as one of the only gifts they had to offer in situations of desperate grief. As one physician expressed it:

> I see the peace families get from donating, they feel good about themselves and the donor. And I've seen families who didn't who regretted it later. I had a mother tell me, months after her daughter committed suicide, that she wished she had the courage to donate, that it would have turned her wasted life into something worthwhile . . . And so, no, no I don't feel bad or cruel or like some vulture that we ask [for the organs]— it gives us something we can do for them, at a point when, really, what else can we offer? (Dr. Fernandez, IMSS)

Emerging from this physician's account is an intriguing sense of how organ donation might be imagined to redeem not only the donor, but family members, and perhaps even transplant professionals, as well. This second possibility, the notion that professionals may, themselves, need redemption— perhaps from that ugly image of the vulture that Dr. Fernandez himself summons—is one I take up more directly in the following section.

Meaning-making cuts all ways, of course, and it is a deeply human trait to tell ourselves the stories we can live with—this is true whether we are the relatives of dying patients, the professionals engaged in enacting transplantation, or the anthropologist trying to tell their tales. And so we must attend not just to the instrumentality of the stories that transplant staff tell patients and families, but to the purposes that the stories they tell *about* those stories serve as well. If offering up narratives of redemption and resurrection serves not only to produce organs, but to ease the suffering of families caught up in transplant's interpellations, it seems important also to note the way this is, itself, a story that in turn eases the suffering of transplant staff too. For this is difficult, death-ridden work that they do, and it is not just families who need sense-making stories with which to face the wrenching frailty of human life.

Nor should my own intentionality in seeking to tell these narratives about narratives escape scrutiny. Attending more carefully to the way that transplant professionals may both deploy *and* inhabit more transcendent, mysterious, and spiritual understandings of the work in which they are engaged is, of course, a deliberate choice—an effort to round out some of the ways that anthropology has tended to engage more deeply with the beliefs and experiences and vulnerabilities of patients, rather than with those of professionals in transplantation. In seeking to take seriously the subjectivity, the spirituality, and even the suffering of professionals as well as patients, I, too, am reaching for a story I can live with.

Yet let us not lose sight of the degree to which all of this making meaning, all of this weaving together of the stories we can live by, is a fundamentally unruly endeavor. Though transplant professionals may hold out certain compelling, persuasive narratives, just what patients and families and others choose to do with those resources for meaning-making can take unexpected turns. In one such example, the SSa transplant coordinator Lupe one day found herself faced with a version of resurrection that did not at all smooth the way for organ donation—indeed, in this case those beliefs instead produced quite the opposite effect. She encountered the wife of a brain-dead patient who was strongly sympathetic to the need for organs for transplant, but who was nonetheless gravely worried about how her husband could eventually be raised by God and ascend to Heaven if his body was no longer "whole and as God made him." Such concerns over the link between bodily integrity and eternal salvation were not uncommon, despite official Church doctrine discounting such materially literal interpretations of resurrection. Indeed, they emerged similarly in the fear expressed by a heartbroken mother, struggling to accept the death of her only daughter, that: "If I donate her eyes, how will she see God when he raises her?" Faced with such concerns, transplant staff usually tried to reassure family members that an all-powerful God would surely have no trouble sorting it all out in the end.[14] But in this case, it was the wife herself who eventually produced a strategic reimagining of resurrection logistics, one that enabled the earthly salvational possibilities of organ donation. After a long, thoughtful, and anguished discussion with Lupe, the wife asked for some time alone to think. Several hours later, she sought out the transplant coordinator again and offered the following suggestion: "Don't ask me to *give* you his organs. Why don't you ask me to *lend* them to you? I can't give them to someone else, right? Because God gave them to my husband, and when he is raised by God, he will need them. But surely God won't mind if we *lend* them to someone else for a while?"

With this slight semantic twist, the wife had creatively reworked the contractual possibilities evoked by the very notion of the body as a form of property that can be owned and hence donated. And for her, it was a twist that made all the difference in the world—by converting the imagined contractual terms of organ donation from a permanent transfer into a temporary loan, she found herself able to grant consent.[15] It was a conversion in which the more fluid circulatory logics of reciprocal relationality as a form of iterative exchange seemed powerfully put to work, allowing for an enabling back-and-forth flow to be imagined not only between donor and recipient but between donor and God himself.

These unruly—even *agile*—routes of reasoning remind us that the operation of religious beliefs (and the negotiation of religious "rules") is no straightforward matter. Neither a simply predictable barrier to participation in organ donation, nor an easily manipulated tool to enable it, spiritual understandings of resurrection and redemption and miracles can be mobilized to make meaning in widely disparate ways.[16] Recent ethnographic work on in vitro fertilization in Catholic Ecuador (Roberts 2012) and Hindu India (Bharadwaj 2006) and on organ transplantation in Muslim Egypt (Hamdy 2012) has shown how individual patients and family members and medical professionals—and religious leaders too—all work out their faith in God and in science in creative and contingent ways. And in the face of both rapidly developing technology and lively religious innovation (to wit, the growing cult of El Niño Doctor himself), this working out is always, necessarily, a work in progress.

Such ongoing efforts to work out their own versions of scientific and spiritual faith were highlighted—and complicated—for several of the transplant professionals I knew by one unexpectedly dire example of the redemption narrative at work. A young man turned up in the IMSS intensive care unit following a terrible car accident, and after initial tests showed no brain activity, he was identified as a potential candidate for organ donation. As the formal process for diagnosing brain death swung into action, the transplant coordinator, Aurelia, began to acquaint herself with the case, gathering information about the family situation and preparing herself to approach them with the request for donation. Despite her preparations, however, when she went down to the ICU waiting room to meet the family she was wholly—and unpleasantly—shocked to recognize the boy's mother. For the mother, it turned out, had recently backed out of donating a kidney to her own sister as a living donor. Her withdrawal from the donation process had been abrupt and quite late in the process, and her sudden disappearance left the transplant staff—who were usually quite astute at detecting reluctant, on-the-fence donors—completely surprised and considerably distressed. The ailing sister died from her kidney disease a few months after the donation was halted, and the transplant staff had not had any contact with the family since her death.

Upon recognizing the recalcitrant former donor—someone with whom she had spent a great deal of time previously—the transplant coordinator paused in the doorway of the ICU, suddenly not quite sure about how to proceed in this unprecedented situation. Before she could make a decision, however, the grief-stricken mother recognized her and drew her insistently into the room. Tearfully clutching her hands, the mother told Aurelia: "You already know what I am going to say, don't you? *Of course* we will donate his organs. Maybe he is paying now for what I refused to do. I couldn't give to my sister, but I *can* give through him." Aurelia told me later that she had to fight the urge to physically recoil from those words because they struck her as such a cruel and distorted vision of divine retribution. But to pull back, to reject the meaning this mother had managed to wrest from the loss of her son, seemed, to Aurelia, its own form of cruelty. Fervently embracing this framing in which she herself was being both punished and redeemed through the broken body of her son, the mother was clearly determined to see this donation through. And in doing so, she rendered her brain-dead son as both tragic victim and powerful savior—a transformation of him, in fact, into a figure not unlike El Niño Doctor himself. For evident in both the sacrificial body of this young man and that wheelchair-enthroned son of God was a similar potent commingling of terrible human frailty and the transcendent salvational power which that frailty can—at least potentially—enable.

Though many of the transplant staff involved in the case were deeply un-comfortable with the mother's directly punitive interpretation of her son's death, the donation did, in fact, go through. And, in the aftermath, many of the involved transplant professionals remained unsettled. In part, the mother's punishing meaning-making revealed an ugly underside to the power of the stories they themselves were so quick to proffer. Made all too painfully clear here was the way that notions of redemption through organ donation could be both compellingly productive and awful to witness, bringing forth organs that might not otherwise have been offered—but doing so, at least sometimes, at a terrible cost. Yet such ethical questioning of the efficacy of their own tactics was not the only disturbing dimension of this case. For while many of the transplant staff generally resisted the mother's reading of her son's death as a form of divine punishment, some were, in fact, troublingly struck by the uncanny coincidence of a failed liv-ing donor being so soon confronted with such a painful decision about her own brain-dead son. It was a case, in the end, that left many transplant staff uneasy both that their own tactics might work all too well *and* that those tactics might rest upon a deeper, more relentless spiritual accounting than they themselves wanted entirely to admit.

In considering the kind of unsettling questions foregrounded in this painful case, I want to return us to the figure with which I opened this section, to that iconic image of Frankenstein. Though he appears in the diagnostic label of "Frankenstein syndrome" as a specter of *patient* experience gone monstrously wrong, I want to suggest that the figure of Frankenstein haunts the professionals of transplant medicine in other, more immediately, intimately personal ways as well. For Mary Shelley's classic tale is as terrifying and cautionary about the recklessly ambitious, arrogant scientist *Doctor* Frankenstein, as it is about the tragic—vengeful, but also deeply suffering—being that he creates.[17] Indeed, though popular convention poses the creature stitched together from dead body parts as the monster, closer reading of the novel suggests that it is Frankenstein himself who is truly monstrous in his callow, callous disregard for his own creation. The doubled uneasiness of transplant staff over this case of the donor's mother who had declined to donate her own living kidney echoes many of the anxieties about both science and scientists themselves portrayed so long ago in Shelley's classic narrative. For this was a case that raised, for many of the staff involved, the possibility that there might be something monstrous in their own work—and, hence, in themselves—if it could be turned to such darkly retributive effect. And further, it was a case that raised the possibilities for horror beyond the merely human, for a world in which the eager work of science could raise a darker power beyond its own ability to entirely comprehend or control. In short, it was a case that hauntingly raised for transplant professionals a question I turn to more explicitly in the next section: in the world of transplantation, just who is the monster?

Instrument of God or Black Market Butcher?: The Slippery Work of Transplantation

Having summoned the specter of doctor as monster in the figure of Frankenstein, I want to tack back to an earlier, oppositional image of the transplant professional, one that appeared in the story of Alma's leaping liver. Recall how the surgeon, as Alma was being anxiously wheeled off to surgery, took her hands in his and soothed her with a promise that in the operating room it was God's hands that were at work. As he recounted to me later, he told her: "Do you see these hands? These are not my hands. When I operate, they are God's hands and I am just His instrument. These are God's hands in there, not mine. Do not be afraid, because whatever happens in there, God will be with us" (Dr. Paredes, transplant surgeon, SSa). Such a statement could, of course, be interpreted as an extreme example of the infamous hubris of surgeons. Yet subsequent conversations with this surgeon suggested that the notion of operating with God's hands was a critical—and enabling—source of comfort and confidence not only for the patient, but for him as well. An exquisitely trained, deeply ambitious man, this surgeon explained that while both technical skill and a certain personal fortitude—even arrogance—were indeed necessary to take a scalpel to the human body, for him these were not sufficient. Taking up that scalpel—with all of its attendant possibilities for healing and for harming—was, for this surgeon, really only possible because of his sense that what happens during surgery, good or bad, is simply God's will. As he put it: "Without that faith, I don't know how we would dare to even attempt the work that we do in there." It was a sentiment with echoes in the statements heard earlier from the transplant coordinator Lupe when she reassured anxious donor families—and herself—that transplantation only works because God allows it. For both surgeon and social worker then, this was a vision in which God authorizes transplant and transplant, in turn, provides powerful proof of God's work in the world.

Moreover, this is a vision that sacralizes not just the transplant endeavor, but those who make it possible as well. That striking image of Dr. Paredes operating with the hands of God offers a compelling counterpoint to the haunting figure of the monstrous Doctor Frankenstein, after all. And while this precise imagery may have been particular to Dr. Paredes, it seemed nonetheless in keeping with a powerful, shared sense of reverence frequently evident in the transplant surgeries I observed. During each of these surgeries there came a moment when the kidney was finally fully "connected up" with its new body, and almost invariably a momentary, reverent hush fell over the operating room. During other, less charged phases of the surgical process, the room was full of bustling activity and collegial—often ribald, highly gendered—banter among the surgeons, nurses, trainees, and even observing anthropologist. Yet, at a certain, critical point in the surgery, all of that halted. We all leaned in, nearly holding our collective breath, to watch as a spreading, healthy pink color crept up over the surface of the kidney, shifting it from the greyish cast it had acquired while outside the human body (and cut off from a blood supply) and marking it as a living, integral part of the recipient's body. It was almost invariably a tense and transformative moment, offering the first, necessary, and visible sign of successful connection between the flesh of donor and recipient.

During one such moment, the lead surgeon turned to me and with a slight catch in his voice said: "The kidney is just so *beautiful*, isn't it? There is always something sacred about this part for me." (Dr. Ruiz, private hospital). Many other critical moments in the transplant process were yet to come, some inside the operating room and some beyond it: when the kidney first began to produce urine, when the first signs of immune rejection appeared and were (hopefully) suppressed, and when the patient could be allowed to return home, for instance. But this moment commanded a collective, shared attention and affect that was distinctive, and that struck me each time I observed—indeed, shared—it. It was a moment that bore witness to the resurrection of the kidney itself, returned to vivid—and revivifying— life in the ailing body of the transplant recipient. Such open expressions of a sense of the sacred, uttered over that high altar of medicine—the operating table itself—were both remarkable and, at the same time, utterly ordinary, a moving, yet routine part of the daily work in which these clinicians engaged. Indeed, beyond the charged symbolic specificity of the transplant procedure itself, such utterances remind us of the way that the operating room has long been recognized as a space where both ritual and reverence are central to how the work of medicine proceeds (Katz 1981).

Although such hints of the surgically sacred seemed most often focused on the in-need-of-salvation figure of organ recipient, they could emerge as well over the supine body of the living donor. In fact, the first time I entered the operating room for a living donor procedure in Guadalajara, I stared in shocked fascination at the unconscious body of the donor arranged on an operating table to which special extensions had been added so that his arms could be stretched straight out to either side in what looked for all the world like an eerie echoing of a crucifixion pose.[18] Noting my expression, one of the several nurses moving swiftly and efficiently around the room as they prepared for the surgery paused beside me, and resting her eyes momentarily on the donor, observed: "So vulnerable like that, no? Like Christ, almost, I think at times. I don't really even see it anymore, just to get the right access is all . . . but it catches you, reminds you, no? What they do, these donors . . ." (Martita, nurse, IMSS). And with a slight shake of her head she moved smoothly back into the choreography of arranging instruments and supplies and lighting and the like. It was a rare moment in which the sacrifice of living donors was openly acknowledged—in this place so very dependent on them—as not just a to-be-expected form of familial love, but as something more extraordinary, perhaps even bordering on the saintly. And in doing so, she invoked both the vulnerability and the power contained in the donor's act of self-sacrifice, and produced a resonance we might discern between that prone body offered up on the operating table and the talismanic figure of El Niño Doctor himself.

The actual space of surgery itself has not yet made much of an appearance in this book, in part because for the patients and family members whose experiences have occupied much of the foregoing chapters that space is largely a kind of blank—closed off from direct, conscious experience. And so I have focused more on the often-terrible times of illness and hope that led up (for some) to the moment of entering the operating room, as well as on the frequently fraught realities that led out from it. Yet for the transplant process as a whole, and for the professionals who most occupy us here, the operating room was utterly central. For those professionals it was in one sense a more private space, protectively closed off from the direct gaze of all those lay constituencies to whom they felt subject: anxious patients and families, calculating hospital administrators, suspicious government officials, and media reporters who could be alternately fawning and muck-raking, among others. But it was also a profoundly performative space. It was the place where transplantation proved itself (or failed to) each time anew. And it was also the space where transplant clinicians performed before one another, enacting surgical prowess and clinical hierarchies, but also, in certain moments, a more transcendent, spiritual sense of purpose as well.

Such performances—both surgical and spiritual—did not remain contained within the sealed-off space of the operating room, however, but leaked out into the wider world of hospital and community in all kinds of ways. The postsurgery bodies of both transplant recipient and organ donor bore embodied witness to transplantation's work (and sometimes, to its failures). When they fared well, returning to their lives and families and work (those sometimes elusive forms of transplanted health and (re)productivity explored in chapter 4), the rescued bodies wrought by transplantation could be imbued with an almost talismanic quality, as transplant staff summoned them in to talk to frightened patients and families, or invited them to deliver their testimonios in public presentations of various kinds, or even just took their pictures to be kept in a desk drawer as a private re-minder of why they do the difficult work that they do. And beyond such surgical bodies themselves, certain surgical narratives also circulated out-side of the operating room as well, stories, for instance, of the particular prowess of a vascular surgeon, renowned for his brilliant manipulation of the renal arteries so critical for enabling that beautiful pinking-up of the reconnected kidney. Aurelia, the transplant coordinator, on hearing that I would be observing a transplant one day, told me to "Watch Dr. Martinez, what he does with those tiny blood vessels . . . it's like magic, like noth-ing you'll see, his hands, so delicate, so beautiful . . ." (IMSS). Or inspiring stories might emerge from the operating room of a particularly harrowing, but ultimately triumphant case, in which things looked grim, but the team bravely pressed on and the patient was saved.

Yet sometimes, of course, the patient was not saved. Sometimes even the most delicate of hands faltered. Sometimes the body that emerged from the operating room was dead. Or sometimes it was irreparably damaged, with a transplant that had failed to take hold and a fierce rejection reaction to the foreign organ that threatened the life of the patient who had been so hopeful upon entering the operating room. Such failures could have wider effects, beyond the immediate, overwhelming personal tragedy for patient and family. They could, in some instances, touch off a scandal that could spread, as examination of failure in one patient case could lead to scrutiny of other failures and other cases as well. And in the process, the questioning could shift from a matter of technical mistake to one of moral compromise instead. The potential for such scandals seemed always simmering just below the surface of everyday transplant practice in this setting where the specter of corruption and profiteering was a quotidian part of the health-care scene writ large, where exposés of diverted pharmaceuticals and tainted blood sup-plies and the nefarious influence of greedy politicos erupted in the news with almost numbing regularity. Transplant scandals were both part of this wider landscape of the slippery State and also a distinctively disturbing variation on familiar narratives of criminality and embodied vulnerability.

Such a spreading form of scandal, radiating out from one patient death into scrutiny of other cases and other transplant practices beyond the strictly surgical, in fact engulfed the very surgeon we met earlier, operat-ing with the hands of God to provide Alma with her joyfully leaping liver. Some time after I left the field, a patient died following complications from a liver transplant surgery performed by Dr. Paredes. The grieving, furious family lodged a formal *denuncio* (accusation) against the surgeon with local authorities. They charged that he had demanded an illegal payment from them to carry out the liver transplant—over and above the formal hospital costs incurred at the public charity SSa hospital where he was operating and directed to a personal account. After the initial denuncio hit the newspapers and the authorities began a formal investigation, other stories began to emerge telling of similar payments extracted from other patients as well, up to an amount of 800,000 pesos (approximately $73,000). The case was widely reported in the local and national media as it continued to unfold over several months, with twenty-seven separate denuncios eventually registered against Dr. Paredes for organ trafficking and improper accounting practices (Alarcón 2013; Ramírez 2009; "Rodríguez Sancho augura que librará 27 acusaciones." El Informador, November 10, 2005). Throughout, he continued to staunchly defend his innocence, claiming that he had never done anything but work hard to bring transplantation to the Mexican people. Ultimately, Dr. Paredes was suspended from his position in the SSa Hospital Civil, though the threatened criminal charges and possibility of imprisonment never materialized.

As I tracked the unfolding case from a distance through news stories and e-mail communications with friends, it seemed hard to sort out just what had happened—and what *would* happen. To some, it seemed the downfall of this formerly widely lauded surgeon proved just what they had known all along, that transplant in Mexico was awash with mafiosos and traficantes, as rotten as the rest of the system, or perhaps even more egregiously, gruesomely so. To others, the unfolding scandal looked less like a downfall than a take-down, the deliberate destruction of a revered surgeon who had grown too personally powerful for the comfort of his corrupt superiors and competitors in the murky, intertwined world of health care, politics, and the criminal underworld. The families coming forward, one after another, to lodge the mounting count of denuncios were deeply compelling. But so too were the patients and families who came surging forward to the surgeon's defense, offering in counterpoint heartfelt testimonios of Dr. Paredes's skill and generosity and selflessness in saving their lives, and denying any experience of impropriety.

I thought that when I returned to Mexico and was able to talk to people in person that perhaps this illegible picture would become clearer, as I imagined that the durability and traceability of committing comments to written e-mail form had made candor more difficult. One clear effect of living in a slippery State, as I had come to know during my time in Guadalajara, was to breed a certain kind of caginess, an abiding sense that one never knows just who might be listening (or watching or reading)—and just which one of the many possible "sides" they might be on. But private, in-person conversation, even with some of Dr. Paredes's former colleagues, produced little more in the way of true clarity. Almost everyone—whether they came down more on the downfall or more on the take-down interpretation of things—hastened to point out that it is almost impossibly hard to know what "really happened" amid the complex play of power and interests and personalities in what I've been calling the slippery State of Mexico. And I came to understand that this reserve, this unwillingness to say definitively that this or that is what happened, was a stance oriented not just toward the uncertainties of understanding what had already occurred but also of anticipating what was yet to come. For if past events seemed difficult to interpret, future unfoldings could be equally hard to predict.

And so it came as a surprise to me—but not, I think to many of my Mexican interlocutors—when several years after Dr. Paredes was dismissed from the SSa hospital in disgrace over organ trafficking he was invited to return to rebuild the transplant program. He had set up practice, in the meantime, in another, smaller city in Mexico and so had not ever actually been prevented from continuing to transplant patients, despite the furor over the scandal in Guadalajara. And while the invitation to return to his former position did reawaken accounts of the former scandal in the papers, the director of the SSa hospital countered such criticisms with the rather blithe statement that "it is time to turn over a new leaf, and begin a new chapter in organ transplantation in Jalisco" (Alarcón 2013). Emergent here, among many other hard-to-pin-down influences at work, is the pull and the pressure of transplant's iconic status, of the way that being able to offer transplantation stands as such a marker of a certain level of medical modernity and technological prowess that much—apparently—can be forgiven in its pursuit.

Though the scandal that engulfed this surgeon was of the spectacular nature we have, perhaps, come to expect from the keen media attention to the global market in human organs, there were other, more mundane forms of doubt, other quieter intimations of disgrace to which transplant professionals could also find themselves subject. In one such example, the IMSS transplant coordinator, Aurelia, had been working for a long time to increase the program's ability to capture cadaveric organ donations. Among her many efforts was implementing something she had learned from a training workshop delivered by some visiting Spanish transplant coordinators, whose authority—as representatives of the most successful organ procurement system in the world—was impeccable. From those Spanish coordinators, Aurelia had gleaned the importance of providing a calm, private place to talk to the grieving families of brain-dead patients, a space conducive to being able to hear and carefully consider the organ donation request. For Aurelia, this image of a protected space in which to conduct the conversations about organ donation grew into, as she described it, "a dream, it was a dream to give our families a good place, a nice place to be while we talk to them." With her highly attuned skills at *agilizando* almost everything required to make transplantation work in the IMSS setting, Aurelia set about making this dream a reality. She wheedled some precious space from the hospital administration, a small room just off the area of the hospital that housed both operating rooms and intensive care. And she drew on her long-standing relationships with the local pharmaceutical representatives to extract donations to purchase furnishings for the room—a pair of comfortable couches, a round table for working on the endless forms entailed in organ donation, even a framed pastoral print for soothing decoration.

When it was complete, she was pleased and proud of what she had wrought. She spoke of the room as a sign of respect and compassion they could now offer donor families in their grief, and recounted the care that had gone into each item chosen for the effect of comfort and consideration she intended to create. And so, when the room was ready and began to be used, she was taken aback by the murmurings of criticism among hospital staff that began to filter back to her—even, in a few cases, from among members of the transplant team itself. Some such mutterings were about the devotion of yet more of the scarce resources of the hospital world—both physical space and pharmaceutical generosity—to the high-profile cause of transplantation. These she expected and could set aside with relative ease as the inevitable jealousies of institutional life. Yet other forms of critique were harder to ignore. Some wondered why the grief of the families of potential organ donors deserved so much more compassion, consideration, and comfort than all of the other devastated families left behind in the stark, public space of the ICU waiting room. At stake, they suggested, was not really the comfort of these families but rather the success of the donation request, making Aurelia's room more a matter of strategy—even manipulation—rather than care. And in such insinuations, that earlier-invoked image of transplant professional as vulture hovering hungrily over the bodies of the brain dead, loomed all too dangerously near. What had seemed for Aurelia like a moment of proud personal commitment and professional accomplishment quickly came to seem instead like an achievement tainted by suspicion, and thus tainting by association.

What made that second criticism so hard to shake off was, on some level, its undeniability. Having a private room in which to ask about donation *was* a matter of strategy, of trying to get more families to give up more organs. Making those families feel more cared for was not just a simple act of human compassion, though it contained that as well. It was, fundamentally, a calculated means of building transplantation by way of building the trust of families in a position to surrender those all-too-scarce organs. Though for Aurelia, as for most professionals engaged in transplant work, this goal too was about care and compassion—that is, for the suffering, sometimes dying patients in need of a new organ. But even with a wholehearted belief in the righteous, even sacralized, nature of that work, the darker underside to the means of its accomplishment remained.

Aurelia's experience foregrounded an uneasy trap in which transplant professionals seem caught. Being good at the work of transplantation requires considerable strategic skill and powers of persuasion in order to induce people to surrender the organs—whether from living bodies or dead ones—upon which this form of medicine depends. And being good at this work carries with it always the risk of being *too* good, of seeming to wrest organs inappropriately from their bodily homes, whether by means of brute pressure or more subtle manipulation. Because while many people around the world have come to agree that donating organs (living or dead) is something that ought to be allowed, there is also general consensus that it ought not be compelled. This is thus the unstable ground transplant professionals were left to occupy as they carried out their daily work, knowing that the line between being good and *too* good, between operating with the hands of God and being cast out as corrupt criminal, can be ruinously hard to pin down. It is in this sense that the role of transplant professional in Mexico—and, I suspect, in many other places as well—could feel like its own kind of slippery state.

Scientists, Saints, Monsters, and Selves

One Friday evening toward the end of my main fieldwork stay I escaped the overwhelming press of the transplant wards for a much-needed break, and headed off to one of the glossy multiplex cinemas in an upscale suburb to see a movie with a group of friends. The film was Spanish director Pedro Almodóvar's All about My Mother (1999), and my friends (all local medical—though not transplant—professionals) were insistent that we see it together, as the trailers had hinted at a transplant-related plotline in the movie. An admirer of Almodóvar's, I was happy to comply and soon found myself nestled in the darkness and drawn into the story of Manuela, a Spanish transplant coordinator whom we first meet as she participates in filming a training video about how to ask devastated families to consider donating the organs of a brain-dead loved one.

In the first few moments of the film I felt a shock of recognition as I realized that the opening scenes of the movie were intimately familiar, a depiction of the exact Spanish organ procurement training seminar I had recently experienced at a conference in Guadalajara. The IMSS program had brought Rocío, a highly experienced Spanish transplant coordinator, to Mexico to deliver a training workshop on just what was being portrayed in the film: the simultaneously death-ridden and death-defying business of asking for organs. I learned later that Almodóvar, reflecting a widespread nationalist pride in the extraordinary success of the Spanish organ procurement system, had been so keen to get this scene just right that he worked closely with real-life transplant professionals as key consultants on the film.

As the film proceeds, the central character of Manuela finds herself brutally thrust onto the other side of the procurement relationship, when her beloved son is hit by a car and she herself is asked to donate his organs. She does so, and then makes an anguished decision that touches off a convoluted series of twists and turns that follow. She sets off to find the man who received her son's heart, driven by a deep need to see this stranger in whom part of her son still lives. In the process, she is reconnected with her own complicated past in a story that involves love and loss, betrayal and redemption, and our embodied selves as fragile sites of suffering, destruction, and creative reinvention.[19] As a mother who gives up the organs of a lost son and, through the course of the film, regains a kind of healing grace, we might discern an eerie echo between the filmic Manuela and the Mexican mother encountered above who also came to feel herself redeemed through the broken body of her son.

As we sat over steaming cups of chocolate atole discussing and dissecting the movie afterward, several of my companions expressed some distaste for the portrayal of Manuela's need to see the recipient of her son's heart. For them it was a moment in the film that undermined the authenticity of her character as a transplant *professional*, someone whose expertise meant that she ought not partake in such popular, superstitious notions of her son living on in the body of another. Yet, for me, that moment too had borne a shock of recognition, for Manuela's story rang so very true to precisely the kinds of stories and experiences explored throughout this chapter, where both the allure and the daily, grinding work of transplantation were underwritten by a complex mixture of scientific authority and a sense of transcendence.

Thinking later about that moment I was intrigued by what one set of medical professionals (my friends) seemed to be looking for in this filmic representation of another (the transplant coordinator Manuela). In one sense their reading of the story was rendered from the position of medical *insiders*, impatient with the irrational fantasizing of pop culture renderings of medical science. Yet, it struck me at the same time as a view very much *outside* of the daily experiences and meaning-making practices of so many of the transplant staff I had come to know. Though the narrative of Almodóvar's film might not be one those transplant professionals would be likely to invoke in meetings with hospital administrators and government officials, it was one I thought they too would recognize as both intimately familiar and emotionally accurate in many ways. What was, from one angle, a sort of insider commentary offered up by my clinician friends worked, in that particular moment, to produce a new set of insider/outsider lines between us, underscoring for me the way the particular medical worlds they themselves inhabited were at once connected to and distinctive from the specific clinical, emotional, and imaginative world of transplant medicine in which I had been (at least provisionally, observationally) immersed. My own sense of self suddenly, if subtly, shifted in that brief conversational turn, distancing me slightly from those friends through a surge of identification with Manuela and the real-life transplant professionals she represented.

It was such a small moment. Yet it seemed a telling one as well, revealing the insider/outsider shifts in forms of identification—theirs *and* my own—that emerged both through processes of storytelling and story reading, and couched specifically in a register of relations between science and the supernatural. That postmovie moment with my friends crystallized for me the richly contingent microprocesses by which we are all, always, taking endless "detours through the other to the self" (Fuss 1995: 2), locating ourselves through the innumerable interactions and identifications (and dis-identifications, and misidentifications) of daily life. It also brought me back to an earlier moment, one I had shared with the real-life Spanish transplant coordinator who had come to Guadalajara to deliver that training seminar captured in Almodóvar's film.

Rocío had been invited to Guadalajara by the IMSS transplant group to deliver a workshop on organ procurement strategies to the regional medical community. After a long day in the packed hotel conference ballroom, she was eager to experience something of the city beyond the bland upscale hotel zone where the conference was held. Aurelia, the IMSS transplant coordinator, arranged an evening out in one of the most picturesque local tourist areas and insisted that I join her and another of the IMSS transplant coordinators, Isabel, in helping to entertain the visiting transplant dignitary. After a leisurely evening of gracious dining and strolling amid the stately colonial architecture of the little town of Tlaquepaque, Rocío made one last request. She asked if we might finish up the evening in a cantina, citing the desire to see something, as she put it, a bit more *cotidiana* (everyday) during her brief time in Mexico.

Aurelia, ever the gracious hostess, smoothly agreed with a warm smile and started ushering us back to the car. It was a smile that turned into a briefly ironic smirk, however, as she exchanged a quick glance with Isabel and me, in a split-second moment of acknowledgment full of charged meaning. Referenced in that glance was, in part, the cultural misreading such a request represented, for cantinas were traditionally a highly masculinized, working-class male space in Guadalajara—decidedly *not* a social location where our group would likely have gone on our own. Her humorous glance seemed to skewer both the predictability of the Spanish visitor's desire to see this particular iconic version of Mexican authenticity enacted *and* her own (albeit ironic) submission to it, despite its absurdity as a stand-in for experiencing some sort of "real Mexico." Animating her brief glance was also the complex play of power dynamics with which the whole evening had been shot through. For the course of conversation throughout the night had been cordially collegial but also dense with the obligations, expectations, and privileges attendant to the roles of guest and host, first-world expert and developing world trainee, and even, at a more subtle, subterranean level, former colonizer and formerly colonized that surfaced at different moments and in a whole host of small ways.

My own positioning as a gringa anthropologist within those relations had left me feeling slightly off-balance throughout the evening. Pointedly including me in her ironic glance, Aurelia had marked me as a kind of insider, privy to understanding the stereotyped silliness of Rocío's request—and there was an undeniable flush of ethnographic pleasure to that feeling of inclusion. In a different moment, however, the Spanish visitor Rocío marked me with a very different, more uncomfortable form of inclusion when she jokingly scolded me, sotto voce, for using a common and characteristically Mexican turn of phrase. "Don't say mande [pardon me—literally, command me]," she told me, "it makes your Spanish sound so old-fashioned, so subservient." It was yet another small moment, but one in which the shock of still-relevant colonial dynamics seemed to suddenly surface, along with Rocío's expectation that I belonged on her side of an imagined modern Spain/backward Mexico divide.

Amid such subtle pulls of power, of identification and disidentification, our group settled into the dark, cave-like setting of a largely empty cantina in the city center—one of the few where women did sometimes go—and ordered up the glasses of locally produced tequila that served to complete the image. Rituals for how the liquor should be properly drunk were obligingly shared and laughingly enacted. And after a round or two, Rocío leaned forward with a somewhat conspiratorial, confessional air to ask a rather blunt question: "So, what are the superstitions people have here about donation, really?" Aurelia, looking a little taken aback, responded a bit tartly that it was not so much a question of "superstition" as simple lack of education, that most people just don't understand brain death. Rocío pressed a bit, saying yes, yes, but even the least educated can be brought to understanding if you take the time to work with them. "Understanding isn't really a barrier," she said, "I'm talking about beliefs, what are the beliefs that you see here?" Sitting in the gritty cantina she'd been obliged to come to, Aurelia visibly bridled a bit, responding only with a tight smile and shrug of her shoulders at what seemed to be Rocío's digging for just another kind of Mexican exoticism. Reading her resistance, Rocío laughingly chided, "Come on, we all have them, you know, the stories we get in this work . . . !"

And with that, Rocío began to regale us with tales of the forms of resistance she encountered in her own organ procurement work in Spain, stories in which both moros (Moors, as Muslims are still often referred to in Spain) and gitanos (Gypsies, as Roma people are often designated) figured prominently. Central to her stories were what she framed as the self-serving superstitions, couched as religious beliefs, that often drove what she saw as the ungenerous—even antisocial—tendency of both groups to resist giving organs, even while being all-too-willing to take them when sick. At one level, Rocío's racially charged account seemed yet another example of that familiar distancing work that so often renders threats both *of* and *to* transplant always "out there" in some unruly, uneducated—and often magically religious—Other. Yet at another level, her storytelling seemed also aimed at a kind of inclusion, at reassuring Aurelia that her request for such belief-bound stories was *not* angling for some exoticizing evidence of the out-of-placeness of transplant in Mexico. Rather, Rocío's own stories seemed to suggest, it was a request meant to establish a sort of kinship between them as professionals whose work rendered them privy to the profound complexities and absurdities of this death-dependent form of life-giving medicine.

Softening just a bit, Aurelia allowed that in Mexico too there were certain groups, certain regions from which resistance to organ donation was more likely to emanate. She offered up some rather vague comments about people from *la sierra* (the mountainous regions surrounding the city) practicing a more naively literal form of Catholicism, one that made them more likely to imagine spiritual resurrection in problematically material terms. "You know," she said with a shrug, "not being able to see God when they're raised if they give the eyes, that sort of thing." As she trailed off, Rocío responded laughingly with a tongue-in-cheek, comradely commiseration that indexed the shared cultural history between their two countries, saying: "Ah, the trouble the Catholic Church has caused!" She then went on to share the observation—culled from her globe-trotting career as an organ procurement expert—that transplant coordinators from different countries tell characteristically different kinds of organ donation stories. The Italians, she told us, revel in heart-breaking stories of high drama, for instance, while Spaniards tend to spin out tales tinged with dark comedy instead. Our conversation in the cantina was an opportunity, it seemed, to add a Mexican variant to the *wunderkammer* of her collection of tales.

Quietly observing from the edges of the conversation at our dark corner table, I sat there listening as Rocío offered up what amounted to a tour of national character by way of organ donation narratives with a slightly queasy mixture of fascination and something bordering on repulsion. On the one hand, this visiting transplant dignitary was essentially enacting one of the central interests of this book, the way that transplantation so readily becomes caught up with—indeed rendered iconic of—notions of national identity. It was one of those moments of ethnographic frisson, one that I knew immediately I would likely want to write about later in some way. But

I also felt distinctly uncomfortable with Rocío's unabashed angling for—and use of—those titillating transplant stories. There was a sense of a narrative acquisitiveness, even greed, underlying the whole conversation that seemed, somehow, a bit unseemly. Part of my discomfort was, of course, a kind of knee-jerk liberal reaction to the kind of glib stereotyping with which many of Rocío's stories were rife. But part of my queasiness, I had to admit, had more to do with an undeniable sense of identification: I could see myself all too uncomfortably in the mirror of Rocío's story-seeking and storytelling. She was eager, after all, for the juicy bits, the meaning-full stories of strangeness and mystery and heartbreak and humor with which transplant is so compellingly rich. So too was I.

For that is, of course, precisely why I was sitting there, head aching from the combination of fiery tequila and fierce concentration on all the details I wanted to be sure to get just right. The whole purpose of my presence there, of the ethnographic enterprise itself, was similarly bent on collecting stories in order to be able to tell them anew, here, in my own work. To be sure, I was after not just those strikingly, stereotypically strange sorts of stories, but the everyday ones as well, the ones that likely would not even register to those I was studying *as stories*, per se. And my purpose, of course, had scholarly aspirations beyond the mere collection of quirky conversational material. And yet the queasiness I felt, observing Rocío only to feel my analytic gaze forced back on myself as observer, marked—in a literally visceral way—the slippery state of the anthropological endeavor itself.

I have, in this chapter, unfolded a whole series of those ethnographic stories I collected, doing so as a means of exploring the unstable territory occupied by transplant professionals, staked out among the figures of scientist, saint, and monster. Bearers of the nation's modernist ambitions, operating with the hands of God, yet haunted always by the specter of the traficante, I have sought to spin out what seem to me some compelling resonances between the work (and workers) of transplantation and the powerfully ambiguous icon who opened this chapter, El Niño Doctor. Sainted, scientific, and tinged with the danger of both awesome power and his own future suffering, that image of the baby Jesus dressed in his doctor's whites seemed to offer such a richly polysemic and vividly Mexican image with which to make the work of transplantation come to matter in an anthropological register. In doing so, however, I come face-to-face with a mirror-image sort of question; that is, how does anthropology, in turn, come to matter through the medium of transplantation?

This is a question that resonates and demands reflexivity at the level of intimate, ethnographic practice. In observing and recounting the way that image of the hovering vulture—drawn by the scent of death from which it hopes to make life—haunts the transplant profession, surely my own uncomfortable kinship with that carrion creature must also be acknowledged. For I, too, have hovered over those life-and-death scenes of transplantation, after all, drawn by the depth of human drama from which I, in turn, hope to make anthropological meaning. In observing and writing about the Janus-faced world of transplantation I am also participating in, indeed *enacting* it, to use Annemarie Mol's term for the way medical objects come into being across a diverse array of sites from clinic to pathology lab to—as here—scholarly analysis (Mol 2003). That is, I am also implicated—at least in some small way—in how transplantation comes to matter, inextricably part of the network I seek to observe.

This is true, of course, not just for me but for what has become an expanding anthropology of transplant. Considerable anthropological attention has been drawn by the high stakes of transplant medicine as it operates at both embodied, interpersonal levels and on a global scale. And anthropologists have exercised a powerful voice in ongoing public debates over the practices and ethics of transplantation—particularly with regard to the global organ trade—affording our discipline an important and often-elusive relevance beyond its own bounds. Yet it seems to me that even as we critique transplant as an iconic example of the biomedical privileging of high-drama "rescue medicine," we would do well to remain alert to the politics and effects and affects of the privileging implicit in our own scholarly choices. Drawn ourselves to the attention-grabbing scene of transplantation, how are we at risk of practicing what we might call in turn a kind of rescue anthropology, partaking of the very dynamics we seek to problematize? For anthropology is not immune to the iconic allure of transplantation that has occupied so much of this book, after all, and our own work must be understood as both subject to and constitutive of that symbolic power—even as we bring our critical powers of analysis to bear upon it. There is no way, I think, to write a book about transplantation as a kind of icon without also participating in those processes of icon formation.

In the end, I have come to find those haunting figures of scientist, saint, and monster useful signposts for staking out not only the dearest hopes and gravest fears of the transplant endeavor, but of the anthropological one as well. For we too trade on claims of authoritative knowledge, we too hold out hopes for a kind of salvation, and harbor fears about our own exploitative potential. Acknowledging a certain kinship between the slippery state of both transplant professional and anthropologist, I want to hold us suspended between those complex figures of possibility, open to the productively unstable nature of their moral push and pull. That is, I want to hold together both deep concern about the lives risked and the hierarchies inscribed in the processes and politics of organ transfer, along with a sense of the joyous possibility alive in Antonio's face-splitting smile as he urinated for the first time in years, or in Ana's powerful postsurgical awakening to a body whose every limb and hair follicle no longer pained her. Similarly, I cannot ignore the way the work of ethnography proceeds by means that feel often intrusive, extractive, and potentially exploitative and yet can put stories in the world that are deeply, effectively *moving*—that can serve both to stir emotions and, sometimes, to shift politics. Ultimately, both transplant and anthropology seem to me simultaneously fraught and fertile, flawed, even dangerous, yet also full of hopeful possibility. Eyes wide open to their respective perils, I find nonetheless that I do not quite want to do without either one in the world.

Coda

Live donor kidney transplantation is emerging as the predominant practice of kidney transplantation around the world.
—Francis Delmonico and Mary Amanda Dew

I began this book with a German mother who became *más mexicana*. I will end with a Mexican nephrologist going global. In 2010 I was invited back to Mexico to speak at an international conference on chronic kidney disease, drawing on my research in Guadalajara to address cultural issues in dialysis and transplantation for a largely clinical audience. I arrived not quite sure what to expect but delighted by the opportunity to spend some time with the conference organizer who had invited me, one of the key transplant professionals I had come to know during my main fieldwork stint. I had known him as a dedicated but often beleaguered and deeply tired man. Building the SSa nephrology program from one abandoned dialysis machine languishing in the hospital basement into a functioning kidney transplant program had required tenacity, commitment, and nearly boundless patience with the daily round of setbacks both small and large, challenges that his mentors in the U.S. program where he had trained could never even have imagined. Back when I first knew him he would joke ruefully with me about how he had started his day trying to figure out how to get soap stocked for scrubbing in to surgery, and then moved on to the glamorous task of scrounging around among his pharmaceutical representative acquaintances to try to acquire some donated filters to keep the hemodialysis machines running. His daily clinical life was a lesson in the *agilizando* required to materialize transplantation—as well as other more mundane forms of kidney care—in Guadalajara at the turn of the millennium. The comparison he drew between his own daily routines and those of his U.S. colleagues was laced with frustration and humor, but also a certain note of pride—achieving transplant in Mexico required a vital set of skills over and above what those U.S. mentors could ever have taught him.

Yet in other, darker moods, this same clinician had shared with me a demoralizing sense of peripherality in the realm of global scientific research. He was welcome to contribute raw data from his patients in Guadalajara to an international transplant registry and did so. But he had many ideas for studies of his own, particularly studies that would explore the possibilities for lowering the costs of treating kidney patients. Could expensive immunosuppressive medications be combined with other cheaper agents that might amplify their effects and reduce the quantity (and costs) needed to maintain a transplant, for instance? Such ideas, he had found, seemed to gain little purchase in garnering the interest of funding agencies or getting on the program at international scientific meetings. Given voice in such conversations was a painfully personal version of living on what Nancy Stepan has described as the "problematic periphery" of scientific knowledge production (Stepan 1991).

And so it was a particularly deep pleasure to find him, years later, at the head of what turned out to be a prestigious international research meeting held in the jewel-like colonial city of Guanajuato. At an elegant dinner on the first night of that conference I found myself flanked on one side by a hotshot Canadian researcher with whom my Mexican friend had been collaborating for several years, and on the other side by a top-level director from the U.S. National Institutes of Health (NIH), who had been following their work together with great interest. From those early, often rather lonely days of unearthing that dusty dialysis machine from the hospital basement, he clearly had come a long way indeed.

But it was not just the individual aspirations and contributions of one Mexican transplant professional that had come so far. Rather, the very problem of kidney disease—and particularly kidney transplantation—has gone dramatically global in the years since I first began this research. Chronic kidney disease has increasingly come to be recognized by the World Health

Organization (WHO) as a massive (and surely massively underestimated) global public health problem, one for which both the burdens of disease and the costs of treatment are extraordinarily high (García García et al. 2012; White et al. 2008). Linked in close relation with other critical epidemics of chronic disease now understood to be sweeping across the global South, particularly diabetes and cardiovascular disease, kidney disease has thus been newly framed as a "global health priority."

As kidney failure thus comes to register as a global health problem, policy rhetoric increasingly poses transplantation as the most pragmatic solution in low-income settings, given the astronomical costs and burdensome nature of dialysis. We are thus in the midst of a deliberate realignment of those technology-out-of-place assumptions about transplantation in "a place like Mexico" with which I began. The boundaries of what—and who—transplantation is imagined to be for, and where it might most appropriately be practiced, are clearly on the move. Yet, at the same time, anxious attention to the dystopic possibilities for organ markets run amok in the poorer parts of the world has hardly disappeared, surfacing spectacularly once again on the front page of the *New York Times*—in a story about the buying and selling of organs in Costa Rica—as I write these very words, for instance (Sack 2014).

With powerful bodies like the WHO pushing to increase kidney transplant rates worldwide, the central questions engaged in this book regarding how decisions are made about where organs come from and to whom they go only intensify in scope and scale. These are, as we have seen, questions that are both intensely personal, a matter of embodied experience and intimate emotion, and deeply political, involving the investment of political, economic, and cultural capital in saving some lives through risking others. It remains true, as that opening tale of the German mother who became más mexicana first alerted us, that neither the clinical practices nor the biopolitics of transplantation are everywhere the same. Yet it is also true that present pressures to grow transplantation—in both poorer and more privileged parts of the world—look likely to lean heavily on the bodies of living donors for some time to come (Delmonico and Dew 2007; Horvat et al. 2009).

Amid the mounting policy statements and scholarly analyses acknowledging this growing global dependence on living donors, familiar forms of framing are also widely in evidence. Reflections on the problems with brain death in poorer parts of the world frequently flag "religious and cultural constraints" as key barriers working against the successful entrenchment of cadaveric donation programs—often highlighting, in the process, a few vivid details of such obstructive beliefs as a compelling splash of color in the otherwise dry discourse of global health analysis. The view from Mexico helps us to see how such arresting invocations of cultural attitudes and religious belief may offer an explanatory device that is both expedient and distancing, one that works to both neatly contain doubt and apportion blame in powerful ways. And while more material problems of uneven infrastructures of technology and training do certainly enter such policy discussions as well, what continues to go largely unspoken are many of the more unruly slippery state/State issues explored here, those unsettling conceptual, logistical, and political uncertainties that shape the way this utilitarian form of death comes to matter (or does not) in Mexico and elsewhere.

Such global biounavailabilities of cadaveric donors condition the burgeoning bioavailability of living ones in our present moment, in both material and imaginative terms. And global health discourse tends to render this increasing resort to the resource of living donors as worrisome primarily—and reductively—as a matter of organ trafficking. What this leaves less visible and less examined, of course, are the considerable and complex vulnerabilities of the vast majority of other, noncommercialized but not unconstrained, living donors upon whom transplant in Mexico (and many other places) depends. The WHO estimates that 10 percent of organ transplants worldwide involve illegal activity of some kind—a stripped-down but indisputably urgent statistic (Shimazono 2007). Yet we may want to be wary of the iconic effects of the grim glamour of that murky world of organ buying and selling. Be wary that it not exert such pull on our attention—clinically, ethically, politically, even anthropologically—that we fail to look as deeply into those other more seemingly familiar, familial forms of bodily sacrifice. For the hypervisibility of organ commodification is refracted through and reflective of the moral economy of the gift/commodity analytic and produces, in turn, what we might call a crucial economy of attention.

Indeed these are economies—both moral and attentive—that seem all too obviously at work in the global health discourse on transplantation, emerging, for instance, in the words of one of the key WHO officials involved in transplantation policy when he asserted that: "There are two prevailing concepts of transplantation. One relies on money and leads to increased inequality, besides putting a price on the integrity of the body and human dignity. The second is based on solidarity and the donor's sole motivation to save a life. We should seek a common global approach to donation and transplantation characterized by respect for the donors, so that they are proud of what they have done" (Luc Noël, quoted in Garwood 2007: 3). This seems to me a somewhat stunning statement, with the goal of donors "being proud of what they have done" an almost absurdly inadequate accounting of what is at stake in the face of the complex, constrained, and consequential stories of living donation unfolded throughout this book.

Working against such striking inadequacies, it will be critical to track the shifting forms of bioavailability and biounavailability that emerge and diverge as organ transplantation expands its aspirational reach both within local clinical settings and across a wider global health imaginary. What kinds of bodies will become more available to the needs of transplant for organs—and more subject to its medically mediated forms of salvation—in specific context and under global regimes of clinical and ethical practice? What kinds of bodies may become less so? And what iconic figurings will be used to make sense of those unevenly distributed bodily economies? Such sense-making can work in a variety of registers and to distinctive effect, as we have seen, sometimes rendering the work of organ transfer culturally legible, economically defensible, ethically domesticated, and politically useful. The operation of the iconic mujer sufrida as the emblematic—though not necessarily the actual—source of living donor organs in Mexico offers one situated example of how this might go. Or, of course, stories can be told also that work to opposite effect, figuring some transplant practices as culturally illegible, economically irresponsible, ethically alien, and politically volatile, in much the way those initial technology-out-of-place reactions to my research so often seemed to do.

In either case, such storytelling is both deeply entwined with and reflective of existing alignments of power and vulnerability and often works to reentrench them in all too predictable ways. Yet stories told offer always the opportunity for retellings, as we have seen, in ways that can open up spaces for interruption and even reinvention, and that may—sometimes—serve to disrupt existing arrangements and expectations. In much this way, the local dependence on living related donors in Mexico could be spun from one angle as a technology-out-of-place problem driven by a "backward" lack of cadaveric donors and then retold in more triumphal terms as a form of technical and ethical expertise, one that emerges from and asserts a sense of national identity and pride. Such retellings are never entirely straightforward nor wholly subversive, of course, but may nonetheless offer productively unsettling opportunities to intervene in some of the ongoing processes of domestication and exoticization, heroization and demonization traced out here—to intervene, that is, in how the ideas and practices of transplantation, of national identity, and of anthropology itself come to matter.

Indeed, anthropology has a role to play in these intimately intertwined processes of narrativization and materialization. Returning to the scene of that prestigious conference to which my nephrologist friend invited me, it matters not just that *he* was now at the table of global scientific knowledge production. It matters that so too was I. It matters, that is, that my own forms of situated knowledge—as someone who works in anthropology, in transplant, in Mexico—were imagined as useful to the public health discussion, as meriting a seat at the table. And not just at that table, but at the other tables in various geographic and disciplinary locations where I have since found myself interpellated, sometimes in the company of my Mexican friend, and sometimes feeling relatively alone in a sea of very unlikeminded clinicians and scientists and policy makers. Such encounters are always both exciting and uneasy for me, as someone full of hope for the ways anthropological work might matter in the world, but also wary of the risks for that work to be turned to purposes not just predictably exoticizing, but disturbingly domesticating as well. How to contribute and even collaborate without being co-opted is a question that, like the ethnographic stories I have offered here, will continue to unfold over time.

Ultimately, the questions raised in this book about the symbolic processes by which transplant comes to matter in particular ways (and not others) is a story that reaches beyond the specific time and place explored here. Indeed, this is a story relevant well beyond the bounds of transplant itself, for questions of how medicine draws on the resources of some bodies to save others, and how ailing individual bodies pull on the wider social body (and vice versa) are hardly restricted to the clinical and political and ethical particularities of the transplant endeavor. In our anthropological tellings and retellings of such wider stories, the notions of bioavailability and biounavailability, of slippery states and ethical domesticity explored here may offer productive angles of insight and useful analytic purchase. Paying attention, in the process, to the iconic dimensions of our own scholarly choices seems worthwhile as well. For we too are drawn to icons of all sorts, and in our analytic efforts to open up and reveal and complicate those icons we are also, always, participating in their polysemy, helping to make them anew.

Notes

Introduction

1. Various terms have been used in the biomedical and social scientific literatures to describe brain-dead organ donors, reflecting the considerable cultural work and semantic politics that have gone into constituting these entities as "dead" despite their continued breathing and fluid circulation when maintained by medical technologies such as the ventilator (see chapter 2). Although the term most commonly employed in the United States is now *deceased donor*, I use the term *cadaveric donor* throughout this study as it is closest to the term *donante cadaverico* used to denote these donors in Mexico during the time of this research.

2. For example, the United Network for Organ Sharing reports comparative graft survival rates for cadaveric vs. living donor transplants in the United States from 1997–2004 as 89 percent vs. 95.1 percent in the first year posttransplant, 77.8 percent vs. 89.9 percent in the third year, and 66.5 percent vs. 79.7 percent in the fifth year (UNOS 2007).

3. My own positioning as a "gringa anthropologist" is a necessary part of this ethnographic account and is taken up more explicitly in the Tracking Transplantation section later in this chapter (see also Nelson 1999: 41–73 for an extensive theorizing of the pleasures and perils of a gringa anthropology).

4. This is precisely the kind of symbolic, celebratory allure mobilized by the pioneering transplant surgeon Joseph Murray in the 1960s when he imagined organ transplantation as a means for enabling space travel, suggesting that the ability to replace worn-out body parts might be just what was needed to bridge the vast, beckoning distances of the cosmos (Murray 1966). At a time when faith in science was perhaps at an all-time high and the international space race was a charged site of nationalist

pride and anxiety, organ transplantation seemed to hold out tantalizing possibilities for pushing the frontiers of both human frailty and outer space alike.

5. The anthropology of transplant now spans an increasingly wide ethnographic range including North America, Japan, Germany, India, Egypt, Pakistan, Eastern Europe, Brazil, Turkey, Malaysia, China, Bangladesh—and, of course, Mexico as well (see, for example, Cohen 1999, 2011; Crowley-Matoka 2005; Hamdy 2012; Hogle 1999; Kierans 2015; Lock 2001; Moazam 2006; Moniruzzaman 2012; Sanal 2011; Scheper-Hughes 2000, 2005; Sharp 2006).

6. The political and moral economies surrounding the distribution and movements of bodies and medical technologies across the U.S.-Mexico border in the context of transplantation emerged with particularly explosive force in the 2003 case of Jesica Santillan, a young Mexican immigrant to the United States who received a disastrous heart-lung transplant at Duke University Medical Center. See Wailoo et al. (2006) for a detailed exploration of that case.

7. See Julie Livingston's eloquent account of how a particular imaginary of place and the diseases thought to characterize it can have material effects on how attention is concentrated and resources are distributed—from medications to research efforts to international aid (Livingston 2012). She explores how a persistent, pernicious image of Africa as a site of infectious disease has rendered cancer on that continent less visible, and hence the whole apparatus required to treat it less available.

8. See Sherine Hamdy's work on kidney transplantation in Egypt for a chilling account of the "political etiologies" of renal disease in that setting, where contaminated food and water supplies, as well as unregulated and dangerous working conditions, are a necessary part of the epidemiological and ethnographic story (Hamdy 2008).

9. "Solid organ" transplantation refers to the transplantation of organs such as kidneys, livers, hearts, and lungs. Other bodily tissues such as skin, bones, cartilage, and corneas can also be transplanted and these forms of transplantation were also in use in Mexico at the time of this research. However, because such tissues can be obtained from cadavers (e.g., those who meet the traditional standards of "heart/lung" death, not just "brain" death), the clinical, logistical, and cultural work involved in these forms of donation and transplantation are substantially different and are not dealt with in this book.

10. The Catholic Church has a long history in Mexico as a dominant cultural and political force, though like much of Latin America, Mexico has also seen the rise of a host of evangelical sects in recent years, including such groups as the Jehovah's Witnesses and the Luz del Mundo (Light of the World) (Burdick 1992; De La Torre 1997; Napolitano 2002).

11. The postrevolutionary crafting of the figure of el mestizo drew also on much longer-standing anticolonial critiques in Mexico and Latin America more broadly, particularly one that explored botanical notions of "hybrid vigor" and sought to push back against Spanish rule through a revaluing of an imagined Aztec past (Alonso 2004).

12. I pull here on the notion of the "illegibility of the state" from Veena Das and Deborah Poole (2004). The depth of these uncertainties emerged for me on an un-

settlingly personal level when I was emphatically advised by local officials, during an orientation session in Mexico held by one of the funding agencies supporting my work, that if I ever got into trouble or found myself the victim of a crime during my time there, "the last thing you want to do here is call the police . . . you'll only get yourself in more trouble, put yourself in more danger that way."

13. See Finkler 1991; Hunt 1995; Mesa-Lago 1978; and Wilson 1995 on the distribution of health-care resources in Mexico. See also Soberón Solís and Villagómez 1999 for a contemporaneous overview of the Mexican health-care systems in general.

14. There was strong precedent in Mexico for this model of attracting U.S. health-care business, even in these days before the more robust global development of what is now often termed *medical tourism*. In Tijuana, for example, there has been a long-standing tradition of people being drawn across the border from the United States in search of more accessible and less expensive health-care services (pharmacy and dentistry, in particular).

15. The article, which ran in the (unabashedly named) *Colony Reporter*, reads as follows: "Although all the liver recipients in Guadalajara have so far been Mexican, foreigners could be candidates . . . A transplant in Guadalajara would cost half as much as in the United States. 'It's an advantage for both the patients and the insurance companies,' notes the surgeon" (Miller 1999: 5). This scenario was purely speculative at the time of this research—no such cases had (yet) taken place.

16. Spain at the time was the only country in the world whose waiting lists for organ transplants were actually shrinking because they procured enough cadaveric organs to meet demand. For more detail on the fascinating Spanish case, see Matesanz 1996 and Matesanz and Miranda 1996a, b, c.

17. In addition to the IMSS and the SSa (which was also sometimes referred to as the Secretaría de Salubridad y Asistencia—Ministry of Health and Welfare), there are also several other smaller government-run social security systems in Mexico, including those set up at different historical points to provide coverage for federal workers such as civil servants, teachers, and members of the police force (Instituto de Seguridad y Servicios Sociales de los Trabajadores del Estado—ISSTE, Institute of Social Security and Services for State Workers) and for workers in PEMEX, the nationalized oil industry (Mesa-Lago 1978). However, at the time of this research, transplantation was not offered within these systems in Guadalajara, although patients in need of transplantation were sometimes sent on to either the IMSS or SSa hospitals for such services.

18. The public health-care landscape described here has been shifting in recent years under a series of successive reforms knows as the *Seguro Popular* (Popular Health Insurance) meant to extend public health access more fully in Mexico (or, as some argue, to shift costs more directly onto the private shoulders of the poor), though the two main institutions, hospital sites, and transplant programs depicted here remain largely intact. See Knaul et al. 2012 and Laurell 2001, 2011, for contrasting accounts of the Seguro Popular reforms more generally, and Kierans et al. 2013 and Kierans 2015 for an account of its emerging effects specifically on kidney care in Mexico.

19. In addition, formal and informal mechanisms existed by which people without employment or who worked in the informal sector (such as domestic workers or the ubiquitous street food vendors) could sometimes arrange to obtain rights to the IMSS system, at least temporarily (see also Kierans 2015).

20. Cuba offers an intriguing contrast with this set of relations between idealism, expectation, national identity, and health in Mexico, where the IMSS system represents a never-quite-fulfilled promise of the Revolution now under increasing threat from privatizing pressures. As Sean Brotherton (2012) has explored, comprehensive and high-quality cradle-to-grave health care in Cuba was a more fully realized and central achievement of the Revolution—as well as a core element of the nation's identity—until the collapse of the Soviet Union and the economic crises of the 1990s began to seriously erode the existing health-care system in both its material and symbolic dimensions.

21. Medicine is not an automatically lucrative profession in Mexico, due in part to a glut of physicians trained in the public medical school system who are heavily concentrated (and hence competing with one another) in the urban areas.

22. The IMSS hospital maintained a daily clipping service, to which I was graciously granted access, that tracked health-care-related articles in ten national and regional newspapers: El Informador, El Occidental, Mural, Público, Ocho Columnas, El Financiero, Siglo 21, Reforma, La Jornada, and Mi Pueblo.

1. Living Organ Donation, Bioavailability, and Ethical Domesticity

1. Though not a form of "bare life," kidneys of course must still be rendered as "extra" and hence extractable in new ways in order to enable transplantation. This set of transformations is explored in more detail in chapter 5.

2. I am indebted to Lesley Sharp for encouraging me to make greater analytic use of the presence of The Two Fridas in this ethnographic space.

3. The medical literature on kidney donor risks over the long term is notoriously dependent on small sample sizes and narrowly defined follow-up data. Recognizing this issue, the National Institutes of Health in the United States has initiated a special research program designed to collect and analyze long-term outcome data on living donors. Of course, it will take quite some time for these data to accrue the necessary volume and duration to be clinically useful.

4. There is some dispute in the anthropological literature on Mexico about whether the practice of keeping such a casa chica is actually common, or merely a commonplace (and highly exaggerated) stereotype of Mexican masculinity. Matthew Gutmann reports finding little evidence of the practice in his study of a working-class colonia in Mexico City (1996), while Emily Wentzell encountered it among some of her informants in Cuernavaca who worked in specific jobs like long-haul trucking (2013). Whether social reality or social imaginary, however, what interests me here is the way the notion of la casa chica functioned as a commonly shared understanding of sociality beyond (or even in seeming contradiction to) the hallowed norm of la familia mexicana.

5. I focus here on the responses of members of the transplant community to this naturalized discourse of women as organ donors because at the time of my research there was virtually no public awareness of this issue in wider society. Media attention to transplantation (much like in North America) has focused either on the dearth of cadaveric donations or on heroic, heartrending stories of individual patients either saved or awaiting salvation through transplantation, with little sustained attention to or critique of issues of gender in living organ donation and transplant. It remains to be seen whether this will change with the increasing routinization of transplantation in Mexico.

6. During the time of my research, all kidney donations in the transplant programs I studied were performed using an open surgical procedure. A laparoscopic procedure for donor kidney removal has become increasingly widespread in the United States and Europe, which requires a much smaller incision and hence reduces postoperative pain and recovery time, but this technique was not yet being used in Mexico (Bartlett and Schweitzer 1999; Bishoff and Kavoussi 2002).

7. This notion of living organ donors as "not the patient"—despite the fact that they are undergoing major abdominal surgery—because they are always necessarily the "healthy" side of the donor/recipient dyad is a compelling conceptual, ethical, and clinical problem in living donor transplantation writ large, which I explore more fully elsewhere (Crowley-Matoka 2005).

8. This is, of course, only one limited and situated way of conceiving of the female experience of heterosexual intercourse. A different reading might position the female body not as being passively penetrated, but as actively taking in or engulfing the male body, imagery that would evoke very different power relationships and hierarchies.

9. Such gendered patterns of labor in Mexico are, of course, hardly static. Matthew Gutmann (1996), Valentina Napolitano (2002), and Emily Wentzell (2013) have documented the shifting roles of men inside the house and family, and of women outside the domestic sphere in Mexico. During the period of this research women were also increasingly joining the flow of migrants northward in search of work in the United States (Cerrutti and Massey 2001).

10. The IMSS database contained data on 685 kidney transplants performed between August 1976 and January 2000. The SSa program database contained data on 60 kidney transplants in total, for the period of December 1991 to January 2000.

11. Some additional information on how these databases were constructed and maintained is useful. The IMSS database was computerized and aimed to represent a complete record of all the transplants performed in the program since its inception. Since this was a project begun only about two years before the initiation of my fieldwork, however, this has required a great deal of "reconstituting" data from the past out of a combination of paper patient files and staff memory. The director of the program brought in a part-time intern with computer training specifically to take on this project because he viewed the marshaling of comprehensive data as critical for the program's self-evaluation and its self-promotion. The much smaller SSa database was initially constituted primarily because the program was enrolled in an international research

protocol, to which it submitted standardized data on an ongoing basis. The program director maintained this database himself, updating it on a case by case basis. While not infallible by any means, I am confident that these data are useful for identifying broad-stroke gender patterns, in part because I was able to check gender against patient and donor names (from which gender is usually easy to discern in Mexico) in the database as an internal check on validity. In the case of both databases, I would be extremely reluctant to rely on them for *outcome* data, however, since the degree of patient follow-up in these programs was often minimal beyond the first few months (see chapter 4). As a result, data on long-term transplant outcomes were often "filled-in" on the basis of little more than gossip, informal hearsay, and the optimistic hope that patients were doing well unless otherwise heard from.

12. An examination of the records for patients referred to the IMSS transplant program from January to December 2000, for example, revealed that of the 342 new patients registered in the program, only 138 were female.

13. Farhat Moazam, writing on transplantation in Pakistan, notes a similar feminine role in protectively blocking (some forms of) organ donation when she describes how women are sometimes characterized as *chalak* (cunning, clever) in thwarting the efforts of transplant staff to identify a living donor (Moazam 2006: 65), and Sherine Hamdy also describes the protective prohibition that senior female family members sometimes exert over living donation, particularly donation by young, unmarried women (Hamdy 2012: 196).

14. This is not the only instance of hypervisibility of women's (potentially) exploited bodies and simultaneous invisibility of the exploitation of men's bodies; similar patterns have been identified in discussions of both reproduction and commercial sex work (Sharp 2000; Ebron 1997).

15. Currently in the United States minors typically are not permitted to donate solid organs as living donors as neither they nor their parents are regarded as able to provide sufficiently autonomous and informed consent. This is, however, a norm that has developed over time—in the early days of transplantation in the United States (and before the rise of the informed consent model in American biomedicine), minors were sometimes used in living donation (Simmons et al. 1987). Most donors in the fourteen to twenty age category in the IMSS database were sixteen and older, but younger donors were occasionally used as well. This is likely due at least in part to the still-emergent character of transplantation in Mexico, as well as to the fact that the notions of informed consent and patient rights operated somewhat differently in Mexico, where it was still not uncommon, for instance, for family members and medical staff to withhold a cancer or other terminal diagnosis from a patient "for his own good." Perhaps even more important, norms surrounding the category (and boundaries) of childhood in Mexico were distinctive from those contained in the U.S. legal notion of "minor." There is both a long rural and a more recent urban tradition of children being expected to work in order to contribute to family survival—in just one example, children as young as eight or nine were employed in a recent state-run labor program in Tijuana, Mexico (Aitken et al. 2006). Within this context the fourteen- to twenty-

year-old donor category is perhaps not surprising, representing the figuration of organ donation as another form of labor on behalf of the family, to which both younger and older members were expected to contribute.

16. Scholars working in the United States have also noted the conflicting pull of natal and marital family ties and responsibilities on potential donors (Gordon 2001; Simmons et al. 1987), but have not generally explored in detail the kind of interactions of gender, class, age, and family structure that seemed so vital in producing (or withholding) living donations in Guadalajara.

17. For example, in 2011 the male to female donor ratio in the United States was 2,219:3,554, in 2012 it was 2,107:3,513, and in 2013 it was 2,212:3,522 (UNOS 2014c).

18. The notion of domestication as a process at once biological, social, and intensely political is central to classic understandings of the history of human-animal relations in anthropology and elsewhere (Franklin 2007; Russell 2007).

2. Cadaveric Organ Donation, Biounavailability, and Slippery States

Epigraph: Michel Foucault, *Discipline and Punish: The Birth of the Prison*, 142.

1. Donation from brain-dead patients was the only form of cadaveric donation routinely practiced for solid organs in Guadalajara at the time of this research, though the use of what are called "non-heart-beating donors" has become increasingly common in the United States and elsewhere as a way to further expand the pool of available organs for transplant (Institute of Medicine 2014).

2. Indeed, data provided by the Departamento de Tránsito (Department of Transit) for the state of Jalisco showed that out of 122,932 license recipients during the period of June 1999 to March 2000, 33,183 registered their desire to serve as an organ donor upon their death. This registration rate of 27 percent is comparable to contemporaneous registration rates in similar state driver's license programs in the United States, where fourteen individual states reported anywhere from 1 percent to 56 percent of license recipients registering themselves as organ donors, with an average of approximately 31 percent (Office of the Inspector General 2002: 19–20).

3. Japan has also maintained a similarly contradictory law regarding the removal of patients from a ventilator (Lock 2001: 3).

4. Note that the patient in the second of the donation-gone-wrong cases was removed from a ventilator *not* in order to end his life in a situation of perceived hopelessness, but as a result of a triage decision made in the context of scarce resources. While another patient was thought more likely to benefit from the use of the ventilator, it wasn't until several days after his continued survival without ventilator support that the coma patient came to be perceived (by the local ICU doctor) as truly "hopeless" and hence a potential candidate for organ donation.

5. This apparatus includes the existence of a "presumed consent" law in Spain (a matter taken up later in this chapter), as well as public investment in the infrastructure of the Organización Nacional de Trasplantes (ONT).

6. See also Kaufman 2000 and Slomka 1995 on the slippery status of personhood in the severely brain-injured.

7. Lesley Sharp reports something similar among some U.S. donor families, who may describe their loved ones as having died "on the operating table," not at the time of the brain-death diagnosis (Sharp 2006: 86; see also Crowley-Matoka and Arno 2004).

8. See also Elizabeth Roberts's incisive work on in vitro fertilization in Ecuador and the profound interpenetration of science and religion in the daily practices of both patients and medical practitioners (Roberts 2012).

9. See chapters 3 and 5 for more on the deep patterns of reciprocal relationality in Mexico as they unfold and are reworked in the context of transplantation.

10. See Oktavec (1995) for a detailed study of present-day practices surrounding mandas.

11. Due to the time pressures created by the medical instability of the potential donor coupled with the unpredictable delays of testing and bureaucratic processes, multiple potential recipients were often summoned to the hospital on the basis of only a blood-type match (and position on the wait list) before human leukocyte antigen typing on the potential donor was available.

12. See chapter 3, on the process of seeking a transplant, for additional detail on the local conditions of medical record-keeping in Mexico.

13. In countries like the United States with more long-term experience in maintaining brain-dead patients—as well as more abundant resources—these patients have been successfully maintained for much longer periods of time, extending into weeks, months, and even years (Shewmon 1998).

14. These time pressures on the scheduling of recipient surgeries in relation to the donor surgery were rendered particularly acute because the perfusion machines commonly used in the United States to sustain extracted organs for longer periods of time outside the human body were not readily available.

15. Though this is not to ignore that the PRI has also exercised more directly brutal forms of power through strategic acts of violence (see, for example, the Tlatelolco massacre of student protesters in 1968 and the armed clashes with the Zapatista uprising in Chiapas in 1994 and beyond) (Knight 1999; Stephen 2002).

16. In brain death, patients exhibit no brain activity. Patients in coma (or persistent vegetative state) *do* exhibit brain activity and for this reason cannot serve as organ donors.

17. The larger amendment also included new language outlawing living organ donation from unrelated donors, intended to inhibit organ sales. This section, however, received relatively little attention in either the transplant community or the popular media—where organ selling was perceived as an occasional problem, but not a well-established practice. See chapter 5 for more on the issue of organ sales.

18. This controversial enrollment of a biotechnology into the political manipulation of modernizing imagery was not unique. More recently, the use of RU-486 (the so-called morning after pill) was legalized via similarly precipitous political processes in Mexico, in a move that also produced great public furor and established a clear (and

clearly intended) distance between the State and the outraged Catholic Church (Maldonado 2004). At a broader level, see Bartra 1992, García-Canclini 1995, and Lomnitz 2002 for trenchant and often lyrical examinations of Mexico's troubled national relationship with an ever-elusive modernity.

3. Being Worthy of Transplant, Embodying Transplant's Worth

1. Insightful work on aging, digitized, and racialized bodies by (respectively), Lawrence Cohen (1998), Stefan Helmreich (1998), and Diane Nelson (1999) has particularly informed the way in which I take up Butler's theory of materialization here.

2. See also Emily Wentzell's recent study of aging and masculinity in Mexico for her description of the perpetually stressed conditions of the IMSS urology clinic in Cuernavaca, where patients were more likely to be deflected from, rather than enticed into, specialty care (2013).

3. The story of how dialysis did, eventually, become more available in Mexico is a complex tale largely beyond the bounds of this analysis. In brief, dialysis is big business the world over, with high-cost peritoneal and hemodialysis supplies bringing in huge profits for multinational pharmaceutical companies. Indeed, dialysis in the United States is a notorious cash cow, due largely to the fact that all renal replacement therapy is federally funded by an act of Congress. This sociohistorically unique arrangement in American health care allows both pharmaceutical companies and for-profit private hemodialysis center networks (but not necessarily patients or taxpayers, as some point out) to benefit (Fox and Swazey 1974; Kassler 1994). Historically, the development of a lucrative dialysis market in the United States seems to have produced the familiar formula of capitalist expansion in which increasingly advantageous economies of scale generate the need for new markets in which to grow. It is in this context that dialysis therapies eventually became more financially feasible (and aggressively marketed) in Mexico. Unlike the United States, however, where federal funding produced incentives for the spread of hemodialysis, the institutional structures and material constraints of health care in Mexico initially shaped a preference for the lower-tech option of peritoneal dialysis.

4. These numbers were provided by the director of medical services for the IMSS Centro Médico. Note that the number of active transplant patients reported here does not reflect the full number of patients actually transplanted: see chapter 4 for more on the distribution of care for posttransplant patients and chapter 1 for data on the number of patients transplanted in the IMSS program overall.

5. It should be noted that there is growing debate over the heavy reliance on hemodialysis in North America and elsewhere, with some indications that morbidity and mortality rates on the more cost-effective peritoneal dialysis may, in fact, be comparable to those on hemodialysis, and even superior for some groups (see, for example, Lamiere and Van Biesen 2010; Murphy et al. 2000). Some speculate that the unique funding structure of kidney care in the United States—rather than therapeutic benefit—is responsible for the dominance of hemodialysis (Fox and Swazey 1974; Kassler 1994; Rothman 1997).

6. This situation of extreme scarcity and the difficult decisions it forced upon hospital staff painfully recalls the early days of dialysis in the United States, when "God committees" were set up to make agonizing choices about who would receive the then-limited resource of dialysis, and who would be left to die (Fox and Swazey 1974: 201–65).

7. Such deeply held cultural beliefs about the centrality of blood to vitality and homeostasis emerge as well in the story of Mexico's blood supply. The model of generalized altruistic blood donation (common to the United States, for example) is rare in Mexico, and most blood donations are collected from family and friends in the name of a specific patient who must "bank" a certain amount of blood to cover what may be needed for transfusion during a particular surgery (Mauleon 2000; "Promoverán Instituciones de Salud la donación altruista de sangre," El Informador, August 4, 2000). To ensure that there is some blood supply available for emergency cases, hospitals generate back-up supply by requiring that patients bank more units of blood than will likely be needed in their own procedure—kidney transplant patients in the IMSS hospital, for instance, typically were required to bank six units of blood, although it was rare that more than four would be required during the transplant surgery. Even when bound by familial ties, however, people were often reluctant to donate blood, and many patients struggled to find enough willing donors to meet their blood unit quota. When pressed about why they had not provided sufficient blood donors, patients were likely to allude to family members' fear of needles, of infection, and especially of losing strength through blood donation. Notably, these are fears reinforced by recurrent media reports of contamination by blood transfusions (Atilano 2000; "Gran Número de Contagios por Sangre." Público, April 11, 2000). Suggested here is a local world in which connections "by blood" are not always sufficient to summon forth a danger-ridden sacrifice of blood. Charlotte Ikels recounts similar problems in maintaining the blood supply in China, which she also links to local understandings of the importance of blood in bodily health (Ikels 1997).

8. This fear has echoes in the anxieties reported by Aslihan Sanal among dialysis patients in Turkey that the process of fluid exchange with the machine was slowly robbing them of their humanity and turning them in to a terrifying form of robot or cyborg (Sanal 2011).

9. Reasons for such high mortality on dialysis in Mexico are complex, ranging from factors such as comorbidities, age, and nutritional status to problems with the quality of dialyzing equipment and environment. The situation is further complicated by the political economy of Mexican health care in general (and kidney care in particular) described above, such that many patients simply were not diagnosed with kidney failure until their health had already irretrievably deteriorated.

10. In general, patients in Mexico had far greater and more routine access to their own medical charts than do their U.S. counterparts, in part because of the realities of record-keeping in the overcrowded and resource-strapped hospitals. Patients were often responsible for carrying their own charts around to various appointments within the hospital and, in many cases, kept test results, X-ray films, and other medical documentation in their own homes. Some of the more savvy patients kept careful track

(and back-up copies) of all of their own records, to guard against the common occurrence of paperwork being lost in the hospital records. For less savvy patients, however, such losses could mean endless delays as tests were repeated and new appointments made due to misplaced test results or physician notes. Ciara Kierans captures this still-common situation in Mexico compellingly in her description of patients as "their own mobile archives" (Kierans 2015).

11. One might discern, in this notion of "agility," a certain affinity with what Emily Martin has termed the "flexibility" that characterizes both late capitalism and late modern immunological figurations of the body (1994). Yet it seems to me that the notion of *agilizar* here is grounded in a different sociohistorical specificity and references not a shift in the logics governing flows of both capital and bodies, but rather a continuity with longer-standing socioeconomic and political arrangements in Mexico.

12. Patients cannot receive a transplant while they have any sort of infection, because the massive immunosuppression they must undergo after the transplant could permit even a minor infection to rage out of control and become life-threatening. As a result, patients with a cold, an infection at their dialysis site, or just an unfilled dental cavity at the time of a donation are passed over even if they are next up on the list.

13. The materiality of Lidia's body, its heaviness, clearly mattered here, both indexing her more advanced disease and impairing (at least symbolically) her potential agility. And of course Lidia's vulnerable economic position powerfully conditioned not only the size and shape of her physical body but also the unchecked advance of her kidney disease that went so long undiagnosed, as well as her skill in navigating clinical interactions. While Lidia's ungainly form emerged from and reinscribed a set of entrenched class hierarchies, it also seems worth remarking that the weight of female bodies in Mexico did not signify in quite the same aesthetic and moral terms that U.S. readers might anticipate. This is, after all, a context in which *mi gordita* (my little chubby one) remained a commonplace term of warm endearment.

14. I refer here to the meaning-making framework of one individual, without claiming "natural selection" as a generalized grid of intelligibility for all transplant program staff. For more detailed explorations of the particular ways in which forms of Darwinism (social and otherwise) have been taken up, reworked, and/or resisted in Mexico and Latin America more generally, see Glick 1974 and Stepan 1991.

15. Lesley Sharp writes movingly about this exclusionary force in her account of the policing of what transplant patients and donor families are permitted to express publicly about their experiences in such forums as the U.S. Transplant Games (2006: 107–61).

4. The Unsung Story of Posttransplant Life

1. See Sherine Hamdy's exploration of the relationship between medical mistrust and the transplant endeavor in Egypt for a similar dynamic (Hamdy 2012: 21–45).

2. And this North American logic of (organ) scarcity is also, of course, distinctive from the logic of scarcity described in chapter 3 that drove the director of an HIV clinic

in southern Mexico to hope that patients would never find their way to his door (from Gutmann 2007).

3. Note that Lawrence Cohen and Nancy Scheper-Hughes have observed a similar reversal of the usual logic of scarcity in the transplant realm in relation to global organ trafficking where it seems to be willing and (financially) able transplant patients/purchasers—rather than organ donors/sellers—who have become increasingly scarce (Cohen 1999; Scheper-Hughes 2005).

4. Transplant patients in Mexico often experienced characteristic swelling of the face ("moon face"), hirsutism, and hand tremors from the steroids used as part of their immunosuppression regimen, and many also wore a surgical mask covering their mouth and nose when outside the home for the first several months posttransplant. See section on Transplanted Health later in chapter 4.

5. It should be noted that such hopes for a miracle are neither unique to the Mexican setting nor necessarily irrational, as evinced by the numerous documented cases of unexplained (in biomedical terms) healing both in the historical record and in the contemporary North American medical literature (see, for example, Duffin 2009 and Weil 2000).

6. This is due to the sensitization of the immune system—once exposed to the foreign body of a transplanted organ, it attacks any subsequent transplant with even greater vigor.

7. The notion of persistent or lingering liminality in chronic illness as used here in relation to patients' dearly held hopes for normality achieved through transplantation also evokes Joseph Dumit's notion of "dependent normality" (Dumit 2005). Yet Dumit's interest is in an understanding of "normality" that can *only ever* be achieved through psychopharmaceutical intervention (such that dependence on such medications is rendered utterly ordinary), while here what is at stake is a longed-for normality through biomedical intervention that can perhaps *never* be fully achieved, in part because of the precariousness of that very intervention.

8. I use the slightly less familiar term *reproductivity* here in its meaning as "the state of or capacity for being reproductive" (Gove 1993), which usefully captures that what is at stake for transplant recipients is not just the effects of *actual* reproduction, but the effects of their perceived reproductive *potential* as well.

9. Such medication-related personality changes could raise uneasy questions, for some patients, about the possibilities for changes to self wrought by the incorporation of another's organ in transplant. Such possibilities, and the fears, fantasies, embodied experiences, and clinical politics surrounding them, are addressed further in chapter 6.

10. The scheduling of follow-up visits for transplant recipients varied substantially, from every one to four weeks for recent recipients to every six to twelve months for those several years posttransplant and/or those living in remote areas.

11. Fox and Swazey describe a similar dynamic with the early patients of dialysis programs in the United States and their clinicians, based both on the closer bonds forged through the experience of being collaborators in an experimental endeavor (rather than merely doctor and patient) and on the talismanic property of those first, uncertain successes (1974: 87–107). This is a pattern of extraordinary effort extended

to "special" patients (often "firsts") that has remained common throughout transplant (see also Sharp 2006: 93).

12. Because a central tenet of Jehovah's Witness doctrine is that Scripture enjoins the acceptance of blood from another person into one's body, transfusion with blood (or blood products) is often rejected by its practitioners, even in the case of surgery. This often puts Jehovah's Witnesses in difficult conflict with surgeons, who are unwilling to put a patient at risk of death on the operating table if a needed blood transfusion cannot be given. In the case of transplantation, several transplant team members expressed a degree of skepticism about the Jehovah's Witness position on blood products, given that (at least some) believers were nonetheless willing to accept transplanted organs. Manuel's interpretation of this apparent contradiction was to draw a fascinating analogy with eating meat. He said: "The important thing is the *intention*. In a transplant, mostly the organ is washed, so there is very little blood, but you are not taking the organ in order to get blood. It is like eating meat—when you eat meat you are eating a little bit of blood too, but you are not eating it to get the blood, that is just an unavoidable part of what you get."

13. Such medication-sharing efforts were further complicated by a recent move from liquid to pill forms of cyclosporine, which can be less easily (and precisely) divided and thus less easily shared. The change in medication format, driven by the pharmaceutical companies, frustrated not just patients but also physicians, who found it more difficult to make minute adjustments to patients' medication levels as a result.

14. The sexualized imagery here regarding a priest may seem somewhat surprising to North American readers, particularly following the sex abuse scandal that has engulfed the Catholic Church in the United States since the late 1980s. Though that scandal did eventually erupt in Mexico (and in the Catholic Church elsewhere around the world) as well, it had not yet gained widespread public attention at this time in Mexico. Moreover, the imagery invoked here of stallions and geldings was of a piece with the highly masculinized identity that Padre Tomás generally affected, one that drew directly on his privileged upbringing and involvement in the horse culture of *charrería* (a highly stylized form of Mexican rodeo). We will return to Padre Tomás again in chapter 5.

15. These figures were based on an internal cost analysis from 1997 that listed annual recurring institutional costs for kidney transplantation versus both forms of dialysis.

5. Gifts, Commodities, and Analytic Icons in the Anthropological Lives of Organs

Epigraph: William Shakespeare, *Four Comedies: The Taming of the Shrew, A Midsummer Night's Dream, The Merchant of Venice and Twelfth Night*, ed. David Bevington, 4.1.298–308.

1. "Mexico"—operating as sign of the beckoning riches of the imagined Americas—is one of the destinations for which Antonio's trading ships are bound, the very ships whose failure to come in leave him so catastrophically unable to pay off his debt to Shylock (Shakespeare 1988: 1.3.20).

2. Of course transplantation and the bodily exchanges it entails constitute just one among a long history of instances in which the relationships between personhood, the body, and the market have been called into question (Hogle 1999; Kimbrell 1993; Sharp 2000; Simmel 1978). Slavery, adoption, prostitution, reproductive technologies, and various traditional and contemporary African witchcraft practices all raise similar problems about the shifting boundaries between persons, things, and money (Collier, Maurer, and Suarez-Navaz 1995; Pashukanis 1978; Radin 1996; Scheper-Hughes 2002b; Sharp 2000; Strathern 1996).

3. I am indebted to Bill Maurer for (among many other things) first suggesting that Portia's argument might be "good to think with."

4. Antonio's pound of flesh that cannot be gotten without a "jot of blood" recalls the explanation offered up by the transplant patient who was a Jehovah's Witness from chapter 4, when he described why receiving an organ did not violate his religion's prohibition of accepting blood from another person. He acknowledged that it was impossible to accept the organ without receiving some accompanying blood, but it was believed it was the intention that mattered, the intention of receiving the organ, of which the blood was merely an unavoidable by-product.

5. One notable exception to this overall pattern is Margaret Lock's work on brain death and organ transplantation in Japan, a setting that is certainly culturally distant from "the West," and yet perhaps more familiar along the gradients of economic privilege and technological sophistication than many of the more economically constrained "Other" settings where more commodification-focused anthropology of transplant has been concentrated (Lock 2001).

6. For the purposes of this chapter's analysis, I have largely bracketed the social lives of cadaveric organs in part because living donors so dominated the Mexican transplant scene. Moreover, although those organs of course may also be more gift-like or more commodity-like in different contexts, it is on the possibilities for the buying and selling of live donor organs that the most acute anxieties (anthropological and otherwise) have focused. The case of cadaveric donation is taken up more directly in chapter 2, and again in chapter 6.

7. This logic of refusal to donate based on one's own children's possible future claims to the "extra" kidney has been reported in the United States as well (Gordon 2001).

8. Such cases of material rewards for familial donations are not uncommon; for example, Scheper-Hughes reports a similar case from Brazil, in which a niece was promised a house in return for her kidney (2000: 32). This kind of unabashed mixing of familial connection, economic value, and bodily sacrifice might ring oddly to Euro-American ears, given the sharp distinctions often drawn between the familial sphere and the economic one, between Kantian notions of "dignity" and "value," and more colloquial ideas about "love" and "money." Yet such distinctions are not always held so dear in other settings, as Elizabeth Roberts has shown in her work on IVF in Ecuador, where the high cost of those deeply desired babies is an integral part of how love is demonstrated and dignity constituted (Roberts 2012).

9. At the time of my research, for example, only 8 percent of all transplants done in the IMSS program had used nonrelated living donors, for a total of 44 such cases since 1976. Of course, it is impossible to know for sure how many other cases of nonrelated living donation may have been disguised as living-related donations. I knew of one case, for instance, in which a now-transplanted patient and his donor admitted to me that they lied to hospital staff and told them that the donor, a close friend, was actually a cousin. The two were worried that the donation might not go through if they were not blood relatives and thought that the lie might increase their chances of being accepted into the transplant program. This practice of producing "kin with a wink" to get potential donors accepted into transplant programs has been widely reported in India after the implementation of new legislation designed to halt organ trafficking (Cohen 2002; Marshall and Daar 2000; Scheper-Hughes 2000, 2004). Yet during the period of my fieldwork in Mexico nonrelated living donors were openly accepted in the IMSS and SSa transplant programs (as several of the cases later in the chapter illustrate), so there is good reason to believe that such misrepresentation of familial relatedness was not widespread at the time of this research.

10. "Emotionally related" is a term that has gained greater currency in the United States in an effort to make the increasing use of nonrelated living donors more palatable as transplant programs search for ways to bridge the perceived ever-widening gap between organ supply and demand (Crowley-Matoka and Switzer 2005).

11. This is a point observed by other scholars of transplantation as well; see, for example, Lock 2001 and Sharp 2006.

12. Such unexpected twists and turns in the ethnographic stories we try to follow and tell also emerge in Elizabeth Roberts's rich study of IVF in Ecuador (2012), serving as an acute reminder of the profoundly partial and always situated nature of any such accountings.

13. The sexualized imagery of penetration here recalls the symbolic connections explored in chapter 1 between organ donation and loss of virginity, though here it is the donor's desire (and kidney) that are violating.

14. Pablo was not the only kidney donor I encountered in Mexico to report this. Another woman I knew, who had donated to her mother, complained about the weight she had subsequently gained due to a similar feeling of urgent hunger that she also attributed to the void left by her donated kidney. The embodied experience and imagery here are provocative—echoing back to Lawrence Cohen's (1999) classic image of the nephrectomy scar as "where it hurts" with a sense of the donor body here as "where it hungers"—and merit more sustained analytic attention than I can accommodate here.

15. Though this is not to say, of course, that such a possibility—of the wife also converting her kidney into a form of economic resource—might not now be rendered more thinkable in the moral field of action expanded by Pablo's giving up of his kidney. As noted in chapter 1, others have reported similar—but also shifting—gender patterns in organ selling, as in Lawrence Cohen's account of the way rural men in India are more likely to sell their kidneys in times of agricultural crisis, while in urban areas it is female sellers who predominate in a context of pervasive precarity rather than acute crisis (Cohen 1999: 138–40).

16. This is the reciprocal relationality so central to the culturally resonant notion of *agilizar* explored in chapter 3.

17. Though both Don Jaime and Faustina expressed their sense of a fictive kinship in biologized relations of father/son and sister/sister, one might imagine other forms of kinship-making through which the connection (potentially) created by organ transfer could be culturally elaborated and naturalized—the bonds of social obligation and mutual assistance produced by marriage might also provide an older model through which the experience of organ transfer could be imagined, for instance.

18. In the constant, constitutive moving back and forth between the two, I have in mind something akin to Marilyn Strathern's notion of the merographic, that is, the way that in describing things we are always making connections that work to produce distinction or separation *and* marking out disconnections whose very description then becomes a form of connection (Strathern 1992).

6. Scientists, Saints, and Monsters in Transplant Medicine

1. The image I saw most frequently in Guadalajara was of the El Niño Doctor *de los Enfermos*, a sculpture housed in the pueblo of Tepeaca, in the state of Puebla. The statue, originally made by nuns and housed in a local hospital in the 1940s, is thought to have performed miracles by visiting the sick and dying (visits first discovered by the evidence of mud on his slippers and reports of his comforting, healing appearance in patients' dreams). The statue now resides on the high altar in the Church of Tepeaca and has become a pilgrimage site for supplicants asking for healing miracles. There is also a similar icon known as the *Santo Niño de la Salud* (Holy Child of Good Health), based on a venerated wood carving of the infant Jesus reported to have granted healing favors in the city of Morelia in Michoacan, Mexico. That original image is currently housed in the Santo Niño de la Salud parish church in Morelia, along with a pilgrimage replica that is used in public devotion ceremonies that have been Church-approved and practiced since 1946 (Lawrence 1996).

2. The designation of "narco-saint" is somewhat controversial, but has been used to characterize (and sometimes critique) a collection of contemporary patron saints recently emergent in Mexico, of which La Santa Muerte is perhaps the most prominent (Hughes 2012).

3. Though the biblical canon is relatively silent on this period of Jesus's life (up until the age of 12), such stories are recounted in apocryphal books like the Infancy Gospel of Thomas and speak to an abiding popular interest in the infant Jesus (Ehrman 2003).

4. Such racialized stories of robbery, dismemberment, and consumption of bodies are not unique to Latin America, of course, but emerge throughout the postcolonial world (see, for example, Adams 1997; Jarosz 1994; Scheper-Hughes 1998b; Vargas Llosa 1995).

5. At the time of this research live donor liver transplants were not yet being done in Mexico. Although the liver transplant surgeon had been trained in this technique in both the United States and Japan, the significantly higher risk profile of the procedure for the donor (a clinical reality that has also slowed the growth of the procedure in the

United States and Europe) made him reluctant to use living liver donors until he had first firmly established a successful cadaveric donor liver program.

6. Although strict anonymity of cadaveric donors is upheld in many places as a central ethical tenet of transplantation, such standards are unevenly embraced in many settings—particularly in places where the effort to materialize transplantation is still tenuous and may be usefully bolstered by anonymity-breaking appeals to the popular media fascination with this iconic biotechnology. Note, however, that Lesley Sharp reports that the norm of anonymity is being increasingly challenged by donor families and recipients in the United States, who have both developed clandestine channels for finding one another and begun to pressure publicly for an end to transplant professionals' efforts to keep them apart (Sharp 2006: 159–205). This movement to challenge an institutionally imposed norm of anonymity in organ donation and transplant also has intriguing resonances with the recent shifts described by Barbara Yngvesson and others in the norms and ethics surrounding "open" versus "closed" adoptions (see, for example, Yngvesson 2010).

7. Intriguingly, food issues seem particularly common in these reports—a matter that merits deeper exploration than I can afford here.

8. There are, however, numerous reports in the medical and social scientific literature of transplant recipients who did indeed experience distress related to their donor's identity and its potential effect on their own (see, for example, Fox 1996; Fox and Swazey 1974; Youngner 1996). Such reports often focus on North American recipients of cadaveric donor organs, for whom anxiety and guilt about the cause of donor death was often deeply implicated in this distress. Further, it is intriguing to note that there are, apparently, often different levels of distress attendant to the incorporation of an internal transplanted organ and the experience of receiving one of the growing number of transplant procedures for externalized body parts, such as hands and faces. Hand transplants, in particular, have produced such upsetting experiences of body/self dissonance that some recipients have requested to have them amputated (Slatman and Widdershoven 2010).

9. There is a wealth of scholarship on the Cartesian logics of biomedicine, and on the implications of the vision of body as machine (see, among many examples, Hogle 1995, 1996; Joralemon 1995; Kirmayer 1988; Osherson and AmaraSingham 1981).

10. Some scholars have argued that the very model of altruistic organ donation is, at its very foundation, a profoundly Christian one (Ohnuki-Tierney 1994).

11. See Claudio Lomnitz's *Death and the Idea of Mexico* for a masterful exploration of the cultural history of death in Mexico and in how Mexico has been perceived by outsiders (2005). These relations are being further explored in Angela Garcia's current work on *anexos*—an unregulated form of residential treatment center for substance abuse in Mexico City—where she is delving into the ways these centers operate on a culturally resonant logic of bringing death into life (through deliberately inflicted pain and terror) in order to access healing (Garcia 2013).

12. By their own accounts, many organ recipients did, in fact, pray consistently for their donors and their donors' families.

13. The possibilities for "revaluing" donors in this way exist in other settings as well, of course, offering an opportunity for the conversion of spiritual/social value by transforming (as Lesley Sharp has put it) "trash" or "waste" into the "treasure" of much-needed organs for transplantation (Sharp 2006: 96 on the United States; see also Ben-David 2005 on Israel).

14. For example, one transplant coordinator often reassured family members that "God created us and all of our parts, and He knows what belongs to each person. When He raises us, those organs will surely be returned to their original owner" (Martina, IMSS). Such words and worries bring to mind the fascinating medieval debates over the material, logistical, and philosophical problems of resurrection traced in detail by Caroline Walker Bynum in *Fragmentation and Redemption* (Walker Bynum 1991). Offering one possible solution to such problems, some of the paintings from this period show beasts vomiting up severed legs and heads to be returned to their rightful owners at the moment of resurrection. A strikingly similar scene was sometimes conjured up for the comfort of donor family members, a scene in which organs go whizzing back to their original owners so that they may be raised whole and complete.

15. There are powerful resonances here with the debates over organ donation that Sherine Hamdy traces in Muslim Egypt over the implications of understanding the body as "owned by God," an understanding that for some—but not all—seems to prohibit organ donation (Hamdy 2012).

16. See chapter 2 on brain death for the way religious beliefs may be—often inaccurately—indicted for holding back the transplant endeavor specifically, and modernity more generally.

17. Shelley's original text does not refer to Victor Frankenstein as Dr. Frankenstein but does describe his medical studies at the University of Ingolstadt, and he is frequently portrayed in both scholarship and popular culture representations as a medical doctor and scientist, forming part of a larger tradition of the mad doctor literary genre that includes the characters of Dr. Jekyll and Dr. Moreau (see, among many examples, Goulding 2002; Helman 1988; Kilgour 1998; Roszak 1974).

18. As noted earlier, living kidney donors in Guadalajara at this time all received an open nephrectomy procedure (rather than the laparoscopic version increasingly common for donor procedures in the United States); thus the patient was prepared in one of the positions common for an open procedure.

19. The film merits a much more detailed exegesis of its own, for it veritably teems with complex themes of gender, sexuality, kinship, religiosity, performativity, contamination, and purity (among others) tangled together to tell a tale that is at once madcap and deeply moving, in true Almodóvar style.

Coda

Epigraph: Francis Delmonico and Mary Amanda Dew, "Living Donor Kidney Transplantation in a Global Environment": 608.

References

Adams, Abigail. 1997. "Los cosechadores de organos y Harbury: Relatos transnaciona-les de impunidad y responsabilidad en Guatemala despues de la guerra." *Mesoa-mérica* 34: 595–632.

Adams, Abigail. 1999. "Gringas, Ghouls and Guatemala: The 1994 Attacks on North American Women Accused of Body Organ Trafficking." *Journal of Latin American Anthropology* 4 (1): 112–33.

Ad Hoc Committee of the Harvard Medical School to Examine the Definition of Death. 1968. "Definition of Irreversible Coma." *Journal of the American Medical Association* 205: 337–40.

"Afirman que 'Hay infraestructura; faltan donadores.'" 2000. *Mural*, March 11, 10A.

Agamben, Giorgio. 1998. *Homo Sacer: Sovereign Power and Bare Life.* Stanford, CA: Stanford University Press.

Aitken, Stuart, Silvia Lopez Estrada, Joel Jennings, and Lina María Aguirre. 2006. "Reproducing Life and Labor: Global Processes and Working in Tijuana, Mexico." *Childhood* 13 (3): 365–87.

Alarcón, Norma. 1981. "Chicana's Feminist Literature: A Re-vision through Malintzin/ or Malintzin: Putting the Flesh Back on the Object." In *This Bridge Called My Back: Writings by Radical Women of Color,* ed. Cherrie Moraga and Gloria Anzaldua, 182–90. Watertown, MA: Persephone Press.

Alarcón, Roberto. 2013. "El escándalo en trasplantes de Rodrigo Sancho." *El Informador,* June 27, 2013. Accessed June 25, 2014. http://www.informador.com.mx/jalisco/2013 /463263/6/el-escandalo-en-los-trasplantes-de-rodriguez-sancho.htm.

Alonso, Ana María. 2004. "Conforming Discomformity: 'Mestizaje,' Hybridity and the Aesthetics of Mexican Nationalism." *Cultural Anthropology* 19 (4): 459–90.

Althusser, Louis. [1970] 1984. *Essays on Ideology*. Brooklyn, NY: Verso Books.

Amaral, Carlos Alberto. 2000. "Más muertes 'por error.'" *El Occidental*, April 10, 1A.

American Academy of Neurology. 2010. "Evidence-based Guideline Update: Determining Brain Death in Adults: Report of the Quality Standards Subcommittee of the American Academy of Neurology." *Neurology* 74: 1911–18.

Appadurai, Arjun. 1986. "Introduction: Commodities and the Politics of Value." In *The Social Life of Things: Commodities in Cultural Perspective*, ed. Arjun Appadurai, 3–62. Cambridge: Cambridge University Press.

Atilano, Alejandro. 2000. "Invierte el gobierno en sangre segura." *Mural*, August 4, 11B.

Ayora-Diaz, Steffan I. 2000. "Response to Nancy Scheper Hughes, The Global Traffic in Human Organs." *Current Anthropology* 41 (2): 191–224.

Baez-Jorge, Felix. 1995. "La Virgen de Guadalupe." In *Mitos Mexicanos*, ed. Enrique Florescano, 139–46. Mexico City: Aguilar.

Bakhtin, Mikhail. 1981. *The Dialogic Imagination*. Austin: University of Texas Press.

Barajas, Esperanza. 2000. "Presentan iniciativa de Ley de Trasplantes." *Mural*, March 28, 4A.

Bareño Martinez, Rosario. 2000a. "Mueren niños: Sin trasplante, fallece 90% de menores enfermos." *El Occidental*, March 3, 1A.

Bareño Martinez, Rosario. 2000b. "Espera mortal de un trasplante que no llega." *El Occidental*, March 27, 18A.

Bartlett, Stephen T., and Eugene J. Schweitzer. 1999. "Laparoscopic Living Donor Nephrectomy for Kidney Transplantation." *Dialysis and Transplantation* 28 (6): 318–31.

Bartra, Roger. 1992. *The Cage of Melancholy: Identity and Metamorphosis in the Mexican Character*. New Brunswick, NJ: Rutgers University Press.

Bataille, Georges. [1957] 1986. *Erotism: Death and Sensuality*. San Francisco: City Lights Books.

Becker, Marjorie. 1995. *Setting the Virgin on Fire: Lázaro Cárdenas, Michoacán Peasants, and the Redemption of the Mexican Revolution*. Berkeley: University of California Press.

Beidel, Deborah C. 1987. "Psychological Factors in Organ Transplantation." *Clinical Psychology Review* 7: 677–94.

Ben-David, Orit Brawer. 2005. *Organ Donation and Transplantation: Body Organs as an Exchangeable Socio-Cultural Resource*. Westport, CT: Praeger.

Bhabha, Homi K. 1994. "The Other Question: Stereotype, Discrimination and the Discourse of Colonialism." *The Location of Culture*. New York: Routledge.

Bharadwaj, Aditya. 2006. "Sacred Conceptions: Clinical Theodices, Uncertain Science and Technologies of Procreation in India." *Culture, Medicine and Psychiatry* 30 (4): 451–65.

Biehl, João. 2005. *Vita: Life in a Zone of Social Abandonment*. Berkeley: University of California Press.

Bishoff, Jay T., and Louis R. Kavoussi. 2002. "Laparoscopic Surgery of the Kidney." In *Campbell's Urology, 8th Edition*, ed. Meredith F. Campbell, Patrick C. Walsh, and Alan R. Retik, 3645–81. Philadelphia: W. B. Saunders.

Boulware, Ebony L., Lloyd E. Ratner, Julie Ann Sosa, Lisa A. Cooper, Thomas A. LaVeist, and Neil R. Powe. 2002. "Determinants of Willingness to Donate Living

Related and Cadaveric Organs: Identifying Opportunities for Intervention." *Transplantation* 73 (10): 1683–91.

Bowers, Siobhan, and Diego Bonaparte. 1999. "Refacciones de vida: Donación de organos, una manera de ayudar a vivir." *Muy Interesante*, November, 56–64.

Brading, D. A. 2001. *Mexican Phoenix: Our Lady of Guadalupe, Image and Tradition across Five Centuries.* Cambridge: Cambridge University Press.

Briggs, Charles, and Clara Mantini Briggs. 2004. *Stories in the Time of Cholera: Racial Profiling during a Medical Nightmare.* Berkeley: University of California Press.

Brodwin, Paul. 2000. "Biotechnology on the Margins: A Haitian Discourse on French Medicine." In *Biotechnology and Culture: Bodies, Anxieties, Ethics,* ed. Paul E. Brodwin, 264–84. Bloomington: Indiana University Press.

Brotherton, P. Sean. 2012. *Revolutionary Medicine: Health and the Body in Post-Soviet Cuba.* Durham, NC: Duke University Press.

Browner, Carole. 1986. "The Politics of Reproduction in a Mexican Village." *Signs* 11 (4): 710–24.

Burdick, John. 1992. "Rethinking the Study of Social Movements: The Case of Christian Base Communities in Urban Brazil." In *The Making of Social Movements in Latin America,* ed. Arturo Escobar and Sylvia Alvarez, 171–84. Boulder, CO: Westview Press.

Butler, Judith. 1993. *Bodies That Matter: On the Discursive Limits of "Sex."* New York: Routledge.

Caldeira, Teresa. 2001. *City of Walls: Crime, Segregation, and Citizenship in São Paulo.* Berkeley: University of California Press.

Callender, Clive O., Lannis E. Hall, Curtis L. Yeager, Jesse B. Barber Jr., Georgia M. Dunston, and Vivian W. Pinn-Wiggins. 1991. "Organ Donation and Blacks: A Critical Frontier." *New England Journal of Medicine* 325 (6): 442–44.

Callender, Clive O., Patrice V. Miles, Gwendolyn D. Maddox. 2004. "The Impact of a National Minority Community Based Transplant Education Program: A National Comparative Analysis." *American Journal of Transplantation Supplement* 4 (Supplement 8): 416.

Callon, Michael. 1998. "Introduction: The Embeddedness of Economic Markets in Economics." In *The Laws of the Markets,* ed. Michael Callon, 1–57. Oxford: Blackwell.

Campbell, Howard. 2014. "Narco-propaganda in the Mexican 'Drug War': An Anthropological Perspective." *Latin American Perspectives* 41: 60–77.

Campion-Vincent, Véronique. 1997. "Organ-Theft Narratives." *Western Folklore* 56 (1): 1–37.

Candelaria, Cordelia. 1993. "Letting La Llorona Go, or Re/Reading History's Tender Mercies." *Heresies: A Feminist Publication on Art and Politics* 7 (27): 111–15.

Carrero, Juan Jesús. 2010. "Gender Differences in Chronic Kidney Disease: Underpinnings and Therapeutic Implications." *Kidney and Blood Pressure Research* 33: 383–92.

Carrillo, Héctor. 2002. *The Night Is Young: Sexuality in Mexico in the Time of AIDS.* Chicago: University of Chicago Press.

Cavell, Stanley. 1976. *Must We Mean What We Say? A Book of Essays.* Cambridge: Cambridge University Press.

Cerrutti, Marcela, and Douglas S. Massey. 2001. "On the Auspices of Female Migration from Mexico to the United States." *Demography* 38 (2): 187–200.

Chakkera, Harini A., Ann M. O'Hare, Kirsten L. Johansen, Denise Hynes, Kevin Stroupe, Philip M. Colin, and Glenn M. Chertow. 2005. "Influence of Race on Kidney Transplant Outcomes within and outside the Department of Veterans Affairs." *Journal of the American Society of Nephrology* 16: 269–77.

Chant, Sylvia. 1991. *Women and Survival in Mexican Cities: Perspectives on Gender, Labor Markets, and Low-Income Households.* Manchester, UK: Manchester University Press.

Chavez, Leo. 2013. *The Latino Threat: Constructing Immigrants, Citizens, and the Nation,* 2nd ed. Stanford, CA: Stanford University Press.

Cohen, Lawrence. 1998. *No Aging in India: Alzheimers, the Bad Family, and Other Modern Things.* Berkeley: University of California Press.

Cohen, Lawrence. 1999. "Where It Hurts: Indian Material for an Ethics of Organ Transplantation." *Daedalus: Journal of the American Academy of Arts and Sciences* 128 (4): 135–66.

Cohen, Lawrence. 2002. "The Other Kidney: Biopolitics beyond Recognition." In *Commodifying Bodies,* ed. Nancy Scheper-Hughes and Loïc Wacquant, 9–30. Thousand Oaks, CA: Sage.

Cohen, Lawrence. 2005. "Operability, Bioavailability and Exception." In *Global Assemblages: Technology, Politics, and Ethics as Anthropological Problems,* ed. Aihwa Ong and Stephen J. Collier, 79–90. Malden, MA: Blackwell Publishing.

Cohen, Lawrence. 2011. "Migrant Supplementarity: Remaking Biological Relatedness in Chinese Military and Indian Five-Star Hospitals." *Body and Society* 17: 531–41.

Collier, Jane. 1986. "From Mary to Modern Woman: The Material Basis of Marianismo and Its Transformation in a Spanish Village." *American Ethnologist* 13 (1): 100–107.

Collier, Jane, William Maurer, and Lydia Suarez-Navaz. 1995. "Sanctioned Identities: Legal Constructions of Modern Personhood." *Identities: Global Studies in Culture and Power* 2 (1–2): 1–27.

Correa-Rotter, Ricardo, and Luis González-Machaca. 2005. "Early Detection and Prevention of Diabetic Neuropathy: A Challenge Calling for Mandatory Action for Mexico and the Developing World." *Kidney International Supplement* 98: s69–75.

Crowley, Megan. 1998. "Troubling Boundaries: Organ Transplantation and Liberal Law." *Political and Legal Anthropology Review* 21 (1): 26–41.

Crowley-Matoka, Megan. 2005. "The Problem of Living Liver Donors as 'Non-Patients': An Anthropological Perspective." In *Ethical Issues in Living Donor Transplantation,* ed. Veronique Fournier. Paris: Centre Ethique Clinique.

Crowley-Matoka, Megan. 2015. "Cultural Factors in Death and Dying." *Oxford Handbook of Ethics at the End of Life,* ed. Robert A. Arnold and Stuart J. Youngner. New York: Oxford University Press.

Crowley-Matoka, Megan, and Robert M. Arnold. 2004. "The Dead Donor Rule: How Much Does the Public Care . . . And How Much Should We Care?" *Kennedy Institute of Ethics Journal* 14 (3): 319–32.

Crowley-Matoka, Megan, and Sherine F. Hamdy. 2015. "Gendering the Gift of Life: Family Politics and Kidney Donation in Egypt and Mexico." *Medical Anthropology: Cross-*

Cultural Studies in Health and Illness, June 17. Accessed December 11, 2015. http://www.tandfonline.com/doi/full/10.1080/01459740.2015.1051181#.VI4HIdCRNYM. doi: 10.1080/01459740.2015.1051181.

Crowley-Matoka, Megan, and Margaret Lock. 2006. "Organ Transplants in a Globalized World." Mortality 11 (2): 166–81.

Crowley-Matoka, Megan, Mark Siegler, and David Cronin. 2004. "Long-Term Quality of Life Issues among Adult-to-Pediatric Living Liver Donors: A Qualitative Exploration." American Journal of Transplantation 4 (5): 744–50.

Crowley-Matoka, Megan, and Galen Switzer. 2005. "Nondirected Living Donation: A Preliminary Survey of Current Trends and Practices." Transplantation 79 (5): 515–19.

Das, Veena. 2000. "The Practice of Organ Transplants: Networks, Documents, Translations." In Living and Working with the New Medical Technologies: Intersections of Inquiry, ed. Margaret Lock, Allan Young, and Alberto Cambrosio, 263–87. New York: Cambridge University Press.

Das, Veena, and Deborah Poole. 2004. "State and Its Margins: Comparative Ethnographies." In Anthropology in the Margins of the State, ed. Veena Das and Deborah Poole, 3–34. Santa Fe, NM: School of American Research Press.

Delaney, Carol. 1991. The Seed and Soil: Gender and Cosmology in Turkish Village Society. Berkeley: University of California Press.

De la Torre, Ramon. 1997. Los hijos de la luz: Discurso, identidad y poder en la luz del mundo. Guadalajara, Mexico: Centro de Investigación y Estudios Superiores en Antropología Social, Universidad de Guadalajara.

Delmonico, Francis, and Mary Amanda Dew. 2007. "Living Donor Kidney Transplantation in a Global Environment." Kidney International 71: 608–14.

Diaz, Alejandro. 2000. "¿Donar la vida . . . a fuerzas?" El Occidental, April 13, 6A.

Diaz del Castillo, Bernal. 1956. The Discovery and Conquest of Mexico 1517–1521, trans. A. P. Maudslay. New York: Farrar, Straus and Giroux.

Diaz-Loving, Rolando. 2006. "Mexico." In Families across Cultures: A 30-Nation Psychological Study, ed. James Georgas, John W. Berry, Fons J. R. van de Vijver, Çigdem Kagitçibasi, and Ype H. Poortinga, 394–401. New York: Cambridge University Press.

DiGirolama, Ann M., and V. Nelly Salgado de Snyder. 2008. "Women as Primary Caregivers in Mexico: Challenges to Well-being." Salud Pública de México 50 (6): 16–20.

Dominguez, Gloria. 2000. "Belen: Sueño que causa orgullo." Mural, February 28, 10B.

Douglas, Mary. 1966. Purity and Danger: An Analysis of the Concepts of Pollution and Taboo. New York: Routledge.

Douglas, Mary. 1970. Natural Symbols: Explorations in Cosmology. New York: Pantheon.

Duffin, Jacalyn. 2009. Medical Miracles: Doctors, Saints, and Healing in the Modern World. London: Oxford University Press.

Dumit, Joseph. 2004. Picturing Personhood: Brain Scans and Biomedical Identity. Princeton, NJ: Princeton University Press.

Dumit, Joseph. 2005. "The Depsychiatrization of Mental Illness." Journal of Public Health 4 (3): 8–13.

Durkheim, Emile. [1915] 1964. *The Elementary Forms of Religious Life*. London: George Allen and Unwin Ltd.

Ebron, Paulla. 1997. "Traffic in Men." In *Gendered Encounters: Challenging Cultural Boundaries and Social Hierarchies in Africa*, ed. Maria Grosz-Ngate and Omari H. Kokole, 223–44. New York: Routledge.

Ehrman, Bart. 2003. *Lost Scriptures: Books That Did Not Make It into the New Testament*. New York: Oxford University Press.

Englehardt, H. Tristan. 1975. "Defining Death: A Philosophical Problem for Medicine and Law." *American Review of Respiratory Disease* 112: 587–90.

Englehardt, H. Tristan. 1992. "The Search for a Universal System of Ethics: Post-Modern Disappointments and Contemporary Possibilities." In *Ethical Problems in Dialysis and Transplantation*, ed. Carl M. Kjellstrand and John B. Dossetor, 3–19. Dordrecht, Netherlands: Kluwer.

Ewald, Francois. 2001. "The Return of Descartes' Malicious Demon: An Outline of a Philosophy of Precaution." In *Embracing Risk*, ed. Tom Baker and Jonathan Simon, 273–302. Chicago: University of Chicago Press.

Farmer, Paul. 1993. *AIDS and Accusation: Haiti and the Geography of Blame*. Berkeley: University of California Press.

Fassin, Didier. 2001. "Culturalism as Ideology." In *Cultural Perspectives on Reproductive Health*, ed. Carla Makhlouf Obermeyer, 300–317. Oxford: Oxford University Press.

Feldman, Deborah, Adam Borgida, John Rodis, and Winston Campbell. 2000. "Irreversible Maternal Brain Injury during Pregnancy: A Case Report and Review of the Literature." *Obstetrical and Gynecologial Survey* 55 (11): 708–14.

Finkel, Michael. 2001. "Complications—This Little Kidney Went to Market." *New York Times Magazine*, May 27, 26–33, 40, 52, 59.

Finkler, Kaja. 1991. *Physicians at Work, Patients in Pain: Biomedical Practice and Patient Response in Mexico*. Boulder, CO: Westview Press.

Finkler, Kaja. 1994. *Women in Pain: Gender and Morbidity in Mexico*. Philadelphia: University of Pennsylvania Press.

Foucault, Michel. 1963. *The Birth of the Clinic: An Archeology of Medical Perception*. New York: Vintage Books.

Foucault, Michel. 1975. *Discipline and Punish: The Birth of the Prison*. New York: Vintage Books.

Foucault, Michel. 1976. *The History of Sexuality: Volume 1, An Introduction*. New York: Vintage Books.

Fox, Renee C. 1978. "Organ Transplantation: Sociocultural Aspects." In *Encyclopedia of Bioethics*, vol. 3, ed. W. T. Reich, 1166–69. New York: Free Press.

Fox, Renee C. 1996. "Afterthoughts: Continuing Reflections on Organ Transplantation." In *Organ Transplantation: Meanings and Realities*, ed. Stuart Youngner, Renee Fox, and Laurence O'Connell, 252–72. Madison: University of Wisconsin Press.

Fox, Renee C., and Judith Swazey. 1974. *The Courage to Fail: A Social View of Organ Transplants and Dialysis*. Chicago: University of Chicago Press.

Fox, Renee C., and Judith Swazey. 1992. *Spare Parts: Organ Replacement in American Society*. New York: Oxford University Press.

Frammolino, Ralph. 1997. "Harvest of Corneas at Morgue Questioned." *LA Times*, November 2.

Franklin, Sarah. 1997. *Embodied Progress: A Cultural Account of Assisted Conception*. London: Routledge.

Franklin, Sarah. 2007. *Dolly Mixtures: The Remaking of Genealogy*. Durham, NC: Duke University Press.

Fried, Linda, J. Bernardini, and B. Piraino. 1996. "Neither Size Nor Weight Predicts Survival in Peritoneal Dialysis Patients." *Peritoneal Dialysis International* 16 (4): 357–61.

Friedrich, Paul. 1987. *Princes of Naranja: An Essay in Anthrohistorical Method*. Austin: University of Texas Press.

Frow, John. 1997. *Time and Commodity Culture: Essays in Cultural Theory and Postmodernity*. Oxford: Clarendon Press.

Fuss, Diana. 1995. *Identification Papers: Readings on Psychoanalysis, Sexuality, and Culture*. New York: Routledge.

Galvez, Alicia. 2011. *Patient Citizens, Immigrant Mothers: Mexican Women, Public Prenatal Care, and the Birth Weight Paradox*. New Brunswick, NJ: Rutgers University Press.

Garcia, Angela. 2010. *The Pastoral Clinic: Addiction and Dispossession along the Rio Grande*. Berkeley: University of California Press.

Garcia, Angela. 2013. "Questions of Rupture: Violence as Recovery in Mexico City's Peripheral Zones." Paper presented at the American Anthropological Association Annual Meeting, November 23, Chicago.

García Canclini, Néstor. 1995. *Hybrid Cultures: Strategies for Entering and Leaving Modernity*. Minneapolis: University of Minnesota Press.

García García, Guillermo, Gregorio Briseño-Rentería, Victor Luquín-Arrellan, Zhiwei Gao, John Gill, and Marcello Tonelli. 2007. "Survival Among Kidney Patients in Jalisco, Mexico." *Journal of the American Society of Nephrology* 18 (6): 1922–27.

García García, Guillermo, Paul Harden, and Jeremy Chapman. 2012. "The Global Role of Kidney Transplantation." *Nephrology* 17: 199–203.

García García, Guillermo, Francisco Monteon-Ramos, Hector García-Bejarano, Benjamin Gomez-Navarro, Imelda Hernandez-Reyes, Ana Maria Lomeli, Miguel Palomeque, Laura Cortes-Sanabria, Hugo Breien-Alcaraz, and Norma Ruiz-Morales. 2005. "Renal Replacement Therapy among Disadvantaged Populations in Mexico: A Report from the Jalisco Dialysis and Transplant Registry (REDTJAL)." *Kidney International* 69 (97): S58–S61.

García García, Guillermo, Karina Renoirte-Lopez, and Isela Marquez-Magaña. 2010. "Disparities in Renal Care in Jalisco, Mexico." *Seminars in Nephrology* 30 (1): 3–7.

García Partida, Juan Carlos. 2000. "Impunes Errores Médicos." *El Occidental*, March 13, 1A.

Garwood, Paul. 2007. "Dilemma over Live-Donor Transplantation." *Bulletin of World Health Organization* 85: 3–5.

Gaspar de Alba, Alicia. 2010. *Making a Killing: Femicide, Free Trade and La Frontera*. Austin: University of Texas Press.

Gauthier, Frédéric. 2004. "The Point of View of a French Pediatric Transplant Surgeon." Paper presented at Les Enjeux Ethiques des Trasplantations Hepatiques avec Donneur Vivant, October, Paris, France.

Giacomini, Mita. 1997. "A Change of Heart and a Change of Mind? Technology and the Redefinition of Death in 1968." *Social Science and Medicine* 44 (10): 1465–82.

Glantz, Margo. 1995. "La Malinche: La Lengua en la Mano." In *Mitos Mexicanos*, ed. Enrique Florescano, 119–38. Mexico City: Aguilar.

Gledhill, John. 1999. "Official Masks and Shadow Power: Toward an Anthropology of the Dark Side of the State." *Urban Anthropology and Studies of Cultural Systems and World Economic Development* 28 (3/4): 199–251.

Glick, Thomas, ed. 1974. *The Comparative Reception of Darwinism*. Austin: University of Texas Press.

Goffman, Erving. 1963. *Stigma: Notes on the Management of Spoiled Identity*. Englewood Cliffs, NJ: Prentice Hall.

Golgowski, Nina. 2013. "Syracuse Hospital Patient Awakens Just before Organs Were to Be Harvested." *New York Daily News*, July 9. Accessed January 30, 2015. http://www.nydailynews.com/news/national/woman-wakes-organs-harvested-article-1.1393821.

Gonzalez de la Rocha, Mercedes. 1994. *The Resources of Poverty: Women and Survival in a Mexican City*. Cambridge, MA: Blackwell.

Good, Byron. 1977. "The Heart of What's the Matter: The Semantics of Illness in Iran." *Culture, Medicine and Psychiatry*. 1: 25–58.

Gordon, Elisa J. 2001. " 'They Don't Have to Suffer for Me': Why Dialysis Patients Refuse Offers of Living Donor Kidneys." *Medical Anthropology Quarterly* 15 (2): 1–22.

Goulding, Christopher. 2002. "The Real Dr. Frankenstein?" *Journal of the Royal Society of Medicine* 95 (5): 257–59.

Gove, Phillip Babcock, ed. 1993. *Webster's Third New International Dictionary of the English Language*. Springfield, MA: Merriam-Webster.

"Gran Número de Contagios por Sangre." 2000. *Público*, April 11, 10.

Grosz, Elizabeth. 1994. *Volatile Bodies: Toward a Corporeal Feminism*. Bloomington: Indiana University Press.

Gupta, Akhil, and James Ferguson. 1997. *Anthropological Locations: Boundaries and Grounds of a Field Science*. Berkeley: University of California Press.

Gutierrez-Padilla, Juan Alfonso, Martha Mendoza-García, Salvador Plascencia-Perez, Karina Renoirte-Lopez, Guillermo García-García, Anita Lloyd, and Marcello Tonelli. 2010. "Screening for CKD and Cardiovascular Disease Risk Factors Using Mobile Clinics in Jalisco, Mexico." *American Journal of Kidney Disease* 55 (3): 474–84.

Gutmann, Matthew C. 1996. *The Meanings of Macho: Being a Man in Mexico City*. Berkeley: University of California Press.

Gutmann, Matthew C. 2002. *The Romance of Democracy: Compliant Defiance in Contemporary Mexico*. Berkeley: University of California Press.

Gutmann, Matthew C. 2007. *Fixing Men: Sex, Birth Control, and AIDS in Mexico*. Berkeley: University of California Press.

Hamdy, Sherine. 2008. "When the State and Your Kidneys Fail: Political Etiologies in an Egyptian Dialysis Ward." *American Ethnologist* 35 (4): 553–69.

Hamdy, Sherine. 2012. *Our Bodies Belong to God: Organ Transplants, Islam, and the Struggle for Human Dignity in Egypt.* Berkeley: University of California Press.

Hamdy, Sherine. 2013. "Political Challenges to Biomedical Universalism: Kidney Failure among Egypt's Poor." *Medical Anthropology* 32 (4): 374–92.

Haraway, Donna. 1991. "A Cyborg Manifesto: Science, Technology, and Socialist-Feminism in the Late Twentieth Century." In *Simians, Cyborgs, and Women: The Reinvention of Nature,* 149–82. New York: Routledge.

Harding, Sandra. 1991. "'Strong Objectivity' and Socially Situated Knowledge." In *Whose Science? Whose Knowledge?,* 138–63. Ithaca, NY: Cornell University Press.

Heath, Deborah. 1998. "Locating Genetic Knowledge: Picturing Marfan Syndrome and Its Traveling Constituencies." *Science, Technology, and Human Values* 23 (1): 71–97.

Heinemann, Laura Lynn. 2014. "For the Sake of Others: Reciprocal Webs of Obligation and the Pursuit of Transplant as a Caring Act." *Medical Anthropology Quarterly* 28 (1): 66–84.

Helman, Cecil. 1988. "Dr. Frankenstein and the Industrial Body: Reflections on 'Spare Part' Surgery." *Anthropology Today* 4 (3): 14–16.

Helmreich, Stefan. 1998. *Silicon Second Nature: Culturing Artificial Life in a Digital World.* Berkeley: University of California Press.

Helms, Mary W. 1982. *Middle America: A Cultural History of Heartland and Frontiers.* New York: University Press of America.

Hogle, Linda. 1995. "Tales from the Cryptic: Technology Meets Organism in the Living Cadaver." In *The Cyborg Handbook,* ed. Chris Hables Gray, 203–18. New York: Routledge.

Hogle, Linda. 1996. "Transforming 'Body Parts' into Therapeutic Tools: A Report from Germany." *Medical Anthropology Quarterly* 10 (4): 675–82.

Hogle, Linda. 1999. *Recovering the Nation's Body: Cultural Memory, Medicine, and the Politics of Redemption.* New Brunswick, NJ: Rutgers University Press.

Horvat, Lucy Diane, Salimah Shariff, and Amit Garg. 2009. "Global Trends in the Rate of Living Kidney Donation." *Kidney International* 75 (10): 1088–98.

Hughes, Jennifer Scheper. 2012. "The Niño Jesús Doctor: Novelty and Innovation in Mexican Religion." *Nova Religio: The Journal of Alternative and Emergent Religions* 16 (2): 4–28.

Hunt, Linda. 1995. "Inequalities in the Mexican Health Care System: Problems in Managing Cancer in Southern Mexico." In *Society, Health, and Disease: Transcultural Perspectives,* ed. Janarden Subedi and Eugene Gallagher, 130–49. Upper Saddle River, NJ: Prentice Hall.

Ikels, Charlotte. 1997. "Kidney Failure and Transplantation in China." *Social Science and Medicine* 44 (9): 1271–83.

Ikels, Charlotte. 2013. "The Anthropology of Organ Transplantation." *Annual Review of Anthropology* 42: 89–102.

IMSS (Instituto Mexicano del Seguro Social). 1995. *Nueva Ley del Seguro Social.*

INEGI (Instituto Nacional de Estadística Geográfica e Informática). 2000. "Derechoha-
bientes del Sistema Nacional de Salud por Institución segun Ambito Geográfico."
Accessed October 24, 2004. http://www.inegi.gob.mx/est/contenidos/espanol
/rutinas/ept.asp?t=msa102&c=3351.

Ingham, John M. 1986. *Mary, Michael, and Lucifer: Folk Catholicism in Central Mexico*. Austin:
University of Texas Press.

Institute of Medicine. 2014. *Non-Heart-Beating Organ Donation: Practice and Protocols*.
Washington, DC: National Academy Press.

Jackson, Jean E. 2000. *"Camp Pain": Talking with Chronic Pain Patients*. Philadelphia: University of Pennsylvania Press.

Jarosz, Lucy. 1994. "Agents of Power, Landscapes of Fear." *Environment and Planning D:
Society and Space* 12: 421–36.

Jimenez, Hugo. 2000. "Aprueba el Senado ley para aumentar donación de organos."
El Occidental, April 27, 7B.

John Paul II (pope). 2000. "Address to the International Congress on Organ Transplantation." Delivered August 29, 2000, Rome, Italy.

Joralemon, Donald. 1995. "Organ Wars: Battle for Body Parts." *Medical Anthropology
Quarterly* 9 (3): 335–56.

Joralemon, Donald, and Kim Mika Fujinaga. 1996. "Studying the Quality of Life after
Organ Transplantation: Research Problems and Solutions." *Social Science and Medicine* 44 (9): 1259–69.

Jordan, Brigitte. 1980. *Birth in Four Cultures: A Cross-Cultural Investigation of Childbirth in
Yucatan, Holland, Sweden, and the United States*. Montreal: Eden Women's Press.

Kassler, Jeanne. 1994. *Bitter Medicine: Greed and Chaos in American Health Care*. New York:
Birch Lane Press.

Katz, Pearl. 1981. "Rituals in the Operating Room." *Ethnology* 20 (4): 335–50.

Kaufman, Sharon. 2000. "In the Shadow of 'Death with Dignity': Medicine and Cultural Quandaries of the Vegetative State." *American Anthropologist* 102: 69–83.

Kaufman, Sharon, Ann J. Russ, and Janet K. Shim. 2006. "Aged Bodies and Kinship Matters: The Ethical Field of Kidney Transplant." *American Ethnologist* 33 (1): 88–99.

Keller, Heidi, Bettina Lamm, and Monika Albes. 2006. "Cultural Models, Socializa-
tion Goals, and Parenting Ethnotheories: A Multicultural Analysis." *Journal of Cross-
Cultural Psychiatry* 37 (2):155–72.

Kelly, Patty. 2008. *Lydia's Open Door: Inside Mexico's Most Modern Brothel*. Berkeley: University
of California Press.

Kher, Vijay. 2002. "End-stage Renal Disease in Developing Countries." *Kidney International*
62: 350–62.

Kierans, Ciara. 2011. "Anthropology, Organ Transplantation and the Immune System: Resituating Commodity and Gift Exchange." *Social Science and Medicine* 73
(10): 1469–76.

Kierans, Ciara. 2015. "Biopolitics and Capital: Poverty, Mobility, and the Body-in-
Transplantation in Mexico." *Body and Society*, April 24. doi: 10.1177/1357034X13508457.

Kierans, Ciara, Cesar Padilla-Altamira, Margarita Ibarra-Hernandez, Guillermo Garcia-Garcia, and Francisco Mercado. 2013. "When Health Systems Are Barriers to Care: Challenges Faced by Uninsured Mexican Kidney Patients." PLoS. One 8 (1): e54380. doi: 10.1371/journal.pone.0054380.

Kilgour, Maggie. 1998. "Dr. Frankenstein Meets Dr. Freud." In American Gothic: New Interventions in a National Narrative, ed. Robert K. Martin and Eric Savoy, 40–56. Iowa City: University of Iowa Press.

Kimbrell, Andrew. 1993. The Human Body Shop: The Engineering and Marketing of Life. San Francisco: Harper.

Kirmayer, Lawrence. 1988. "Mind and Body as Metaphor: Hidden Values in Biomedicine." In Biomedicine Examined, ed. Margaret Lock and Deborah Gordon, 57–93. Dordrecht, Netherlands: Kluwer.

Knaul, Felicia Marie, Eduardo González-Pier, Octavio Gómez-Dántes, David García-Junco, Hector Arreola-Ornelas, Mariana Barraza-Lloréns, Rosa Sandoval, Francisco Caballero, Mauricio Hernández-Avila, Mercedes Juan, David Kershenobich, Gustavo Nigenda, Enrique Ruelas, Jaime Sepúlveda, Roberto Tapía, Guillermo Soberón, Salomón Chertorivski, and Julio Frenk. 2012. "The Quest for Universal Health Coverage: Achieving Social Protection for All in Mexico." Lancet 380 (9849): 1259–79.

Knight, Alan. 1990. "Racism, Revolution and Indigenismo: Mexico 1910–1940." In The Idea of Race in Latin America 1870–1940, ed. Richard Graham, 71–113. Cambridge: Cambridge University Press.

Knight, Alan. 1999. "Political Violence in Post-Revolutionary Mexico." In Societies of Fear: The Legacies of Civil War, Violence and Terror in Latin America, ed. Kees Koonigs and Durk Krujit, 105–24. London: Zed Books.

Kopytoff, Igor. 1986. "The Cultural Biography of Things: Commoditization as Process." In The Social Life of Things: Commodities in Cultural Perspective, ed. Arjun Appadurai, 64–94. Cambridge: Cambridge University Press.

Kristeva, Julia. 1982. Powers of Horror: An Essay on Abjection. New York: Columbia University Press.

Lafaye, Jacques. 1976. Quetzalcoatl and Guadalupe: The Formation of Mexican National Consciousness 1531–1813. Chicago: University of Chicago Press.

Lamiere, Norbert, and Wim Van Biesen. 2010. "Epidemiology of Peritoneal Dialysis: A Story of Believers and Nonbelievers." Nature Reviews: Nephrology 6: 75–82.

Latour, Bruno. 1987. Science in Action: How to Follow Scientists and Engineers through Society. Cambridge, MA: Harvard University Press.

Latour, Bruno. 1993. We Have Never Been Modern. Cambridge, MA: Harvard University Press.

Latour, Bruno, and Steve Woolgar. 1979. Laboratory Life: The Construction of Scientific Facts. Beverly Hills, CA: Sage.

Laurell, Asa Cristina. 2001. "Health Reform in Mexico: The Promotion of Inequality." International Journal of Health Services 31 (2): 291–321.

Laurell, Asa Cristina. 2011. "Los Seguros de Salud Mexicanos: Coberatura Universal Incierta." Ciencia y Saude Colectiva 16 (6): 2796–806.

Lawrence, Rev. Ralph J. 1996. "The History of the Devotion." Our Lady of the Holy Spirit Center. Accessed December 11, 2006. http://www.olhsc.org/cjgh.htm.

Lester, Rebecca J. 2007. "Critical Therapeutics: Cultural Politics and Clinical Reality in Two Eating Disorder Treatment Centers." Medical Anthropology Quarterly 21 (4): 369–87.

LeVine, Sarah. 1993. Dolor y Alegría: Women and Social Change in Urban Mexico. Madison: University of Wisconsin Press.

Levinsky, Norman G., and Richard A. Rettig. 1991. "The Medicare End-Stage Renal Disease Program: A Report from the Institute of Medicine." New England Journal of Medicine 324: 1143–48.

Lévi-Strauss, Claude. 1962. The Savage Mind. Chicago: University of Chicago Press.

Lewis, Oscar. 1959. Five Families: Mexican Case Studies in the Culture of Poverty. New York: Basic Books.

Lewis, Oscar. 1961. The Children of Sanchez: Autobiography of a Mexican Family. New York: Vintage Books.

"Ley General de Salud." 2000. salud.gov.mx, April 28. http://www.salud.gob.mx /unidades/cdi/legis/lgs/LEY_GENERAL_DE_SALUD.pdf.

Lindenbaum, Shirley, and Margaret Lock. 1993. Knowledge, Power, and Practice: The Anthropology of Medicine and Everyday Life. Berkeley: University of California Press.

Little, Miles, Christopher F. C. Jordens, Kim Paul, Kathleen Montgomery, and Bertil Philipson. 1998. "Liminality: A Major Category of the Experience of Cancer Illness." Social Science and Medicine 47 (10): 1485–94.

Livingston, Julie. 2012. Improvising Medicine: An African Oncology Ward in an Emerging Cancer Epidemic. Durham, NC: Duke University Press.

Lock, Margaret. 1993. Encounters with Aging: Mythologies of Menopause in Japan and the United States. Berkeley: University of California Press.

Lock, Margaret. 2000. "On Dying Twice: Culture, Technology and the Determination of Death." In Living and Working with the New Medical Technologies: Intersections of Inquiry, ed. Margaret Lock, Allan Young, and Alberto Cambrosio, 233–62. New York: Cambridge University Press.

Lock, Margaret. 2001. Twice Dead: Organ Transplants and the Reinvention of Death. Berkeley: University of California Press.

Lomnitz, Claudio. 1995. "Ritual, Rumor and Corruption in the Constitution of Polity in Modern Mexico." Journal of Latin American Anthropology 1 (1): 20–47.

Lomnitz, Claudio. 2002. Deep Mexico, Silent Mexico: An Anthropology of Nationalism. Minneapolis: University of Minnesota Press.

Lomnitz, Claudio. 2005. Death and the Idea of Mexico. New York: Zone Books.

Lomnitz, Larissa Adler. 1977. Networks and Marginality: Life in a Mexican Shantytown. New York: Academic Press.

Lomnitz, Larissa Adler, and Marisol Pérez-Lizaur. 1987. A Mexican Elite Family 1820–1980. Princeton, NJ: Princeton University Press.

Lomnitz-Adler, Claudio. 1992. Exits from the Labyrinth: Culture and Ideology in the Mexican National Space. Berkeley: University of California Press.

Lupton, Deborah. 1999. Risk. New York: Routledge.

Maldonado, Sara. 2004. "Understanding Mexican Bioethics." Paper presented at the 2004 American Society of Bioethics and Humanities Annual Meeting, Baltimore.

Malinowski, Bronislaw. 1948. *Magic, Science, and Religion and Other Essays*. Glencoe, IL: Free Press.

Marshall, Patricia A., and Abdallah S. Daar. 2000. "Ethical Issues in Human Organ Replacement Technologies: A Case Study from India." In *Global Health Policy, Local Realities: The Fallacy of the Level Playing Field*, ed. Linda Whiteford and Lenore Manderson, 205–32. Boulder, CO: Lynne Rienner.

Martin, Emily. 1987. *The Woman in the Body: A Cultural Analysis of Reproduction*. Boston: Beacon Press.

Martin, Emily. 1994. *Flexible Bodies: The Role of Immunity in American Culture from the Days of Polio to the Age of* AIDS. Boston: Beacon Press.

Martinez, Manuel. 2000. "Sí a la donación de organos con fines de caridad: Rivera." *El Occidental*, March 11, 3B.

Marx, Karl. [1867] 1990. *Capital: A Critique of Political Economy (Volume One)*. London: Penguin Books.

Matas, Arthur J., Stephen T. Bartlett, Alan B. Leichtman, and Francis Delmonico. 2003. "Morbidity and Mortality after Living Kidney Donation, 1999–2001: Survey of U.S. Transplant Centers." *American Journal of Transplantation* 3 (7): 830–34.

Matesanz, Rafael. 1996. "Transplantation and the Mass Media." In *Organ Donation for Transplantation: "The Spanish Model,"* ed. Rafael Matesanz and Blanca Miranda, 19–34. Madrid: Grupo Aula Medica.

Matesanz, Rafael, R. Marazuela, B. Dominguez-Gil, E. Coll, B. Mahillo, and G. de la Rosa. 2009. "The 40 Donors Per Million Population Plan: An Action Plan for Improvement of Organ Donation and Transplantation in Spain." *Transplantation Proceedings* 41 (8): 3453–56.

Matesanz, Rafael, and Blanca Miranda. 1996a. *Organ Donation for Transplantation: "The Spanish Model."* Madrid: Grupo Aula Medica.

Matesanz, Rafael, and Blanca Miranda. 1996b. "Organ donation: The 'Spanish Model.' " *Transplantation Proceedings* 28 (1): 11.

Matesanz, Rafael, and Blanca Miranda. 1996c. "Organ Donation: The Role of the Media and Public Opinion." *Nephrology, Dialyisis, Transplantation* 11: 2127–28.

Mauleon Lee, Montserrat. 2000. "Necesario Aumentar Altruismo en la Donación de Sangre." *Ocho Columnas*, April 8, 4A.

Mauss, Marcel. [1924] 1976. *The Gift: Forms and Functions of Exchange in Archaic Society*. New York: W. W. Norton.

Mercado Martinez, Francisco Javier. 1996. *Entre el infierno y la gloria: La experiencia de la enfermedad crónica en un barrio urbano*. Guadalajara: Universidad de Guadalajara.

Merry, Sally. 1995. "Gender Violence and Legally Engendered Selves." *Identities* 2 (1–2): 49–73.

Mertz, Elizabeth. 2007. "Semiotic Anthropology." *Annual Review of Anthropology* 36: 337–53.

Mesa-Lago, Carmelo. 1978. *Social Security in Latin America: Pressure Groups, Stratification and Inequality*. Pittsburgh: University of Pittsburgh Press.

"México establece liderazgo en materia de legislación sobre trasplantes de organos." 2000. *El Informador*, April 28, 10A.

Michielsen, Paul. 1996. "Presumed Consent to Organ Donation: 10 Years' Experience in Belgium." *Journal of the Royal Society of Medicine* 69: 663–66.

Miller, Grady. 1999. "New Hope for Liver Patients." *Colony Reporter*, July 17–23, 5.

Mitchell, W. J. T. 1986. *Iconology: Image, Text, Ideology*. Chicago: University of Chicago Press.

Moazam, Farhat. 2006. *Bioethics and Organ Transplantation in a Muslim Society: A Study in Culture, Ethnography, and Religion*. Bloomington: Indiana University Press.

Moazam, Farhat, Riffat Moazam Zaman, and Aamir M. Jafarey. 2009. "Conversations with Kidney Vendors in Pakistan: An Ethnographic Study." *Hastings Center Report* 3: 29–44.

Mohanty, Chandra. 1988. "Under Western Eyes: Feminist Scholarship and Colonial Discourse." *Feminist Review* 30: 61–88.

Mol, Annemarie. 2003. *The Body Multiple: Ontology in Medical Practice*. Durham, NC: Duke University Press.

Moniruzzaman, Monir. 2012. "Living Cadavers in Bangladesh: Bioviolence in the Human Organ Bazaar." *Medical Anthropology Quarterly* 26 (1): 69–91.

Monteon, Francisco. 2000. "Trasplante renal: Mundial, nacional y en el Hospital de Especialidades Centro Medico del Occidente." Paper presented at the III Curso Teórico Práctico: Tratamientos Substitivos de la Insuficiencia Renal Crónica, Donación y Trasplante de Organos, April, Guadalajara, Mexico.

Morales, Jose Luis, and Josef Maria Camposol. 1999. "El modelo Español." Talk presented at the Hospital de Especialidades Centro Medico Occidental, October, Guadalajara, Mexico.

Morgan, Lynn. 2009. *Icons of Life: A Cultural History of Human Embryos*. Berkeley: University of California Press.

Morton, Peggy. 1971. "A Woman's Work Is Never Done." In *From Feminism to Liberation*, ed. Edith Altbach, 211–27. Cambridge, MA: Schenkman.

Muehlmann, Shaylih. 2013. *When I Wear My Alligator Boots: Narco-Culture in the U.S.-Mexico Borderlands*. Berkeley: University of California Press.

Murphy, Sean W., Robert N. Foley, Brendan J. Barret, Gloria M. Kent, Janet Morgan, Paul Barre, Patricia Campbell, Adrian Fine, Marc B. Goldstein, S. Paul Handa, Kailash K. Jandal, Adeera Levin, Henry Mandin, Norman Muirhead, Robert M. A. Richardson, and Patrick Parfrey. 2000. "Comparative Mortality Rates on Hemodialysis and Peritoneal Dialysis in Canada." *Kidney International* 57 (4): 1720–26.

Murray, Joseph. 1966. "Organ Transplantation: The Practical Possibilities." In *Ethics in Medical Progress: With Special Reference to Transplantation*, ed. G. E. W. Wolstenholme and M. O'Connor, 54–64. Boston: Little, Brown.

Napolitano, Valentina. 2002. *Migration, Mujercitas, and Medicine Men: Living in Urban Mexico*. Berkeley: University of California Press.

Napolitano, Valentina. 2009. "The Virgin of Guadalupe: A Nexus of Affect." *Journal of the Royal Anthropological Institute* 15 (1): 96–112.

Navon, Liora, and Abraham Morag. 2004. "Liminality as Biographical Disruption: Unclassifiability Following Hormonal Therapy for Advanced Prostate Cancer." *Social Science and Medicine* 58 (11): 2337–47.

Nelkin, Dorothy, and M. Susan Lindee. 1996. *The DNA Mystique: The Gene as Cultural Icon.* Ann Arbor: University of Michigan Press.

Nelson, Diane M. 1999. *A Finger in the Wound: Body Politics in Quincentennial Guatemala.* Berkeley: University of California Press.

Nigenda, Gustavo. 1997. "The Regional Distribution of Doctors in Mexico 1930–1990: A Policy Assessment." *Health Policy* 39: 107–22.

Notimex. 2000a. "Aprueba el Senado ley de trasplantes." *Ocho Columnas,* April 27, 11A.

Notimex. 2000b. "Aprueban iniciativa en materia de trasplantes." *Público,* April 27, 21.

Notimex. 2000c. "Al menos 100 mil mexicanos requieren algun trasplante de organo." *Ocho Columnas,* March 23, 24A.

Nutini, Hugo G. 1995. *The Wages of Conquest: The Mexican Aristocracy in the Context of Western Aristocracies.* Ann Arbor, MI: University of Michigan Press.

Nutini, Hugo G., and Betty Bell. 1980. *Ritual Kinship: The Structure and Historical Development of the Compadrazgo System in Rural Tlaxcala, Volume 1.* Princeton, NJ: Princeton University Press.

Oakley, Ann. 1984. *The Captured Womb: A History of the Medical Care of Pregnant Women.* Oxford: Basil Blackwell.

Office of the Inspector General. 2002. *Organ Donor Registries: A Useful, but Limited, Tool.* Department of Health and Human Services, U.S. Government.

Ohashi, H., H. Oda, M. Ohno, S. Sakata. 1999. "Predictors of Survival in Continuous Ambulatory Peritoneal Dialysis Patients." *Advances in Peritoneal Dialysis* 15: 87–90.

Ohnuki-Tierney, Emiko. 1994. "Brain Death and Organ Transplantation: Cultural Bases of Medical Technologies." *Current Anthropology* 35 (3): 233–54.

Oktavec, Eileen. 1995. *Answered Prayers: Miracles and Milagros along the Border.* Tucson: University of Arizona Press.

Orozco García, Octavio. 2000. "Iatrogenia criminal." *El Occidental,* April 30, 3D.

Ortiz, Ruth, Sara Ruelas, Miguel Angel Palomeque, Graciela Paredes, and Jose Luis Canales. 2000. "Sobrevida del paciente con insuficiencia renal crónica en alguna modalidad de tratamiento sustitutivo." Paper presented at the III Curso Teórico Práctico: Tratamientos Substitivos de la Insuficiencia Renal Crónica, Donación y Trasplante de Organos, April, Guadalajara, Mexico.

Osherson, Samuel, and Lorna AmaraSingham. 1981. "The Machine Metaphor in Medicine." In *Social Contexts of Health, Illness, and Patient Care,* ed. Elliot G. Mishler, 218–49. New York: Cambridge University Press.

Paredes, Graciela Figueroa. 1999. "Cultura de donación de organos (sensibilización)." Paper presented at the Curso Taller: Donación de Organos, Una Esperanza de Vida, October, Guadalajara, Mexico.

Partida, Juan Carlos G. 2000a. "Ningun caso documentado pero . . . Descartan tráfico de organos." *El Occidental,* May 22, 1A.

Partida, Juan Carlos G. 2000b. "Cuestionan especialistas viabilidad de tráfico de organos." El Occidental, May 22, 10A.

Pashukanis, Evgeny. 1978. Law and Marxism: A General Theory. London: Ink Links.

Paz, Octavio. 1959. El laberinto de soledad. Mexico City: México Fondo de Cultura Económica.

Peirce, Charles S. 1974. Collected Papers of Charles Sanders Peirce, Volumes I and II, ed. Charles Hartshorne and Paul Weiss. Cambridge, MA: Harvard University Press.

Petryna, Adriana. 2005. "Ethical Variability: Drug Development and Globalizing Clinical Trials."American Ethnologist 32 (3): 183–97.

Poovey, Mary. 1998. A History of the Modern Fact: Problems of Knowledge in the Sciences. Chicago: University of Chicago Press.

"Promoverán Instituciones de Salud la donación altruista de sangre." 2000. El Informador, August 4, 2B.

Rabinow, Paul. 1996. "Artificiality and Enlightenment: From Sociobiology to Biosociality." In Essays on the Anthropology of Reason, 91–111. Princeton, NJ: Princeton University Press.

Radcliffe-Richards, Janet, Abdallah S. Daar, Ronald D. Guttmann, Raymond Hoffenberg, Ian Kennedy, Margaret Lock, Robert A. Sells, and Nicholas Tilney. 1998. "The Case for Allowing Kidney Sales." Lancet 351: 1950–52.

Radin, Margaret. 1987. "Market Inalienability." Harvard Law Review 100: 1849–937.

Radin, Margaret. 1996. Contested Commodities. Cambridge, MA: Harvard University Press.

Ramírez, Victor. 2009. "Multan a Hospital Civil de Guadalajara por escándalo de trasplantes." Terra, July 17, 22–25.

Ramirez-Rubio, Oriana, Michael D. Maclean, Juan José Amador, and Daniel R. Brooks. 2013. "An Epidemic of Chronic Kidney Disease in Central America: An Overview." Journal of Epidemiology and Public Health 67: 1–3.

Rapp, Rayna. 1999. Testing Women, Testing the Fetus: The Social Impact of Amniocentesis in America. New York: Routledge.

Rapp, Rayna, Deborah Heath, and Karen-Sue Taussig. 2001. "Genealogical Dis-Ease: Where Hereditary Abnormality, Biomedical Explanation and Family Responsibility Meet." In Relative Values: Reconfiguring Kinship Studies, ed. Sarah Franklin and Susan McKinnon, 384–412. Durham, NC: Duke University Press.

Richardson, Ruth. 1996. "Fearful Symmetry: Corpses for Anatomy, Organs for Transplantation?" In Organ Transplantation: Meanings and Realities, ed. Stuart Youngner, Renee Fox, and Laurence O'Connell, 66–100. Madison: University of Wisconsin Press.

Richardson, Ruth. 2001. Death, Dissection and the Destitute. New York: Routledge and Kegan Paul.

Rithalia, Amber, Catriona McDaid, Sara Suekarran, Lindsey Myers, and Amanda Snowden. 2009. "Impact of Presumed Consent for Organ Donation on Donation Rates: A Systematic Review." British Medical Journal 338: a3162–70.

Robben, Antonius C. G. M. 2004. Death, Mourning and Burial: A Cross-Cultural Reader. Malden, MA: Blackwell.

Roberts, Elizabeth F. S. 2012. *God's Laboratory: Assisted Reproduction in the Andes*. Berkeley: University of California Press.

Rodriguez Gonzalez, Perla. 2000. "Oposición familiar impide concretar donación de organos." *Ocho Columnas*, March 8, 5A.

"Rodríguez Sancho augura que librará 27 acusaciones." 2005. *El Informador*, November 10, 6A.

Romero Diaz, Esperanza. 2000. "De quienes esperan riñon, mueren 70%." *Público*, February 27, 14.

Rose, Nikolas. 2001. "The Politics of Life Itself." *Theory, Culture and Society* 18 (6): 1–30.

Ross, Lainie Friedman, Mark Siegler, and Robert Thistlethwaite. 2007. "We Need a Registry of Living Kidney Donors." *Hastings Center Report* 36 (5): 49.

Roszak, Theodore. 1974. "The Monster and the Titan: Science, Knowledge and Gnosis." *Daedalus* 103 (3): 17–32.

Rothman, David J. 1997. *Beginnings Count: The Technological Imperative in American Healthcare*. New York: Oxford University Press.

Rothman, David J., and Sheila M. Rothman. 2003. "The Organ Market." *New York Review of Books* 50 (16): 49–51.

Rubel, Arthur J., Carl W. O'Nell, and Rolando Collado Ardón. 1984. *Susto: A Folk Illness*. Berkeley: University of California Press.

Rull, Juan A., Carlos A. Aguilar-Salinas, Rosalba Rojas, Juan Manuel Rios-Torres, Francisco J. Gomez-Pérez, Gustavo Olaiz. 2005. "Epidemiology of Type 2 Diabetes in Mexico." *Archives of Medical Research* 36 (3): 188–96.

Rus, Andrej. 2008. " 'Gift vs. Commodity' Debate Revisited." *Anthropological Notebooks* 14 (1): 81–102.

Russell, Nerissa. 2007. "The Domestication of Anthropology." In *Where the Wild Things Are Now: Domestication Reconsidered*, ed. R. Cassidy and M. H. Mullin, 27–48. Oxford: Berg.

Sack, Kevin. 2014. "Kidneys for Sale." *New York Times*, August 17, A1.

Salinas Galvan, Abelardo. 2000. "Esperan un Riñon 800 Jalicienses." *El Occidental*, May 3, 10A.

Sanal, Aslihan. 2011. *New Organs among Us: Transplants and the Moral Economy*. Durham, NC: Duke University Press.

Sandoval Iñiguez, Cardenal Juan. 1997. *Carta del Arzobispado de Guadalajara*. Guadalajara: Ediciones Populares.

Sandoval Iñiguez, Cardenal Juan. 1999. "Los avances de la medicina y la moral catolica." *Investigación en Salud* 1 (2): 112–19.

Schemo, Diana Jean. 1994. "Death's New Sting in Brazil: Removal of Organs." *New York Times*, January 15, A4.

Scheper-Hughes, Nancy. 1998a. "The New Cannibalism: A Report on the International Traffic in Human Organs." *New Internationalist* 300: 14–17.

Scheper-Hughes, Nancy. 1998b. "Truth and Rumor on the Organ Trail." *Natural History*, October, 48–57.

Scheper-Hughes, Nancy. 2000. "The Global Traffic in Human Organs." *Current Anthropology* 41 (2): 191–224.

Scheper-Hughes, Nancy. 2002a. "Commodity Fetishizing in Organs Trafficking." In *Commodifying Bodies*, ed. Nancy Scheper-Hughes and Loïc Wacquant, 31–62. Thousand Oaks, CA: Sage.

Scheper-Hughes, Nancy. 2002b. "Bodies for Sale—Whole or in Parts." In *Commodifying Bodies*, ed. Nancy Scheper-Hughes and Loïc Wacquant, 1–8. Thousand Oaks, CA: Sage.

Scheper-Hughes, Nancy. 2004. "Parts Unknown: Undercover Ethnography of the Organs-Trafficking Underworld." *Ethnography* 5 (1): 29–73.

Scheper-Hughes, Nancy. 2005. "The Last Commodity: Post-Human Ethics and the Global Traffic in 'Fresh' Organs." In *Global Assemblages: Technology, Politics, and Ethics as Anthropological Problems*, ed. Aihwa Ong and Stephen J. Collier, 145–68. Malden, MA: Blackwell.

Scheper-Hughes, Nancy. 2006. "Mr. Tati's Holiday: Seeing the World via Transplant Tourism." Paper presented at the American Anthropological Association Annual Meeting, November, San Jose, California.

Scheper-Hughes, Nancy. 2007. "The Tyranny of the Gift: Sacrificial Violence in Living Donor Transplants." *American Journal of Transplantation* 7 (3): 507–11.

Scheper-Hughes, Nancy, and Margaret Lock. 1987. "The Mindful Body: A Prolegomenon to Future Work in Medical Anthropology." *Medical Anthropology Quarterly* 1 (1): 6–41.

Schwaller, John F. 2011. *The History of the Catholic Church in Latin America: From Conquest to Revolution and Beyond.* New York: NYU Press.

Segev, Dorry L., Abimereke D. Muzaale, Brian S. Caffo, Shruti H. Mehta, Andrew L. Singer, Sarah E. Taranto, Maureen A. MacBride, and Robert A. Montgomery. 2010. "Perioperative Death and Long-Term Survival Following Live Kidney Donation." *Journal of the American Medical Association* 303 (10): 959–66.

Selby, Henry A., Arthur D. Murphy, and Stephen A. Lorenzen. 1990. *The Mexican Urban Household: Organizing for Self-Defense.* Austin: University of Texas Press.

Shah, Seema K., Robert D. Truog, and Franklin G. Miller. 2011. "Death and Legal Fictions." *Journal of Medical Ethics* 37: 719–22.

Shakespeare, William. 1988. *Four Comedies: The Taming of the Shrew, A Midsummer Night's Dream, The Merchant of Venice, and Twelfth Night*, ed. David Bevington. New York: Bantam Books.

Sharp, Lesley A. 1999. "A Medical Anthropologist's View of Post-Transplant Compliance: The Underground Economy of Medical Survival." *Transplantation Proceedings* 31 (Supplement 4A): 31S–33S.

Sharp, Lesley A. 2000. "The Commodification of the Body and Its Parts." *Annual Review of Anthropology* 29: 287–328.

Sharp, Lesley A. 2001. "Commodified Kin: Death, Mourning and Competing Claims on the Bodies of Organ Donors in the United States." *American Anthropologist* 103 (1): 112–33.

Sharp, Lesley A. 2006. *Strange Harvest: Organ Transplants, Denatured Bodies, and the Transformed Self.* Berkeley: University of California Press.

Sharp, Lesley A. 2007. *Bodies, Commodities, and Biotechnologies: Death, Mourning, and Scientific Desire in the Realm of Human Organ Transfer*. New York: Columbia University Press.

Sharp, Lesley A. 2013. *The Transplant Imaginary: Mechanical Hearts, Animal Parts, and Moral Thinking in Highly Experimental Science*. Berkeley: University of California Press.

Sheehy, Ellen, Suzanne L. Conrad, Lori E. Brigham, Richard Luskin, Phyllis Weber, Mark Eakin, Lawrence Schkade, and Lawrence Hunsiker. 2003. "Estimating the Number of Potential Organ Donors in the United States." *New England Journal of Medicine* 349: 667–74.

Shewmon, Allan. 1998. "Chronic 'Brain Death': Meta-analysis and Conceptual Consequences." *Neurology* 51: 1538–45.

Shimazono, Yosuke. 2007. "The State of the International Organ Trade: A Provisional Picture Based on Integration of Available Information." *Bulletin of the World Health Organization* 85: 955–62.

Siminoff, Laura A., Renee H. Lawrence, and Robert M. Arnold. 2003. "Comparison of Black and White Families' Experiences and Perceptions Regarding Organ Donation Requests." *Critical Care Medicine* 31 (1):146–51.

Simmel, George. 1978. *The Philosophy of Money*. London: Routledge.

Simmons, Roberta G., Susan Klein Marine, and Richard L. Simmons. 1987. *The Gift of Life: The Effect of Organ Transplantation on Individual, Family, and Societal Dynamics*. New Brunswick, NJ: Transaction Books.

Slatman, Jenny, and Guy Widdershoven. 2010. "Hand Transplants and Bodily Integrity." *Body and Society* 16 (3): 62–92.

Slomka, Jacqueline. 1995. "What Do Apple Pie and Motherhood Have to Do with Feeding Tubes and Caring for the Patient?" *Archives of Internal Medicine* 155: 1258–63.

Soberón Solís, Fernando, and F. Alejandro Villagómez, eds. 1999. *La seguridad social en México*. Mexico City: Fondo de Cultura Económica.

Soto Laveaga, Gabriela. 2009. *Jungle Laboratories: Mexican Peasants, National Projects, and the Making of the Pill*. Durham, NC: Duke University Press.

Stepan, Nancy. 1991. *The Hour of Eugenics: Race, Gender, and Nation in Latin America*. Ithaca, NY: Cornell University Press.

Stephen, Lynn. 2002. *Zapata Lives! Histories and Cultural Politics in Southern Mexico*. Berkeley: University of California Press.

Strathern, Marilyn. 1992. *After Nature: English Kinship in the Late Twentieth Century*. Cambridge: Cambridge University Press.

Strathern, Marilyn. 1996. "Potential Property: Intellectual Rights and Property in Persons." *Social Anthropology* 4: 17–32.

Tambiah, Stanley Jeyaraga. 1990. *Magic, Science, Religion, and the Scope of Rationality*. New York: Cambridge University Press.

Taylor, Janelle S. 2008. *The Public Life of the Fetal Sonogram: Technology, Consumption, and the Politics of Reproduction*. New Brunswick, NJ: Rutgers University Press.

Townsend, Janet Gabriel, Emma Zapata, Joanna Rowlands, Pilar Alberti, and Marta Mercado. 1999. *Women and Power: Fighting Patriarchies and Poverty*. New York: Zed Books.

Trostle, James A. 1997. "The History and Meaning of Patient Compliance as an Ideology." In *Handbook of Health Behavior Research II: Provider Determinants*, ed. D. S. Gochman, 109–24. New York: Plenum Press.

Truog, Robert. 1997. "Is It Time to Abandon Brain Death?" *Hastings Center Report* 27 (1): 29–37.

Turner, Victor. 1969. *The Ritual Process: Structure and Anti-Structure*. Ithaca, NY: Cornell University Press.

UNOS (United Network for Organ Sharing). 2007. "Kidney Kaplan-Meier for Graft Survival Rates for Transplants Performed 1997–2004." optn.org, January 19. http://www.optn.org/latestData/rptStrat.asp.

UNOS (United Network for Organ Sharing). 2014a. "Transplant Center Membership." unos.org, July 27. http://www.unos.org/whoWeAre/transplantCenters.asp.

UNOS (United Network for Organ Sharing). 2014b. "Donors Recovered in the U.S. by Donor Type." optn.org, August 5. http://optn.transplant.hrsa.gov/latestData/rptData.asp.

UNOS (United Network for Organ Sharing). 2014c. "Living Donors Recovered in the U.S. by Donor Gender." optn.org, August 5. http://optn.transplant.hrsa.gov/latestData/rptData.asp.

Van Gennep, Arnold. 1906. *The Rites of Passage*. London: Routledge and Kegan Paul.

Vargas Llosa, Mario. 1995. *Death in the Andes*. New York: Farrar, Straus and Giroux.

Vasconcelos, José. [1925] 1979. *La Raza Cósmica: Bilingual Edition*, trans. Didier Tisdel Jaén. Los Angeles: Centro de Publicaciones, California State University.

Veatch, Robert. 1993. "The Impending Collapse of the Whole-Brain Definition of Death." *Hastings Center Report* 23 (4): 18–24.

Vega, Irené. 2000. "Medicinas robadas al IMSS fueron vendidas a narcos." *Público*, June 4, 19.

Vega, Margarita. 2000. "Contempla nueva ley 'desconectar' pacientes." *Mural*, March 29, 2A.

Verdery, Katherine. 1999. *The Political Life of Dead Bodies*. New York: Columbia University Press.

Villa Herrejon, Luis E. 2000. "Transplante y donación de organos." *El Informador*, March 28, 5A.

Voekel, Pamela. 2002. *Alone before God: The Religious Origins of Modernity in Mexico*. Durham, NC: Duke University Press.

Vrame, Anton. 2003. "Never as Gods: Lessons from a Millenium of Icons." *Religious Education* 98 (1): 108–23.

Wachtel, Nathan. 1994. *Gods and Vampires*. Chicago: University of Chicago Press.

Wailoo, Keith, Julie Livingston, and Peter Guarnaccia. 2006. "Introduction: Chronicles of an Accidental Death." In *A Death Retold: Jesica Santillan, the Bungled Transplant, and Paradoxes of Medical Citizenship*, ed. Keith Wailoo, Julie Livingston, and Peter Guarnaccia, 1–16. Chapel Hill: University of North Carolina Press.

Walker Bynum, Caroline. 1991. *Fragmentation and Redemption: Essays on Gender and the Human Body in Medieval Religion*. New York: Zone Books.

Weil, Andrew. 2000. *Spontaneous Healing: How to Discover and Embrace Your Body's Natural Ability to Heal and Maintain Itself.* New York: Ballantine Books.

Weiner, Annette. 1992. *Inalienable Possessions: The Paradox of Keeping While Giving.* Berkeley: University of California Press.

Wentzell, Emily. 2013. *Maturing Masculinities: Aging, Chronic Illness, and Viagra in Mexico.* Durham, NC: Duke University Press.

White, Sarah, Steven Chadban, Stephen Jan, Jeremy Chapman, and Alan Cass. 2008. "How Can We Achieve Global Equity in Provision of Renal Replacement Therapy?" *Bulletin of the World Health Organization* 86: 229–37.

Wilkie, James W. 1967. *The Mexican Revolution: Federal Expenditure and Social Change since 1910.* Berkeley: University of California Press.

Wilson, Carter. 1995. *Hidden in the Blood: A Personal Investigation of AIDS in the Yucatan.* New York: Columbia University Press.

Wolf, Eric. 1958. "The Virgin of Guadalupe: A Mexican National Symbol." *Journal of American Folklore* 71 (279): 34–39.

World Development Report. 2012. "Gender Differences in Employment and Why They Matter." Washington, DC: World Bank.

Yen, E. F., K. Hardinger, D. C. Brennan, R. S. Woodward, N. M. Desai, J. S. Crippin, B. F. Gage, M. A. Schnitzler. 2004. "Cost-Effectiveness of Extending Medicare Coverage of Immunosuppressive Medications to the Life of a Kidney Transplant." *American Journal of Transplantation* 4 (10):1703–8.

Yngvesson, Barbara. 2010. *Belonging in an Adopted World: Race, Identity, and Transnational Adoption.* Chicago: University of Chicago Press.

Youngner, Stuart J. 1990. "Organ Retrieval: Can We Ignore the Dark Side?" *Transplantation Proceedings* 22 (3): 1014–15.

Youngner, Stuart J. 1996. "Some Must Die." In *Organ Transplantation: Meanings and Realities,* ed. Stuart Youngner, Renee Fox, and Laurence O'Connell, 32–55. Madison: University of Wisconsin Press.

Youngner, Stuart, Seth Landenfield, Claudia J. Coulton, Barbara W. Juknialis, and Mark Leary. 1989. "'Brain Death' and Organ Retrieval: A Cross-Sectional Survey of Knowledge and Concepts among Health Professionals." *Journal of the American Medical Association* 261: 2205–10.

Index

Page numbers followed by *f* indicate a figure; those followed by t indicate a table.

biomedical approach to health, 5, 63, 171–72

biopolitics of transplantation, 6, 30, 55, 71–105; government corruption and, 91–99; iconicity in, 3–6, 28–30, 93, 105, 237n4; modernity in, 102, 258, 274n18; in slippery states, 14–15, 71–72, 249–50, 268n12; U.S.-Mexico relations and, 6, 268n6

biosociality, 175

biounavailability, 29, 52, 65–72, 100–105, 273n1; brain-death controversies and, 72–81, 94–95, 98–99, 264; cultural explanations of, 67–68, 72, 103–5; logistical challenges and, 81–91, 274n11, 274nn13–14; medical complications of, 68–71; presumed consent system and, 100–105, 274nn17–18; skepticism about government corruption and, 91–99

birth analogies, 42–43, 49

blood supply, 276n7

bodily commodification, 35, 187–89, 270n1. See also commodification frame in transplantation

brain death, 29, 65–99, 237n1, 263–64, 273n1; conceptual slipperiness of, 73–81, 94–95, 98–99, 280n5; definition of, 72; "donor" versus "patient" terminology of, 86–87, 90; experiential contradictions in, 75–76; Lazarus signs and, 70; legal and legislative arena of, 75, 84; logistical challenges of, 81–91, 274n11, 274nn13–14; medical diagnosis of, 68–71, 79, 82–84, 93, 274n16; religious and personhood considerations in, 76–81, 274nn7–8; skepticism about government corruption and, 91–99. See also cadaveric donor transplants

Butler, Judith: on coming to matter, 4, 111–12, 275n1; on girling, 145

cadaveric donor transplants, 1–3, 10, 237n1, 280n6; biounavailability of, 29,

52, 62, 65–72, 100–105, 264; family decisions in, 29, 86–96, 103, 231–33, 251–52; national procurement system for, 67, 75; non-heart-beating donors in, 273n1; outcomes of, 1, 68t, 237n2; presumed consent systems for, 100–105, 273n5, 274nn17–18; rates of, 33, 59; resurrection and redemption themes of, 238–44, 283–84nn10–14; Spain's program of, 18, 33, 251, 253–57, 269n16. See also brain death

cardiopulmonary death, 76, 81

la casa chica, 38–39, 370n4

Catholic Church, 25, 268n10, 274n9; on brain death, 76–81, 95–97; on cadaveric organ donation, 79–80, 95–96; Church-State relationship of, 95; on fetal life, 98–99; La Guadalupe and, 11–15, 95; El Niño Doctor de los Enfermos and, 12, 225–29, 238, 242, 258, 282n1, 282n3; priest sex abuse scandal of, 279n14; on resurrection, 241; La Santa Muerte and, 228, 282n2

Cavell, Stanley, 220

childbearing, 179–80, 278n8

child donors, 50t

China, 115

chronic kidney disease. See kidney disease

Cohen, Lawrence, 7; on bioavailability, 33, 65; on ethical experimentation, 63; on "good" and "bad" families, 39; on living unrelated donation, 219; on organ donation and "where it hurts," 281n14; on organ trafficking, 61–62, 192, 278n3, 281n15; on transcendent ethics, 222. See also India

Collier, Jane, 12

comatose patients, 274n15. See also brain death

coming to matter, 4, 111–12

commodification frame in transplantation, 187–95, 222–25; developing-world settings of, 193, 223; modern alienation and, 190–92; moral politics of, 188–89, 199, 216–23, 249–50, 264–65, 280n8; social lives of commodities in, 191; social lives of kidneys in, 195–204, 280nn6–8; temporal and relational perspectives of, 194–95, 211–22, 281nn14–15, 282n17. *See also* anthropology of transplantation; organ trafficking

Cortés, Hernán, 12–14

Cuba, 270n20

cultural value: of blood, 119–20, 276n7; of the kidney, 115

curandería (folk healing), 23

cyclosporine, 166–67, 279n13. *See also* immunosuppressive drugs

Das, Veena, 124, 181, 268n12. *See also* India

deceased donors, 237n1. *See also* brain death

Delaney, Carol, 42, 49

dependent normality, 278n7

developing world, 7–10, 62, 188, 265–66, 268nn7–8

diabetes, 9, 211

dialysis, 117–22; availability in Mexico of, 114–15, 275n3, 276n6; rates of use of, 117, 275n4; risks and side effects of, 119–21, 275n5, 276nn8–9; stable patients on, 152; types of, 117–19

disability status, 173–74

doctors. *See* transplant professionals

domestication: of bioavailability, 60–61; of biounavailability, 105; gift/commodity frames of transplantation and, 223–24; of posttransplant life, 184; of transplantation, 28–29, 59–64, 184, 273n18

donors: actual gender of, 47–55; ages of, 56t, 272n15; anonymity considerations for, 283n6; family contexts of, 28–29, 33–41, 46–55; gendered imaginings of,

41–46, 271nn8–9; men as, 47–48, 50t, 55–59; pain experienced by, 43, 214, 271nn6–7; relationship type of, 50–53, 56, 62, 272–73nn12–16; risks to, 37, 52–53, 370n11; self-sacrificial Mexican mother narratives of, 2–3, 11–15, 28–29, 54–55; transformed value of bodies of, 196–98; unrelated individuals as, 33–34, 47, 200–201, 213–22, 281nn9–10. *See also* cadaveric donor transplants; living donor transplants

Las Dos Fridas (Kahlo), 34f, 35–37, 40, 52, 201

Douglas, Mary, 7–10, 62

Dumit, Joseph, 278n7

economics of transplantation, 181–82, 279n15

Egypt: debates on brain death in, 73, 92; living organ donation in, 42, 66; posttransplant pregnancy in, 155; religious restrictions on cadaveric donation in, 66, 80, 242, 284n15. *See also* Hamdy, Sherine

ethical domestication of transplantation, 28–29, 59–64, 273n18; aspirational moments in, 62–64; posttransplant challenges and, 184; sanctioned privacy of, 61

ethical variability, 63

ethnographic gaze, 26–28, 237n3

ethnographic Other, 193

exchange-value, 200

familialization of living donation, 59–64

families, 2, 10–11, 15; brain-dead organ donation decisions by, 29, 86–96, 103, 231–33, 251; caregiving for patients by, 45–46, 59, 110, 118, 135, 163; as center of moral values of, 38–41, 270n4; ethical domestication of transplantation and, 28–29, 59–64, 184, 273n18, 280n8; impact of neoliberalism on,

living donor transplants (*continued*)
284n18; from unrelated donors, 33–34,
47, 200–201, 213–22, 281nn9–10. *See
also* donors
Livingston, Julie, 268n7
living with a transplant. *See* posttransplant life
La Llorona, 13
Lock, Margaret, 227; on brain death, 75,
92, 280n5; on living organ donation,
59, 66. *See also* Japan
Lomnitz, Claudio, 283n11

male donors, 47–48, 50t, 55–59; age of,
56–57, 272n15; emotion-driven logic
of, 57–58; relationship type of, 50–53,
56
La Malinche, 12–15, 36, 44
Manuela (character), 253–54
maquiladoras, 174
Martin, Emily, 277n11
Marx, Karl, 190, 200
Mauss, Marcel, 190–91
media review, 25, 270n22
medical professionals. *See* transplant
professionals
medication collectives, 169–70, 279n13.
See also immunosuppressive drugs
The Merchant of Venice (Shakespeare),
187–89, 279n1, 280nn3–4
the merographic, 282n18
mestizaje, 13–14, 16–17, 22, 268n10; racialized imagery of, 128–29; reproductive logic of rape in, 55
Mexican culture and identity, 2–4, 10–15;
belief in miracles in, 77, 80–81, 232,
242, 278n5; la casa chica in, 38–39,
370n4; families' central place in,
10–11, 15, 38–41; German mother
story of, 1–3, 8, 10, 23, 30, 35, 37–38; in
Guadalajara, 15–19; iconicity of bodily
sacrifice in, 6; impact of neoliberal
reforms on, 14–15, 59–60; mestizaje

in, 13–14, 16–17, 22, 55, 268n10; popular Catholicism in, 11–12, 228, 268n10;
self-sacrificial Mexican mother icon
of, 2–3, 11–15, 28–29, 54–55. *See also*
transplantation in Mexico
minors as donors, 56, 272n15
miraculous beliefs, 77, 80–81, 232, 242,
278n5
Mitchell, W. J. T., 5
Moazam, Farhat, 47, 272n13
Mol, Annemarie, 259
Moldova, 44
moral politics of transplantation,
188–89, 199, 216–23, 249–50, 264–65,
280n8
moral requiredness, 130
Morgan, Lynn, 5
mothers' bodies, 2–4; birth analogies of,
42–43, 49; expectations of suffering
and, 49; German mother story and,
1–3, 8, 10, 23, 30, 35, 37–38; housework
analogies of, 45–46, 271n9; self-
sacrificial Mexican mother icon of,
2–3, 11–15, 28–29, 36–37, 54–55
Murray, Joseph, 237n4

Napolitano, Valentina, 271n9
narco-saint (La Santa Muerte), 228,
282n2
national identity, 3, 256–57
neoliberalism: biomedical approach
to health of, 5, 63, 171–72; blame of
individual patients in, 170–72, 184;
impact on families of, 14–15, 59–60;
patients' potential production of value
in, 109–10, 127–29, 134–37, 141–46;
public health-care system reforms of,
34–35, 269n18
El Niño Doctor de los Enfermos, 12,
225–29, 238, 242, 258, 282n1, 282n3
non-family living donors, 33–34, 47,
200–201, 213–22, 281nn9–10
non-heart-beating donors, 273n1